Praise from

A Workbook

"If the Text of *A Course in Miracles* is to get the message clear in our heads, the Workbook is to bring it home to our hearts. In their *Workbook Companion* series, Allen and Robert speak straight to our hearts, complementing the spirit and meaning behind the lessons. Their work resonates with intellectual honesty, building our relationship with the Course on the solid ground of their years of dedicated study."
—TIM SCHOENFELDER, M.D.

"Sometimes it seems as though Allen is reading my mind when he writes his Workbook commentary for the day. He has an uncanny way of addressing precisely the questions and objections that occur to me. I find Allen's commentaries unique in spanning the distance between the peace and truth of the real world and the dramatic distractions of the illusory world of separation. He is never just theoretical; he knows the terrain on this path, and he is a great travelling companion."
—MILLI GRAVEL

"Encouraging, stimulating…a beautiful and extremely important work."
—ARMANDO BRONS

"The return of the Workbook commentaries is like the return of a long departed friend. When I started the Course several years ago, the commentaries got me through the difficult but very rewarding process of completing the Workbook."
—DENNIS WESTON

"Robert and Allen are companions in a very real sense. Robert's support in terms of practice, and Allen's inspired commentaries, have been my travelling friends in my study of the Course for nearly two

years. They deliver genuine and often mind-expanding insights throughout the series. I keep the *Workbook Companion* alongside my copy of the Course."
—CLIVE BAYNE

"The lesson commentaries have been very helpful. I have been doing the Workbook for over fifteen years, and the additional insight has expanded my understanding of the Course. Thank you very much!"
—JUDY JUNGHANS

"Since I started to use these lesson commentaries, I have gained a much deeper understanding of the Course's teachings. Allen's brilliant insights have helped me immensely, opening many new doors of understanding for me. He one of the most down to earth, loving, gifted Course scholars living today."
—REV. LEE POEPPING, UNITY CHURCH OF SANTA CLARITA

"I have found the *Workbook Companion* books to be valuable tools in helping me gain a greater understanding of each lesson. They reinforce the goal for the day and encourage dedication to the actual exercise instructions so we can apply them to 'in the world' use. The commentaries enrich and enhance what can initially feel unclear. Any confusion about what each lesson might mean or how to apply it is clarified beautifully. I highly recommend these tools to anyone who has an interest in using the lessons in their daily lives."
—KATHY SMITH

"Allen brings a perspective to the lessons that has helped me to understand them at a deeper level. I have also found that his references to appropriate sections of the Text have deepened my appreciation for the importance of the Text to understanding the messages in the Workbook. Instruction in how to practice the lessons also makes a wonderful contribution. A very valuable aid to anyone starting out with the Course."
—SARAH HUEMMERT

"Allen's explanations and commentaries are so helpful. When I am not clear about a lesson I can refer to the practice summary and lesson commentary. What a godsend they are. The *Workbook Companion* books are valuable and important tools in my understanding and living *A Course in Miracles*."

—ALLISON CRAIG

A Workbook Companion

Volume I

Other Books by Allen Watson:

The Journey Home
Seeing the Bible Differently

By Allen Watson & Robert Perry:

Everything You Always Wanted to Know about Judgment but Were
    Too Busy Doing It to Notice
The Answer Is a Miracle
Let Me Remember You: God in *A Course in Miracles*
Bringing the Course to Life: How to Unlock the Meaning of *A Course
    in Miracles* for Yourself

A Workbook Companion

Commentaries on the Workbook
for Students from *A Course in Miracles*

Volume I
Lessons 1 - 180

Second Edition
Revised and Expanded

Lesson Commentaries by Allen Watson
Practice Instructions and Cameo Essays by Robert Perry

Published by Circle Publishing
A division of The Circle of Atonement Teaching and Healing Center
P.O. Box 4238 • West Sedona, AZ 86340
(928) 282-0790 • Fax: (928) 282-0523
E-mail: info@circleofa.org • Website: www.circleofa.org

Cover design by George Foster; www.fostercovers.com
Design and layout by Phillips Associates UK Ltd
Printed in the USA

ISBN 1-886602-24-7

Library of Congress Cataloging-in-Publication Data

Watson, Allen, 1940-
 A workbook companion : commentaries on the Workbook for students from
A course in miracles, second edition, revised and expanded / lesson
commentaries by Allen Watson ; practice instructions and cameo essays
by Robert Perry.
     p. cm.
 Summary: "A practice aid for students doing the Workbook of A Course
in Miracles, containing lesson commentaries, practice summaries, and
essays on practice methods"--Provided by publisher.
 Includes bibliographical references.
 ISBN 1-886602-24-7 -- ISBN 1-886602-25-5
 1. Spiritual life--New Age movement. I. Course in miracles. Workbook
for students. II. Perry, Robert, 1960- III. Title.
 BP605.C68W37 2005
 299'.93--dc22
                                    2005005515

A Workbook Companion

Thus what you need are intervals each day

in which the learning of the world

becomes a transitory phase;

a prison house from which you go into the sunlight

and forget the darkness.

Workbook, Lesson 184

Contents

Contents

Introduction to the Second Edition

I've been happily amazed at the strong positive response from readers of *A Workbook Companion*. I had no idea that this series would turn out to be the most popular books published so far by Circle Publishing. What delights me most of all is that people who read *A Workbook Companion* are reacting to it just as I hoped they would react—by truly putting the lessons of the Workbook for Students into practice.

The Second Edition has some substantial changes from the First Edition. The lesson commentaries themselves (by Allen Watson) remain the same, but the practice instructions (by Robert Perry), previously called "practice summaries," have been completely rewritten. Rather than just condense the practice instructions found in the Workbook lessons, Robert has expanded on them, adding commentary and explanation, so that these pieces really coach you in detail on how to actually practice the lessons. Additionally, Robert has written a number of cameo essays on different aspects of Workbook practice. These are related to the specific instructions given at various points in the Workbook, and so are interspersed throughout the volume at the appropriate places. These cameo essays can be read as separate pieces, although they will add to the richness of your practice experience if you incorporate them as you go.

The other main change to the Second Edition is that the original three-volume set is being turned into two larger-format volumes. This means that the new Volume I contains Lessons 1-180 (the original Volume I and the first half of the original Volume II). Volume II of the Second Edition contains Lessons 181-365 (the second half of the original Volume II and the whole of the original Volume III).

In the original introduction to this series of commentaries, I declared that the most important thing I could say about them is that they are definitely not intended as a replacement for the Workbook for Students that makes up Volume II of *A Course in Miracles*. My commentaries are meant, rather, as companions to the Workbook, aids for students to assist them through a spiritual program that some people have found intimidating and confusing. Most of all, they are intended to assist you, as a student, in actually doing the Workbook lessons as the author intended for us to do them.

How delighted I have been to hear from one student after another that the effect of reading these books has been that, for the first time, the student has actually completed the entire set of Workbook lessons! Some have written to say that they had tried to go through the Workbook several times, and never made it, but with the help of *A Workbook Companion* they are thrilled to have done so.

One student did confess to me, sheepishly, that she often read my commentary and did not read the lesson it was discussing. But she was the exception. Numerous people told me that the *Companion* had motivated and helped them to apply themselves to the full program of the Workbook, something they would not have done without it.

The Course portrays the Workbook as absolutely essential and crucial for its curriculum in spiritual mind training. It says:

> A theoretical foundation such as the text provides is necessary as a framework to make the exercises in this workbook meaningful. Yet it is doing the exercises that will make the goal of the course possible. An untrained mind can accomplish nothing. It is the purpose of this workbook to train your mind to think along the lines the text sets forth. (W-pI.In.1:1-4)

Adhering to the Workbook's structured program will train our minds to "think along the lines the text sets forth." Mere study alone cannot accomplish that, although study of the Text is also a necessary part of the training. Nor can simply *reading* through the Workbook lessons bring the benefits it promises. What trains our minds is actually *doing* the exercises. *A Workbook Companion* is designed to help you to understand and practice the exercises—nothing more than that.

In Robert's and my experience, many people have read the Workbook without actually attempting to carry out the practice instructions as they are set forth. We believe that in failing to make a serious attempt to do the practice, students get only a miniscule fraction of the possible benefits. We hope that these two volumes will help students to avoid that pitfall and to enjoy the promised benefit: realigning their minds from fear to love.

Each day's lesson in *A Workbook Companion* contains two parts: a summary of practice instructions (written by Robert Perry), which extracts and condenses the actual instructions for practice given in the Workbook and gives helpful suggestions on putting them into practice, and a commentary (written by Allen Watson), which attempts to highlight and clarify some of the teaching given in the lessons. The commentary does not, in most cases, attempt to comment on everything in the lessons; that could fill four or five sets of books the size of these. Rather, I highlight things that have spoken to me in my reading, or things that seem most central to the lesson. You may find that a different part of the lesson speaks more directly to you; that is entirely appropriate.

How should you use this book in conjunction with the Workbook for Students? I recommend reading the lesson for the day from the Workbook and then, if time permits, reading the corresponding section from *A Workbook Companion*. The *Companion* comments on the practice instructions, often clarifying them and helping your practice to be more focused and meaningful. If, however, you must choose between taking time to read the commentary and taking that same time to actually do the practice, by all means skip the commentary and do the practice. Read the commentary later in the day, whenever you find time.

A few notes on some formatting details in the book. I have chosen to include a date at the top of each lesson; this shows the day of the year the lesson will fall on if you begin with Lesson 1 on January 1. This is purely a convenience for people who choose to do the Workbook in synchronization with the calendar. There is nothing in the Workbook itself to suggest that this is necessary or even desirable. You can start the Workbook on any day of the year you choose.

Although it isn't necessary to follow the calendar if you are working alone, it can greatly facilitate doing the Workbook along with a group of friends. The distribution of these commentaries by electronic mail resulted in hundreds of people doing the same lessons each day. In Sedona, in our local Course community, we chose to do the same thing. We found that doing so adds enormously to our ability to support one another, to encourage one another in doing the Workbook, and to discuss the lessons together.

I highly recommend that anyone setting out to follow the Workbook program also obtain a copy of *Path of Light: Stepping into Peace with 'A Course in Miracles,'* by Robert Perry (available from Circle Publishing). Chapter 7 gives a wealth of practical advice about making these lessons a part of a consistent, daily spiritual practice, and the book as a whole shows how the Workbook fits into the total spiritual program presented by the Course. You can find even more detailed help online at our website: www.circleofa.com.

These commentaries were written informally over a period of four or five years. They began as written meditations on the lessons in my personal journal, with no thought of publication. I covered nearly half the Workbook lessons in this manner over a period of three years. Some of the comments refer to events in my life that were current at the time, but now are long past. I have chosen to leave in many of these personal references because they illustrate so well how the general theme of a lesson can be applied to one's immediate circumstances. Many readers have told me that these personal anecdotes are often the most helpful thing in the commentaries.

In 1994, I began sharing the commentaries by electronic mail (e-mail) on America Online, writing new commentaries for lessons not covered previously, day by day. In 1995, I expanded to the general Internet, with the help of James Hale of Latrobe University in Australia, who offered his computer system to host my electronic mailing list. A companion electronic discussion group about the Workbook lessons was also begun that year. That lasted for several years. We have since set up our own mailing lists for the Workbook lessons and discussion groups with a commercial e-mail list service. Over time I also added the practice summaries (since revised and renamed "practice instructions") written by Robert Perry for each lesson. In addition, during 1996 I posted the commentaries on the Internet newsgroup talk.religion.course-miracle.

In 1996 and 1997, I repeated the mailings, beginning with Lesson 1 on January 1. The actual daily work of sending that day's commentary was taken over beginning in 1997 by several volunteers: Valda Gostautas, of Brazil, distributed the lessons during most of 1997; Pierre Caron, a Canadian volunteer, took over late that year; and finally, Susan Carrier, in New Jersey, has been distributing the lessons for us for the last six years. In part, these volunteers have given me more time to devote to other work, so I am very grateful to them all. The enthusiastic response of those receiving these commentaries by e-mail is what originally prompted us to make them more widely available in book form.

The Internet distribution of these commentaries still continues as of this writing (June 2004), without any further effort on my part. If you have Internet access and would like to receive the commentaries via e-mail on a daily basis, you can subscribe to the Workbook mailing list on our website.

My prayer is that these daily readings will encourage you to put the daily thoughts offered by the Workbook into practice, filling your mind with them until you begin to experience the inner peace and joy promised by *A Course in Miracles*.

Your companion on the journey,
Allen Watson
Portland, Oregon, July 2004
E-mail: allen@circleofa.org

Note: A Course in Miracles, which includes the Workbook for Students on which these commentaries are based, can be purchased at any major bookstore, or at a number of outlets on the Internet, including our online bookstore: www.circlepublishing.org.

Preliminary Notes on Workbook Practice

To begin with, I'd like to share some thoughts about what Workbook practice really is, and what it is intended to accomplish. From my study of the Course, I believe the Workbook is intended to train us in the formation of a habit of spiritual practice. This habitual practice is meant to continue until we have nearly completed our spiritual journey. Let me try to explain what I mean by this *habit* of spiritual practice.

In the Manual for Teachers, Section 16 ("How Should the Teacher of God Spend His Day?"), the Course discusses what daily practice should be like for those who have completed the Workbook. This gives a clear picture, then, of the results of the Workbook's training program, or the kind of daily practice for which the Workbook is the training program.

The discussion of daily practice in this section becomes more understandable if we set it in the context of the various categories the Course discusses within its curriculum:

- pupils
- teachers of God
- advanced teachers of God
- Teachers of teachers

We begin as pupils or students, those who have begun to study the

Course. Next, after a certain level of "accomplishment," we become "teachers of God." What qualifies us as a teacher of God?

> A teacher of God is anyone who chooses to be one. His qualifications consist solely in this; somehow, somewhere he has made a deliberate choice in which he did not see his interests as apart from someone else's. Once he has done that, his road is established and his direction is sure....He has entered an agreement with God even if he does not yet believe in Him. He has become a bringer of salvation. He has become a teacher of God. (M-1.1:1–3, 6–8)

By this definition, all it takes to become a teacher of God is a moment in which we realize we share common interests with another person. That common interest must, by implication, be "salvation," because in that moment we have entered an agreement with God and have become a "bringer of salvation." Another way of seeing this, perhaps, is that we have experienced a holy instant, or a moment of true forgiveness.

And yet, in Section 16, there seems to be a different set of criteria. This section states clearly: "He cannot claim that title [teacher of God] until he has gone through the workbook, since we are learning within the framework of our course" (M-16.3:7). So, although in general a teacher of God can be said to be anyone who has made a decision that involved common interests with another, *within the framework of the course* (that is, within this particular form of spiritual curriculum) a "teacher of God" is someone who has completed the Workbook for Students.

The Course appears to be making a distinction between a teacher of God in the general sense, and a teacher of God who is sharing with another person the specific goal of learning the Course. To be a teacher in that special sense, one needs to complete the Workbook. Since the Workbook in many places assumes we have studied the Text, we can therefore assume that completing the Workbook also includes completing the Text. To be a teacher of God in the framework of the Course, then, means having completed both volumes. It seems only common sense that one should complete a course—any course—before claiming to teach it.

I should note, for people unfamiliar with the Course, that it is all right to do the Workbook before reading all of the Text, if you feel guided to do that. I would say that the "normal" order would be to read the Text first, or at least most of it, before doing the Workbook, but that is by no means a strict rule. If you have been led to begin the Workbook, it isn't necessary to read all of the Text first. I would recommend beginning to read it as soon as possible, however.

Beyond the level of "teacher of God" lies "the advanced teacher of God" (M-16.1:1). That phrase describes someone who is nearing the end of his or her personal journey, living on the verge of or within the real world—that is, with spiritually clarified perception of the world—as Jesus lived while on earth. Every student of the Course is in training to become an advanced teacher of God; Section 4 of the Manual describes the characteristics of an advanced teacher (M-4:2:2), a list of ten very fundamental character traits, including trust, honesty, gentleness, patience, and defenselessness. This section also tells of the often long process a person goes through in developing these characteristics.

And even beyond that exalted level are the "Teachers of teachers" (M-26.2:2); beings who have "laid the body down merely to extend their helpfulness to those remaining behind" (M-26.3:9) and who retain "no trace of worldly limits...[while] remembering their own Identity perfectly" (M-26:2:1); beings who are "no longer visible" (M-26.2:2) yet who "appear when and where it is helpful for them to do so" (M-26.2:3).

With that understood, let's turn back to Section 16. (All of the Course quotations in the following discussion are from that section, unless otherwise indicated.) It begins with describing what the day is like for an *advanced* teacher of God; to such a person, the question of how to spend the day "is meaningless" (1:1). He or she lives without a program. These teachers keep in constant touch with the Holy Spirit and are told, moment to moment, what to do (1:1–10). Of course, we all aspire to such a state, but few, if indeed any, have yet attained it. I don't know of anyone who has. So the section then addresses itself to the more common level of the less-than-advanced teacher of God, who is still in the process of developing those ten characteristics. It says: "But what about those who have not reached his [the advanced teacher of God's] certainty?" (2:1).

And now the section begins to discuss how a *teacher of God* (as opposed to an *advanced* teacher) spends his day. Unlike the advanced teacher, the day for a teacher of God is not entirely without structure: "They are not yet ready for such lack of structuring on their own part" (2:2). What is going to be described here is the *post-Workbook* practice, the habit of practice which the Workbook is designed to teach us. This practice is meant to continue until we reach the state of advanced teachers of God, where structure becomes meaningless and we live in a spontaneous partnership with the Holy Spirit. Even after completing the Workbook, we are not yet ready for complete lack of structure.

Workbook practice is *very* structured. Post-Workbook practice is *loosely* structured. And the practice of an advanced teacher is characterized by *lack of structuring*.

The post-Workbook practice, in simple outline, is this:

1. Begin the day right, as soon as possible after waking. "As soon as possible after waking take your quiet time, continuing a minute or two after you begin to find it difficult" (4:7). The goal in this time is to join with God, and we should spend as long as it takes (the length of time is not a major concern) until it becomes difficult (4:4–8).

2. Repeat the "same procedures" (5:1) at night; just before sleeping if possible (5:6).

3. Remember God all through the day (6:1–14).

4. Turn to the Holy Spirit with all your problems (7:4–5).

5. Respond to all temptations by reminding yourself of the truth (8:1–3; 10:8; 11:9).

Developing the habit of this fivefold practice is the purpose of the highly structured practice of the Workbook. The practice given in its lessons begins very easily, with just a minute or two in the morning. Very quickly, it introduces the other practices: morning and evening times, hourly remembrances, frequent reminders between the hours, listening to the Holy Spirit for guidance, and responding to every temptation with the day's lesson. The Workbook verbally sounds a trumpet each time it introduces a new practice. The duration and intensity of these practices steadily increases as we progress. We meet first one, then another. There will be a brief period of intense practice, than an easing up, letting us catch our breath, before the pace picks up again.

If we follow the instructions of the Workbook carefully we will, at the end of the year, have formed the steady habit of daily practice the Manual speaks about. If we do not follow the instructions of the Workbook carefully, and simply "do it" however we feel like doing it, we will *not* develop that habit. Habits are formed by disciplined repetition, and no other way. Therefore, watch, as you read, for both the instructions for practice *and* for the passion with which Jesus urges us to really *do the practice*. He isn't casual about it at all! He pleads with us; he cajoles us; he sympathizes with our difficulties but calls us back to a renewed effort after failure. And at one point in the introduction he tells us that "it is doing the exercises that will make the goal of the course possible" (W-In.1:2).

In the Text, in a section talking about daily practice, he says, "The speed by which it [the goal] can be reached depends on this one thing alone; your willingness to practice every step" (T-30.In.1:3).

And in a passage that is reminiscent of a TV pitchman trying to sell us an amazing slicer/dicer along with a set of knives, he tries to impress on us the importance and value of the disciplined practice to which he calls us:

> Is it not worth five minutes of your time each hour to be able to accept the happiness that God has given you? Is it not worth five minutes hourly to recognize your special function here? Is not five minutes but a small request to make in terms of gaining a reward so great it has no measure? You have made a thousand losing bargains at the least.
>
> Here is an offer guaranteeing you your full release from pain of every kind, and joy the world does not contain. You can exchange a little of your time for peace of mind and certainty of purpose, with the promise of complete success. And since time has no meaning, you are being asked for nothing in return for everything. Here is a bargain that you cannot lose. And what you gain is limitless indeed!
> (W-pI.98.5:1–6:5)

To me, there is no doubt that the author of the Workbook really desires and expects us to make every effort to follow his instructions. As he says in the Workbook's introduction:

> You are merely asked to apply the ideas as you are directed
> to do....It is their use that will give them meaning to you,
> and will show you that they are true.   (W-pI.In.8:3, 6)

As an aid to those who want to follow the practice of the Workbook, this book includes with each lesson a condensed summary of the practice instructions which apply to the day. (Often a set of instructions is given in one lesson and carries over for several weeks, without being restated daily.) These summaries were written by Robert Perry.

Now, I'm not saying that everyone who reads the Workbook has to engage in a disciplined practice of the Workbook. I'm not trying to tell you what you should do; that is a matter of individual guidance. But I do mean to point out that, if you want to make the Course your path, these are the instructions given by the author, and he heavily stresses their importance within the curriculum he gives us.

I do believe that the Workbook lessons were written in a particular order for a reason, and that there is an intelligently planned approach in the way they work cumulatively to transform our thoughts as we study them. Therefore I always recommend that people do the lessons in order, 1 to 365. Nevertheless, if the imposition of such minimal "structure" or the submitting of oneself to this very slight amount of authority raises the level of fear in us, then a compromise approach, doing it however you please, may be better.

I believe that the resistance we have to following Jesus' instructions in the book is nothing more than a manifestation of the basic "authority problem" that is said, in the Text, to be the root of all "evil" (see T-3.VI.7:2–3). Even so, doing the lessons out of order, or ignoring the instructions for practice to do them however we feel comfortable, is certainly better than not doing them at all! And, if trying to force myself to follow the practice instructions disturbs me so much it threatens to cause me to stop altogether, then throw that approach out the window.

> And if you find resistance strong and dedication weak, you
> are not ready. *Do not fight yourself.*   (T-30.I.1:6–7)

To summarize: I believe that the instructions in the lessons are very explicit for a reason. We are meant to follow these instructions to the letter, as much as we possibly can. We will not be able to do so, especially in the beginning, but the whole intent of the exercises is to form a habit of spiritual practice that will endure for a lifetime. You can't do that without some persistent effort over a long period of time.

> The goal is clear, but now you need specific methods for attaining it. The speed by which it can be reached depends on this one thing alone; your willingness to practice every step. Each one will help a little, every time it is attempted. And together will these steps lead you from dreams of judgment to forgiving dreams and out of pain and fear....So now, we need to practice them awhile, until they are the rules by which you live. We seek to make them habits now, so you will have them ready for whatever need.
>
> (T-30.In.1:2–5, 7–8)

A note on reading Course references

All references are given for the Second Edition of the Course, and are listed according to the numbering in the Course, rather than according to page numbers. Each reference begins with a letter, which denotes the particular volume or section of the Course and its extensions (T = Text, W = Workbook for Students, M = Manual for Teachers, C = Clarification of Terms, P = *Psychotherapy*, and S = *Song of Prayer*). After this letter comes a series of numbers, which differ from volume to volume:

> T, P, or S-chapter.section.paragraph:sentence; e.g., T-24.VI.2:3–4
> W-part (I or II).lesson.paragraph:sentence; e.g., W-pI.182.4:1–2
> M or C-section.paragraph:sentence; e.g., C-2.5:2

A Workbook Companion
Volume I

I

The Introduction to the Workbook

The Workbook's introduction is something everyone doing the Workbook should definitely read thoughtfully. In my opinion we could profit from reading it over once a month or so as we do the Workbook to remind ourselves of its basic instructions.

The first paragraph explains the interrelationship of the Text and the Workbook. *Both* are essential for anyone doing the Course. According to the first sentence, without the "theoretical foundation" of the Text, the exercises of the Workbook are "meaningless." We should all pay careful attention to the Text; it is "necessary" to do so if we want the benefits of the Workbook exercises. Does that mean that one should study the Text before doing the Workbook? Not necessarily. The Manual discusses the order in which the volumes should be used, and says it differs from person to person. Some, it says, "might do better to begin with the workbook" (M-29.1:6). It is evident from this introduction, however, that if one begins with the Workbook, the Text should follow, or perhaps be read along with the Workbook.

On the other hand, studying the Text without doing the Workbook is equally useless because "it is doing the exercises that will make the goal of the course possible" (1:2; all references in this discussion will be from the Workbook's introduction, unless otherwise indicated). To simply study the theoretical foundation without practical application results in little more than empty head knowledge. You may understand intellectually what the goal is, but you will not be able to attain it without the exercises. In Chapter 30 of the Text, the Course puts forth this same idea. It says there:

> The goal is clear, but now you need specific methods for attaining it. The speed by which it can be reached depends on this one thing alone; your willingness to practice every step. Each one will help a little, every time it is attempted. And together will these steps lead you from dreams of judgment to forgiving dreams and out of pain and fear. (T-30.In.1:2–5)

The "one thing alone" that determines how fast we reach the goal is our "willingness to practice every step." In terms of doing the Workbook I think this can be aptly applied to how willing we are to practice the daily exercises *as instructed*. If the lesson calls for four or five repetitions during the day, how willing are we to actually do that? Each time we remember to practice it may not seem as if much is happening, but every time helps a little. It is all the little, repeated times of practice that, when added together, will lead us out of our dream of judgment. The Workbook does not promise to change us overnight; rather, it says that if we are willing to practice every step of the exercises, each such attempt will, little by little, purify our minds of the ego's darkness.

The purpose of the Workbook is "to train your mind to think along the lines the text sets forth" (1:4). The word *train* calls to mind things like piano practice, sports exercises and drills, and even military training. It definitely carries with it the idea of manifold repetitions, of disciplined effort, of pushing beyond the envelope of our present abilities. When you train in a gym or health club the whole idea involves pushing past the limits you now have and learning to do things you cannot now do. Yet at the same time it also carries with it the idea that what is being developed is something latent, the calling out of an undeveloped potential, and not the addition of something heretofore entirely lacking.

What is being trained is our minds. The separation is nothing more than a mistaken mindset, and

> all mistakes must be corrected at the level on which they occur. Only the mind is capable of error.   (T-2.IV.2:3–4)

> Correction belongs at the thought level.   (T-2.V.1:7)

> The purpose of the workbook is to train your mind in a systematic way to a different perception of everyone and everything in the world.   (4:1)

So this is a very thorough mind training, intended to affect the way you perceive literally *everything*. That we are learning a "different" perception clearly implies that our existing perception is mistaken.

Notice some of the very simple "rules" for doing the Workbook:

1. "Do not undertake to do more than one set of exercises a day" (2:6).

2. The exercises are to be practiced with "great specificity" (6:1) (one of those words I never used until I began studying the Course!). This means that we are to pay great attention to details, and to applying the general ideas of the lessons specifically to many different things in our lives. The purpose is to help us generalize the ideas and to see that they apply to "everyone and everything in the world" (4:1).

3. Do not deliberately exclude anything from the application of the ideas (6:3).

Having 365 lessons, one for each day of the year, implies that we should do the lessons in order. (There is nothing wrong with doing some out of order at random times, but in following the training program, they should be done in order.) As you move through the lessons, it becomes obvious that the later lessons build quite squarely on earlier ones; doing them in order is the most effective way, therefore, to learn.

Some people wonder about doing one lesson per day. They wonder if, perhaps, they should repeat a lesson if they feel they did not "get" it, or did not do the practice correctly. The wisdom of many students who have worked with the book can be summed up like this: Don't "guilt yourself" about the lessons. In general, there is no need to repeat. Later lessons will repeat the same concepts in many cases. If you want to repeat a lesson because you found it beneficial, by all means do so. If you are repeating because you are trying to do it perfectly, you may be subconsciously resisting moving on to the next lesson, which will free you. It is usually better to forgive yourself and move on.

We are asked to remember that "the overall aim of the exercises is to increase your ability to extend the ideas you will be practicing to include everything" (7:1). I'd like to linger a little on those words "exercises" and "practicing." We are not just *reading* these ideas. "Doing the Workbook" is not just reading the lessons. It is *practicing* the lessons. Each lesson gives "specific procedures by which the idea for today is to be applied" (3:3). Your following those procedures is what is meant by practicing, and practicing is "doing the Workbook." How much chemistry would you learn if all you did was read the lab manual but never performed the experiments?

If we do the exercises, the results are guaranteed:

> This [extension of the ideas] will require no effort on your part. The exercises themselves meet the conditions necessary for this kind of transfer. (7:2–3)

Our part is to do the exercises; the extension of the benefits derived from exercise will happen automatically, without additional effort on our part. You may practice with certain specific things or individuals or thoughts; the benefits of that practice will extend, without your effort, to everything in your world.

Like working out in a health club, you don't have to even like the program. If you work out, your body will benefit whether or not you like working out. So here, in doing these mental exercises, it isn't necessary that we believe the ideas at first, or like them, or accept them, or welcome them. You can even actively resist them. It doesn't matter what we think about them. "You are asked only to use them" (8:5). "Nothing more than that is required" (9:5). That is, apply them to your life as instructed. Notice that applying the ideas *is required* for the program to work. If you do so, they will be effective. Using the ideas is what will give them meaning to us and will show us that they are true.

No one can read this carefully without realizing what is being asked of us. Reading the Text isn't enough to reach the goal of the Course. Reading the Workbook as well is also not enough. We have to carry out the instructions in each lesson, the specific procedures for applying the idea during the day. It is our willingness to practice every step, to follow every instruction, and to do the exercises, that will determine the speed with which we reach the goal.

II

Lessons 1 - 50

9/6/06

LESSON 1 ✦ JANUARY 1

"Nothing I see in this room [on this street, from this window, in this place] means anything."

Practice instructions

Purpose: To teach that everything you see is equally meaningless, that no real differences exist between any of the things you see.

Exercise: Two times—morning and evening, preferably, for one minute (but do not hurry).

Look leisurely about you, applying the idea specifically and indiscriminately to whatever you see, first in your immediate area and then farther. Say, for example, *"This table does not mean anything."*

Remarks: It is essential to specifically exclude nothing. Do not, however, try to include everything. Do not hurry; leisure is essential.

Commentary

The early lessons do not seem particularly inspiring to most people, but they are carefully planned to begin undermining the ego thought system. "Nothing I see…means anything." We are so certain, in our ego arrogance, that we really understand a lot of things. The lesson is trying to plant the idea that we don't really understand anything we see, that our vaunted understanding is an illusion. As long as we think we understand what something is and what it means, we will not begin to ask the Holy Spirit for its true meaning. Our belief that we understand closes our mind to any higher understanding. We need to become like little children, who realize they do not know, and ask someone who does know.

Zen Mind, Beginner's Mind[1] is the title of a wonderful little book that introduces Zen thought. The idea is that we grow most rapidly and reliably when we admit we are beginners who do not know, and need instruction in everything. A "beginner's mind" is an open mind, ready to find unrecognized meaning in everything.

---

1. Shunryu Suzuki, *Zen Mind, Beginner's Mind* (Trumbull, Conn.: Weatherhill Inc., 1972).

10/6/06

LESSON 2 ✦ JANUARY 2

"I have given everything I see [on this street, from this window, in this place] all the meaning that it has for me."

Practice instructions

Exercise: Two times—ideally morning and evening, for one minute.

Same basic instructions as yesterday, just using a new idea. In selecting subjects for today, look side to side and behind you.

Remarks: Like the previous lesson, this one focuses on being totally indiscriminate in your selection of subjects. The comments in paragraph 2 about avoiding "selection by size, brightness, color, material, or relative importance to you" (2:1) are a brief reference to the Course's theory of selective attention. According to the Course, we are highly selective in what we attend to visually. We pay attention to things that visually stand out and therefore catch our eye (see M-8.1) and we pay attention to things we value (see M-8.3:7). Notice that both of these factors—things that visually stand out and things we value—are included in the sentence I just quoted. This implies that we are supposed to practice the lesson without our usual habit of selective attention, because that habit assumes that the different things in our visual field are *truly* different, and this lesson is meant to teach us that they are not.

Commentary

The meaning of yesterday's lesson is now a little clearer; "Nothing I see means anything" can be understood to say, "The only meaning anything has for me is the meaning that I give to it; there is no intrinsic meaning in anything."

When I first practiced Lesson 1, I recall that the first object my eyes lit on was an excellent new photograph of my two children. At first, my mind rebelled at saying, "That photograph does not mean anything," because it sure meant something to me. But the next morning, on Lesson

11

2, I began to see what the lessons were getting at. The photo, in itself, has no meaning at all. To the vast majority of people in the world it really would mean nothing; but to me, it meant something because I had given meaning to it.

When we begin to realize that our perception is formed by our minds, and not vice versa, it can be a startling revelation. If this lesson seems trivial or obvious to you, try applying it the next time "everything I see" includes someone who, in your perception, is betraying you, lying to you, or abandoning you: "I have given this situation all the meaning that it has for me." Not so trivial!

11/6/06

LESSON 3 ✦ JANUARY 3
"I do not understand anything I see in this room [on this street, from this window, in this place]."

Practice instructions

Purpose: To clear away the thick film of past associations which you project onto everything, so that you see things afresh and realize that you do not really understand them at all.

Exercise: Two times—ideally, morning and evening, for one minute.

Same basic instructions as the previous two days, only with a new idea.

Remarks: Being indiscriminate in selecting subjects is a direct reflection of the lesson's purpose, which is to clear your mind of the interpretive film which you lay over things and which claims to tell you what those things really are. It is that same film which would also tell you there are some things to which the lesson does not apply. The very act, therefore, of applying the lesson to absolutely anything is also an act of setting aside that interpretive film.

Commentary

If nothing I see means anything, and I have given everything I see all the meaning that it has for me, then obviously I do not understand anything I see. The Workbook is laying the groundwork for our learning. To learn a new understanding of anything we must let go our belief that we already understand it.

I find this lesson useful in many situations. When something happens that I interpret as unpleasant or upsetting, I can realize that my judgment of "unpleasant" or my upset comes not from the thing or person or situation, but from my imagined understanding of it. By repeating, "I do not understand anything I see," I open my mind to a new understanding from the Holy Spirit. I use variants of the idea at times, such as "I don't know what this means" or "I have no idea what this is all about."

In the Course, the beginning of understanding is understanding that I don't understand anything.

Remember this is an exercise. Don't expect to perform it perfectly! You are practicing the realization that you don't understand, which means you are coming from a state of mind that believes it does understand. That's okay.

12/6/06

LESSON 4 ✦ JANUARY 4

"These thoughts do not mean anything. They are like the things I see in this room [on this street, from this window, in this place]."

Practice instructions

Purpose: To train you to lump all your normal thoughts, both "good" and "bad," as well as all the things you see outside you, into one category: they are meaningless, and they are outside you (outside your real nature). This will open your mind to the fact that there is a whole other realm than that which you are aware of, which is fundamentally different, which is truly meaningful, and which lies deep within.

Exercise: Three or four times (no more), for one minute or so.

- For roughly one minute, watch your thoughts. Include both "good" and "bad" ones.
- Then apply the idea specifically to each thought you noticed, saying, *"This thought about [name of central figure or event] does not mean anything. It is like the things I see in this room [on this street, and so on]."* You may also include unhappy thoughts you were aware of before the practice period.

Response to temptation: Optional.

In addition to (not instead of) the formal exercises, feel free throughout the day to use the idea as a way of dispelling specific unhappy thoughts. This is the first instance of a practice that will become a major focus of the Workbook.

Commentary

The introduction to the Workbook states, "The purpose of the workbook is to train your mind in a systematic way to a different perception of everyone and everything in the world" (W-pI.In.4:1). This lesson begins to teach us to work directly with our thoughts, and the first lesson is: They don't mean anything.

There is an assumption in this lesson that we are very inexperienced (5:4) and therefore completely, or nearly completely, out of touch with what the lesson calls our "real thoughts" (2:3). The thoughts it is referring to as meaningless are the thoughts of the ego. It is the contention of the Course that our minds are nearly completely ego-directed (see T-4.VI.1:4). The tone of this lesson is based on that assumption; therefore, whatever thought you focus on, you can regard it as meaningless.

Our real thoughts are the thoughts of the Christ within us; they are not meaningless. What we call thinking, however, is not really thinking at all (this is made clear in Lesson 8). We have identified with our egos. The ego is like a tiny corner of our minds that we have cordoned off from the rest; we have convinced ourselves that it is the whole thing. The thoughts that swirl around in this little pocket of mind are totally unrepresentative of our true Self, and therefore, whether "good" or "bad," they are meaningless. When we have trained ourselves to look at these thoughts objectively we will realize how true this is (1:6–7).

The ego thoughts cover up our real thoughts. The "good" ones are at best shadows of the real, and shadows make it difficult to see. The "bad" ones are outright blocks to sight. "You do not want either" (2:6). Realizing that we don't want the "bad" ones is fairly easy; realizing we don't want the "good" ones is much more disconcerting and difficult.

The lesson calls itself "a major exercise" (3:1) and promises to repeat the exercise later. It says that the exercise is fundamental to three long-range goals, and serves to begin implementing these goals:

- to separate the meaningless from the meaningful
- to see the meaningless as outside you, and the meaningful within
- to train our minds to recognize what is the same and what is different

First, it helps us learn to separate meaningless thoughts from meaningful ones, our ego thoughts from our real thoughts. Note that there is a kind of judgment going on here, and even separation, although these are two terms usually given negative connotations. This kind of looking at our thoughts is one form of what the Text calls "the right use of judgment" (T-4.IV.8:6).

Second, we are learning to see the meaningless as outside us. We may ask how, if it is our thoughts that are meaningless, we can see them as outside us; aren't thoughts within us? Here, I believe, the Workbook means our true Self when it speaks of "you." Our meaningless ego thoughts are not representative of our true Self; they are not really part of it, but outside it.

Third, we are learning to recognize what is the same and what is different. We think "good" thoughts are different from "bad" thoughts, but this lesson is training us to see that they are really the same, both different forms of madness.

In suggesting that we might use the idea for today "for a particular thought that you recognize as harmful" (5:1), the Workbook is introducing a new form of practice, one that will become part of its regular repertoire. Besides scheduled morning and evening practice, we can use the idea as a response to random "temptation" in the form of a harmful thought. Response to temptation will be brought in as a practice exercise many more times as we go on. In asking us to do the exercise three or four times, the lesson also introduces midday practice sessions in addition to the morning and evening ones.

LESSON 5 ✦ JANUARY 5   13/6/06
"I am never upset for the reason I think."

Practice instructions

Purpose: To teach you that the cause of your upset is not the external situation, person, or event you think it is. Also, to teach you that your negative emotions are not truly different from one another.

Exercise: Three or four times, for one minute or so.

- Optional beginning: Say, *"There are no small upsets. They are all equally disturbing to my peace of mind."* This is designed to correct your tendency to dismiss some upsets as too insignificant to bother with.
- For a minute or so, search your mind for any persons, situations, or events that are distressing you, however mildly.
- Then apply the idea indiscriminately to each one by saying, *"I am not [angry, worried, depressed, etc.] about [source of upset] for the reason I think."*
- If you want to hang on to certain upsets because they seem justified, say, *"I cannot keep this form of upset and let the others go. For the purposes of these exercises, then, I will regard them all as the same."*

Response to temptation: Optional.

In addition to the formal practice periods, feel free during the day to apply the idea to any upset you are experiencing, as a way of restoring your peace of mind. Say, *"I am not [angry, worried, depressed, etc.] about [source of upset] for the reason I think."*

Commentary

This lesson is, to me, one of the most useful tools for jarring my thinking loose from a deeply worn track. "This lesson, like the preceding one, can be used with any person, situation or event you think is causing you pain" (1:1). Try to remember it today when, for whatever

18

reason, you get upset. That slowpoke driver on the road in front of you. The person who puts you down. When the job you've been hoping for falls through. When someone tracks dirt on your freshly mopped floor, or breaks your favorite keepsake. "I am never upset for the reason I think."

Notice that the lesson does not identify what it is that you really are upset about. That comes later. For now the Course is simply trying to undermine your belief that you know what is upsetting you. Notice, too, that it does not ask you not to be upset! "Fear, worry, depression, anxiety, anger, hatred, jealousy..." (1:3): The lesson does not ask you to be without these feelings, simply to recognize that they are not occurring for the reasons you think. Yes, of course, the eventual goal is to let them all go. But to do that we have to break our belief that they are different things with different causes. All of them stem, ultimately, from the same cause; all of them are meanings we project onto the world we see.

These first five lessons have been tough, if you think about them. Lesson 1 was about letting go of what I see. Lesson 2, letting go of my judgments about meaning. Lesson 3, letting go of my understanding. Lesson 4, letting go of my thoughts. And this lesson is leading me to let go of my entire thought system, the root cause behind all of my upsets.

LESSON 6 ✦ JANUARY 6 ¹⁴/₀₆/₀₆
"I am upset because I see something that is not there."

Practice instructions
Exercise: Three or four times, for one minute or so.

Same instructions as yesterday, only using a new idea.

Tip: The lessons speak as if you should *first* search your mind for a minute, and *then* apply the lesson to everything uncovered in your search. However, you may have difficulty remembering all the things you uncovered. If so, rather than practicing in these distinct two phases, you may want to practice in a slightly different way: Search your mind, find a single upset, apply the idea to it, then search your mind for another upset, apply the idea to that one, and so on.

Response to temptation: Optional.

The idea can be used throughout the day to dispel your upsets. But do not substitute this for the practice periods.

Commentary
This begins to explain why I am really upset. I am never upset for the reason I think; I am upset because I see something that is not there. (Once again the Workbook builds its case piece by piece; it does not tell us just what we are seeing, only that it is something that isn't there. If you're curious, go ahead, peek at the next lesson.) We can't begin to imagine how much of what we see, things we think of as "real" and "objective facts," are really things that are not there. The case being built here is that all of our upset comes from things that aren't there. Only what God creates is real, and nothing He creates is upsetting, and if those are facts, today's idea must be true. So when I feel upset I can say to myself, "I'm upset because I'm seeing something that isn't there."

We are asked to recall the "two cautions stated in the previous lesson" (3:1). Since they are repeated they are obviously important, so let's think a little about each.

20

There are no small upsets. They are all equally disturbing
to my peace of mind.   (3:2–3)

I find I have to remind myself of this a lot. It is so easy to overlook "small" upsets and leave them undealt with. A rage at someone who betrays me and steals my job is no different than a "minor" annoyance at slow service in a restaurant. Both have the power to disturb my peace of mind. If my goal is a mind at peace I must learn to deal with all upsets as being of equal importance; I must learn to "recognize what is the same and what is different" (W-pI.4.3:4).

I cannot keep this form of upset and let the others go. For
the purposes of these exercises, then, I will regard them all
as the same.   (3:5–6)

At least during the practice periods of the Workbook, we need to regard all upsets as the same, and apply the lesson to them. If I insist on not applying the lesson to some "minor" upset or to an upset that seems justified to me, I won't really be able to let any of the upsets go. I will be holding on to the principle behind all of them. It would be like saying you are going to lose weight by cutting out sugar and fat, except for that half gallon of ice cream every night. The Course insists that we be thorough and absolute in our practicing.

"I am upset because I see something that is not there."

LESSON 7 ✦ JANUARY 7 15/06/06
"I see only the past."

Practice instructions

Purpose: To begin to change your ideas about time, which are the foundation for all that you see and believe. Your mind will resist this change, in order to maintain the stability of your world, yet it is that world which keeps you bound.

Exercise: Three or four times, for one minute or so.

Look about you and apply the idea specifically and indiscriminately to whatever catches your eye, saying: *"I see only the past in [this shoe, that body, etc.]."* "Do not linger over any one thing in particular, but remember to omit nothing specifically" (5:1).

Commentary

As the lesson says, this "is the rationale for all of the preceding" lessons (1:2). "It is the reason why nothing that you see means anything" (1:3), and so on through the previous six thoughts. Because we see only the past, every one of those previous ideas is true. It makes this lesson an extremely important one, one we need to take in and consider very seriously.

Notice how absolute the thought for today is: "I see *only* the past." We may find this "particularly difficult to believe at first" (1:1). If anything, that is an understatement. If you find the concept difficult to accept, be reassured that the Teacher realizes your difficulty and accepts it in you.

The Course lays an unusually heavy emphasis on this concept, not only here, but also in the Text. For instance, three sections of Chapter 13, from "The Function of Time" (T-13.IV) through "Finding the Present" (T-13.VI), deal with how we see time and the fact that "the ego invests heavily in the past, and in the end believes that the past is the only aspect of time that is meaningful" (T-13.IV.4:2). It speaks of the shadow figures from the past, built upon illusions, that completely block out our sight of present reality. It says:

> To be born again is to let the past go, and look without
> condemnation upon the present.   (T-13.VI.3:5)

"Everything you believe is rooted in time, and depends on your *not* learning these new ideas about it" (2:1, my emphasis). Whatever we have learned, we learned from the past; that cannot be disputed.

Therefore, everything we think we know is based on the past. We look at the present through the filter of our past learning. The Course urges us not to let our past learning be the light that guides us in the present (see T-14.XI.6:9). Instead we need to turn, in the moment, and inquire of the Holy Spirit to show us His vision of the present.

The illustration in the lesson about the cup makes the point that our identification of things depends on the past, and our reactions to things come from past experiences. "You would have no idea what this cup is, except for your past learning" (3:6). And, "This is equally true of whatever you look at" (4:2).

What we are "seeing" is the past, pure and simple. At the moment there may seem to be no alternative to this; we may wonder what other way of seeing is possible. But there *is* another way; the Course will bring us to that eventually. For now, simply let this lesson sink in: "I see only the past."

LESSON 8 ✦ JANUARY 8 /6/ɔ6/ɔ6
"My mind is preoccupied with past thoughts."

Practice instructions

Purpose: To teach you that your mind spends all of its time empty, because it is always contemplating what is not there (the past). While it thinks about the empty, it itself is empty. Recognizing this emptiness makes way for something new to come in: real thoughts, which will produce real vision.

Exercise: Four or five times (three or four if you find the practice irritating), for one minute or so.

- Close your eyes and search your mind for a minute or so without investment, noting the thoughts you find and naming them by the central figure or theme of each one. Say, *"I seem to be thinking about [name of person], about [name of an object], about [name of an emotion]...."*
- Conclude with, *"But my mind is preoccupied with past thoughts."*

Remarks: If you find the exercise arousing feelings in you—for instance, irritation—you may want to apply the idea to those feelings just as you would to anything else. This is a helpful tip for many of the lessons.

Commentary

"This idea is, of course, the reason why you see only the past" (1:1). This clearly assumes that what we see simply reflects the thoughts occupying our minds. If that is so, then because our minds are preoccupied with past thoughts, we perceive pictures from the past in the outside world. "No one really sees anything. He sees only his thoughts projected outward" (1:2). This idea is so central to the Course, yet here it is simply slipped into this discussion of the past and time. We don't really see anything! Everything we see is "the outside picture of an inward condition," as the Text puts it (see T-21.In.1:1–5).

I've always loved the first line of the second paragraph: "The one

24

wholly true thought one can hold about the past is that it is not here." Ponder that a moment. You may have some extremely clear memories of the past, especially the very recent past. Yet if several people who experienced the same thing firmly disagreed with you, you would probably begin to doubt your memory—because you cannot really be completely certain it is reliable. You know very well from experience that your memory can deceive you. We think, "I could have sworn I left that key on the table!" Or we say, "Didn't I tell you about that? I thought I did." We say that sort of thing all the time without realizing how shaky our memory really is. But there is one absolutely trustworthy thought you can have about the past: "The past is not here. This is the present." Now, if the past isn't here, how can it have present effects? "To think about it at all is therefore to think about illusions" (2:2). You are thinking about something that no longer exists, which by definition is an illusion.

Okay, so if my mind is preoccupied with past thoughts, and all thoughts about the past are thoughts about illusions, and all that I see is a projection of my thoughts—where does that leave what I am "seeing"? Nowhere. We are seeing reflections of memories of an illusion. When we are picturing the past or anticipating the future, the Course says our mind is actually *blank*, because it is thinking about nothing (2:4).

This lesson is trying to get us to recognize when our mind is not really thinking at all, but is full of what it calls "thoughtless ideas." This is why "these thoughts do not mean anything" (Lesson 4). To open ourselves to "vision" we have to stop blocking the truth with these meaningless mental images of something that isn't here. The first step towards vision is becoming aware of the things that are *not* vision, which are the thoughts that normally fill our minds.

I find this kind of exercise helps develop a kind of mental detachment. You step back, as it were, from your thoughts and observe them. Don't make the mistake I made at first: Trying to force these thoughts out of the mind and make it blank. We don't need to do that because it is blank already! Just observe your thoughts and apply the lesson, saying, "My mind is preoccupied with past thoughts." Be willing to let go of your investment in the thoughts, or in having them be real thoughts, or deep ones, or important ones. Unclasp your fingers from them, let them go, be willing to see that they are without real meaning if they are based on the past, and thus based on something that is not here.

The lesson is a gentle wedge, prying loose our attachment to what we think of as our thoughts.

LESSON 9 ✦ JANUARY 9 17/06/06

"I see nothing as it is now."

Practice instructions

Exercise: Three or four times, for one minute.

Look about you, applying the idea without discrimination or exclusion to whatever you see. Begin with things near you: *"I do not see this [telephone, arm, etc.] as it is now."* Then extend the range outward: *"I do not see that [door, face, etc.] as it is now."*

Remarks: You may accept this idea, but you do not really understand it, nor are you expected to. Understanding is not the prerequisite for this practice; rather, understanding is the *goal* of this practice. These exercises are meant to undo your illusion that you understand things and, by clearing this blockage away, allow true understanding to finally dawn on your mind. So at this point simply practice the idea, even if you do not understand it, find it disturbing, or even actively resist it.

Commentary

If I see only the past, and my mind is preoccupied with past thoughts, then obviously I see nothing as it is now. I love the fact that the lesson goes on to say, "But while you may be able to accept it intellectually, it is unlikely that it will mean anything to you as yet" (1:2). The Course clearly recognizes a vast difference between intellectually accepting an idea and truly understanding it, so that it has become a part of us. I think of the stages of grief when a loved one dies. Immediately after the death, we may intellectually accept that our beloved is gone, but we have not truly grasped and assimilated that fact. It takes time for the reality of it to sink in.

Likewise, we can accept the idea that we see nothing as it is now, but it may be some time before the meaning of that fact truly begins to dawn on us. Fortunately, the lesson goes on to say that our understanding, at this stage, is not necessary. In fact, what *is* necessary is the recognition that we *do not* understand! You might say that one of the things we are

27

to grasp from this lesson is that we don't understand it!
It makes a kind of sense if you think about it.

> These exercises are concerned with practice, not with understanding. You do not need to practice what you already understand. (1:5–6)

Some people may feel that it doesn't make sense to work with an idea you don't fully understand or believe. I've heard people ask questions such as "How can I work with a lesson like 'I am the holy Son of God Himself' if I don't really believe that?" And the answer is, if you believed it already, you wouldn't need to work with the lesson! Helping you understand or believe is what the practice is for.

The attitude of recognizing our real ignorance is vital to learning. Without it, our false "understanding" gets in the way of learning. So when a lesson such as this one, "I see nothing as it is now," rubs you the wrong way or leaves you feeling that you don't really know what it is talking about—just be honest that you feel that way. Don't make the mistake of pretending you already understand when you don't. The lessons are designed with our ignorance in mind.

"It is difficult for the untrained mind to believe that what it seems to picture is not there" (2:1). Difficult? Nearly impossible is more like it. The idea is disturbing; most of us will actively resist it in some way or another. *That's okay.* That does not keep you from applying the idea anyhow, and that is all that is asked of us. (Remember the introduction to the Workbook and its last two paragraphs? If not, read them over in this regard.) Just do the exercises anyhow, even if your mind is resisting the entire idea; it will still have the desired effect.

Notice how the lesson talks about "each small step" (2:5) clearing away a little darkness until understanding finally comes. The tone of these lessons, and indeed the entire Course, should not lead us to believe that we will reach enlightenment quickly. It comes in small steps, little by little. The Course does say that full enlightenment could come to any of us in any instant, if we could but open to it; it is nearer to us than our own hands and feet. But it also says that it will take much longer to make us willing to open than it will take for that final transformation of mind to occur. It says:

> By far the majority are given a slowly-evolving training

program, in which as many previous mistakes as possible are corrected. Relationships in particular must be properly perceived, and all dark cornerstones of unforgiveness removed. (M-9.1:7–8)

Notice: a "slowly-evolving training program" is the norm. So don't be so restless or feel like you're working against some deadline; take things at the pace they come, and work with the exercises in this Workbook. Be content to slowly evolve. Don't worry if understanding does not leap full-blown into your mind tomorrow!

The exercises are again deceptively simple, things like "I do not see this computer screen as it is now." How does saying this help me? I can't say for sure. I do know that the more often I repeat an idea, the more reasonable it starts to seem. Maybe that's all there is to it. I know it has helped me, at times, to remind myself in some situation that seems fearful or out of control that "I do not see this situation as it is now in reality." I can reassure myself that what I am seeing, which seems to be causing my fear, is not the reality of things. I may not have any idea what the reality is, but it helps to know that what I am seeing ain't it! The idea is less reassuring when I apply it to something that I *do* like: "I do not see this romantic relationship as it is now." Hmmm, not sure I like that. But if it does nothing more than begin to shake my faith in what I see, the lesson is doing its job even if I don't fully understand it or like it.

LESSON 10 ✦ JANUARY 10
"My thoughts do not mean anything."

Practice instructions

Purpose: To show you that all of your current thoughts are meaningless and are, in fact, not real thoughts at all. Recognizing that you have been preoccupied with nonexistent thoughts will pave the way for uncovering your real thoughts.

Exercise: Five times, for one minute or so (no more; cut in half if you are uncomfortable).

- Close your eyes and repeat the idea very slowly. Then add, *"This idea will help to release me from all that I now believe."*
- Then search your mind for all available thoughts. Avoid selection or classification, seeing your thoughts as an odd procession which has no meaning to you. As each one crosses your mind say, *"My thought about _____ does not mean anything."*

Remarks: It is important to stand back from your thoughts and observe them with detachment. Do not think of them as different from one another in any real way. You might want to imagine you are watching a strange parade of disorganized, meaningless objects. Another helpful metaphor (not mentioned in the Course) might be to imagine that you are watching leaves float by on a stream.

Response to temptation: Optional—whenever you have a distressing thought.

Feel free to apply the idea to any upsetting thoughts you have throughout the day, using the form: *"My thought about _____ does not mean anything."*

Commentary

Lesson 4 said, "These thoughts do not mean anything," and it promised the exercise would be "repeated from time to time in somewhat different form" (W-pI.4.3:1). This lesson is the first repetition. It explains that the reason the idea is true is that

> all the thoughts of which you are aware…are not your real
> thoughts.   (1:1–2)

That is particularly difficult to accept at first. How can my thoughts not be my real thoughts? It explains that we don't have any basis for comparison *as yet*, but that when we do, "you will have no doubt that what you once believed were your thoughts did not mean anything" (1:5). So once again the Workbook is asking us, to a certain degree, to take this idea by faith for the time being.

A basis for comparison implies that before long we will experience our real thoughts, and when we do, we will know that what we believed to be our thoughts were not our real ones. It's like we've been eating carob all our lives thinking it was chocolate. Once we taste real chocolate, we know that carob was not chocolate; but until we have a basis for comparison, we can only take our teacher's word for it.

The difference between Lesson 10 and Lesson 4 is in the first word: "*My* thoughts" instead of "*These* thoughts." In addition, the lesson does not go on to link the thoughts with things around us, as Lesson 4 did: "They are like the things I see in this room." So the emphasis in this lesson is on the thoughts themselves: "The emphasis is now on the lack of reality of what you think you think" (2:4).

The third paragraph points out the different aspects about our thoughts that have been emphasized so far:

- they are meaningless
- they are outside rather than within
- they concern the past rather than the present

"Now we are emphasizing that the presence of these 'thoughts' means that you are not thinking" (3:2). This rephrases the earlier concept that our mind is simply blank. Before we can have vision, we have to learn to recognize nothingness when we think we see it.

The exercises given make it clear that what the Course is talking about closely resembles many Eastern meditation teachings. What is being cultivated is a kind of detachment from our "thoughts," becoming "the witness" or taking the position of an observer in regard to our thoughts. We watch the thoughts as if "you are watching an oddly assorted procession going by, which has little if any personal meaning to you" (4:6).

One book I read about meditation (Stephen Levine's *A Gradual Awakening*,[1] a wonderful little book) used the analogy of watching a train going by, each car containing a thought or set of thoughts. "Oh, there goes a thought of hatred! There goes some worry. There is a carload of sadness." It also used the picture of watching clouds floating by in the sky, with the expanse of sky being the mind itself. Levine emphasizes that we do not let ourselves cling to any of the thoughts or allow them to drag us along with them, but likewise we do not push them away or resist them. If they are "meaningless," as the lesson says, we need not respond to them at all.

As you do this kind of mental exercise you become aware of your mind as something independent of the thoughts that appear to cross it. You dis-identify with the thoughts. They lose their emotional charge for you. The thoughts become less and less of a "big deal" to you. You begin to recognize the vast expanse of mind in which these thoughts come and go, and to realize that they have no effect on that "sky of mind" in which they float.

Notice in the practice instructions that the pace is stepping up a bit. "Five practice periods are recommended" (5:2) in addition to using the idea during the day for any thought that distresses us.

The closing added thought can be helpful to reinforce our belief that what we are doing is really worthwhile. We may need such reinforcement, since the actual practice of the exercise may induce discomfort at times. It isn't comfortable to repeatedly tell oneself, "My thoughts do not mean anything." It may seem demeaning. So reminding myself that "this idea will help to release me from all that I now believe" (4:3) can be a needed step in strengthening our motivation to do the exercises. The Workbook is cognizant of how entrenched the ego is in our minds, and works with us very gently in its attempts to dislodge us from our fixed position.

---

1. Stephen Levine, *A Gradual Awakening* (New York: Anchor Books, 1979, 1989).

LESSON 11 ✦ JANUARY 11
"My meaningless thoughts are showing me a meaningless world."

Practice instructions

Purpose: To reverse how you see cause and effect in your perception. You think that the outside world imprints itself on your mind, causing your perceptions, yet causation travels the other way: from the inside out. What you see outside you is the projection of your thoughts. This is the first lesson that deals with this major Workbook theme.

Exercise: Three times (four or five if you find that comfortable and desirable), for one minute or so.

- With eyes closed repeat the idea *slowly* and *casually*, to reflect the peace and relaxation contained in the idea.
- Then open your eyes and look about, up and down, near and fear, letting your eyes move rapidly from one thing to another. During this time repeat the idea leisurely and effortlessly.
- To conclude, close your eyes and repeat the idea slowly.

Remarks: Unlike most of the previous exercises, in this one you do not apply the idea specifically to the objects around you, naming them as you do. In fact, the repeating of the idea is not synchronized with the shifting of your glance. The two happen at different paces. The relative *rapidity* with which you look around is contrasted with the *slowness* with which you repeat the idea.

Commentary

The lesson introduces "the concept that your thoughts determine the world you see" (1:3), a major theme in the Course. It is the reason for the famous line, "Seek not to change the world, but choose to change your mind about the world" (T-21.In.1:7). The mind is primary and the world secondary. We believe that the world causes (or at least affects) what we think; the Course teaches that mind is the cause, and the world, effect.

The idea, we are told, "contains the foundation for the peace, relaxation and freedom from worry we are trying to achieve" (3:4).

> In this idea is your release made sure. The key to forgiveness lies in it. (1:4–5)

Why is that? If what I see outside is being caused by my own meaningless thoughts, then there is nothing to "blame" in the outside world; all that is needed is to correct my thoughts. I can forgive what I see *because* it is meaningless. I condemn and judge only when I think I see something that means something—something bad or evil or terrible. But if it is meaningless there is no ground for condemnation. And if my mind is the cause of what I see, then how can I judge it? All I can do is recognize that, as the Text says, "I *am* responsible for what I see" (T-21.II.2:3), and choose to change my own mind.

LESSON 12 ✦ JANUARY 12
"I am upset because I see a meaningless world."

Practice instructions

Purpose: To realize that you are upset because you instinctively sense that the world is content-free, a blank slate. This makes you afraid that the truth will be written on it. This exercise will help you accept that the world truly is a blank slate, erase what you have written on it, and then see what God has written on it.

Exercise: Three or four times, for one minute or less (stop whenever you feel strain).

- Look about slowly, shifting your glance at regular time intervals. As you look about, say, *"I think I see a fearful world, a dangerous world, a hostile world,"* and so on, using whatever descriptive terms occur to you. This includes positive ones, which imply the possibility of their opposite. They imply a world in which both positive and negative are present and battle for supremacy. This is not the world God would have you see.
- At the end add, *"But I am upset because I see a meaningless world."*

Remarks: Shifting your glance at regular intervals reflects today's idea. By giving the same amount of time and attention to each thing, you teach yourself that the things you see are all equally meaningless. This is the same thing today's idea is trying to teach you.

Commentary

What upsets us is an empty slate, a canvas without paint; we can't resist, we have to paint *our* meaning on it, and when we do, what we see is frightening, sad, violent, or insane. We can't simply accept the world as meaningless and "let the truth be written upon it for you" (5:3); instead, "you are impelled to write upon it what you would have it be" (5:4). We can't allow God to give the world, and ourselves, our meaning; we want to make our own. The result is an upsetting view of everything.

This idea, that what I think is upsetting me is not really the cause of my upset (see Lesson 5 again), is an incredibly useful one. It can work miracles in our experience. I recall the first time this really sank in. I had just gone through a disappointing exchange with my girlfriend, one in which I realized that she didn't want to spend time with me as much as I did with her, and she had an interest in someone else. I was feeling spit upon, put down, a second-class citizen; I was angry at her for not realizing what a prize I was and for making me spend my Saturday evening alone. I was miserable.

All of a sudden the thought came to me: "I'm doing this to myself; it isn't her." I thought of the song from *My Fair Lady* where Rex Harrison sings, "I was supremely independent and content before we met. Surely I could always be that way again…and yet." I realized that I was *choosing* to see her as the cause of my upset, but it was the way *I* was thinking about the situation that was making me miserable. If I wanted to, I could still be happy. It was a major revelation to me! I wasn't sure I liked it, to be honest, but my inner sense kept telling me, "This way lies real liberty." That was a big beginning for me.

Let the world be meaningless to you today. Don't be so quick to impose your meaning on it. Just let what is so be what it is, without any meaning, and let the Holy Spirit have a chance to write His meaning on it.

> When your words have been erased, you will see His. That is the ultimate purpose of these exercises.　　(5:8–9)

There is a Workbook-like saying given in the Text that runs along the same line:

> When your peace is threatened or disturbed in any way, say to yourself:
>
> *I do not know what anything, including this, means. And so I do not know how to respond to it. And I will not use my own past learning as the light to guide me now.*
>
> By this refusal to attempt to teach yourself what you do not know [or to write your meaning on the blank slate], the

Guide Whom God has given you will speak to you. He will take His rightful place in your awareness the instant you abandon it, and offer it to Him.   (T-14.XI.6:6–11)

LESSON 13 ✦ JANUARY 13
"A meaningless world engenders fear."

Practice instructions

Purpose: The same as yesterday.

Exercise: Three or four times, for one minute or so (no more).

- Close your eyes and repeat the idea.
- Open your eyes and look slowly around you. While doing so repeat over and over, *"I am looking at a meaningless world."*
- Close your eyes and say, *"A meaningless world engenders fear, because I think I am in competition with God."*

Remarks: Do not worry if you do not believe the closing statement. You may think it is crazy and you may resist it. All of that is fine. Simply note your resistance, whatever forms it takes, and tell yourself that the real reason for it is that this statement awakens your underlying fear of God's vengeance. Deep inside you believe that by rushing in and writing your meaning on the world's blank slate you have temporarily defeated God. As a result, you believe you now face His wrath. To cope with this belief you have shoved it down into your unconscious, but today's concluding statement brings it back toward the surface. This is why you fear the statement and are eager to dismiss it. Because of all this, do not dwell on it or even think of it except during the exercises.

Commentary

More specifically than upsetting us, the meaningless world we see sparks fear within us. After spending several days convincing us, so it seems, that the world is meaningless, the Course "reverses course":

> Actually, a meaningless world is impossible. Nothing without meaning exists. (1:2–3)

The introduction to the Text states that "nothing unreal exists"

(T-In.2:3), and now we are told nothing meaningless exists. The situation is not that meaningless things exist and we are afraid because we see them; what is happening is that we *think* we perceive things without meaning, and rush to write our meaning on them. We see no meaning because we are unwilling to see the meaning already written on them by God.

When we see the meaningless it arouses anxiety in us:

> It represents a situation in which God and the ego "challenge" each other as to whose meaning is to be written in the empty space the meaninglessness provides. The ego rushes in frantically to establish its own ideas there, fearful that the void may otherwise be used to demonstrate its own impotence and unreality. And on this alone it is correct. (2:2–4)

If the ego did not rush in to give its meaning to things, the meaning established by God would, indeed, demonstrate the unreality of the ego. That is why the ego imagines it sees an empty space of meaninglessness to write in; it fears the meaning God has already given. We assign our own meaning to everything.

The Course is insistent that if we did not rush in to write our own meaning, the message we would hear would be one of love and beauty. This is true no matter what the outside "situation" appears to be. For instance, a brother may be totally deceived by his own ego and verbally attacking us. The message we hear in his words, no matter their form, is the message we *choose* to hear. We assign the meaning we think our brother is giving us. If my mind were attuned to the Holy Spirit, no matter what anyone did or said, I would hear a message that affirms the Christ in me and engenders my love. (For a long—and somewhat complex—section on this very topic, see Text, Chapter 9, Section II, "The Answer to Prayer," which says, in part, "The message your brother gives you is up to you. What does he say to you? What would you have him say? Your decision about him determines the message you receive" [T-9.II.5:1–4].)

The idea that we are in competition with God and fear His vengeance because of our competition may, as the lesson admits, seem preposterous. It asks us to practice the lesson anyhow. At this level we are mainly trying to become aware that we are afraid to leave anything without meaning, although we don't realize fully *why* we are afraid of that. It is asking us to work at being willing to say, "I do not know what this means." We really are afraid of that! The lesson also asks us to note any form of fear carefully. Not to try to overcome it; just notice it. Notice that leaving something without an assigned meaning makes you anxious, and let yourself consider that maybe the reason is that somehow, somewhere deep down in the darkness of your unconscious, you are afraid of the meaning God might write there if you let Him.

LESSON 14 ✦ JANUARY 14
"God did not create a meaningless world."

Practice instructions

Purpose: To erase the interpretations you have put on the world so that you can see God's interpretation (just as with the previous two lessons). This process will save you. In its early stages, however, you may often feel as if you are being led into terror. This is only temporary. You will be led through fear and then beyond it forever.

Exercise: Three times (unless you find more comfortable), for one minute at most.

- With eyes closed, think of all the horrors in the world that cross your mind, anything you are afraid might happen to you or anyone. For each one say, *"God did not create that [specify the horror], and so it is not real."* Be very specific in naming the horror or disaster.
- Conclude by repeating the idea.

Response to temptation: Optional—when anything disturbs you.

Feel free to apply the idea to dispel your upsets during the day. A special form has been provided for this: "God did not create a meaningless world. He did not create [specify the situation which is disturbing you], and so it is not real." This is a very effective practice for regaining peace of mind. You may, in fact, want to give it a try now: Choose a situation that is weighing on you and apply the practice to it. See if at least some of the weight of it does not lift immediately.

Commentary

Today's idea should come as a welcome relief after four days of being told our thoughts are meaningless and are showing us a meaningless world that is upsetting and frightening. The meaningless world we are seeing was not created by God, and "what God did not create does not exist" (1:2).

In the book *Awaken from the Dream*[1] by Gloria and Kenneth Wapnick, Gloria wrote about how this idea first attracted her to the Course:

> Hearing firsthand about the devastating effects World War II had on people personally, I concluded that if this world were the best that God could create, I wanted nothing more to do with Him...
>
> As I read Jesus' words explain that God did not create the world, it was as if "lightning bolts" crashed through my head. "Why hadn't I thought of that?" I kept thinking to myself. "It is so simple; that is the answer." Finally, after twenty-three years the puzzle in my mind was solved. The Course had supplied the missing piece, and I no longer had to blame God for a world He did not create.

To some, the message that God did not create the meaningless world we see comes as salvation; to others, it may be "quite difficult and even quite painful" (3:2). For recognizing that He did not create it entails a corollary truth: we made it up. We are responsible for the world we see. That can lead us "directly into fear" (3:3). The Course faces up to this in many different places through all three volumes. The message it is giving to us, especially in the "early steps" (3:2), can be difficult, painful, and fearful.

Many people wonder if something is wrong because they have strong negative reactions to this line of thought in the Course. The answer is, not at all. Perhaps it is those among us who *do not* have any negative reactions who should be wondering if they are apprehending the Course's message correctly and realizing its implications. A negative reaction is far more common than a positive one: that I can say with confidence.

Be glad, however, that the lesson goes on to say:

> You will not be left there [in fear]. You will go far beyond it. Our direction is toward perfect safety and perfect peace.
>
> (3:4–6)

The Course calls our path a journey "through fear to love" (T-16.IV.11:1–2). The early distress is avoided by very few indeed, but the direction of the journey is towards a warmth and breadth of love that can barely be imagined as we start out.

One word of caution about the particular form of practice today. Notice carefully that the lesson is asking you to say these thoughts *to yourself* about "your personal repertory of horrors" (6:1). It is not advocating telling another person who is going through some tragedy that it isn't real; for instance, "Cheer up! God didn't create the death of your husband, so it isn't real." In most cases that is not a loving message but an attack, placing you in a "superior" spiritual position to the other person. The lesson is talking about giving this message to yourself.

Note also the mention here about our illusions, that "some of them are shared illusions, and others are part of your personal hell" (6:3). Things such as famine and AIDS fall in the "shared illusion" category. There is clear support here for the idea that the illusion of the world is a shared responsibility, not just your personal creation, or mine.

---

1. Gloria and Kenneth Wapnick, *Awaken from the Dream*, 2nd Ed. (Temecula, Cal.: Foundation for *A Course in Miracles*, 1995).

LESSON 15 ✦ JANUARY 15
"My thoughts are images that I have made."

Practice instructions

Purpose: To introduce you to the process of image making, by which your inner thoughts appear as outer images.

Exercise: Three times (four if comfortable), for one minute (less if you feel uneasy).

- Repeat the idea to yourself.
- Then look about and apply it randomly to whatever you see, saying quite slowly, *"This [name of object] is an image that I have made."* Let your eyes rest on the object the whole time you are repeating this.

Response to temptation: Optional—whenever you are upset.

You may want to use this form: *"This [name of situation] is an image that I have made."* This will remind you that the "upsetting" situation you are seeing is not objectively real, but is just your own thoughts appearing in image form.

Commentary

Our perception is composed of images made from our thoughts. Because the thoughts appear as images, we do not recognize the thoughts as nothing. Physical sight is nothing more than this, and this is the purpose of physical sight. We gave our body's eyes the function of seeing these thought images, in order to validate the thoughts we think we are thinking.

> It is not seeing. It is image making. It takes the place of seeing, replacing vision with illusions. (1:5–7)

The Course is quite consistent in its view of our physical sight. It says, for instance:

> Everything the body's eyes can see is a mistake, an error in perception, a distorted fragment of the whole without the

> meaning that the whole would give.   (T-22.III.4:3)

> The body's eyes see only form. They cannot see beyond
> what they were made to see. And they were made to look
> on error and not see past it.   (T-22.III.5:3–5)

What our eyes show us is a mistake. What our eyes show us is an image we have made, and does not portray the truth. They were "made to look on error and not see past it." Part of what we must begin to learn is to look past the bodily level, to begin to realize that what our eyes are showing us is not necessarily the truth. Our eyes are showing us only the errors of our own minds.

There is something *beyond* the physical that vision can show us. That is the meaning of the "edges of light" (2:2) the lesson refers to. In a workshop I attended, Ken Wapnick remarked that this mention of "light episodes" (3:1) was included in part as an answer to a friend of Helen's who was seeing light around people and wondering if there was something wrong. The lesson explains that such experiences "merely symbolize true perception" (3:5). The lesson is not trying to say that everyone should have such experiences. It is saying merely that, if such experiences do occur, we should not be disconcerted by them; they are a sign of progress. It is not the symbol of true perception we seek, however, but true perception itself. The meaning of "edges of light" is simply that there is something there to be seen that is beyond the physical. It is to this realization that the lesson is leading us.

LESSON 16 ✦ JANUARY 16
"I have no neutral thoughts."

Practice instructions

Purpose: A beginning step in learning that every thought has effects and that each one produces either fear and war or love and peace.

Exercise: Four or five times (three if there's strain), for one minute each (reduce if there's discomfort).

- Close your eyes and repeat the idea.
- Then search your mind for any thoughts present. Try to make no distinctions among them. Try especially not to overlook any "little" thought. As each thought crosses your mind, hold it in mind and say, *"This thought about _____ is not a neutral thought."*

Response to temptation: Whenever you are aware of an upsetting thought.

Apply the idea to it using this specific form: *"This thought about _____ is not a neutral thought, because I have no neutral thoughts."* The point is to make you realize that, by entertaining this thought, you are actively causing yourself fear.

Commentary

This could seem like a scary idea, but the main intent is for us to realize how effective our thoughts are. This is an empowering idea, not a threatening one, unless we choose to see it that way.

> Everything you see is the result of your thoughts. There is no exception to this fact. (1:2–3)

Like many of the ideas the Course presents, this one is difficult to believe at first because we are so convinced that our thoughts have nothing to do with most of the things we see. Just in case we let the idea slip by, the lesson adds that there are no exceptions. True thoughts create true things; false thoughts make false things, or illusions. There is

46

nothing to be afraid of here because only the true thoughts create realities; false thoughts only make illusions.

No thought, however, is "idle." "What gives rise to the perception of a whole world can hardly be called idle" (2:2). Every thought in our mind is producing *something* all the time, contributing to truth or to illusion. The Course is a mind-training course. Its aims to make us aware of our thoughts and their effects. It desires us to be intimately involved in the process of choosing the thoughts that occupy our minds and produce their effects in the world around us.

We are asked to recognize that no thought is neutral, no thought does nothing to affect the growth of truth or illusion. Every thought expresses either love or fear; there is no in-between. If I look at the way I treat my own thoughts I can see the lesson is correct: I really do tend to slough off certain thoughts as unimportant and not worth bothering about. Every thought is worth bothering about; all fear thoughts are equally destructive. *They are also equally unreal*. Thus, we need not be guilty about them.

Some students of the Course are quick to latch on to the "unreal" part but very slow to acknowledge the "destructive" side; the Course always maintains this balance. Just because something is unreal or illusory does not mean it is unimportant and can be ignored! For instance, at one point the Text says that delay is impossible in eternity but is *tragic* in time (T-5.VI.1:3). The Course is not advocating an attitude of indifference to the world simply because it is an illusion. Remarks such as "AIDS? It's only an illusion" or "What starving children? It isn't real," are not representative of the true spirit of the Course, although you may hear them in some circles. If AIDS and starvation are in our perception, the thoughts that manifest them must be in our minds, individually or collectively, and therefore we are responsible for healing those thoughts. But I digress from the lesson; time to step off the soapbox.

The lesson is pointing out that no thought can be dismissed as trivial, and no thought is neutral. As you practice the lesson there will be some thoughts that will easily be seen to be "not neutral." If someone steals your car it is fairly easy to acknowledge that your thoughts about it are not neutral. But if you are thinking of which breakfast cereal to eat it is a bit more of a stretch to believe that "This thought about Wheaties is not a neutral thought," that it is expressing either love or fear. Believe it; it is. As the instructions say, do not "make artificial distinctions" (4:3).

The mind is like a light bulb, which is either on or off and never in-between; our minds are expressing fear or love, and never something in-between, never both, and never nothing.

LESSON 17 ✦ JANUARY 17
"I see no neutral things."

Practice instructions

Purpose: To continue teaching you the real cause and effect relationship between what you think and what you see. You think that outer events cause your perceptions, but in fact your perceptions are caused by your thoughts.

Exercise: Three or four times (three are required), for one minute (less if there's resistance).

Remarks: As usual, it is crucial to treat whatever you see as the same. The carpet may be neutral in itself, but you do not see it that way, because your perception of it arises from thoughts that are inherently non-neutral. Even if the carpet is black and white, figuratively speaking, your thoughts always color it.

Commentary

The true meaning of cause and effect in this world, according to the Course, is that thoughts are the cause and the world is the effect. We tend to believe that events or actions in the world cause us to think in certain ways; the Course says the opposite. "It is always the thought that comes first, despite the temptation to believe that it is the other way around" (1:3). We have no neutral thoughts and therefore we see no neutral things.

What is our usual tendency when we find ourselves having certain thoughts? We ask ourselves, "What made me feel this way? What made me depressed, or angry, or bored?" But the thought always comes first. It was not anything outside of your mind that caused you to think in a certain way. Rather, your mind caused the world you see.

The lesson becomes quite radical in its statements at times:

> Regardless of what you may believe, you do not see anything that is really alive or really joyous. That is because you are unaware as yet of any thought that is really true, and therefore really happy. (3:2–3)

I've been studying the Course now for ten years and I still have trouble fully accepting the idea that I don't see anything really alive. I know that the Course states that the body (which is what I see with my eyes) does not die because it has never lived, and so I know intellectually that the Course defines "alive" quite differently than we normally do. By "alive" it obviously must mean something nonphysical, because it writes off the physical body as not being alive at all. But I have to admit that I still need to practice with this lesson because my instinct is still to regard bodies as alive. I have to work at it to remember otherwise.

I recall speaking with my friend Lynne a little over a year before her body "died." She was a student of the Course. Her body had deteriorated rapidly during the preceding year, and after several surgeries was only a shell of what it had been. She remarked to me that she was really learning the truth of what she really was. I said, "I guess you have a little more understanding of what the Course means when it says, 'I am not a body.'"

"I damn well better not be!" she exclaimed, laughing.

These two ideas—that nothing I see with my eyes is really alive, and that nothing I see is neutral because my thoughts are not neutral—can be disconcerting. Even so, they have their plus side. The lesson is the same for us all, although for some, like Lynne, it seems to be accelerated. Yet our bodies will wither and decay just as hers did, only a little more slowly. It is a welcome relief to realize that the body's only meaning is given it by our mind. The mind and spirit are what are alive and real; they are the cause, and the body and its world are only the effects of thoughts.

LESSON 18 ✦ JANUARY 18
"I am not alone in experiencing the effects of my seeing."

Practice instructions

Purpose: To continue to teach you that your thoughts are not without effect. The preceding lessons have emphasized that they always affect your mind. This lesson emphasizes that they always affect *all* minds.

Exercise: Three or four times, for one minute or so (perhaps less).

- Look around you, randomly selecting subjects and resting your glance on each one long enough to say, *"I am not alone in experiencing the effects of how I see _____."*
- Conclude by repeating the idea.

Commentary

The concept that "minds are joined" (1:2) is easy to grasp, but literally far-reaching in its implications. How I see things affects other minds, not just my own. The miracles that the Course can bring into our lives will prove this to us time and time again. A shift in the way *I* see things can bring about miraculous effects in people around me:

> A miracle is never lost. It may touch many people you
> have not even met, and produce undreamed of changes in
> situations of which you are not even aware. (T-1.I.45:1–2)

The fact that how I see things affects more than just myself makes the thoughts that give rise to my seeing even more important. How I think and perceive things affects, quite literally, the entire world. By opening my mind to love I can be a conduit of love for the world.

LESSON 19 ✦ JANUARY 19

"I am not alone in experiencing the effects of my thoughts."

Practice instructions

Purpose: To teach you that all minds are joined. Despite being initially unwelcome, this idea must be true for salvation to be possible.

Exercise: Three or four (at least three), for one minute or so (shorter if necessary).

- Close your eyes and repeat the idea.
- Search your mind carefully for the thoughts it contains now. As you consider each one in turn, hold it in your mind and say, *"I am not alone in experiencing the effects of this thought about [name central person or theme of thought]."*

Remarks: Today's lesson includes the last major mention of a theme that is quite familiar by now: the need to be indiscriminate and random in selecting practice subjects. These early lessons have drilled this into us (it has been mentioned in every lesson except 8, 13, and 14), and so in this lesson the author announces that he will no longer emphasize it. This is not because it is no longer relevant, but because he expects that we have internalized it by now. He now expects us to maintain this practice throughout the rest of the Workbook. He also mentions why it is so important. Being able to apply the idea just as easily to our partner's body as to a speck on the floor will ultimately enable us to heal cancer just as easily as a cold.

Response to temptation: As needed.

Apply the idea in response to any unwanted thought. Just realizing that this thought affects everyone will help you let it go.

Commentary

Yesterday it was about seeing; today about thinking. "Thinking and its results are really simultaneous, for cause and effect are never separate" (1:4). Thinking is cause; seeing is effect, and they are simultaneous. A baseball flying through your window causes the glass to be broken. Which happens first? The baseball passing through the plane of the glass, or the glass breaking? Obviously both happen at once.

So it is with thinking and seeing. When we think, we perceive. The simultaneity is part of what makes it so difficult for us to recognize thought as the cause. It is fairly easy for the ego to play the trick of reversing cause and effect, so that we believe that what we see is the cause of what we think. But that isn't the way it works at all.

The idea that minds are joined is exciting, but also, especially at first, quite threatening. There are thoughts I have that I do not want to have shared, but "there are no private thoughts" (2:3). My "private" thoughts affect everyone and everything just as every thought does that engages my mind. The idea can be disconcerting. The lesson tells us that despite resistance, eventually we will all recognize that the idea—of joined minds in which no thought is private—is inevitable "if salvation is possible at all" (2:4). It does not explain why it is inevitable, but just says that we'll all see it that way before long.

Let's think about it for a minute. If other minds are truly separate from mine, then different wills are also truly possible. That places me in competition with the world, alone against the universe. How can I then be free from fear, if outside forces can at any moment turn against me in vicious attack?

If, however, minds are joined, and if what I think affects all of this unified mind, then salvation is possible. Then one choice for peace can affect the entire joined mind towards peace. Salvation is possible; I am not an effect of the world, but the world is my effect. I am empowered to choose. I can choose peace for all of Mind. This is how, in the Course's view of things, I can become a savior of the world.

Let me then determine this day to choose for peace, for healing, and for forgiveness. As I begin to realize that I am not alone in experiencing the effects of my thoughts, I will begin to care about what I think, and as I begin to care, I will begin to heal myself and the world along with me.

LESSON 20 ✦ JANUARY 20
"I am determined to see."

Practice instructions

Purpose: To be determined to have vision and so to receive vision.

Exercise: Two per hour (preferably on the half hour).

- Repeat the idea. *How* you repeat it makes all the difference. The lesson asks you to do so "slowly and positively" (5:1), remembering that you are determined to exchange your present state for one you really want. (In fact, you may want to try saying it this way just once right now, and see if that makes a difference.)
- If you find at some point that you have forgotten to practice, "do not be distressed...but make a real effort to remember" (5:2) from then on.

Remarks: This lesson marks a major shift in the Workbook. If the Workbook has seemed easy up until this point, that was intentional. It cannot stay that easy, however, and reach its goal of the total transformation of your thinking. So beginning now it will give you more of a structure within which to practice. This will include more frequent practice, set times in which to practice, and longer practice. Today's lesson includes the first two of those. How you respond to this structure is crucial. If you see it as an imposition, as an outside will forcing itself on you, you will either actively or passively rebel against it. Instead, try to see it as the expression of your true will. You want all the things the Course offers you. And you will only get them through having a trained mind, and you will only get that through doing the practice. Therefore, doing the practice today is your own true desire.

Response to temptation: Whenever you become upset about a person, situation, or event.

Repeat the idea as an emotional remedy. You may want to specify it: *"I am determined to see this situation."* If you really want to see this situation differently, you will.

Commentary

Today's lesson does not really ask all that much of us: Every half hour, remember to repeat the words "I am determined to see." If we are studying the Course this is something we probably truly want.

> You want salvation. You want to be happy. You want peace.
> (2:3–5)

Why then all the foofaraw about our feeling coerced, resentful and opposed to the instructions?

Because "this is our first attempt to introduce structure" (2:1), and it will not be the last. Our undisciplined minds have a built-in resistance to structure. So what if it's good for us? Actually something we want? If someone *tells* us to do it in a certain way, at certain times, we rebel. We drag our feet. We don't like being told what to do or how to do it. Our mind is "totally undisciplined" (2:6) and wants to remain that way to protect the ego's vested interests.

The practice asked is extremely simple. So try it. You'll probably be amazed at how often you forget, how the thought of doing it may flash into your mind only to be postponed because it isn't convenient at the moment, or because "it isn't really important," and then forgotten completely. This is why the Workbook approaches the whole idea of structure with great caution; it knows there will be resistance, and is trying to make us realize just how important this deceptively simple practice really is. This is why it says: "Do not be distressed if you forget to do so, but make a real effort to remember" (5:2).

"Your decision to see is all that vision requires" (3:1). If we could really get this lesson, in other words, and truly mean what we are saying, the job would be done. Vision would be ours. "In your determination to see is vision given you" (3:8). This is *not* a trivial lesson; it is the core of everything the Course is teaching. So let's put our heart into it today! Let's do this joyfully, even—dare I say?—religiously, every half hour. Let's repeat the idea "slowly and positively" (5:1). Let's "make a real effort to remember" (5:2). Let's apply it "to any situation, person or event that upsets" us (5:3).

> You can see them differently, and you will. What you desire you will see. Such is the real law of cause and effect as it operates in the world. (5:4–6)

LESSON 21 ✦ JANUARY 21

"I am determined to see things differently."

Practice instructions

Exercise: Five times, for one full minute each.

- Repeat the idea.
- Then close your eyes and search your mind carefully for any situation at any time that arouses anger in you, no matter how mild. Hold each one in mind and say, *"I am determined to see [specify person or situation] differently."* Give "little" and "big" thoughts of anger the same attention. Be very specific, even to the point of naming specific attributes in specific people that anger you: *"I am determined to see [specify the attribute] in [name of person] differently."*

Remarks: In this practice, we are meant to avoid the fallacy that the degree of our anger matters. This fallacy takes two forms. The first is thinking that tiny bits of anger—for instance, mild irritation—are too small to bother including in the exercise. The second is emphasizing certain "obvious" sources of anger, which implies that in these particular cases our anger is truly justified. The truth is that *all* anger is maximal and *none* of it is justified.

A second fallacy is mentioned as well. This is the belief that our anger is confined to a particular personality trait in someone: "I basically love Jim. I am not angry at him across the board, just at this one particularly annoying trait of his." This lesson is implying that our anger toward this person is *not* safely confined in this way; it *is* across the board. With this fallacy, rather than not letting it influence our practice (as with the previous fallacy), we are supposed to *use* it in our practice. We are supposed to apply the idea specifically to that trait (see 5:4).

Response to temptation: Whenever a situation arouses anger.

Repeat the idea, specifying the perceived source of the anger: *"I am determined to see [specify person or situation] differently."*

Commentary

In this lesson we apply the idea of being determined to see to specific situations that arouse anger, with an emphasis on seeing these situations differently. The meaning of these exercises in connection with transforming our perceptions is quite obvious.

One thought from this lesson is particularly striking. It is a thought that makes more and more sense to me the longer I work with the Course, studying the Text and practicing the mental disciplines it teaches us: "You will become increasingly aware that a slight twinge of annoyance is nothing but a veil drawn over intense fury" (2:5).

The very first "miracle principle" presented in Chapter 1 of the Text says, "There is no order of difficulty in miracles" (T-1.I.1:1). The idea expressed in this lesson closely parallels that concept. There is no order of severity in anger, either; a slight twinge of annoyance is the same as intense fury, and in fact *is* disguised rage. All forms of anger stem from the same source.

Some schools of psychology have long maintained that everyone carries around a deeply suppressed, primal anger. It may be tempered by a veneer of civilization, but underneath, in the subconscious, lies a violent fury. Many have attributed this to our animalistic origins in evolution, but the Course sees the anger in a metaphysical sense. Within us we carry a blinding anger at ourselves because we believe we have attacked reality and succeeded; we have somehow managed to separate ourselves from God and have destroyed the unity of Heaven. We think that in a childish fit of pique over not receiving special treatment and special love, we have ruined our own home and can never go back.

We are enraged at ourselves, but, unable to endure the guilt of our own self-hatred, we broadcast our rage outward and deflect our anger onto other objects we believe to be separate from ourselves. The term used for this displacement of anger is "projection." The ego within us is constantly "cruising," looking for situations onto which anger can be projected with seeming justification, in order to convince our minds that the cause of the anger is without, and not within.

Every flash of anger, ranging from mild irritation up to rage, is a symptom of this same, deep, primal self-hatred, projected onto the world. They are all the same thing. This is why the Course is advising us not to believe that some forms of attack are more justified than others, and not to overlook the "little" thoughts of anger. By making no distinction between "degrees" of anger we are helping ourselves learn that they are, in reality, all the same, and all equally unjustified.

LESSON 22 ✦ JANUARY 22
"What I see is a form of vengeance."

Practice instructions

Exercise: Five times (at least), for one minute (at least).

- Look about you. As your eyes move slowly from one thing to another say, *"I see only the perishable. I see nothing that will last. What I see is not real. What I see is a form of vengeance."*
- Conclude by asking yourself, *"Is this the world I really want to see?"*

Remarks: The four lines that we are asked to repeat do not seem to logically follow from each other, even though it seems like they are meant to. Based on paragraph 2, I would say they do follow from each other, only *in reverse order*—meaning, the conclusion comes first and the argument's foundation comes last. The logic all rests on the idea (mentioned in paragraph 1) that we see the world through angry eyes. As a result, we are convinced that the world *must* want to get revenge on us for the daggers that came out of our eyes, so to speak. This (unconscious) conviction on our part makes us perceive ourselves surrounded by a world thirsting for vengeance on us. (That explains the fourth line.) The vengeful world we see, therefore, is our own projection. It exists only in our imagination. It is not a real world. (That explains the third line.) And, because it is not real, it does not have the *attributes* of reality; in this case, permanence. (That explains the first and second lines.) To make this fully clear, let me place the original lines and my explanation side by side:

Original lines	Explanation
I see only the perishable. *I see nothing that will last.*	I see a world that has no permanence.
What I see is not real.	It has no permanence because permanence is an attribute of reality, and the world I see is not real. It is only a picture in my imagination.
What I see is a form of vengeance.	This picture is painted by my attack thoughts. They cause me to imagine a world poised to get revenge on me for my attack on it.

Commentary

This is a lesson that I simply did not understand the first few times I went through the Workbook. I'm not entirely sure I understand it now, but it makes a certain sense to me, and to the degree that I do understand it, I'd like to share that understanding with you. Notice one thing, however, as you read through the lesson. What you are asked to actually practice with is *not* simply the thought that heads the lesson, but quite a bit more, ending with the question: "Is this the world I really want to see?" (3:8). So understanding the lead thought isn't really the purpose of this lesson; rather, the purpose is to help us realize that we do not really want what we are seeing.

We are seeing it, however, because in some part of our mind, a part we have hidden from consciousness, we do want it. We always see what we want to see, and we are seeing what we are seeing because we want to see it.

> You see what you believe is there, and you believe it there because you want it there. Perception has no other law than this. (T-25.III.1:3–4)

If we are seeing what we are seeing because we want to see it, then if this lesson can help us learn we don't *really* want it—that we really want something else—it will help us change what we see. Change what we want, and our perception changes with it.

If we hold attack thoughts in our mind we must see the world as a vicious place, a dangerous place. It is a world of pain, and "pain is but witness to the Son's mistakes in what he thinks he is. It is a dream of fierce retaliation for a crime that could not be committed" (W-pI.190.2:3–4). As I said yesterday, we are angry at ourselves over what we think we have done, and as a result we are having "a dream of fierce retaliation" for our crimes. As egos we are also angry at reality for not being what we want it to be, for not supporting our wish for separation and specialness. We cannot face our own anger at ourselves, and we cannot support the guilt of our insane rage at reality, so we project it: "Having projected his anger onto the world, he sees vengeance about to strike at him" (1:2).

The anger and attack we see in the world is only the reflection of the intensity of our inner rage, the rage we cannot see in ourselves *precisely because* we have denied it and projected it outward. The world I see thus shows me what I am thinking. "What I see is a form of vengeance" because vengeance is what fills my own mind, although I am unaware of it. That I see vengeance in the world is the proof it is in my mind, because that is the law of perception.

> He will attack, because what he beholds is his own fear external to himself, poised to attack, and howling to unite with him again. Mistake not the intensity of rage projected fear must spawn. It shrieks in wrath, and claws the air in frantic hope it can reach to its maker and devour him.
>
> (W-pI.161.8:2–4).

"It is from this savage fantasy that you want to escape" (2:1). The words the Course uses—"savage fantasy," "a dream of fierce retaliation"—are so evocative! If the world looks like this—and surely it does, quite often at least—what must be the state of our minds that spawn it? "This becomes an increasingly vicious circle until he is willing to change how he sees" (1:4).

We *do* want to escape from this savage fantasy. That is the goal of today's lesson, to help us become willing to change how we see. None of what we are seeing exists, and if we are willing to change how we see, we will no longer see it.

The Course's definition of "real" is "eternal, everlasting, change-less." What does not last is not real, by definition. "I see nothing that will last" (3:4). Therefore none of it is real, by this definition. If it is not real, what is it? "A form of vengeance" (3:6). Ken Wapnick said once that the world is simply crystallized guilt. This lesson is saying that the world is crystallized attack thoughts, vengeance solidified into a world of attack and counterattack.

> *Is this the world I really want to see?*
> The answer is surely obvious.   (3:8–9)

Bear in mind that this lesson is working at the level of motivation. It is not telling us *how* we can see something differently. It knows that if it can get us to the point of *wanting* something different the battle is over, because what we want, we will see. So if this lesson leaves you thinking, "God! No, I don't want to see the world like this anymore, but what can I do about it?" then the lesson has been successful. The question will be answered as the lessons progress.

LESSON 23 ✦ JANUARY 23
"I can escape from the world I see by giving up attack thoughts."

Practice instructions

Purpose: To learn "that you are not trapped in the world you see, because its cause can be changed" (5:1).

Exercise: Five times, for about one minute.

- Repeat the idea slowly as you look about you.
- Then close your eyes and search your mind for thoughts of attack and being attacked. Hold each one in mind and say, *"I can escape the world I see by giving up attack thoughts about _____."*

Remarks: It is important to include thoughts of attack coming *from* you and thoughts of attack coming *at* you. The lesson says that these are just two different forms of the same thought. In fact, if you look closely, you will notice that every attack thought contains both aspects. When you are angry with someone, there is always an element of "He caused me pain in some way (which means he somehow attacked me) and that's why I am angry." And whenever you see someone attacking you, there is an accompanying anger, displeasure, or frustration directed *at* him. Thus, it is all the same, and it is all attack. Seeing this can motivate us to let it all go.

Response to temptation: Whenever you notice yourself having attack thoughts.

Repeat the idea as a way of dispelling those thoughts. You might want to make it specific by using the same form as above: *"I can escape the world I see by giving up attack thoughts about _____."*

Commentary

This is one example of a statement that sums up the message of ACIM for us. We do not escape from the world by controlling it, manipulating it, fixing it, or trying to make it better. We escape by an act of mind, by giving up attack thoughts. The world I see is the effect of attack thoughts in my mind, and therefore I can "escape" from it by changing my mind. This is "the only way out of fear that will ever succeed. Nothing else will work; everything else is meaningless" (1:1–2).

"It is with your thoughts, then, that we must work" (1:5). The Text puts it like this:

> You must change your mind, not your behavior, and this *is* a matter of willingness. You do not need guidance except at the mind level. Correction belongs only at the level where change is possible. Change does not mean anything at the symptom level, where it cannot work.
>
> (T-2.VI.3:4–7)

The world is the symptom level; the mind is the level of causation.

It is very hard for most people to accept this dictum of the Course: "There is no point in trying to change the world" (2:3). As often as I have read this I keep running my head up against it. I find myself trying to change some outward factor, something in the world around me, thinking that such a change will somehow make things better. All this accomplishes is to alleviate some symptoms, like taking a cough drop when I have a cold. It cures nothing. Or, as Marianne Williamson has said, it is like trying to solve the problems on the Titanic by rearranging the deck chairs. What works is changing my thoughts about the world, because my attack thoughts are the cause of the world I see.

"You see the world that you have made, but you do not see yourself as the image maker" (4:1). We don't recognize the power of our mind; we use the very images made by the mind to mask the mind's power. We resist being tagged as the image maker. We want it to be someone else's fault, even God's.

> Vision already holds a replacement for everything you think you see now. Loveliness can light your images, and so transform them that you will love them, even though they were made of hate. For you will not be making them alone. (4:4–6)

Every single thing we made out of our hate, our attack, and our rage can be transformed if we join with the Holy Spirit to let His light shine on them. Every special relationship, whether it seems hateful or loving, can become a source of blessing to the world. Every act of vengeance can be turned into salvation. This is what a miracle does. "The holiest of all the spots on earth is where an ancient hatred has become a present love" (T-26.IX.6:1).

We are not trapped in the world "because its cause can be changed" (5:1). Then follows a wonderfully brief summary of the process, which Ken Wapnick has labeled the three steps of forgiveness. It is found in a single sentence: "This change requires, first, that the cause be identified and then let go, so that it can be replaced" (5:2).

1. "This change requires, first, that the cause be identified...." We must recognize mind as the cause. We must become aware that we are constantly "making" the ego every moment within our own minds, by our thoughts. We must become aware that we are responsible for what we see.

2. "...and then let go...." Having recognized the mind as cause, we must choose to change our mind about the world. We must realize that the thoughts we have been thinking are not the thoughts we want because, as the lesson said yesterday, we have realized this is not the world we want to see. It does not say anything here about coming up with new thoughts; it merely says we let go of the old ones. All that is needed is a willingness for change, a recognition that "I no longer want this."

3. "...so that it can be replaced." The third step is the replacement of attack thoughts with holy thoughts, thoughts of love and peace. The next sentences are extremely important here: "The first two steps in this process require your cooperation. The final one does not" (5:3–4). The replacement step is not our job! We cooperate in identifying the cause, uncovering the ego within our minds, and we cooperate in letting go of those ego thoughts, but the replacement with God's thoughts is not our job. That just happens.

When something happens to upset me, this is all I need to remember:

1. The cause is not outside, but is instead my own thoughts.

2. I do not want these thoughts.

Step 3 takes care of itself, for if I take the first two steps, I will see that my false images have *already* been replaced. The true thoughts spoken of earlier are already in my mind, but they are masked by the false ones. Remove the false, and the true is seen to be already there.

Within the practice instructions there is one other idea worth singling out:

> Be sure to include both your thoughts of attacking and being attacked. Their effects are exactly the same because they are exactly the same. (7:1–2)

An "attack thought" is not just a thought I have about attacking another; it is also a thought of *being* attacked. If everything I see is a reflection of my thoughts, then what seems to be attack coming at me from outside is really my own thought of attack bouncing back at me.

Fears of all kinds are attack thoughts. Uneasiness when a highway patrol car cruises by is an attack thought. Worry about competition at work, or in a relationship, is an attack thought. Cheering when the Death Star blows up is an attack thought. Watch your mind on Super Bowl Sunday!

We have a lot of giving up to do. The result is worth it.

LESSON 24 ✦ JANUARY 24
"I do not perceive my own best interests."

Practice instructions

Exercise: Five times, for two minutes.

- Repeat the idea.
- With eyes closed, search your mind for unresolved situations that you've been concerned about. When you find one, name all the goals you hope this situation will end up meeting for you, all the outcomes you are desiring, at least all that you can find. Say, *"In the situation involving _____, I would like _____ to happen, and _____ to happen...."* Once you cannot find any more, say, *"I do not perceive my own best interests in this situation."* This line should simply articulate what you have already observed in uncovering your goals. You should see that many of them cannot be met together, by the *same* situation, and that others cannot be met by *this* situation.
- After saying that line, repeat the whole procedure with a new situation, and so on until the time is up.

Remarks: The important thing in these exercises is to be honest with yourself. It can be humiliating to admit just how many impossible and contradictory hopes you have crammed into a single situation. But admitting that is the whole point of this exercise. That is what will show you that today's idea really is true for you. So be unusually honest, as well as careful and patient, in uncovering all the goals you have stuffed into the pockets of this situation.

Commentary

Our actions in any situation are determined by our perception of the situation, and as we have been seeing for the last twenty-three lessons, our perceptions are, to put it mildly, unreliable. The lesson says it more bluntly: our perceptions are "wrong" (1:3). There is no way, then, that we can possibly know what our own best interests are in any situation.

The exercises for today are designed to bring four things to our attention (paragraph 6):

- We are making a large number of demands on the situation that have nothing to do with it.
- Many of our goals are contradictory.
- We have no unified outcome in mind.
- We must be disappointed in regard to some of our goals no matter what the outcome is.

We have all experienced this, particularly in making major decisions. Suppose I receive a fabulous job offer that pays me more money than I ever dreamed of and involves doing something I like. Sounds good at first. Then I realize I will have to relocate to a part of the country I don't like, I'll have to be willing to travel extensively, and I will frequently be required to work long hours and weekends. My mind suddenly becomes filled with all the conflicting goals. I may find I am expecting the job to make me happy, somehow. Perhaps I am thinking the job should provide me with spiritual companions. I'll have to leave my friends behind. And so on, and so on...

The more I have worked with the Course, the more I realize that this is not just a beginning lesson; it is something that applies to nearly every situation I get into. I am constantly reminding myself that I don't know what my own best interests are in one situation after another. I find it most important to do so when things seem to be relatively clear, when I think I *do* know what I want and need. If I think I know my best interests, I cannot be taught what they really are. The best mental state I can maintain, then, is "I don't know."

I can acknowledge my preferences, I can admit that I think I would like certain things to happen, but I need to learn to add, "I'm not certain this is the best." If I pray for something, I can add, "Let X happen, or something better." I remain open-minded, ready to accept that what I think about the situation may not cover all the bases, and probably does not. That is the intent behind today's idea: to open our minds to the possibility that we may not know, and may need assistance.

LESSON 25 ✦ JANUARY 25
"I do not know what anything is for."

Practice instructions

Purpose: To begin to learn that the purposes you assign things are totally meaningless. This will help you give up those purposes.

Exercise: Six times, for two minutes.

- Repeat the idea slowly.
- Then look about you and let your glance rest on each thing that catches your eye. Keep looking at it long enough to say quite slowly, *"I do not know what this _____ is for."* Then move on to the next thing. Make no distinctions between things near or far, important or unimportant, human or nonhuman.

Remarks: As you look at an object and repeat the idea, you may become aware of just how much you see that object as existing to serve your personal interests. This includes inanimate objects as well as animate ones, such as human bodies. We see everything in our environment as having the purpose of serving this separate self. That simply *cannot* be what its true purpose is.

Commentary

Have you noticed how the pace of recommended practice is accelerating? Yesterday we moved from five one-minute periods to five two-minute periods; today we increase to six two-minute periods. How many of us are making a serious effort to follow these instructions? Remember how the introduction said that we aren't asked to believe the ideas, accept them, or welcome them; even active resistance is okay. All that is asked is that we "use them" (W-pI.In.9:4), to "apply the ideas as you are directed to do" (W-pI.In.8:3). Nothing but that is required to make them effective. But applying them as directed *is* required, if we want them to have effect in our lives.

We don't know what anything is for. The obvious question is: "What is it for?" This lesson answers the question. "Everything is for your own best interests" (1:5). Obviously that relates to yesterday's lesson, "I do not perceive my own best interests." What is for my best interests? Everything.

We don't know that and we certainly don't believe it. We evaluate everything "in terms of ego goals" (2:1), and since "the ego is not you" (2:2), that cannot give us any idea of what our best interests are. We are picking and choosing the things that support our ego, which is not our Self, and therefore, clearly, we are actually undermining our true Self. (The statement that "the ego is not you" is particularly important; it isn't something we would realize without being told.)

We look at the world from the ego perspective and we literally "assign" purposes to things, purposes that will support our ego. When things don't live up to our expectations, we get upset. All our goals involve "personal" interests. Yet, "Since you have no personal interests, your goals are really concerned with nothing" (3:2). We don't really have personal interests because the "person" we think of when we say those words isn't real. We have no real goals that we do not share in common with all living things, because all living things are connected, and the sharing is what makes the goals real. Shared goals recognize the reality of who we are. Ego goals do not. This is why we are extremely confused about what things are for.

The lesson points out that, on a superficial level, we do know what things are for; we know a telephone is for talking to someone not physically present. "Yet purpose cannot be understood at these levels" (4:3). For instance, we don't understand why we want to reach someone by phone.

We may think we understand. You might be calling the store to order a book. But why do you want the book? Why call now, at precisely this moment? There is a deeper purpose in everything that we do not understand, nor can we understand it as long as we think our conscious goals are the real ones. We have "to be willing to give up the goals [we] have established for everything" (5:1).

The entire foundation of our judgment is rotten because it rests on the idea that there are "things" outside of us that differ from us. There is nothing outside of us; everything is part of us. As long as we are coming from that false premise, our goals will be skewed and our judgments will be faulty.

I find it very helpful to remember that I don't know what anything means and I don't know what it is for. A phone call may bring "bad news," but I can say, "I do not know what this phone call is for; I do not know what this situation is for, and therefore I cannot judge it."

The Course insists on our total ignorance. "The confusion between your real creation and what you have made of yourself is so profound that it has become literally impossible for you to know anything" (T-3.V.3:2). That's pretty definite, isn't it? "Literally impossible." This isn't any figure of speech. Obviously, if you literally know nothing, judgment is impossible.

Because we've confused ourselves with our egos, we can't know anything. Our belief in our identity as separate beings, located in bodies, has become an unquestioned core belief behind our every thought. We evaluate everything in terms of ego goals (W-pI.25.2:1). Before we even begin to evaluate what anything means we have presupposed that, whatever it is and whatever it means, it is not us; it is *other*. From that premise it is literally impossible to know or understand anything because it is not *other*. It is part of us.

A very young baby in its crib goes through a process of learning that its foot or hand is part of itself. To begin with, the baby does not know that. You can watch the baby, sometimes, treating the foot as if it were a foreign object.

We are all still infants in this sense because we don't recognize parts of ourselves when we see them; we think they are something else. Because we think they are something else, we are unable to form judgments that make any sense. Our judgments are not simply exaggerated or inaccurate, they are so wide of the mark they're ludicrous.

> Let us remember not our own ideas of what the world is
> for. We do not know.   (T-31.I.12:2–3)

If we don't know what anything is for, we can't judge it! We can't evaluate whether or not it is fulfilling its purpose because we don't know what its purpose is.

We aren't being asked to acquire all this knowledge we lack; we are asked to become still and to remember how much we don't know (see T-31.II.6:4). The Text tells us that there is no statement that the world is more afraid to hear than this:

71

I do not know the thing I am, and therefore do not know what I am doing, where I am, or how to look upon the world or on myself. (T-31.V.17:7)

It goes on to say that learning this is the birth of salvation. This is where learning starts: admitting how incapable of judging we are. All of these things we don't know! Recognizing our ignorance is the birth of salvation because, until we admit we don't know, we won't ask for help. As long as we think we know, we block true knowing.

> Little children recognize that they do not understand what they perceive, and so they ask what it means. Do not make the mistake of believing that you understand what you perceive, for its meaning is lost to you....Yet while you think you know its meaning, you will see no need to ask it of Him.
> You do not know the meaning of anything you perceive. Not one thought you hold is wholly true. The recognition of this is your firm beginning. (T-11.VIII.2:2–3, 5; 3:1–3)

LESSON 26 ✦ JANUARY 26
"My attack thoughts are attacking my invulnerability."

Practice instructions

Purpose: To realize that how vulnerable you feel is due not to how the world treats you, but strictly to your own thoughts; specifically, to your attack thoughts. Relinquishing these thoughts is the road to feeling truly invulnerable.

Exercise: Six times, for two minutes (cut in half if you become uncomfortable).

- Repeat the idea.
- Close your eyes and pick a situation that has been concerning you, that has been on your mind. First name the situation: *"I am concerned about _____."* Then go over each potential outcome (ideally, about five or six) that you have been afraid might happen. For each one say, *"I am afraid _____ will happen,"* and then tell yourself, *"That thought is an attack upon myself."* This is the punch line. This is the whole point of the exercise. What is attacking you is not the external outcome, but your thought that you are vulnerable to that outcome.
- When you run out of outcomes for that situation, repeat this procedure with other situations until the time is up.
- Repeat the idea to close.

Remarks: Try to be both honest and thorough. If you only go through two or three situations, that is all right. We do not like to admit to ourselves just how many fearful possibilities we see facing us. Consequently, the outcomes you are really frightened of may only occur to you after you think you have completely exhausted your list. However, as this lesson advises, try to treat the frightening outcomes the same as the mildly worrisome ones. All of them are just different permutations of your belief that you are vulnerable.

Commentary

The American Heritage dictionary defines "invulnerable" as "immune to attack." So to believe I can be attacked means, by definition, that I believe I am not invulnerable. That much is obvious.

There is a little bit of logic in the first paragraph that might slip by without careful reading:

> You see attack as a real threat. That is because you believe
> that you can really attack.   (1:2–3)

It is my belief that *I* am capable of attack that makes me fear attack from without; if I can attack, so can everyone else. My fear of attack, therefore, comes from the projection of my own belief about myself! It comes from my belief that I am not a wholly loving being, but rather I am malicious, malign and wicked. That is what the second paragraph is all about.

"What would have effects through you must also have effects on you" (1:4). This is why, as Lesson 23 said in the last paragraph, thoughts of attacking and thoughts of being attacked are exactly the same. My belief in attack within myself, acting through me, will also have effects *on* me. "It is this law that will ultimately save you" (1:5). What that is referring to is the truth, much emphasized in the Course, that the way I find forgiveness is by giving it; the way I receive healing is to heal others. But we are "misusing" that law now, projecting guilt instead of extending love. So we need to learn how to use it for our own best interests, rather than against them (a reference to Lesson 24).

Attack thoughts weaken me in my own eyes, whether they are fearful thoughts of assault from without, or aggressive thoughts of attack on another. The strong do not have enemies, as it implies elsewhere (see T-23.In.1:5). If I can let go of attack thoughts I will perceive my invulnerability; my "vulnerability or invulnerability is the result of [my] own thoughts" (4:1).

"Nothing except your thoughts can attack you" (4:2). That is a thought I have meditated on for years, and have proved valid in my own experience. It is particularly difficult to believe at first; that's okay. Work with it. It is an empowering thought. (In this light you might want to read over Chapter 10's introduction in the Text.)

The instructions for today's lesson are longer and quite detailed. Read them carefully. This is a real mental process we are to engage in.

In thinking of a situation we are to "go over every possible outcome" (7:3), referring to it very specifically. The lesson emphasizes being thorough, and taking time with each situation.

LESSON 27 ✦ JANUARY 27
"Above all else I want to see."

Practice instructions

Purpose: To bring closer the day when you want vision more than everything else.

Exercise: At least every half hour (three or four times an hour is suggested).

Simply repeat the idea. You can do this even in the middle of conversation. Don't worry if you don't fully mean the idea. Repeat it to bring closer the day when you *will* mean it. If repeating it arouses fear of having to give up something, add, *"Vision has no cost to anyone,"* and, if still afraid, say, *"It can only bless."*

Remarks: This is a very important lesson, the second lesson in frequent practice (the first was Lesson 20). It is clearly serious about this frequency. At the beginning of the day you are supposed to set the interval you will use (e.g., every twenty minutes, every thirty minutes). If you have not done that yet, it would be good to do so now. Then, for the rest of the day, you are asked to do your best to stick to the frequency you yourself chose. The Course realizes that, in all likelihood, you will not do this perfectly. When you forget a practice period, do not get angry with yourself. This eventually makes you feel like giving up (and is, in fact, an ego ploy to engineer just this outcome; see W-pI.95.7:3-5, 10:1-2). Just get back to your practicing as if nothing happened. What is important is not lamenting past failures to practice, but *doing* the practice in the present and future. The benefits of this can be enormous. Just one truly sincere repetition can put you forward years in your development.

Commentary

This is reminiscent of Lesson 20, "I am determined to see," to which a subtle reference is made in the first line: "Today's idea expresses something stronger than mere determination." It puts the desire to see into first place, "above all else." I want to see more than I want anything else. If we mean this, we will choose the path that leads to vision every time, no matter what other lesser goal might be tempting us.

The lesson recognizes that the idea may not be wholly true for us yet. Since desire determines vision, if it were now wholly true you would *already* see, and therefore would not need the lesson! So working with a lesson like this is not hypocritical; it is an exercise intended specifically for people for whom the idea is not yet wholly accepted, designed to move us closer to the day when it will be.

The phrase "above all else" may tempt us to think we are being asked to sacrifice. "Vision at any cost!" Therefore the lesson suggests that if we feel uneasy about unreservedly committing ourselves to vision, we should add this thought: "Vision has no cost to anyone" (2:3). If that isn't enough, add, "It can only bless" (2:5). Put them all together: "Above all else I want to see, and vision has no cost to anyone. It can only bless."

This hints at an idea stated clearly many times in the Course: this path does not believe in sacrifice. It says we are asked only to sacrifice illusions, and that this is in reality only an illusion of sacrifice. "Nothing real can be threatened" (T-In.2:2).

Still, the lesson is leading us toward this kind of single-minded, unreserved determination to have true vision. We *do* need to be willing to put vision above anything that seems to compete with it. It may *seem* at times that we are being asked to give things up, and we may actually have to give them up, but when we do, we will realize we have given up nothing we truly wanted. The entire process is perfectly safe, and entails no real loss of any kind.

The practice requirements suddenly leap into high gear in this lesson: repeat the idea "at least every half hour" (3:2). That's *at least* every half hour, "and more if possible. You might try for every fifteen or twenty minutes" (3:2–3). (Things will ease up again tomorrow.) Specific structure, with a set time schedule, is recommended. All we are asked to do each of these times is to repeat the one sentence to ourselves: "Above all else I want to see." This is not a big deal. There isn't any reason we can't do it, even in the middle of a conversation—if we want to, if we are willing.

The real question is, how often will you remember? How much do you want today's idea to be true? Answer one of these questions and you have answered the other.

(4:1–3)

How often we remember will be the measure of how much we really want to see above all else. This will be a very revealing day!

Notice carefully how we are supposed to deal with the fact that we probably will forget and come nowhere near the ideal of every fifteen minutes. It says a lot about how the Workbook views this whole matter of "practice." Basically it says, "Don't let your 'failure' bother you; just get back on track immediately." All that it takes to save "many years of effort" (4:6) is to, just once during the day, repeat the idea with perfect sincerity. To achieve that one time, many repetitions are needed. Simply do the best you can—but let it be the *best* you can do.

LESSON 28 ✦ JANUARY 28
"Above all else I want to see things differently."

Practice instructions

Purpose: To commit to really seeing, to commit to withdrawing your preconceptions about things and opening your mind to seeing them with true vision. You will make this commitment one object at a time. By committing to seeing one thing truly, you are really committing to seeing everything truly.

Exercise: Six times, for two minutes.

- Repeat the idea.
- Then apply it randomly to whatever you see about you, giving each subject equal sincerity. Let your eyes rest on each one long enough to say, slowly and thoughtfully, *"Above all else I want to see this _____ differently."* Realize that in saying this you are making a request, a request to withdraw the purpose you have laid on this object, and to see the purpose that God has given it, "the purpose it shares with all the universe" (5:3). By seeing this one object truly, then, you could see the purpose of everything. You could gain total vision.

Remarks: Each application of the idea (to the table, to the chair, to the foot) is the making of a commitment. So try to practice in this spirit. With each repetition, try to mean what you are saying. Do not rush through the words thoughtlessly. Try to say them with sincerity. Say them thoughtfully. Do not worry about whether you will follow through with these commitments, for that inhibits you from making them. And you will never *keep* them unless you first *make* them.

Commentary

The thought that I could gain vision from just a table, or any random thing for that matter, if I could look on it with a completely open mind, is staggering. It means that I have been surrounded all my life by people and things, any one of which could have brought me enlightenment, and I have not responded. The computer screen I look at as I write, if seen without any of my own ideas, could open up and show me "something beautiful and clean and of infinite value, full of happiness and hope" (5:2).

I still find that hard to believe. Oh, I don't doubt it, in one sense. Somehow it makes sense to believe that an enlightened being, like Jesus for instance, would see, as the poet put it, "the universe in a grain of sand." But I guess what I doubt is that *I* could see that. I've looked at so many tables in my life and none of them ever spoke to *me*. I look at my desk now and I see—a desk.

"Hidden under all your ideas about it is its real purpose, the purpose it shares with all the universe" (5:3). Ah! A clue as to what this lesson is getting at; we're talking about a shared purpose. We're asking to see a common purpose that binds everything as one. I think a desk is for writing on, a table is for eating on, a fork is for spearing my food, a computer is for sending messages to folks on the Internet. I see a whole bunch of different purposes, each thing with its own, separate purpose. But they all share a purpose. As does my body, the sky, the moon, everything I can see. What is that purpose? That is what I am asking to see.

That is something worth asking for.

> Nothing around you but is part of you. Look on it lovingly, and see the light of Heaven in it. So will you come to understand all that is given you. In kind forgiveness will the world sparkle and shine, and everything you once thought sinful now will be reinterpreted as part of Heaven. How beautiful it is to walk, clean and redeemed and happy, through a world in bitter need of the redemption that your innocence bestows upon it! What can you value more than this? For here is your salvation and your freedom. And it must be complete if you would recognize it.
>
> (T-23.In.6:1–8)

LESSON 29 ✦ JANUARY 29
"God is in everything I see."

Practice instructions

Purpose: "To begin to learn how to look on all things with love, appreciation and open-mindedness" (3:1). To see the holy purpose that resides in everything.

Longer: Six times, for two minutes.

- Repeat the idea.
- Then apply it to randomly chosen objects in your visual field, naming each one. Say, *"God is in this [magazine, finger]"* or *"God is in that [body, door]."* Realize that you are not claiming that God is somehow physically in that object, but that God has assigned His purpose to it, a purpose which is part of Him. Remember your training in this practice. Start near to you and then extend farther out. Keep looking at each object until you are done repeating the sentence. And make sure you avoid "self-directed selection" (4:2), something that might be more challenging with this idea.

Frequent reminders: At least once an hour.

Repeat the idea slowly while looking slowly about you.

Commentary

The idea for today explains why you can see all purpose in everything. It explains why nothing is separate, by itself or in itself. And it explains why nothing you see means anything. In fact, it explains every idea we have used thus far, and all subsequent ones as well. Today's idea is the whole basis for vision. (1:1–5)

Clearly, today's idea is pivotal in the Course's thought system, and not simply a nice, sentimental idea. Nor is it mere pantheism, which teaches that nature and God are the same. Elsewhere the Course clearly teaches, "There is no world!" (W-pI.132.6:2), so this is not saying that nature and God are identical. "Certainly God is not in a table…as you see it" (2:3).

As I see things, nothing means anything. A table is merely a table, a flat surface to eat on or play poker on. It has no eternal purpose; its purposes are all ephemeral. Seen like this, the table does not reveal God, but helps hide Him.

God is not in the physical table, but He can be seen through or by means of the table. If the table shares the purpose of the universe, it must share the purpose of the Creator of the universe. That purpose is our happiness, our joy, our completion, which is necessary to His. "Everything is for your own best interests. That is what it is for; that is its purpose; that is what it means" (W-pI.25.1:5–6).

"Purpose" is the key word in this and the last lesson. God is in everything I see because everything shares God's purpose. My sight is a veil across the truth that shines in everything, but vision can shine through that veil if I allow it. The way I perceive, God is not in everything; in fact, He is in nothing. If mere physical sight were enough we would all have seen God long ago. We made our sight to obscure Him, but seen with the vision of Christ, everything can reveal Him.

> Nothing is as it appears to you. Its holy purpose stands
> beyond your little range.   (3:4–5)

As I first read this lesson I was puzzled by the statement that the idea for the day, "God is in everything I see," explained the earlier idea that nothing we see means anything. On the face of it, if God is in everything I see, it ought to give those things profound meaning; I would see them as sharing the purpose of the universe, the purpose of the Creator. How can I logically proceed from "God is in everything I see" to "Nothing I see means anything?"

Finally I noticed a distinction that should have been obvious from the beginning: the distinction made between "seeing" or "sight" and "vision." The Course makes this distinction quite consistently throughout, but because my mind still tends to think of sight and vision as the same thing, I failed to notice it here. "Sight" refers to our normal mode of seeing, our belief that what our physical eyes show us is real, instead of the result of a desire within the mind and the projection of meaning from the mind, imposed on what is seen. "Vision," on the other hand, is another kind of sense altogether, virtually unrelated to the physical eyes.

Notice that the lesson says, "Today's idea is the whole basis of *vision*" (1:5, emphasis mine). "When *vision* has shown you the holiness that lights up the world, you will understand today's idea perfectly" (3:6, emphasis mine). It is vision that reveals God in everything; mere sight does not reveal Him. God is in everything I see, but sight does not show Him to me; that is why nothing I see means anything. "You do not see them [with vision] now" (3:2). God is there, but sight does not see Him; sight is overlooking the very thing that gives everything the meaning it has. We could therefore revise the earlier statement to say: "Nothing I see means anything, *the way I see it*." Meaning is there but I am blind to it.

> The world you see must be denied, for *sight* of it is costing you a different kind of *vision*. *You cannot see both worlds*, for each of them involves a different kind of seeing, and depends on what you cherish.
> (T-13.VII.2:1–2, my emphasis on the words "sight" and "vision")

The idea that God is in everything is "the whole basis for vision" (1:5). It is the foundation for a "different kind of seeing" (T-13.VII.2:2). In order to see with vision I have to be willing to deny, or disregard, my current mode of seeing, which is limited to the physical and reports back to me only what my ego wants to see. If I recognize that God is in everything, yet I do not see Him with my eyes, there must be a different kind of seeing, and I will be led to desire it. I will ask for vision.

The lesson speaks of the "little range" (3:5) of our kind of seeing. Imagine, as an analogy, that God is only visible in the infrared part of the spectrum (of course He is not visible in any physical manner at all). Our eyes simply do not see infrared radiation, so even if it is present we see nothing. The range of physical sight is very narrow; there are all kinds of "light" we cannot see: infrared, ultraviolet, heat, radiation, radio waves, microwaves, and so on. God is in everything, but He is outside the range of our physical sight; we need a different kind of vision.

I think that in a sense the lesson is trying to arouse a certain discontent within us. It provokes the disturbing question: "If God is in everything, how come I don't see Him?" It makes us aware of the limitations of what we have believed to be "sight." It makes us aware of its limited range, and evokes within us the desire for a new kind of vision that sees beyond this limited range, and sees the purpose of the universe in everything.

Tomorrow's lesson will continue to instruct us in finding vision.

LESSON 30 ✦ JANUARY 30
"God is in everything I see because God is in my mind."

Practice instructions

Purpose: To learn a new way of seeing. In this kind of seeing, what you see does not come in from the external world, through your body's eyes, or from you projecting your illusions onto the world. Rather, it comes from you "projecting" the *truth* that is in your mind onto everything you see.

Exercise: As often as possible throughout the day, for one minute.

Look about you and apply the idea to your visual field and even to what lies beyond that field, out of sight. Make sure that, for several of the exercises, you close your eyes and apply the idea to your inner world.

Commentary

As yesterday's lesson was the "whole basis" (W-pI.29.1:5) for vision, today's idea is "the springboard" (1:1). That God is in everything I see forms the foundation. Knowing that this is so "because God is in my mind" is what can propel us from mere sight into vision.

> From this idea will the world open up before you, and you will look upon it and see in it what you have never seen before. Nor will what you saw before be even faintly visible to you.   (1:2–3)

Fundamental to understanding what the Course is talking about is the fact that what we see is quite directly *caused* by what is in our mind. The commonsense idea of perception is that something outside causes an impression, through my senses, on my mind. The reality is the reverse, according to the Course. The thoughts of my mind are projected outward and cause my perceptions. "Projection makes perception," says the Text in two different places (T-13.V.3:5; T-21.In.1:1; compare with T-10.In.2:7).

What this lesson attempts to teach us is "a new kind of 'projection'" (2:1). We might call it "positive projection." Instead of using projection to get rid of thoughts we are uncomfortable with, we are attempting to see in the world *what we want to see in our own minds*. What I want to see, for one thing, is my own innocence. Therefore I am attempting to see the world as innocent. I am choosing my thoughts and deliberately "projecting" them onto the world. I want to see myself as having God in my mind, and so I choose to see everything as having God in it.

If all things contain God, and I contain God, then we are joined. "Thus, we are trying to join with what we see, rather than keeping it apart from us. That is the fundamental difference between vision and the way you see" (2:4–5). Our kind of seeing emphasizes differences and distinctions; vision emphasizes sameness.

"Real vision is not only unlimited by space and distance, but it does not depend on the body's eyes at all" (5:1). It is becoming clearer with each lesson that the vision being talked about has nothing at all to do with our physical sight. In the Course's thought system, our eyes do not see at all; they are merely the means for deception. We can include in our vision things beyond the range of physical sight. This is a seeing done with our minds, not with eyes. "The mind is its only source" (5:2).

Now I recall our earlier lesson, "Above all else I want to see" (Lesson 28) with a stronger sense of purpose. I want vision; I want this other kind of seeing that sees God everywhere. I want it because somehow I instinctively know that if I can see things that way, I will also be able to see myself that way. If I can see you as a holy child of God, innocent and blameless, I will know that I am seeing a reflection of myself. I want to see myself that way, so I want to see you that way.

God is in my mind. The world mirrors what is in my mind. How, then, do I want to see the world? Am I willing to see the world with God in it? If not, it only reflects the fact that I am unwilling and afraid to see His presence in my mind.

LESSON 31 ✦ JANUARY 31
"I am not the victim of the world I see."

Practice instructions

Purpose: To begin declaring your release.

Longer: Two times, morning and evening, for three to five minutes.

- Repeat the idea two or three times while looking slowly about you.
- Then close your eyes and apply the idea to your inner world, the level of cause. Let whatever thoughts that want to come arise, be noted, and then allowed to pass by. As with Lesson 10, it is important to stay detached from your stream of thoughts. Try seeing it as either a strange parade of disorganized, meaningless objects or as a series of leaves floating by on a stream. Let the stream keep moving; don't stop it to dwell on a particular thought. As you watch it move by, repeat the idea as often as you want, with no hurry.

Frequent reminders: As often as possible (suggestion: several times per hour).

Repeat idea. While doing so, consciously remember that you are declaring your freedom from all outer causation, and freeing other minds in the process. Try a repetition now in that spirit—it will take you five seconds.

Response to temptation: When you feel like anything in the world is victimizing you.

Repeat the idea. You will get more from it if you say it as a declaration that you *refuse* to be slave to outer events and to your ego's reactions.

Remarks: Today's lesson marks an important development. The daily practice now begins to separate out into two levels: longer practice periods, which will generally be done morning and evening; and shorter, frequent practice throughout the day (this includes both frequent reminders and response to temptation). This is a major step toward the eventual fourfold structure of morning and evening practice periods, hourly remembrance, frequent reminders, and response to temptation.

Commentary

As you must have noticed when you read today's lesson, there isn't a lot of metaphysical thought in it. In fact there is almost none, except in the lead thought quoted above. The rest of the lesson is practice instructions. So I'll weight my comments in approximately the same way.

The one sentence that heads the lesson is plenty in itself, however. If you think about it, it is amazing how many ways we see ourselves as victims of the world. We go through life feeling like victims—of the weather, of the jerk who cuts you off in traffic or swerves into the parking space you were aiming for, of your computer disk when "it" loses your file, of your housemate who uses the last of the hot water just before your shower, of the slow service in the restaurant, of the traffic that makes you late for your appointment. Then, of course, there are the people who may deliberately and malevolently terrorize you in our cities (or perhaps in your home).

To assert that "I am not the victim of the world I see" can be liberating and empowering. It is remarkable how these simple words can cause feelings of weakness and helplessness to wash away. Try it! You'll like it.

Oddly enough, we also feel victimized by unseen enemies and even our own thoughts. Ever have an anxiety attack? Or find yourself feeling gouged by the IRS? A victim of an unfair "system"? Plagued by self-doubt? You are not the victim of your inner world any more than of your outer world. "You will escape from both together, for the inner is cause of the outer" (2:5).

This lesson introduces what will become the basic practice outline for most of the Workbook, and for ongoing practice for Workbook graduates:

1. Two longer practice periods, morning and evening, in which you apply the idea for the day on a sustained basis.

2. Frequent repetitions through the day, as often as possible (a study of other references to this indicates that four or five times per hour is intended).

3. Using the idea as a "response to temptation" whenever it arises.

The only element of Workbook practice not present in this lesson is specific hourly or half-hourly periods of shorter practice, in length somewhere in between #1 and #2 above. That appears as the Workbook goes along to build a habit of practice on the structure of the clock, and then is gradually phased out as the habit (presumably) has been established. The three elements presented here in Lesson 31 are retained in recommendations for post-Workbook practice given in the Manual for Teachers (see Section 16, "How Should the Teacher of God Spend His Day?").

Make a point of taking those longer, three to five minute periods morning and evening. This is the first time for them. You wouldn't practice the piano by playing only half the scales, so don't stint here, either. From this point on in the Workbook the practice is going to intensify; like me, I'm sure you'll find it more difficult to maintain and to actually carry out. Remember:

> You are merely asked to apply the ideas *as you are directed to do*. You are not asked to judge them at all. You are asked only to use them. It is their use that will give them meaning to you, and will show you that they are true.
>
> (W-In.8:3–6, emphasis mine)

LESSON 32 ✦ FEBRUARY 1

"I have invented the world I see."

Practice instructions

Purpose: To teach you that you are not the effect of the world; it is the effect of you.

Longer: Two times, morning and evening, for at least three to five minutes.

As with yesterday's lesson, repeat the idea a few times while looking around you slowly. Then close your eyes and apply it to the images that arise in your inner world. Remain detached by reminding yourself that both worlds are equally imaginary.

Remarks: The counsel in 4:3 about when to practice is repeated in different forms several times in the Workbook. For a discussion, see "When Should You Take Your Morning Quiet Time?" Following the Workbook's counsel in this regard will enhance the quality of your practice, so that, as with today's lesson, you may find yourself wanting to go longer than five minutes.

Frequent reminders: As often as possible.

Repeat idea *slowly* while looking about either your outer or inner world.

Response to temptation: Whenever a situation upsets you.

Immediately respond with: *"I have invented this situation as I see it."*

Commentary

If I'm not the victim of the world, what is my relationship to it? I've invented it. If I've invented it, if I made it up, how can I possibly be its victim?

Now, saying that I've invented the world is a pretty heavy statement. Saying that I can give it up as easily as I made it seems even more improbable. Yet that is what the practice of the Workbook is setting out to prove to us, not by rigorous logic but through experiences that demonstrate that it is true. That's what miracles are. Miracles demonstrate that "the world you see outside you" and "the world you see in your mind" are "both...in your own imagination" (2:2–3).

This lesson is simply introducing the idea, not trying to prove it. The Text discusses the same thought in several places (T-21.II.11:1; T-20.III.5:1–5), the most telling of them being:

> What if you recognized this world is an hallucination?
> What if you really understood you made it up?
> (T-20.VIII.7:3–4)

It isn't a concept you can easily avoid if you study the Course; the Course insists on it.

All that is really being asked here is that we open our minds to the idea that we have invented the world we see. It is a concept that can throw our minds into turmoil because it flies in the face of our fundamental beliefs about the world. The world has a few nice things about it, but also a lot of ugly junk. And being told I am responsible for it, I made it up, doesn't sit easily with my mind.

If it raises all kinds of questions in my mind, fine; let the questions bubble up. For today, for the practice periods, just apply the idea as given. It's okay if part of your mind is kibitzing in the background saying, "This is nuts! I don't really believe this." The introduction warned us we might even actively resist the ideas. It said:

> Whatever your reactions to the ideas may be, use them.
> Nothing more than that is required.   (W-In.9:4–5)

It may be difficult to see at first, but we really only have two options. Either I made up the world, or I am its victim. Either I am the cause, or the effect. There aren't any other choices; think about it. Either I am the dreamer, inventing the whole mess, or I am part of someone else's dream (maybe God's). If I am not the cause, I am at the world's mercy. But if I *am* the cause—there is hope! I can change the dream, and perhaps, eventually, stop dreaming altogether.

WHEN SHOULD YOU TAKE YOUR MORNING QUIET TIME?

Morning quiet time is essential for a student of *A Course in Miracles*. That is when we establish our mental set for the day, so that the day becomes about God rather than just survival. Having this time in the morning is an essential part of doing the Workbook. That is when you read your lesson and do your first practice period. Yet even after the Workbook is over, the Course expects you to continue taking this time, as we are told in Section 16 of the Manual, "How Should the Teacher of God Spend His Day?"

The question I want to discuss here is *when*. When should you take this time? If you have not yet established such a time in your life, the question of when is obviously relevant. Yet even if you have regular morning quiet time, you might have nagging questions at the back of your mind: How important is it to take my quiet time the instant I get up? Is it all right to wait until later? How do I know when the ideal time is?

As with so many such questions, the answers are right there in the Course. I am aware of eleven passages that give an answer to this question, and they mention the same three things over and over again:

1. "As soon as possible after you wake" (W–pI.42.3:1)

Ideally, the Course wants us to take this time right as we get up. We will receive more benefits, it tells us, if we do our practice first thing in the morning (W-pI.rIII.8:1). Why? I think it is because when we first awake our mind is a relatively blank canvas. It is not yet cluttered with all the minutiae of the day. At this point, we can paint on it whatever we want. And if we take this opportunity to paint a scene of Heaven on it, that is what will remain for a good part of the day, maybe the entire day. On the other hand, if we wait too long, then our canvas will begin getting crowded with scenes of tasks and worries and plans. And then, by the time we do sit down for our quiet time, we might not succeed in erasing what is already painted there. We might very well spend our quiet time mulling over tasks and worries and plans.

But is this some kind of law that we must have our quiet time the instant we awake? The Course says no:

This course is always practical. It may be that the teacher of God is not in a situation that fosters quiet thought as he awakes. (M–16.4:1–2)

What is important is not the *form* of taking your quiet time the instant you wake up, but the *content* of taking it at a time most conducive to its real purpose. That is why the Course says not "when you wake," but "as soon as possible after you wake" (it mentions this three times). How we gauge what defines "as soon as possible" leads us to the second and third points.

2. "When few distractions are anticipated" (W–pI.32.4:3)

This is so obvious that it hardly needs mentioning. If taking your quiet time the minute you awake would mean children knocking on the door and asking "When's breakfast?" then that is not a suitable time. Instead, find a time with fewer distractions. This means two things in the Workbook:

1. You are by yourself (mentioned twice)

2. You have quiet (mentioned four times)

3. "When you yourself feel reasonably ready" (W–pI.32.4:3)

The previous point is about externals—are you in a noisy room with other people in it? This point is about internals—do you feel ready inside to focus on God? This issue of readiness is mentioned four times and, I think, is primarily a code for "are you fully awake yet?" Let's face it, there are some of us who are not human when we first get up. There are some of us who, when the alarm clock goes off, still can't figure out what that noise is. For us, trying to take our quiet time the instant we get up makes no sense whatsoever.

Summary

When should you take your morning quiet time? The Course provides a simple formula: as soon as possible after you wake, as soon as you feel ready (fully awake) and can get yourself alone in a quiet place.

LESSON 33 ✦ FEBRUARY 2
"There is another way of looking at the world."

Practice instructions

Purpose: To show you that you have the power to change your perception of both the outer and inner world, which are really the same.

Longer: Two times, morning and evening, for five full minutes.

Go back and forth from glancing around your outer world to closing your eyes and observing your inner world. While doing so repeat the idea unhurriedly. Regard both inner and outer worlds with equal casualness, uninvolvement, and detachment, to the point where you feel little transition in shifting between them.

Frequent reminders: As often as you can.

Repeat the idea. Try to be as detached as you were during the longer exercises.

Response to temptation: The instant any situation disturbs you.

When upset, apply the idea specifically, saying, *"There is another way of looking at this."* Do so immediately, rather than waiting until you have tried to fix things on the outside. If your feelings do not clear up right away, don't give up. Spend a minute or more repeating the sentence over and over, closing your eyes and concentrating on the words you are saying.

Commentary

This lesson asserts the power of our minds to choose how we see the world. We can shift our perception of the world! That is not only a personally empowering concept, it is, quite literally, a world-changing realization.

As we begin to examine our thoughts, we will be amazed at the number of situations in which the idea of "another way" of looking at it has simply never occurred to us. With some things, the idea that we could see them differently may actually be offensive. Without realizing it we may be saying, "My mind is already made up; don't confuse me with facts."

That is why following the practice instructions with these lessons is so important. It isn't just the longer five-minute times in the morning and evening: "The shorter exercise periods should be as frequent as possible" (3:1). The more often we bring this idea into our awareness during the day, the more we will become aware of areas of thought that we are protecting from change.

LESSON 34 ✦ FEBRUARY 3

"I could see peace instead of this."

Practice instructions

Purpose: To begin to experience the peace that characterizes true vision.

Longer: Three times, morning, evening, and once in between, for five minutes.

Close your eyes and search your mind for "upsetting" *situations*, *personalities*, and *events* (a typical triad in the Workbook). Repeat the idea slowly as you dispassionately watch the stream of upsets go by. After a couple of minutes, you may run out of upsets. That is all right. Just keep repeating the idea slowly until the five minutes are up.

Response to temptation: Make a point of watching your mind today for upsets. Whenever you notice one, apply the idea to it. There are two forms of upset to watch out for, each requiring a slightly different form of practice:

1. If you are upset about a specific situation, apply the idea specifically: *"I could see peace in this situation instead of what I now see in it."*

2. If your upset is not attached to anything in particular, but consists of a general mood of depression or worry, simply repeat the idea.

If needed, take several minutes, repeating the idea until you feel relief. It will help if you add, *"I can replace my feelings of depression, anxiety or worry [or my thoughts about this situation, personality or event] with peace."*

Remarks: The final sentences of this lesson make a very important point, one to remember throughout the Workbook and afterwards. Repeating the idea just once may not do the trick. Your upset may go away only after you've spent several minutes repeating the idea. Repeating the same line again and again may sound like some kind of brainwashing, in which you just drum your mind into submission. However, I find this to be an exercise not in putting my mind to sleep, but in gradually illuminating it. If I have strong negative feelings, the first few repetitions of the idea may simply bounce off. But if I keep it up, each repetition allows the truth to enter in a little bit further, until I finally see the situation entirely differently. I urge you, therefore, to give this longer form of practice a real try today.

Commentary

The most helpful thought I ever heard in relation to this lesson was this: Notice that it says, "I *could* see peace," and not "I *should* see peace." It is far too easy to take this lesson as another reason for guilt. "Terrible me! I should see peace, but I am seeing this mess instead. What is wrong with me?" That is not how this lesson is meant to be applied.

The opening paragraph contains such a wonderful summation of the Course's philosophy of peace:

> Peace of mind is clearly an internal matter. It must begin with your own thoughts, and then extend outward. It is from your peace of mind that a peaceful perception of the world arises. (1:2–4)

Peace is the motivation for doing this Course (see T-24.In.1:1). Our goal is what a later part of the Workbook refers to as "a mind at peace within itself" (W-pII.8.3:4). Peace must begin with our thoughts and extend outward from our minds. The focus is on the mind.

We can replace our negative feelings and our unloving thoughts with peace. We have that power. We can choose peace if we want peace. Notice that the practice instructions for applying the lesson to "adverse emotions" (6:1) suggest that we repeat the idea "until you feel some sense of relief" (6:2). This practice is meant to have tangible effects.

At times I have found that even in an extremely upsetting situation, repeating these words, "I could see peace instead of this," has a decidedly calming effect on my mind, *even if I cannot, in that very moment, see peace.* In a very subtle way, it helps to convince my mind that the awful things I am seeing are not rock solid, immutable reality. I am seeing something other than peace, but if I really *could* see peace instead, then what I am seeing must not be as real as I think. Even that level of relief is worth the time it takes to practice.

I used to believe that when upsetting situations occurred, I had to deal with the situation and change things around in order to be at peace. Through the practice of this lesson, I have learned that I can respond to any situation much more effectively if my mind is at peace *first*. I have discovered that I can bring my mind to peace without having first "solved" my problems. It really is possible to see peace instead of whatever seems to be upsetting me. And when I do, if response is required, I act calmly and without fear. Panic is not conducive to productive action; far better to seek peace first, then act.

LESSON 35 ✦ FEBRUARY 4
"My mind is part of God's. I am very holy."

Practice instructions

Purpose: To show you who you really are. You see yourself according to the place you occupy in your environment. Since you think your environment is the physical world, your identity seems to be determined by the part you play in this world, by how you behave in earthly situations. Yet your true environment is not this world, it is God's Mind. Your place *there* is what determines your real identity. If you truly believed you were part of that environment, you would instantly understand that you are holy.

Longer: Three times, for five minutes.

Repeat the idea, then close your eyes. Search your mind for descriptive terms you would apply to yourself, positive or negative (do not discriminate). Find them by picking up specific situations that occur to you and identifying the term you think applies to you in that situation. Say, *"I see myself as [failing, helpless, charitable, etc.]."* After each one, add, *"But my mind is part of God's. I am very holy."* If, after a while, no specific terms occur to you, don't strain to dig up more. Relax and repeat the idea until another comes to mind. For complete instructions, see paragraphs 4–8.

Frequent reminders: As often as possible.

This practice can take one of two forms:

1. Notice the attribute you are applying to yourself in the current situation and plug it into the formula you used in the longer practice *("I see myself as...But my mind is...")*.

2. If no attributes occur to you, just repeat the idea slowly with eyes closed.

Commentary

The Text tells us that "you do not understand how lofty the Holy Spirit's perception of you really is" (T-9.VII.4:2). In the following section of the same chapter, it says:

> You did not establish your value and it needs no defense. Nothing can attack it nor prevail over it. It does not vary. It merely *is*. Ask the Holy Spirit what it is and He will tell you, but do not be afraid of His answer, because it comes from God. It is an exalted answer because of its Source, but the Source is true and so is Its answer. Listen and do not question what you hear, for God does not deceive. He would have you replace the ego's belief in littleness with His Own exalted Answer to what you are, so that you can cease to question it and know it for what it is.
>
> (T-9.VIII.11:2–9)

As the lesson points out, we do not normally think of ourselves in terms such as "lofty" and "exalted." Notice, though, that the Course is saying this is true of us, not because of anything we have done, but because of our Source (3:2). What makes us what we are is not ourselves, but God. That is why the Course lays so much stress on the idea "I am as God created me." Our little view of ourselves comes from our attempts to create ourselves; our true grandeur derives from the fact that we are God's creations. Our unwillingness to recognize this connection with our Source is what keeps us locked in our smallness. We resist acknowledging God as our Source because it seems, to our egos, to put us in second place and to make us dependent. It does not *make* us dependent—we *are* dependent. That is not our shame; it is our glory. It is what establishes our grandeur.

We have difficulty believing that "I am very holy." Our refusal to believe it is why we are in this world, in this environment we think we want. We want it because it supports our image of ourselves as separate beings, independent of God.

When we look at the world, and look at ourselves living in the world, the things we see do not support the idea of this lesson. And yet the eyes, ears, nose, and touch we use to gather evidence are part of the very image of this world. They exist within the constraints of the world's image which we have constructed, very carefully, *not* to show us our

100

union with God. Of course, they bring us very little evidence to contradict the ego's image of us; we made them to function that way.

One very strong emphasis of the Course is on looking directly at our darkness and confronting our fears. The more we look at fear, says the Course, the less we will see it. Simply bringing the darkness into the light dispels the darkness. Looking at our ego, and even the full extent of our hatred, is crucial to our growth, it tells us. This lesson reflects the other side, which is sometimes neglected when looking at the ego is overemphasized. The other side is reminding ourselves, firmly, of the truth of our exalted reality: "My mind is part of God's. I am very holy." In the Text we are told:

> Whenever you question your value, say:
>
> *God Himself is incomplete without me.*
>
> Remember this when the ego speaks, and you will not hear it. (T-9.VII.8:1–3)

Reminding ourselves of the truth about us is another powerful technique the Course recommends for transcending our egos.

The list of attributes and terms we use to describe ourselves given in the lesson is just a sample. As you practice the lesson today, try to notice how you think about yourself, and how different all of those thoughts, good and bad both, are from the lesson's statement about you. I could add some of my own terms to the list: forgetful, disorganized, intelligent, clever, falling behind, skillful at what I do. What terms do you think of?

You should have noticed that the lessons are now calling for three longer practice periods of five minutes each. We are getting into heavier practice. Some of us, if we have not meditated previously, may find it difficult to sit for five minutes with our eyes closed doing these exercises. I encourage you to do them anyway. Anything new is difficult at first, but becomes easier with practice; that is what the practice is for.

"MY MIND IS PART OF GOD'S. I AM VERY HOLY"

"I see myself as…"

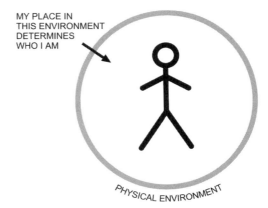

"But my mind is part of God's. I am very holy."

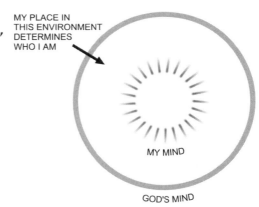

EXERCISE

1. Think of a situation you figure in and select the term you are applying to yourself in that situation, based on how you are taking part in the situation.

2. Write that term inside the upper circle.

3. Now say, *"I see myself as [fill in the term you've written]."* While doing so, look at the upper circle, understanding the circle as the situation you are in and the stick figure as you (or the image of you) operating in the situation.

4. Then say, *"But my mind is part of God's. I am very holy."* While doing so, look at the lower circle, understanding the circle to be God's Mind and the light in the center to be your mind.

LESSON 36 ✦ FEBRUARY 5

"My holiness envelops everything I see."

Practice instructions

Purpose: To realize that the holiness of your mind must lead to holy sight.

Longer: Four times (evenly spaced out), for three to five minutes.

- Close your eyes and repeat the idea several times.
- Open your eyes and look slowly and casually around, specifically applying idea to whatever your glance falls upon. Say, *"My holiness envelops [this rug, that wall, that chair, etc.]."* Several times during the practice period briefly close your eyes and repeat the idea. Then return to open-eyed practice.

Frequent reminders: Frequency is important today.

Repeat the idea with eyes closed, then with eyes open (looking around), then with eyes closed again.

Remarks: Note that you are supposed to evenly space out the longer practice periods and do frequent shorter ones in between. The point is obviously to not leave any long gaps in which you are not practicing, so that your mind is protected all day long. Enclosing your day in this finely woven net, that has no big holes, is a major goal of the Workbook.

Also, as always, repeat the idea very slowly, casually, and without strain. Doing it this way makes all the difference.

Commentary

I've always had a fondness for this lesson, because the first time I did it I had a very real sense of how holiness was emanating from me and surrounding everything, first in my room, then my town, then the world, and finally the universe. For a very brief moment I felt like a Buddha, sitting and blessing the entire world (that's tomorrow's lesson, by the way). The result was so effective for me that often, when I am simply

103

sitting in meditation and not practicing any particular lesson, I think of this one and allow that sense to steal over me again.

Not everyone responds to every lesson, but everyone responds to some of the lessons. Notice the ones that seem particularly effective for you, and remember them. Lesson 194 in the Workbook speaks of building a "problem-solving repertoire" of things that we find helpful:

> If you can see the lesson for today as the deliverance it really is, you will not hesitate to give as much consistent effort as you can, to make it be a part of you. As it becomes a thought that rules your mind, a habit in your problem-solving repertoire, a way of quick reaction to temptation, you extend your learning to the world.   (W-194.6:1–2)

In yesterday's lesson the focus was on the perceiver: "I am very holy." Today the holiness extends to what is perceived. Because I am holy, my perception must also be holy. And I am perfectly holy because God created me that way. Holy means "sinless," and you cannot be partly sinless any more than a woman can be "a little" pregnant. The logic here is quite simple and plain: If I am part of God I must be sinless, or part of God would be sinful. If I am without sin I must have holy perception as well.

How I see myself affects how I see the world. My holiness envelops the world if I see myself as holy. My awfulness envelops the world if I see myself as awful. If I am willing to see the world enveloped in holiness, I can learn to see myself that way.

I know, that sounds like I have it backwards; the order "should be" that I see myself holy first, and then the world. The thing of it is, what keeps me from seeing myself as holy is my unwillingness to see the world that way. From within the ego mindset, it seems as if seeing the world as holy will make me unholy by comparison. The ego always thinks in terms of comparison. The fact is that as I see the world, so I see myself, and as I see myself, so I see the world.

The ego mind will insist it must be one way or the other because it operates on a presumption of separateness. The Holy Spirit presents it both ways at once because He operates on the presumption of unity. There is no separation between myself and what I see; there is only the one.

LESSON 37 ✦ FEBRUARY 6
"My holiness blesses the world."

Practice instructions

Purpose: To introduce you to your true function (this is the first lesson to deal with the topic of function). You are here to bless, and to make no demands. This blessing involves first acknowledging your own holiness, and then seeing others in its holy light. Try to see today's practice periods in this way, as practice in the reason you are here.

Longer: Four times, for three to five minutes.

* Repeat the idea and, for a minute or so, look about you and apply it to the objects you see, saying, *"My holiness blesses [this chair, that window, this body, etc.]."*
* Close your eyes and apply the idea to any person you think of, saying, *"My holiness blesses you, [name]."*
* For the remainder you may continue with this second phase of practice, go back to the first, or alternate between them.
* Conclude by repeating the idea with eyes closed and then once more with eyes open.

Frequent reminders: As often as you can.

This can take one of two forms:

1. Repeat the idea slowly.

2. Apply the idea silently to anyone you meet, using his or her name. Really try to do this. It takes real presence of mind to repeat the idea right when you meet up with someone, but it can be done. Or it can be done after the interaction is over. The Workbook will repeat this practice in several future lessons, which shows the importance it has. This practice has the power to transform an ordinary encounter into a holy encounter.

Response to temptation: Whenever you have an adverse reaction to someone.

Immediately apply the idea to him or her (*"My holiness blesses you, [name]"*). See this as a real act of blessing this person with your holiness. This will keep your holiness in *your* awareness, while your anger will blot it from your mind.

Commentary

There is a principle stated in Chapter 13 of the Text that applies to this lesson: "To perceive truly is to be aware of all reality through the awareness of your own" (T-13.VI.1:1). Or, in terms a bit closer to our lesson for today:

> Since you and your neighbor are equal members of one
> family, as you perceive both so you will do to both. You
> should look out from the perception of your own holiness
> to the holiness of others.   (T-1.III.6:6–7)

Unless we recognize our own holiness we will not see the holiness of all of God's creations. What we perceive is, after all, merely the reflection of how we see ourselves. Conversely, how we perceive others *shows* us how we must be seeing ourselves.

In this lesson we are told that we see "the first glimmerings of your true function in the world, or why you are here" (1:1). Our job is stated simply but with great profundity: "Your purpose is to see the world through your own holiness" (1:2).

Have you ever met someone you would consider very holy? I have. The most remarkable thing about them is that they seem to see everyone as holy. When you are around them, you even feel holy yourself! They seem to be seeing something in you that normally you cannot see; their seeing it draws it out of you. And just exactly that is why we are in the world; just exactly that is what all of us are here to do. We are here to see the world through our own holiness, to draw out of everyone around us their native holiness, to perceive them in such a way that the power of our perception lifts them up out of self-doubt and self-loathing into an awareness of their own magnificence.

We have this power!

> As you share my unwillingness to accept error in yourself
> and others, you must join the great crusade to correct it;
> listen to my voice, learn to undo error and act to correct it.

The power to work miracles belongs to you.

(T-1.III.1:6–7)

"Those who are released must join in releasing their brothers, for this is the plan of the Atonement" (T-1.III.3:3). This is the plan by which we, empowered by God's Spirit within us, can save the world. We release one another by perceiving each other through our own holiness, creating a resonance within them as their own holy nature, long suppressed, responds to our perception of them.

> Thus are you and the world blessed together. No one loses; nothing is taken away from anyone; everyone gains through your holy vision. (1:3–4)

"My holiness blesses the world"; that is what I am here for. I am here to bring blessing to the world, and the message I bring is: *so are you*. No one loses; everyone gains. What an incredible outlook this is!

This undoes the entire idea of sacrifice because it is a message of total equality. We are here to acknowledge each other, and when we do we have achieved our glorious purpose. Any other way of looking at things winds up demanding sacrifice; somebody, somewhere, has to lose. But with the vision of Christ we can look out at all the world and proclaim, "They are all the same; all beautiful and equal in their holiness" (T-13.VIII.6:1).

"Your holiness blesses him by asking nothing of him. Those who see themselves as whole make no demands" (2:6–7). Oh, that we might learn the lesson of asking nothing, making no demands! Have you ever, even perhaps if only for a brief time, been with someone who was so complete they made no demands on you? They had no need they were, overtly or covertly, asking you to fill. They loved you just as you were; they accepted you without expecting anything from you. Isn't that what we all want in our relationships? Isn't that what unconditional love is?

Well, the way to have what you want is to give it away. This is what all of us are destined to do, and will do eventually, even if it seems beyond us now. Aware of your holiness and your own completion, you will stand and bless the world.

> Your holiness is the salvation of the world. It lets you teach the world that it is one with you, not by preaching to

it, not by telling it anything, but merely by your quiet recognition that in your holiness are all things blessed along with you. (3:1–2)

LESSON 38 ✦ FEBRUARY 7
"There is nothing my holiness cannot do."

Practice instructions

Purpose: "To begin to instill in you a sense that you have dominion over all things because of what you are" (5:5).

Longer: Four times, preferably for five full minutes.

- Repeat the idea then close your eyes.
- Search your mind for any suffering or difficulty, whether in your life or someone else's. Do your best to treat these two as the same. For problems of your own, say, *"In the situation involving _____ in which I see myself, there is nothing my holiness cannot do."* For problems of others, say, *"In the situation involving _____ in which _____ sees himself, there is nothing my holiness cannot do."*
- Periodically, feel free to add thoughts of your own that are related to today's idea. Stay close to the idea; don't go too far afield. These thoughts will serve to make that idea more real to you. This is the first occurrence of the important practice of letting related thoughts come, which you will receive more instruction in later.

Frequent reminders: Frequent.

Repeat the idea.

Response to temptation: Whenever a specific problem—your own or someone else's—presents itself or comes to mind, use the specific form from the longer practice period.

Commentary

Toward the end of the lesson there is this informative line: "The purpose of today's exercises is to begin to instill in you a sense that you have dominion over all things because of what you are" (5:5). In a much later lesson (190) the same idea is echoed:

> There is nothing in the world that has the power to make you ill or sad, or weak or frail. But it is you who have the

> power to dominate all things you see by merely re-
> cognizing what you are.   (W-pI.190.5:5–6)

Now, if you are like me, you probably don't feel as though you have the power to dominate all things or that you are "unlimited in power." You probably don't feel as though the power of God is made manifest through your holiness, that because of what you are you can "remove all pain, can end all sorrow, and can solve all problems" (2:4). If you did feel that way, you'd probably suspect in some part of your mind that you were suffering from delusions of grandeur.

That's exactly why we need this kind of lesson. What we are, in reality, is so far above what we normally think we are that when we hear words like this lesson there is a part of us that whispers, "This is getting a little freaky here." We have no idea of the power of our minds, which were created by God and given the same creative power as His. When we get hints of how powerful we are, it scares us, and we try to forget about it.

What we really are is "beyond every restriction of time, space, distance and limits of any kind" (1:2). We really do have the power to solve all problems, our own and anyone else's. If practicing today's lesson simply *begins* to instill this sense in us, it has been successful.

When I face a situation that is troubling me and repeat, "In this situation, there is nothing that my holiness cannot do," even if ninety percent of my mind is protesting against the idea, something shifts within me. A little faith is generated. Maybe the percentage shifts from ten percent belief to eleven percent belief. And when I do it again, twelve percent. We've all read stories of people who overcame unbelievable odds just because they believed in themselves; that only hints at what the Course is talking about, but it illustrates the principle.

The Course is talking about the power of belief, but much more as well; it is talking about the power of what we honest-to-God *are*. And it is talking about the power of our holiness, not just belief. You and I are made out of God-stuff. When we actually get that, we can change the world.

> True learning is constant, and so vital in its power that a
> Son of God can recognize his power in one instant and
> change the world in the next.   (T-7.V.7:5)

LESSON 39 ✦ FEBRUARY 8
"My holiness is my salvation."

Practice instructions

Purpose: To get you in touch with your holiness, which is your salvation from the hell of guilt.

Longer: Four times (more are encouraged), for five full minutes (longer is encouraged).
- Repeat the idea.
- Close your eyes and slowly search your mind for unloving thoughts, thoughts with any kind of negative feeling attached to them. This includes specific situations, events, or personalities associated with angry, worried, or depressed thoughts. Make no exceptions and try to treat each one the same. With each, say, *"My unloving thoughts about _____ are keeping me in hell. My holiness is my salvation."* Your unloving thoughts keep you in hell by producing guilt. Your holiness saves you by showing you that your true nature is untouched by sin and guilt, and it proves this by blessing everything it sees.
- Because sustained concentration is hard for you at this stage, you may want to intersperse this practice with several periods of just repeating the the idea slowly, or relaxing and not thinking of anything. You can also introduce variety, which seems to mean varying the wording of the idea. Make sure, however, that you retain its central meaning: that your holiness is your salvation.
- Conclude by repeating the idea and asking yourself, *"If guilt is hell, what is its opposite?"* (For the answer, see 4:2).

Frequent reminders: At least three or four per hour.

Ask yourself, *"If guilt is hell, what is its opposite?"* Or repeat the idea. Preferably both.

Response to temptation: Whenever you are tempted to give in to unloving thoughts.

Apply the idea specifically: *"My holiness is my salvation from this."*

Commentary

The opposite of hell is salvation; the opposite of guilt is holiness. If guilt is hell, then holiness must be salvation. The question is: Do I believe that guilt is hell? Or do I, perhaps, feel that guilt serves a useful function in my life?

The Course teaches that guilt is at the root of all our problems, and yet at the beginning we don't even suspect guilt as the cause. We lay the problems at the feet of many different things, but rarely at the feet of guilt. "Of one thing you were sure: Of all the many causes you perceived as bringing pain and suffering to you, your guilt was not among them" (T-27.VII.7:4). Guilt *is* hell. This is part of what the Course is trying to teach us—a large part.

> As long as you believe that guilt is justified in any way, in anyone, whatever he may do, you will not look within, where you would always find Atonement. The end of guilt will never come as long as you believe there is a reason for it. For you must learn that guilt is always totally insane, and has no reason. (T-13.X.6:1–3)

> All salvation is escape from guilt. (T-14.III.13:4)

> Guilt is interference, not salvation, and serves no useful function at all. (T-14.III.1:4)

Perhaps we may object. Perhaps it seems that guilt is necessary to keep us from wrongdoing; but that presumes something within us that is inherently evil and perverse, something that will always do wrong unless it is kept caged, or punished when it misbehaves. Guilt serves no useful function; guilt is hell. Guilt is what we need to escape from. Guilt does not keep us from wrongdoing; it keeps us locked into it. It is guilt that has driven us insane.

As this lesson says, if we wholly believed that guilt is hell, we would immediately understand the entire Text and have no need for a Workbook. We would have salvation, full and complete, for salvation *is* escape from guilt. This is not a part of the Course's message; it is the whole of it. This is why my holiness is my salvation; holiness is freedom from guilt.

Notice the emphasis in practice on "unloving thoughts" (6:2; 7:1; 8:3). Unloving thoughts are guilty thoughts; they both stem from guilt and produce more of it. Holiness is lovingness. If my thoughts are unloving, I will be fearful and guilty; my holiness is my salvation from guilt. As we realize that our unloving thoughts are keeping us in hell, we will let them go.

Today's practice instructions are fiercely demanding: a minimum of four sessions of five full minutes each, with "longer and more frequent practice sessions...encouraged" (5:1). Then there are shorter applications, "which should be made some three or four times an hour and more if possible" (11:1). Plus there are responses to temptation. Today's idea must be very important! It must be very hard for our minds to absorb, so that we need to frequently immerse our minds in this thought.

LESSON 40 ✦ FEBRUARY 9
"I am blessed as a Son of God."

Practice instructions

Purpose: To put you in touch with the happy things that you are entitled to as God's Son.

Frequent reminders: Every ten minutes is highly desirable.

Close your eyes (if feasible), repeat the idea, and apply to yourself several attributes you associate with being a Son of God. For example: *"I am blessed as a Son of God. I am happy, peaceful, loving and contented."*

Remarks: You can see that he really means us to do this practice today. He urges us to do our best to keep to the schedule (1:3). He reminds us that the practice takes "little time and no effort" (3:1). And he has three provisions for when we do not or cannot do the practice as instructed:

1. When you notice that you have forgotten to practice, even for a long stretch, rather than feeling guilty and giving up, simply get back to your practicing right away.

2. If it is not feasible to close your eyes—which will often be the case—don't let that keep you from practicing. Just practice with eyes open.

3. If there is not enough time to do the exercise as suggested, simply repeat the idea. That takes about four seconds.

Commentary

There is no escaping the importance the Workbook attaches to actually trying to practice as instructed. In this lesson, whose practice is in one sense a relaxation from yesterday's and in another sense an intensification, you cannot read these words and think that the author believes that it does not matter whether or not we follow the instructions:

No long practice periods are required today, but very frequent short ones are *necessary*. Once every ten minutes would be highly desirable, and you are *urged* to attempt this schedule and to *adhere to it whenever possible*. If you forget, *try again*. If there are long interruptions, *try again*. Whenever you remember, *try again*.

(1:2–6, my emphasis)

Attempt…try…try…try. The more often we can repeat the lesson, the more impact it will have on our mind. How can you have a "course in mind training" (T-1.VII.4:1) without some kind of mental discipline? You can't; it's that simple.

At the same time notice that there is no "guilting" going on here. The author anticipates our indiscipline and expects (or allows for) our forgetting, and for "long interruptions" (1:5). He knows we lack discipline; that is exactly why the practice is so "necessary." But he does not judge us for it. He says, simply, "If you forget, try again." Don't let forgetting, even for long periods of the day, be an excuse to give up for the rest of the day. Every time we remember, we add a link to the "chain of forgiveness which, when completed, is the Atonement" (T-1.I.25:1).

He goes to the trouble of pointing out that just because you can't get alone and close your eyes, that is no excuse for not practicing. "You can practice quite well under any circumstances, if you really want to" (2:4).

The practice for today is, very simply, making positive affirmations as often as possible. "I am blessed as a Son of God. I am calm, quiet, assured and confident" (3:7–8). This might take ten or fifteen seconds, perhaps a little longer to think of a new list of attributes that you might associate with being a Son of God: "I am serene, capable and unshakable." "I am joyful, radiant, and full of love."

Can any of us really consider it a trial to engage in practice like this? Our egos do, and they will resist. I am no longer startled, but still astonished, at the variety of ways my ego finds to distract me and keep me from practicing my own happiness—for that is all we are doing here. Observing my ego's constant opposition to my happiness is one thing that has convinced me of the truth of that line in the Text: "The ego does not love you" (T-9.VII.3:5).

Because of what I am, an extension of God, I am entitled to happiness. The ego *has* to resist that idea because its existence depends upon my believing that I have separated myself from God; therefore the ego wants me to be unhappy. It wants me to believe that I do not deserve to be happy. Maybe it doesn't want me totally miserable—that might prompt me to reconsider everything. Just "a mild river of misery," as Marianne Williamson puts it. Just a vein of sadness and impermanence running through even my best times. Just enough to keep me from listening to The Other Guy Who talks about my union with God. And definitely not *happy*. Happy is dangerous to the ego. Happy says separation isn't true.

And it isn't!

LESSON 41 ✦ FEBRUARY 10
"God goes with me wherever I go."

Practice instructions

Purpose: To get in touch with God's Presence deep within you, so that you experience the fact that He goes with you wherever you go. This is the real cure for all human ills, which are merely symptoms of our illusory separation from God.

Longer: One time, for three to five minutes, as soon as possible after rising.

- Close your eyes, repeat the idea very slowly.
- Then let your mind go blank and focus all your attention on sinking down and inward. Sink past the cloud of insane thoughts on the surface of your mind and toward the Presence of God at the quiet center of your mind. "Try to enter very deeply into your own mind" (6:6). Repeat the idea occasionally if it helps, but spend most of your time gently willing yourself to sink toward the core of your mind, where all is still. Hold in mind the confidence that you can make it, for reaching this place is more natural than anything in this world. When thoughts arise, simply slip past them on your way inward. It will help dispel them if you repeat the idea.

Remarks: This is the Workbook's first meditation exercise. It is labeled "our first real attempt" (5:3) to reach the light within. As this quote suggests, this practice is extremely important in the Workbook. Paragraph 8 clearly signals that we will be engaging in "this kind of practice" (8:6) more, receiving more instruction in it, and growing in it, until we reach the point where "it is always successful" (8:5).

Frequent reminders: Often.

Repeat the idea according to the instructions in paragraph 9. To get a sense for that, I suggest that you repeat it right now following the instructions below, all of which are drawn from paragraph 9:

- Repeat "it very slowly, preferably with eyes closed."
- Repeat it again and "think of what you are saying; what the words mean."
- Repeat the words again and "concentrate on the holiness that they imply about you." If He goes with you and He is holy, then you are holy.
- Repeat them again, concentrating "on the unfailing companionship that is yours."
- Repeat them again, concentrating "on the complete protection that surrounds you."

Response to temptation: Whenever you have fear thoughts.

Remember the idea. If you really connect with its meaning, you will be able to laugh at the fears that seemed so heavy an instant before.

Commentary

Innumerable problems seem to have arisen from our perception of ourselves as separate from God. A sense of loneliness and abandonment, depression, anxiety, worry, helplessness, misery, suffering, and intense fear of loss all stem from this root problem. Most of our lives are spent, if we look at things objectively, with various ways of trying to circumvent and overcome these problems.

> But the one thing [we] do not do is to question the reality
> of the problem. Yet its effects cannot be cured because the
> problem is not real.   (2:2–3)

A spiritual teacher, Adi Da, once wrote a book subtitled *The Imaginary Disease That Religion Seeks to Cure*. That is what separation is: an imaginary disease. How can you cure a disease that does not really exist? The answer is obvious; you cannot. There is no cure because there is no disease. This is why all our attempts to "cure" ourselves do not work. We cannot find the way "back" to God because He has never left us; God goes with us wherever we go. All of our strife and drama is just foolishness, "despite the serious and tragic forms it may take" (2:5).

> Deep within you is everything that is perfect, ready to
> radiate through you and out into the world. It will cure all

sorrow and pain and fear and loss because it will heal the
mind that thought these things were real, and suffered out
of its allegiance to them.   (3:1–2)

We carry the "cure" for our disease deep within us. This cure heals,
not by overcoming the "illness" but by healing our belief in the reality
of the illness. God is always with us. How could we ever, in any way,
ever be separate from the Infinite? How could we ever be apart from All
That Is? The very idea is insane and impossible.

> We understand that you do not believe all this. How
> could you, when the truth is hidden deep within, under a
> heavy cloud of insane thoughts, dense and obscuring, yet
> representing all you see? Today we will make our first real
> attempt to get past this dark and heavy cloud, and to go
> through it to the light beyond.   (5:1–3)

How reassuring to have our Teacher tell us that he understands we do
not believe this as yet. Oh, perhaps we hold an intellectual belief in
God's omnipresence, but we do not believe it to the core, in a way that
banishes all our fear, sorrow, pain and loss. That is the purpose of this
lesson: to get past "this dark and heavy cloud" and to reach the light.

This lesson is the Course's first introduction to the practice of what
we might call traditional meditation. While the Course does not make
such meditation a primary focus, it definitely accords it a place of great
importance. Meditation in the Course consists of sitting with eyes
closed and making "no effort to think of anything" (6:4), but attempting
to enter deeply into our own mind, to sink down and inward while trying
to keep the mind "clear of any thoughts that might divert your attention"
(6:6). The purpose, as has been stated, is to become aware of the light
within ourselves. Or, in more traditional terms, to experience a sense of
God's presence with us. We are attempting to reach God today.

This meditation exercise, says the lesson, can achieve startling
results the very first time you try it. That may not happen for you the
first time, but "sooner or later it is always successful" (8:5). That
certainly implies that we are expected to repeat the exercise, and to
expect *something* as a result.

Clearly, if this idea of God's presence is meant to banish our
loneliness, we can expect to develop a very clear and tangible sense of

Someone Who is always with us, in every moment. When we begin to develop this sense we may be tempted to think it is our imagination. This is no imagination! It is the *absence* of this Presence that is imaginary.

"You can indeed afford to laugh at fear thoughts, remembering that God goes with you wherever you go" (10:1).

MEDITATION IN
A COURSE IN MIRACLES

For thousands of years, meditation has been considered by seekers all over the world to be perhaps *the* royal road to God. It has been sanctified by Hindu gurus, Christian mystics, Sufi masters, and by the Buddha himself. Because many of us have come to *A Course in Miracles* already steeped in traditions that stress meditation, we naturally wonder what role it has in the Course.

There seem to be many answers to this question floating around in the Course community. One says that the Course doesn't teach meditation, but that you can still practice alongside the Course whatever meditation techniques you have picked up elsewhere. Another says that meditation is prevalent in the Course, since we can consider any sort of inner exercise to be a meditation of sorts. Yet another says that the Workbook does have you meditate, but that there is no need to keep up with it once you are done with the Workbook, for meditation is not a permanent part of the Course's path.

I too wondered what role meditation played in the Course. Before I came to the Course I had tried out many different techniques. These techniques were all quite different, but they had some basic things in common. They all had to do with focusing the mind and clearing it of normal contents (or at least detaching it from those contents), so that higher states of mind could arise in the meditator.

Thus, when I came to the Course, I had my eye out for something like this. It wasn't too long before I found it. It was introduced quite clearly in Lesson 41. This lesson first presents a picture of the mind. It explains that deep within your mind is "everything that is perfect, ready to radiate through you and out into the world" (3:1). Yet this inner place of perfection is obscured by a "heavy cloud of insane thoughts" (5:2) that lies on the surface of your mind. To understand this, you might picture the mind as a circle. At a place on the surface of this circle is your normal, superficial awareness, filled with clouds of insane thoughts. At the center of this circle is your real Self and God.

After presenting this view of the mind, the lesson then says, "Today we will make our first real attempt to get past this dark and heavy cloud, and to go through it to the light beyond" (5:3). Apparently, we are about to be introduced to some new form of practice, designed to access this deep place in us.

And that is exactly what follows. We are told to begin our longer practice period by repeating the idea for the day, and then clearing our minds of thoughts. We then turn inward, sinking past our idle thoughts, through their dense clouds, and towards that deep place in our minds where God abides.

This lesson is clearly an exercise in meditation. Like more traditional methods, it involves a focusing and clearing of the mind in an attempt to contact higher states of mind. And this technique is not an incidental sidelight in the Course, as you can see from these remarks, which come right after the practice instructions:

> It is quite possible to reach God....The way will open, if you believe that it is possible. This exercise can bring very startling results even the first time it is attempted, and sooner or later it is always successful. We will go into more detail about this kind of practice as we go along. (8:4-6)

This more detailed instruction begins three lessons later, in Lesson 44. There, we find these words:

> Today we are going to attempt to reach that light. For this purpose, we will use a form of exercise which has been suggested before, and which we will utilize increasingly. It is a particularly difficult form for the undisciplined mind, and represents a major goal of mind training. It requires precisely what the untrained mind lacks. Yet this training must be accomplished if you are to see. (W-pI.44.3:1-5)

After these remarks, we are instructed in the same basic practice that was given in Lesson 41. We repeat the idea for the day, then sink down and inward, past all interference, toward the light in us. This same "form of exercise" is then repeated in Lessons 45, 47, 49, and 50. From there on, as the above passage promises, this exercise is utilized increasingly, becoming a staple of Workbook practice.

So the Course *does* teach meditation. This is not meditation defined so loosely that any sort of inner exercise can be considered meditation. It is a kind of meditation that stands comfortably alongside more ancient forms of meditation from the world's great spiritual traditions.

Why, then, haven't Course students noticed it? There are two reasons that I can think of. First, these lessons never use the word "meditation." Instead, they speak of "this kind of practice" or "this form of exercise." As a result, you can't spot meditation in the Course by name. You have to spot it by *concept.* This leads to the second problem: I think that Course students often do not pay close enough attention to the practice instructions. If they did, they would realize that they are being taught meditation even though the name isn't used.

It struck me as very significant that the Workbook has a particular method of meditation that it both teaches and greatly emphasizes. This prompted me to design an audio tape for Miracle Distribution Center back in 1986. The tape was called *The Holy Instant* and was read by Beverly Hutchinson with music from Steven Halpern. One side of it was a half-hour meditation exercise created from piecing together various Workbook meditation instructions.

I thought that having this tape would be just what I myself needed to really use this technique of meditation. Yet it didn't work out that way. I found that as I listened to the instructions to sink down and inward, I would often end up feeling like my consciousness actually sank down into my stomach. It wasn't a very spiritual feeling at all. In fact, it was quite uncomfortable and disorienting. So I stopped using the tape. I decided that I liked the feeling of ascending in my mind (the technique I had been using), rather than going down and inward (the technique taught by the Workbook). Going upward made me feel, well, more elevated and uplifted. It sure felt better than getting stuck in my liver.

Years passed by without me using the Course's method of meditation. I assumed that it just wasn't for me. Finally, about four years ago, I returned to it. I was practicing the Workbook more intensely, and my "ascending" meditation gave me tension headaches and made me irritable—not exactly what the Workbook is aiming for. So I thought I'd give this sinking down and inward thing another try. And it did cure my tension and irritability, but I remained somewhat confused about the technique. I had mixed results.

Then one morning about three years ago I had a breakthrough. I was going through the Workbook and had reached Lesson 41. I resolved to myself, "This time I am really going to get this method of meditation." I read through the lesson and was drawn to a particular line: "Try to enter very deeply into your own mind" (6:6). Something clicked in me. It is not talking about going down and inward in your *body*, but in your *mind*. I'm sure I knew that, but without realizing it I had been trying to sink down in my body, rather than inward in my mind.

"Try to enter very deeply into your own mind." I finally got it. There is a center of my mind, a core of me, the inmost part of my being. That is what I am trying to find. It really has nothing to do with my body. To get a sense of this, close your eyes for a moment and imagine that you don't have a body at all, that you are just a mind, a disembodied mind. While imagining that, repeat these words over and over, "Try to enter very deeply into your own mind."

Did that work? Did you get a sense that you could enter very deeply into your mind whether or not you had a body? That morning, trying to practice Lesson 41, I finally did. As I closed me eyes and began my meditation, I had a very distinct feeling of gently pushing deeper and deeper toward the center of my being, what the Text calls "the quiet center." It was a new experience, different from all previous meditations. And though it was nothing spectacular (I am not the world's most gifted meditator), it was definitely a more profound and tranquil state of mind than I was accustomed to reaching.

I was pulled out of this state, however, by an unexpected phone call. It was from Roger Walsh, a well-known transpersonal psychologist, a respected authority on the Course, and, incidentally, a devoted meditator. He wanted to express his gratitude for an article I had written. This article recounted my long journey with the Workbook, telling how, after years of fumbling in the dark, I had slowly translated the Workbook's instructions into a living practice in my life, one I found deeply fulfilling and transformative. Roger likened the Workbook practice (done as instructed) to the intensive spiritual practice found in other traditions, especially those of the East. We shared our personal difficulties in doing the Workbook and talked about how crucial we felt it was for Course students to understand the supreme value of practice.

I couldn't help but feel that this phone call was a sign, a confirmation of the breakthrough I had just experienced. Here I had finally managed to turn the Workbook's meditation instructions into a fruitful living practice. And I received a call (from someone who cares deeply both about the Course and about spiritual practice) thanking me for an article about how I had turned the Workbook as a whole into a fruitful living practice. I felt as if the Holy Spirit were saying to me, "Congratulations.You did it. You have made this part of the Course live in your own life."

Since that morning, this form of meditation has become a foundation for my daily practice and for my life. A day without it is a very different, and much worse, day. I find it far more effective than the other techniques I have used over the years. If you haven't already tried it, I highly recommend that you do. The following instructions, drawn from various Workbook lessons, are a great start. I hope your experience of Course-based meditation will be as rewarding as mine has been.

COURSE-BASED MEDITATION
"Down-and-Inward" Meditation

Where taught: Initially, in Lessons 41 and 44, where it is hailed as "our first real attempt" to experience the light within, "a major goal of mind-training," and a practice "we will utilize increasingly." After these two lessons, it becomes a staple of Workbook practice.

Three aspects: I have found it useful to break this method down into three aspects, the first of which is the basic process or motion, which is then enhanced by the second and third aspects.

I. Sink deeply into the center of your mind

Repeat the idea for the day a few times, then let go of it. Clear your mind of all normal thoughts, then try to sink towards the center of your mind. *Sink down and inward*, toward the truth in you, the core of you, the heart of you. My favorite sentence about that is this: "Try to enter very deeply into your own mind."

Rather than specific words or mantras, this sinking toward the quiet center is the focus of this method. This is what you do with your mind while meditating, letting/willing your mind to go to its center, rather than repeating anything, focusing on your breathing, or just sitting there and trying to keep your mind blank.

Please note that this does not mean going to some place in your *body* or anywhere in physical space. It means going to the center of your *mind*. As an experiment, close your eyes, and focus on yourself as a mind—try to forget about your body. Then say to yourself, "Try to enter very deeply into your own mind." Do you get a sense of where that is? Did that evoke any kind of feeling or sense? Personally, this sentence evokes a very specific sense for me, but not of a place in my body; rather, of a place that lies at the heart of whatever I am.

At the beginning of the practice period, repeat today's idea very slowly.
Then make no effort to think of anything.
Try, instead, to get a sense of turning inward,
  past all the idle thoughts of the world.
Try to enter very deeply into your own mind,
  keeping it clear of any thoughts that might divert your attention.
  (W-41.6)

Try to sink into your mind,
  letting go every kind of interference and intrusion
  by quietly sinking past them.
Your mind cannot be stopped in this unless you choose to stop it.
It is merely taking its natural course. (W-44.7)

Try to reach down into your mind to a place of real safety.
You will recognize that you have reached it if you feel a sense of deep
  peace, however briefly. (W-47.7)

From time to time, you may repeat the idea if you find it helpful.
But most of all, try to sink down and inward,
  away from the world and all the foolish thoughts of the world.
You are trying to reach past all these things.
You are trying to leave appearances and approach reality. (W-41.7)

Let go all the trivial things that churn and bubble
  on the surface of your mind,
  and reach down and below them to the Kingdom of Heaven.
There is a place in you where there is perfect peace.
There is a place in you where nothing is impossible.
There is a place in you where the strength of God abides. (W-47.7)

II. Use concrete methods to pull your mind back from wandering

It is absolutely essential to bring your mind back from wandering or your meditation will not accomplish anything. You must be willing to constantly pull your mind back again and again. The Course says, "Do this *as often as necessary*. There is definite gain in refusing to allow retreat into withdrawal [drowsiness], even if you do not experience the peace you seek [italics mine]" (W-74.6). Here are two methods for pulling your mind back.

1. If your mind wanders, repeat the idea for the day. This is the

Workbook's most common method.

2. Repeat: "This thought I do not want. I choose instead [repeat idea for the day]" (W-rVI.In).

III. Hold a heightened sense of intention

This method is very flexible on the level of form. You may visualize yourself going through clouds to a light (Lesson 69), or sinking under churning waters to peaceful depths (47), or going through a doorway deep in your mind (131). The form you use is not important. What *is* crucial, however, is the *attitude* or *intention* you hold about reaching you goal.

> While no particular approach is advocated for this form of exercise, *what is needful* is a sense of the importance of what you are doing; its inestimable value to you, and an awareness that you are attempting something very holy.
> (W-44.8; italics mine)

> For this kind of practice *only one thing is necessary*; approach it as you would an altar dedicated in Heaven to God the Father and to God the Son. For such is the place you are trying to reach. (W-45.8; italics mine)

The following categories are the particular mental attitudes most encouraged in the Course's meditation instructions. I find it helpful to begin my meditations by focusing on one at a time.

CONFIDENCE, because God wants you to reach this place in you and so do you

DESIRE, because reaching that place is your heart's desire

IMPORTANCE (of what you are doing), because this is your salvation and the world's

HOLINESS (of what you are doing), because reaching this holy place in you is a holy thing

LESSON 42 ✦ FEBRUARY 11

"God is my Strength. Vision is His gift."

Practice instructions

Purpose: To realize that vision comes not from you but from the strength of God in you, and that therefore you can receive it under any circumstance and cannot fail to find it eventually.

Longer: Two times, for three to five minutes, (early) morning and (late) evening.

- Repeat the idea slowly, looking about you. Close your eyes and repeat it even slower.
- Then step back and let only thoughts related to the idea come to mind. Do not strain or actively try to think them up. "Try merely to step back and let the thoughts come" (6:2). I find it helpful to repeat the idea and watch for the germ of a related thought to spark in my mind somewhere during that repetition. Then I put words to that germ.
- If your mind wanders, repeat the idea and try again. If related thoughts stop coming, repeat the idea with eyes open and eyes closed as at the beginning. If no related thoughts come at all, just repeat this beginning phase over and over.

Remarks: This is our first lengthy instruction in the practice of letting related thoughts come (which was introduced in Lesson 38). Over time, the Workbook will try to make this practice a habitual part of our overall repertoire.

Frequent reminders: The more often the better.

Repeating this idea, which consists of two parts, will begin to show you that all the parts of the Course come together into a unified whole. It will also remind you that the Course's goal—vision—is a genuine priority for you.

Commentary

Question: Why can we not fail in our efforts to achieve the goal of this course?

Answer: Because God wills us to achieve it.

If that answer sounds somewhat demeaning to you, don't be surprised at having such a reaction. With our minds permeated by ego thinking, it can seem personally insulting to be told that the guarantee of our success is that "God wants it that way," as if we don't have any choice in the matter. But the fact is, we don't.

As the introduction to the Text puts it:

> It is a required course. Only the time you take it is vo-
> luntary. Free will does not mean that you can establish the
> curriculum. It means only that you can elect what you want
> to take at a given time.   (T-In.1:2–5)

The curriculum is learning who we are, and we don't have any say in establishing that; we are what God created, and we cannot change that. The only choice is how long it takes us to accept the fact of what we are, instead of trying to be something we are not.

The Text talks about how separation took root in our minds when we refused to accept ourselves as creations of God and wanted to create ourselves. We're still fighting that same silly battle. It still seems insulting to be told that the outcome is inevitable; we are what God created and can't be anything else, no matter how much we might wish for it.

It is God's strength and not ours that gives us our power. We can't give ourselves vision, but neither can we forever refuse His gift to us. Even if we resist, eventually we will capitulate. And if we cooperate, our success is guaranteed.

Werner Erhard, the founder of Erhard Seminars Training (est), once said that it is easier to ride the horse in the direction in which it is going. That is what the Course is asking us to do; to join our will to God's, and to recognize that we really do want exactly what He wants to give us, and has given already. "What He gives is truly given" (2:1).

If we can accept that our will and God's are the same, we can enter into spiritual life as a sure thing. We can say, "Vision must be possible. God gives truly" (4:5–6). Or "God's gifts to me must be mine, because He gave them to me" (4:7). We can walk through life with a calm assurance. "Those who are certain of the outcome can afford to wait, and wait without anxiety" (M-4.VIII.1:1).

There is an idea that gets tossed into the middle of this lesson, seemingly unrelated, although it is closely related. "Your passage through time and space is not at random. You cannot but be in the right place at the right time" (2:3–4). The more you go on with this path (and similar ones) the more you know this is absolutely true. There are no random events; everything has a purpose. And you cannot miss! You can't screw it up. Oh, you can make mistakes; the Course is quite clear about that. It tells us: "Son of God, you have not sinned, but you have been much mistaken" (T-10.V.6:1). But even our mistakes can be used by the Holy Spirit for our benefit: "The Son of God can make no choice the Holy Spirit cannot employ on his behalf" (T-25.VI.7:5). Even if you make the "wrong" choice, nothing has really happened; no permanent damage has been done. "Nothing is ever lost but time, which in the end is meaningless" (T-26.V.2:1). The Holy Spirit can take whatever you give Him and turn it to your good.

So you can't help being in the right place at the right time; you can just relax in life and enjoy the show, instead of being anxious about it all. Why is this so? Because of the strength of God, and His gifts. Your reaching the goal is His Will, and what God wants, God gets. After all, He's *God*.

One further comment: In the instructions for practice you are asked to let thoughts occur in relation to today's idea; this kind of rehearsing of related thoughts is another type of meditation that is quite common in the Workbook. Then it says, "You may, in fact, be astonished at the amount of course-related understanding some of your thoughts contain" (5:2).

You may, however, instead be very puzzled over what the heck this means! The first time I tried this exercise my mind was virtually blank. Remember that the Workbook often assumes that you have studied—not just read, but studied—the Text before you began these exercises. It isn't a requirement, but it is assumed to be the general case.

For anyone who has done that, related thoughts will indeed come easily, or if you are on a repeat pass through the Workbook, same thing. If, after trying for a minute or two to find related thoughts, you find that they do not come easily, take the advice given a little further on in the lesson: "If you find this difficult, it is better to spend the practice period alternating between slow repetitions of the idea with the eyes open, then with eyes closed, than it is to strain to find suitable thoughts" (6:3). The presence of this kind of instruction shows that the lessons can accommodate people who haven't already studied the Text in depth.

LESSON 43 ✦ FEBRUARY 12
"God is my Source. I cannot see apart from Him."

Practice instructions

Purpose: To remember your function.

Longer: Three times, for five minutes each; morning (early as possible), evening (late as possible), and in between (when readiness and circumstances permit).

- First phase: Repeat the idea, then glance around you, applying it specifically and indiscriminately to whatever you see. Four to five subjects will be enough.
- Second phase: Close your eyes, repeat the idea, and let related thoughts come to you. Their purpose is to enrich the idea "in your own personal way" (5:2). They don't need to be restatements of it, or even obviously related to it, but they can't contradict it. If your mind is wandering or you begin to draw a blank, repeat the first phase of the exercise and then attempt the second phase again. Don't let the practice period become a mind wandering session, so be determined do this as many times as you need to.

Frequent reminders: You have a choice of three forms:

1. When you are with someone, whether friend or "stranger," tell him silently, *"God is my Source. I cannot see you apart from Him."*

2. Apply the idea to a situation or event, saying, *"God is my Source. I cannot see this apart from Him."*

3. If no subjects present themselves, merely repeat the idea.

Remarks: Try to allow no long gaps in remembering the idea. This is an important training goal for the Workbook. The same thing was urged in Lesson 36 (2:2).

Also, do your best to remember to apply the idea to people you encounter. It takes real presence of mind to do this, but it can be done, and it will change the quality of the encounter.

Response to temptation: Whenever you get distressed about an event or situation.

Apply the idea specifically: *"God is my Source. I cannot see this apart from Him."*

Commentary

All of what we call "seeing" is perception; it is not knowledge. Perception does not show us the truth; at best it shows us a clear symbol of truth. "Knowledge" in the Course is something that belongs to the realm of perfection, of Heaven; it is not possible to have knowledge and to be in this world, because this world is not true. The entire aim of the Course is to move us from false perception to true perception; when our perception has been cleaned up, we will be ready for the transfer to knowledge.

Without the Holy Spirit, perception would have remained false. But because God has placed this link with Himself in all of our minds, perception can be purified so that it will lead us to knowledge.

In Heaven or in God, there is no such thing as perception, only knowledge. Perception requires two, a perceiver and the perceived; that is duality and does not exist in truth. Yet "in salvation," our experience in this world, "perception has a mighty purpose" (2:3). Although we made perception for "an unholy purpose" (2:4), to make illusions that we think are real, the Holy Spirit can use it to restore our holiness to our awareness.

Remember Lesson 1? "Nothing I see means anything." That is because "perception has no meaning" (2:5). All of perception is essentially meaningless, "yet does the Holy Spirit give it a meaning very close to God's" (2:6). Rather than trying to understand what we see, we need to step back and let the Holy Spirit write His meaning on it all. Seen with Him, everything reveals God to us.

Without God, we think we see, but we really see nothing. We see nothing that looks like something and we attach our meanings to it all, meanings which deceive us. "I cannot see apart from Him." I may think I see, but what I seem to see is not seeing; it is hallucinating. With God, I can see truly. With God, I can perceive a clear reflection of truth in everything I look upon. It is that perception of truth that is the means by which I can forgive my brother. If I ask, I will see it.

So I cannot see apart from God. But that's a no-brainer, because I cannot *be* apart from God, so the truth is I can't do anything apart from Him. It's like saying, "My hand can't do anything without my body." Of course not; my hand is not separate from my body. "Whatever you do you do in Him" (3:2).

To achieve true vision I do not need to *become* part of God or to join with Him, as if I were making a transition of some kind from a separated condition to a unified condition. No, all I really need to do is acknowledge or recognize that I am already one with Him. As I accept that reality about myself, vision is already mine. It is inherent in my natural condition.

What I see when I think I am apart from God must not be sight, because being apart from God is illusion, so the "sight" must also be illusion. "I cannot see this desk apart from Him" (4:8).

Once again we are led into a period in which we let relevant related thoughts arise in our minds. The Course is clearly encouraging us to put its ideas into our own words, and to extend them and embellish them for our own personal use. Sometimes, the "altered" form of the lesson will prove more effective for your practice than the original version. We should feel free to do this kind of personalizing in all of the Workbook lessons. It is a tool we are meant to use to make the lessons more personally meaningful.

LESSON 44 ✦ FEBRUARY 13
"God is the light in which I see."

Practice instructions

Purpose: To contact the light within that allows you to see with true vision.

Longer: At least three times, for three to five minutes (longer is highly recommended if not a strain).

- Repeat the idea, then close your eyes slowly, repeating the idea several more times.
- The rest of the practice involves a single motion of sinking into your mind. I find it helpful to think of this motion as having three aspects:

1. Sink down and inward, past your surface thoughts and toward the light of God deep within your mind. As you do this, "try to think of light, formless and without limit" (10:2). If your meditation is successful, you will experience a feeling of approaching or even entering light.

2. Do not allow yourself to get sidetracked. This is crucial. As you pass by your thoughts, observe them dispassionately, "and slip quietly by them" (7:5). They have no power to hold you back. If resistance arises, repeat the idea. If actual fear arises, open your eyes briefly and repeat the idea. Then return to the exercise.

3. Hold in mind a heightened attitude about what you are doing, a sense that it has great importance, untold value, and is very holy. This attitude is more important than details of technique.

Remarks: This is the Workbook's second meditation exercise (the first was Lesson 41), and you can see the immense importance given it here, especially in paragraphs 3–5. We may resist this practice, because it requires discipline our minds don't yet have, and because it means leaving our ego's thoughts and beliefs behind. But these are the very reasons why this practice is so important.

Frequent reminders: Often—be *determined* not to forget.

Repeat the idea with eyes open or closed, as seems best.

Commentary

The first paragraph presents a rather amazing picture of what this world we see is. It says we made darkness, and then we thought we could see in it. What we call "seeing," then, is simply imagining that we can see in darkness. "In order to see, you must recognize that light is within, not without. You do not see outside yourself, nor is the equipment for seeing outside you" (2:1–2). What we call light is not true light. Light is not outside of us; it is within us. It is not physical, it is spiritual. And we do not see truly with external eyes but with inner vision.

The light for true seeing is within us, and the goal of today's lesson is to reach that light. Once again the Workbook takes us into an experiential exercise of meditation. This kind of meditation, and the experience it seeks to produce, is clearly a major component of Course practice. The emphasis placed on it is nothing short of amazing.

We are told that it is a form of exercise that "we will utilize increasingly" (3:2). It "represents a major goal of mind training" (3:3). Longer times are "highly recommended" (4:2). We are urged to persist despite "strong resistance" (5:2). It represents a "release from hell" (5:5). We are reminded of "the importance of what you are doing; its inestimable value to you" (8:1), and that "you are attempting something very holy" (8:1). The lesson closes with these words: "But do not forget. Above all, be determined not to forget today" (11:2–3). There is no mistaking the awareness that Jesus, as the author, considers this kind of meditation practice *exceptionally* important.

Why is that? There are a few indications within the lesson. In the third paragraph, the lesson notes that this kind of practice—sitting quietly, sinking inward, slipping by our thoughts without being involved in them—"is a particularly difficult form for the undisciplined mind" (3:3). It is difficult because it "requires precisely what the untrained mind lacks" (3:4). It is the very difficulty that proves our need of it, just as getting out of breath when you jog for fifty yards proves that you need aerobic exercise. "This training must be accomplished if you are to see" (3:5). In other words, meditation practice is a requirement for developing inner vision. How can we see with inner vision if we do not know how to find the inner light?

These are training exercises. We will find it difficult at first. We will encounter resistance. The exercise is clearly labeled an "attempt" (3:1) at reaching the light, indicating an understanding that we may not do so all at once, any more than we will run a marathon the first few times we begin jogging. It is a *goal* of our mind training to reach the light, and we will likely not reach the goal right away, although it is "the most natural and easy [form of practice] for the trained mind" (4:3). We are in the process of acquiring the training that will make reaching the light seem easy and natural, but it is not that way now because our minds are still undisciplined.

We are "no longer wholly untrained" (5:1). If we have been following the instructions we have had forty-three days of practice leading up to this day. Still, we may "encounter strong resistance" (5:2). To the ego what we are doing seems like "loss of identity and a descent into hell" (5:6). But we are attempting to reach God, Who is the light in which we can see; that is not a loss. It is escape from darkness.

When we begin to build up a history of experiences with the light, of feeling relaxation, sensing our approach to it, and even being aware of entering into it, we will know what the Course is talking about. And we will crave more. There is nothing like the experience. These holy instants are foretastes of Heaven, glimpses of reality. They will motivate us in our journey like nothing else. There is a sense of reality so real that what seemed real before pales into insubstantial shadows by comparison. When we have entered the light we will recognize that we have been in darkness, thinking it was light. That is what gives these experiences their "inestimable value."

LESSON 45 ✦ FEBRUARY 14
"God is the Mind with which I think."

Practice instructions

Purpose: To experience your real thoughts, which you think with the Mind of God.

Longer: Three times, for five minutes.

- Repeat the idea as you close your eyes. Then add four to five related thoughts (remember the instruction in letting related thoughts come that you received in Lessons 42 and 43).
- Then repeat the idea again and say, *"My real thoughts are in my mind. I would like to find them."*
- Then employ the same meditation technique you were taught in Lessons 41 and 44. Again, it is helpful to think of it as having three aspects:

1. Sink down through the obscuring layer of your senseless, unreal thoughts; reach past that to the eternal, limitless thoughts you think with God.

2. When your mind wanders, draw it back. It will help if you repeat the idea.

3. Above all, hold a certain attitude in mind. *Confidence*: Don't let your worldly thoughts tell you that you can't make it. You can't fail, because God wants you to make it. *Desire*: Reaching this place in you is your true heart's desire. *Holiness*: Approach it as you would a holy altar in which God and His Son think in perfect unison. "Remind yourself that this is no idle game, but an exercise in holiness" (8:7).

Frequent reminders: Ideally, spend one to two minutes.

Repeat the idea. Then step aside from your usual unholy thoughts and spend some time reflecting on the holiness of your mind. Think about how holy it must be if it thinks with the Mind of God.

Commentary

The lessons are trying, in a way, to cause extreme disorientation in us. Our real thoughts "are nothing that you think you think, just as nothing that you think you see is related to vision in any way" (1:2). If my thoughts aren't real and what I see isn't real, what do I have to hold on to? Not much at all. This can seem quite frightening, almost what it might be like if I were one of those characters in a suspense thriller who is being attacked by someone trying to drive them insane, causing them to believe that they are hallucinating and imagining things that are not there.

Actually, although the attempt to break our mental orientation is similar, the Course's intent is just the reverse. It is trying to drive us *sane*, not insane. We already are insane. We *are* hallucinating and imagining things that are not there, and the Course is trying to break our obsessive belief in their reality.

Underneath the protective layer of delusion we have laid over reality is a wholly sane mind thinking wholly sane thoughts and seeing only truth. Our real thoughts are thoughts we think with the Mind of God, sharing them with Him. Thoughts do not leave the mind, so they must still be there. Our thoughts are God's thoughts, and God's thoughts are eternal. If these thoughts are there we can find them. We can push our feet down through the mushy ooze of our thoughts and find solid bedrock. We may be almost totally out of touch with these original, eternal thoughts, thoughts completely in accord with the Mind of God, but God would have us find them. Therefore we must be capable of finding them.

Yesterday we were seeking the light within ourselves, a very abstract concept. Today we are seeking our own real thoughts. That brings the abstract a little closer to home; not just "the light" but my own thoughts, something that is part of me and representative of my nature.

What would a thought be like that was in perfect harmony with the Mind of God? That is what we are trying to find and experience today. And if we are honest, we will have to admit that the thoughts of which we are mostly aware are not in that league at all. Our thoughts are too riddled with fear, too uncertain, too defensive, too anxious or frantic, and above all too changeable to qualify as thoughts we share with God.

A thought we share with God must be one of complete harmony, absolute peace, utter certainty, total benevolence, and perfect stability.

We are seeking to locate such a thought-center in our minds. We are seeking to find thoughts of this nature *within ourselves*.

Once more we practice the quiet sinking down, going past all the unreal thoughts that cover the truth in our minds, and reaching to the eternal that is within us. This is a holy exercise, and one we should take quite seriously, although not somberly, for it is a joyous exercise. Within me there is a place that never changes, a place that is always at peace, always brilliant with love's shining. And today, O God yes today, I want to find that place! Today I want to touch that solid foundation at the core of my being and know its stability. Today I want to find my Self.

LESSON 46 ✦ FEBRUARY 15
"God is the Love in which I forgive."

Practice instructions

Longer: At least three times, for five full minutes.

* Repeat the idea as you close your eyes. Search your mind for those you have not completely forgiven. This shouldn't be hard—any lack of total love is a sign of unforgiveness. To each one, say, *"God is the Love in which I forgive you, [name]."* This will "put you in a position to forgive yourself" (5:1).
* After a minute or two of this, tell yourself, *"God is the Love in which I forgive myself."* Then spend the rest of the time letting your mind come up with thoughts related to this idea. They need not be a restatement of it, but don't get too far away from it, either. Draw upon the instruction you have received in letting related thoughts come.
* Conclude by repeating the original idea.

Frequent reminders: As many as possible.

Repeat the idea, in original form or in the form of a related thought.

Response to temptation: When you have a negative reaction to anyone, "present or not" (7:3).

Tell that person silently, *"God is the Love in which I forgive you."*

Commentary

The whole of the Course's teaching on the Atonement principle is contained in the first sentence: "God does not forgive because He has never condemned." Over and over the Course emphasizes that God is not a God of vengeance, that God is not angry with us, that He knows nothing of punishment. God does not condemn; He never has. His heart remains eternally open to us all. To me specifically.

In this world of illusions, where mutual condemnation has become a way of life (or death?), forgiveness is necessary—not God's forgiveness, but our own. Forgiveness is the way we release ourselves from illusions. All condemnation is self-condemnation; the guilt we see in others is our own reflecting back at us, and as we release others from our condemnation, we are released. "As you condemn only yourself, so do you forgive only yourself" (1:5).

As later lessons will make clear, our whole purpose in this world is to bring forgiveness to it, to release it from the burden of guilt that we have laid upon it. This is what returns our mind to the awareness of God. We find God by liberating those around us, lifting our judgment from them, and acknowledging them as worthy creations of God along with ourselves. "God...is approached through the appreciation of His Son" (T-11.IV.7:2).

Lifting the chains of judgment from everyone that I know puts me in a position to forgive myself (5:1). It brings a warm feeling inside when I can say, "God is the Love in which I forgive myself" (5:3). I may not even be aware of any guilt consciously, but when I bless myself with forgiveness, something melts, and I know that the forgiveness was needed. There is a subliminal self-criticism that is nearly always going on; and when I break into it, picturing the Love of God pouring over me like molten gold, knowing and accepting (maybe just in that moment) His total acceptance of me, I rarely escape the moment without tears of gratitude.

LESSON 47 ✦ FEBRUARY 16
"God is the strength in which I trust."

Practice instructions

Purpose: "To reach past your own weakness to the Source of real strength" (4:1), so that you gain confidence in the face of all problems and decisions.

Longer: Four times (more are urged), for five minutes (longer are urged).

- Close your eyes and repeat the idea.
- Search your mind for situations about which you have fear. Release each one by saying, *"God is the strength in which I trust."* Do this for a minute or two.
- The remainder is another exercise in meditation. Sink down in your mind, beneath all your worried thoughts, which are based on your sense of inadequacy. Reach down below these to the place in you where nothing is beyond your strength, because the strength of God lives in you. You might imagine you are sinking down beneath the choppy waters on the surface to the peaceful depths where all is still. "You will recognize that you have reached [this place] if you feel a sense of deep peace, however briefly" (7:2). Remember (as previously instructed) to draw your mind back from wandering as often as needed, and to hold in mind an attitude of confidence and desire.

Frequent reminders: Often.

Repeat the idea.

Response to temptation: When any disturbance arises.

Repeat the idea, remembering you are entitled to peace because you are trusting in God's strength, not your own.

Commentary

It is reported in the Gospel of John that Jesus said, "The Son can do nothing of himself, unless it is something He sees the Father doing….I can do nothing on my own initiative, as I hear, I judge" (Jn 5:19, 30). Basically that is what this lesson is telling us: We cannot do anything by ourselves. When the lesson speaks of "trusting in your own strength" (1:1) it is talking about attempting to do anything by ourselves, as an independent unit, separate from God and His creation. It is talking about operating as an ego. The lesson is saying that it is simply impossible.

Another example from the Gospels may help. Toward the end of his time on earth, Jesus compared himself to a vine, and his disciples to branches in the vine. He was speaking, I believe, from the perspective of the Christ; or perhaps it would be better to say the Christ was speaking through the man, Jesus. He said: "As the branch cannot bear fruit of itself, unless it abides in the vine, so neither can you, unless you abide in me....apart from me you can do nothing" (Jn 15:4–5).

Think about it. Where does the vine leave off and the branch begin? The branch is *part of* the vine. That is its whole existence. It cannot operate independently; it cannot "bear fruit" if it is cut off from the vine.

We are parts or aspects of the Sonship, and the Son is one with the Father. "What [God] creates is not apart from Him, and nowhere does the Father end, the Son begin as something separate from Him" (W-pI.132.12:4). Sounds a lot like a vine and its branches, doesn't it?

When we try to operate independently we can do nothing. As we normally think of ourselves, what is there we can wholly predict and control? How can we "be aware of all the facets of any problem" and "resolve them in such a way that only good can come of it?" (1:4). Left to ourselves, left to the limited resources of the self as the ego sees it, cut off from everything, we simply cannot do it. We don't have what it takes. "If you are trusting in your own strength, you have every reason to be apprehensive, anxious and fearful" (1:1).

The lesson is asking us to recognize that we are not limited to what we may think of as our own strength; "God is the strength in which I trust." It is asking us to operate based on our union with God. From where we are at the start of things, it is going to seem as if we are dealing with some kind of external God, a "Voice" that speaks within our minds or operates in circumstances to guide us:

> Since you believe that you are separate, Heaven presents itself to you as separate, too. Not that it is in truth, but that the link [the Holy Spirit] that has been given you to

join the truth may reach to you through what you understand.   (T-25.I.5:1–2)

So it may seem as if we are being asked to "submit" to a superior
force, when in fact all we are doing is aligning ourselves with all the rest
of our own being, from which we have dissociated ourselves. The Holy
Spirit speaks for us, as well as for God, for we are one (see T-11.1.11:1;
T-30.II.1:1–2; W-pI.125.8:1; W-pI.152.12:2).

When we realize we cannot live on our own—when we accept our
dependence on this Higher Power—God becomes our strength and our
safety in every circumstance. His Voice tells us "exactly what to do to
call upon His strength and His protection" (3:2).

When we fear, we must be trusting in our own independent strength,
which is nonexistent. Simply feeling inadequate for some task is a form
of fear, arising from the belief I am on my own. "Who can put his faith
in weakness and feel safe?" (2:3). When fear arises, let me remind
myself that I do not trust in my own strength, but God's. That reality can
pull me up from fear to a place of deep, abiding peace.

To recognize our weakness as independent beings is a necessary
beginning (6:1). If we deceive ourselves into believing we can handle
everything on our own, without God, without our brothers and sisters,
we will crash and burn eventually. But that recognition is not the point
at which to stop; we must go beyond that to realize that we have the
strength of God, and that confidence in that strength "is fully justified in
every respect and in all circumstances" (6:2).

Nearly every time I meditate I repeat, silently or aloud, the words
that come near the end of this lesson:

> There is a place in you where there is perfect peace. There
> is a place in you where nothing is impossible. There is a
> place in you where the strength of God abides.   (7:4–6)

Let us, today, pause frequently to reach down below "all the trivial
things that churn and bubble on the surface of [our] mind" (7:3), to find
that place.

LESSON 48 ✦ FEBRUARY 17
"There is nothing to fear."

Practice instructions

Frequent reminders: Very frequent, as often as possible.
This has two forms. Use the longer whenever you can.

1. Repeat the idea. You can do this with eyes open under any circumstance, even while in conversation. It can take as little as two seconds.

2. Take a minute or so, close your eyes, and repeat the idea slowly several times.

Remarks: The longer practice periods have been cleared away today, so you can focus on *frequency*. We saw the same thing in Lessons 20, 27, and 40. Today's lesson, therefore, is part of a series designed to teach us the crucial habit of frequent practice. Therefore, rather than taking a rest today, really give it your all. The more you put into it, the more you'll get out of it.

Earlier lessons (27, 40) recommended setting a frequency at the beginning of the day and then trying to stick to it. I would recommend doing the same today. What sort of frequency should you set? Let's look at previous lessons that specified a frequency:

20: two per hour

27: two to four per hour

39: three to four per hour

40: six per hour

The average is three to four per hour, but notice also that the frequency goes up as the lessons go up. I would suggest picking a frequency you really think you can maintain, and then setting a firm intention to stick with it, and even taking a moment to imagine yourself practicing it frequently under different circumstances. During the day, when you notice you have lapsed, don't be disturbed; it happens to all of us. Simply get back to practicing—immediately and without guilt.

Response to temptation: When anything disturbs your peace of mind.

Repeat the idea *immediately.*

Commentary

One can understand this simple thought in at least two ways:

1. Nothing exists of which to be afraid.

2. Fear? Nothing to it!

As the third paragraph makes clear, this thought is connected to yesterday's lesson about trusting in God's strength versus trusting in our own strength, apart from Him. "The presence of fear is a sure sign that you are trusting in your own strength" (3:1). As the lesson yesterday said, "Who can put his faith in weakness and feel safe?" (W-pI.47.2:3). So, when we trust in our own strength, we feel fear. When we trust in God's strength, we do not. Fear is nothing to be afraid of, however; it is merely a warning sign indicating that our faith is misplaced, and simply calls for correction, not condemnation.

That there is nothing to fear is a simple fact, from the perspective of the right mind. God is all there is, and we are part of Him; nothing outside Him exists. Of course there is nothing to fear. Fear is a belief in something other than God, a false god, an idol with power that opposes and overcomes God. We secretly believe that we have done so, and so we fear, but what we are afraid of is ourselves. Yet what we think we have done has never occurred. Therefore there is nothing to fear. "Nothing real can be threatened" (T-In.2:2).

If we believe in illusions, fear seems very real, but we are afraid of nothing. The lesson says it is "very easy to recognize" (1:4) that there is nothing to fear; what makes it seem difficult is that *we want the illusions to be true* (1:5). If they are not true, we are not who we think we are and who we wish to be; we are God's creations instead, and not our own. So we hold on to the illusions to validate our egos, and in so doing, hold on to the fear.

When we allow ourselves to recall that there is nothing to fear, when we consciously remind ourselves of that fact throughout the day, it shows that "somewhere in your mind, though not necessarily in a place you recognize as yet, you have remembered God, and let His strength take the place of your weakness" (3:2). This is what the Text calls the "right mind." There is a part of our minds—really the only part there is—in which we have *already* remembered God! That part of our minds is what is waking us up from our dream.

Have you ever wondered how you happened to come upon *A Course in Miracles*, and why it seems attractive to you? Your right mind has created this experience for you; your true Self is speaking to you through its pages to awaken you. Each time we repeat the thought for today, "There is nothing to fear," we are aligning ourselves with the part of us that is already awake, and has already remembered. Since we are already awake, the outcome is inevitable. But we need this appearance of time to "give ourselves time," so to speak, to dispense with our illusions and to recognize the ever-present truth of our reality.

LESSON 49 ✦ FEBRUARY 18
"God's Voice speaks to me all through the day."

Practice instructions

Purpose: To tune into and identify with the part of your mind where God's Voice is always speaking to you.

Longer: Four times (more if possible), for five minutes.

This is yet another meditation exercise, like Lessons 41, 44, 45, and 47. After closing your eyes and repeating the idea (not mentioned today, but standard), go into the meditation. Again, I find it helpful to think of it as having three aspects:

1. Sink past the cloud of frantic, insane thoughts that chokes the surface of your mind. Sink down to the part of your mind where stillness reigns, where you are truly at home, and where God's Voice speaks to you. Sinking down to this part also means listening to this part.

2. Draw your mind back from wandering by repeating the idea.

3. Above all, hold in mind the attitude that this is the happiest, holiest thing you could do, and that you are confident you can make it, because God wants you to.

Frequent reminders: Very frequently.

There is a range of options, which go from practicing under limiting circumstances to the ideal form of practice. This range applies to all the lessons:

1. Repeat the idea with eyes open when you have to.

2. Repeat it with eyes closed when possible.

3. Whenever you can, sit quietly, close your eyes, and repeat the idea. Make this an invitation to God's Voice to speak to you.

Commentary

"God's Voice speaks to me all through the day." Yes, It does! It may seem like wishful thinking to you when you say this sentence, but it isn't. God's Voice really does speak to us all through the day, every day. "The part of your mind in which truth abides [i.e., the right mind] is in constant communication with God, whether you are aware of it or not" (1:2). We aren't usually aware of this communication, although we could be. Our consciousness simply isn't tuned in.

It's like a radio signal. Here in Sedona we have a radio station called KAZM ("chasm," cute, huh?). KAZM is in communication with my radio all through the day, but I may not have my radio tuned to that station. The Holy Spirit is in communication with my mind all through the day, but I may not be tuned in.

There is another part of our mind that carries on the busy-ness of this world. That is the part we are mostly aware of. I'll label it "wrong mind" so we can tell the parts apart. This part really does not exist, and the part tuned in to God (right mind) is really the only part there is (2:2–3). Thus, speaking of "parts" of our mind is really just a helpful fiction.

The wrong mind is an illusion. The right mind is real. The wrong mind is frantic, distraught, filled with a chattering madhouse of "thoughts" that sound like the White Rabbit in Alice in Wonderland. The right mind is "calm, always at rest and wholly certain" (2:1). The right mind is what Lesson 47 spoke of when it said, "There is a place in you where there is perfect peace" (W-pI.47.7:4). In this place, "stillness and peace reign forever" (2:5).

We can choose which voice to listen to, which "part" of our mind to attend to: the frantic voice or the peaceful Voice. Does it seem hard to believe that there is a place in you that is always perfectly peaceful, like the eye of a hurricane? But there is. I found it hard to believe, but when I began looking for it I began finding it.

Often when we first try to find this place, the other voice shrieks so loudly that it seems we can't ignore it (as the lesson instructs us to). Just the other day someone was telling me how when they sat in meditation, the onset of peace was so frightening that they had to jump up and get busy with something. Isn't it weird that we find peace so unacceptable? Sit for a few minutes trying to be peaceful and something inside you is screaming, "I can't stand it!" That's the frantic voice. "Try," the lesson says, "not to listen to it" (2:4).

It's worth the effort! That place of peace is there in all of us, and when we find it—ahhh! I still have some days when I can't seem to stop the *yama yama* of my mind (as Werner Erhard calls that constant mental chatter), but the times when I sink into the peace beyond my thoughts are increasing, for which I am very grateful. You simply have to stop your activity to find it; you can't find it without sitting down, quieting down, and shutting down for a while. The world is far too distracting otherwise, at first.

Eventually we can learn to find this peace any time, anywhere, and even to bring it with us into chaotic situations. At first, however, we need to act out the stillness in order to find it, closing our eyes on the world, going past the stormy surface of our minds and into the deep, calm depths, asking God's Voice to speak to us.

One more thought. You might think, from this lesson, that if God's Voice speaks to you all through the day, it must be easy to hear it. Wrong. The ego's voice is characterized here as "raucous shrieks" (4:3), "frantic, riotous thoughts and sights and sounds" (4:4), and "constantly distracted" (1:4). Listening to God's Voice, at first, is like trying to meditate in the middle of a riot. It's like trying to compose a new tune while a rock band is tuning up. Or like trying to write a careful letter when three people are shouting different things into your ears. It's hard work. It takes focus and concentration. It takes, above all, willingness. "The Holy Spirit's Voice is as loud as your willingness to listen" (T-8.VIII.8:7).

You have to be willing to tune out that other voice. The shrieks of the ego don't just happen without our volition; they do not stem from some malevolent demon trying to frustrate our efforts to hear God. They are our own unwillingness taking form; that's all. We've spent eons turning on the noisemakers in our own minds. We have to start going around and choosing to turn them off.

So hearing the Holy Spirit isn't something that happens overnight—read about it today, start being "divinely guided in all I do" tomorrow. No. It's not that simple. In fact, in the Text, Jesus himself says that learning to listen *only* to that Voice and no other was the final lesson he learned, and that it takes effort and great willingness!

> The Holy Spirit is in you in a very literal sense. His is the
> Voice That calls you back to where you were before and

will be again. It is possible even in this world to hear only that Voice and no other. It takes effort and great willingness to learn. It is the final lesson that I learned, and God's Sons are as equal as learners as they are as sons. (T-5.II.3:7–11)

So, let us begin today to learn this so-very-important lesson. Let us listen.

LESSON 50 ✦ FEBRUARY 19
"I am sustained by the Love of God."

Practice instructions

Purpose: To internalize the idea that you are sustained by God's Love, not by the things of the world, and to feel the protection, peace, and safety His Love brings.

Longer: Two times, morning and evening, for ten minutes.

Spend these ten minutes repeating the idea and really dwelling on it and thinking about it. Let related thoughts come "to help you recognize its truth" (5:2). Do all this with the goal of letting the idea sink more deeply into your mind. Bask in the idea. Feel the benefits it carries for you. Try to feel God's Love covering you like a blanket of peace and safety.

This is not a meditation exercise, but an extended exercise in mentally reflecting on the idea. Your thoughts will tend to wander during lengthy reflection like this. When they do, see those thoughts as intruders that have inappropriately wandered into the temple of the holy mind of God's Son. Repeat the idea to dispel them.

Frequent reminders: Often.

Repeat the idea, not just as rote words, but as a real "declaration of independence" (W-pI.31.4:2)—a declaration that you are free of needing to be sustained by the empty things of this world. Try repeating it once in this spirit right now, and see the effect it has on your mind.

Response to temptation: Whenever you feel confronted by a problem or challenge.

Answer what confronts you by repeating the idea. While doing so, remember that "through the Love of God within you, you can resolve all seeming difficulties without effort and in sure confidence" (4:5).

Commentary

What sustains me? What do I turn to when I feel empty or depleted? God—my eternal Source? Or something else? I have to admit that often it is to something else that I turn for renewal. What would it be like to have a habit of turning to the Love of God? What would it be like to come to rely fully on something so utterly and absolutely dependable?

The list of items in the first paragraph of the lesson contains something that fits nearly every one of us. Whatever my personal preference for "sustainer," the whole bunch of them is just "an endless list of forms of nothingness that [we] endow with magical powers" (1:3). When we turn to them, something in us knows that these things are not really solving anything; they are nothing but palliatives, placebos that may dull the symptoms for a while but in the end cure nothing.

I think it was Saint Augustine who said that every one of us is born with a God-shaped blank in our heart. We may try to fill it with all sorts of things, but nothing fits the blank but the Love of God. We "cherish" the other things because we are trying to preserve our imagined, independent identity as an ego in a body. We are cherishing nothingness to preserve a nothing. Wholeness comes only from union with our Source.

The Love of God can "transport you into a state of mind that nothing can threaten, nothing can disturb, and where nothing can intrude upon the eternal calm of the Son of God" (3:3). [Note: a few early printings of the Second Edition had a typographical error, substituting the word "claim" for "calm."] I want a state of mind like that. I want that kind of inner stability, that serenity of consciousness. What else could bring it to me except knowing that I am connected to an unending supply of bottomless benevolence?

The Psalmist said it well in the First Psalm. The "godly," those who know they are sustained by God's Love, "shall be like a tree planted by the rivers of water, that bringeth forth his fruit in his season; his leaf also shall not wither; and whatsoever he doeth shall prosper" (Ps 1:3). When you become inwardly aware of God's Love sustaining you, it is like being a tree planted by a river, its roots constantly supplied by the water that is always there, always being renewed. Or from the Twenty-third Psalm: "The LORD is my shepherd; I shall not

want…. My cup runneth over. Surely goodness and mercy shall follow
me all the days of my life" (Ps 23:1, 5–6).

> Put all your faith in the Love of God within you; eternal,
> changeless and forever unfailing. This is the answer to
> whatever confronts you today.   (4:3–4)

Again the practice instructions tell us to "sink deep into your
consciousness" (5:1). (Notice that it is for a ten-minute period, morning
and evening; the periods of meditation are getting longer.) We are to
"allow peace to flow over [us] like a blanket of protection and surety"
(5:2). Often I find it helps me establish that sense by visualizing
something—being bathed in golden light, being embraced by my
spiritual guide, or sinking into a warm Jacuzzi. I can let it be a time of
rest, ten minutes in which I simply let go, physically and mentally, and
allow myself to experience peace. I tell myself: "I am okay. I am safe. I
am at home in God. His Love surrounds me and protects me. His Love
nourishes me and makes me what I am."

III

Review I: Introduction and Lessons 51 - 60

INTRODUCTION

In Review I, the third and fourth paragraphs present a theory of practice that is useful in understanding why the Workbook is structured as it is. In fact, the paragraphs imply a lot about the importance of structure itself, which changes as we progress in our practice. Five degrees of structure are indicated here, moving from highly structured to almost none.

1. Highly Structured with Formal Setting

In the beginning of our study, the Course recommends quite highly structured practice, with attention to certain forms. The earlier lessons in the Workbook all go to great lengths spelling out the specific details concerning how the lesson should be practiced. In this review, for instance, we are told that we do not need to review the comments after each of the five daily thoughts in any great detail (3:1). Rather, we are to focus on the central point and think about that, allowing related ideas to come to us as we have been doing in recent lessons.

In addition we are told that "the exercises should be done with your eyes closed and when you are alone in a quiet place, if possible" (3:3). This is what I mean when I say it pays attention to form. It deals with *where* we should be (in a quiet place) and specifically *what* we should do with our eyes. It adds that this kind of instruction is "emphasized for practice periods at your stage of learning" (4:1), which is obviously understood to be the beginning stage.

The idea behind this sort of instruction seems to be that, at the beginning stage, we need structure, and we need physical solitude and quietness. We need to close our eyes to shut out distractions because our minds have not been sufficiently trained to ignore the distractions without doing so. We are training ourselves to have inner peace, and at the beginning it is helpful to encourage that state of mind by arranging our environment.

2. No Special Setting

As we advance, it will become necessary to give up the formal setting and structure, so that we can "learn to require no special settings in which to apply what you have learned" (4:2). Initially, to find peace of mind, we need a quiet place, we need to close our eyes. But as we go on, the intent is that we begin to apply our learning in situations that appear to be upsetting. After all, when is peace most needed? Obviously, it is needed when something happens that seems to upset us (4:3).

We have begun to advance when we learn to generalize, when we are able to take what we have learned in the "laboratory" of quiet practice and apply it in distressing situations. This will happen almost without conscious volition. Suddenly we will notice that things that used to instantly upset us no longer do so. Or we will find ourselves reacting with love instead of anger.

The Workbook practice encourages this "spread" of the lessons into our lives by asking us to remember the thought for the day whenever something happens that upsets us. This takes the lesson out of the laboratory and into our lives. This kind of expanded practice, or "response to temptation," as it is called, is vital if the Course is going to make a noticeable difference in our lives.

3. Bringing Peace with Us

As our practice of the first sort continues, and as we begin to respond to upsets by choosing to experience peace instead of the upset, we begin to move into a third stage: we start to bring peace with us into every situation (4:4). In the second stage we are reacting to a situation and choosing peace; here, we are proactively bringing peace with us into distress and turmoil, healing the situations we find. Our quiet practice has established a certain level of peace within our minds, and now we bring the quiet with us as we move through our days. "This is not done by avoiding [distress and turmoil] and seeking a haven of isolation for yourself" (4:5).

At this level of development we have ended any attempt at monastic isolation and we are reaching out into the world, bringing healing to it. We may still withdraw periodically to "recharge," as it were, but we are no longer fearful of distress and turmoil; we even begin to actively seek out situations in which our healed mind can bring healing to others.

4. Recognizing Peace Is Part of Us

At a higher level still, we begin to realize that peace is not some quality or condition that comes and goes; rather, it is an inherent part of our being (5:1). Here we have realized that peace is not conditional. It does not depend on conditions. It is inherent in our nature; it is what we are. We have become identified with peace so that, simply by being there, we bring peace into every situation in which we find ourselves. We no longer need to get alone or shut our eyes to feel peaceful; we *are* the peace. Conditions around us do not affect our peace; instead, our peace affects the conditions.

5. Peace Seen Everywhere

At the highest level, we will realize that our physical presence is not required to affect any situation. We realize that "there is no limit to where you are, so that your peace is everywhere, as you are" (5:2). This is the state of mind of the advanced teacher of God, or what, in some circles, might be called a realized master. This state of mind will not long abide in a body, because it has transcended bodily limitations.

This broad overview of where the Course is taking us can be very encouraging as we struggle with the elementary level. Look at the scope of the Course's program. Starting with a level at which our peace is so vulnerable that we must close our eyes and shut out the world, it moves to transcend the world entirely. We may long to be at the highest level right away; it doesn't work that way. You can't skip steps, as Ken Wapnick often points out. Don't get caught in the trap of thinking, "I ought to be able to experience peace anywhere," and because of that refuse yourself the support of being alone, quiet, and shutting your eyes. At the beginning those props are necessary and even, in the Course's curriculum, *emphasized.* Don't think you are being untrue to your highest understanding by setting up a formal structure for yourself, perhaps setting an alarm to remember your practice times, writing the lesson on cards and carrying it around, or asking a friend to remind you and check up on you. At the beginning, almost anything that helps you remember is useful.

The structure won't last, and should not last. But you need the structure at the start in order to get to where being unstructured will work for you. Try to skip immediately to unstructured practice and you'll end up not practicing at all. Use structure, but don't get attached to it. Don't make an idol of it. The structure is like training wheels on a bicycle: necessary and useful as you are learning, but to be discarded as soon as you have learned to keep upright on your own.

REVIEW I PRACTICE INSTRUCTIONS

Practice instructions

Purpose: To review the lessons and therefore let them sink in a notch deeper. Also, to see how interrelated they are and how cohesive the thought system is that they are leading you to.

Exercise: As often as possible (suggestion: every hour on the hour), for at least two minutes.

- Alone in a quiet place, read one of the five lessons and the related comments. Notice that the comments are written as if they are your own thoughts about the idea. Try to imagine that they are. It will help if you frequently insert your name. This will set you up for the next phase, in which you generate similar thoughts of your own.
- Close your eyes and think about the idea and the comments. Think particularly about the central point of the commentary paragraph. Reflect on it. Let related thoughts

come (utilizing the training you've received in that practice). If your mind wanders, repeat the idea and then get back to your reflection. This is the same basic exercise as in Lesson 50, in which you actively think about ideas in order to let them sink more deeply into your mind.

Remarks:
- At the beginning and end of the day read all five lessons.
- Thereafter, cover one lesson per practice period, in no particular order.
- Cover each lesson at least once.
- Beyond that, concentrate on a particular lesson if it appeals to you most.

LESSON 51 ✦ FEBRUARY 20
Review of:

(1) "Nothing I see means anything."
(2) "I have given what I see all the meaning it has for me."
(3) "I do not understand anything I see."
(4) "These thoughts do not mean anything."
(5) "I am never upset for the reason I think."

 Practice instructions
> See instructions on page 158.

Commentary

Note first that we aren't simply to read this review; we are meant to spend time morning and evening reviewing all five ideas, and to spend *at least* one two-minute practice period during the day on each of the five. That's five practice periods between the morning and evening, minimum. It will probably take a little planning to schedule those five interim periods, and the planning time is worth the effort. Second, notice that these practice instructions apply to all ten review lessons for the next ten days.

The comments on the five lessons given in Lesson 51 link them together so clearly that little comment is really needed. As the introduction to this review says in the last sentence, the emphasis of this review is on the relationships between the ideas and the cohesiveness of the entire thought system being presented. If you look at them together, they are lessons in "letting go" (the words "let go" or some variant occur in four of the five reviews).

In these first five lessons I am being asked to let go of:

1. What I see

2. My judgments

3. My understanding

4. My thoughts

5. My thought system

What we "see" in the normal sense is nothing; we need to realize it is meaningless and let it go, so that vision may take its place. We are not actually seeing things; rather, we are seeing our judgments on them. If we want vision, we have to realize our judgments are invalid, and cease letting them govern our sight. If we have misjudged, surely we have also misunderstood. Our "understanding" of things is based not on reality, but on our own projections. But we can choose to exchange our misunderstandings for real understanding, based on love rather than judgment.

Like what we see, our conscious thoughts are without any real meaning; we need to let them go, along with judgment-based perceptions. They are thoughts of anger and attack, seeing all things as our enemies. These thoughts which are apart from God require constant justification, and our upset is no more than an attempt to justify our anger with the world and our attacks upon it.

As we read over this review, which is written in the first person, we may want to try reading it aloud, and seeing how we resonate with it. *Am* I really willing to let go of what I see, my judgments and my understanding of everything, my thoughts, and my very thought system? Can I say, "I am willing to let it go"?

LESSON 52 ✦ FEBRUARY 21

Review of:

(6) "I am upset because I see what is not there."
(7) "I see only the past."
(8) "My mind is preoccupied with past thoughts."
(9) "I see nothing as it is now."
(10) "My thoughts do not mean anything."

 Practice instructions

See instructions on page 158.

Commentary

Remember that the general practice for these reviews is to read all five thoughts and comments twice daily, morning and evening, and to spend at least one two-minute period with each of the five ideas during the day.

The thoughts are thick in these reviews, so I offer only a few observations on things that stand out for me.

"Reality is never frightening" (1:2). Reality is, of course, what God created. When I feel frightened, I find it useful to remind myself that I must be seeing something that isn't really there.

I am the one who makes up frightening illusions. How reassuring to be told, "Nothing in God's creation is affected in any way by this confusion of mine" (1:7). That is the basis for letting go of guilt. I may be confused, mistaken, deceived, and deceiving, but none of it affects what is real. What's real is real no matter what I do. The sun doesn't go out when I cover my eyes. So all that I have done has had zero real effects! I have nothing about which to feel guilty.

"If I see nothing as it is now, it can truly be said that I see nothing" (4:2). A thing is as it is now. It isn't as it was yesterday; it isn't as it will be tomorrow. Things exist *now*. That is the only way I can see them. That is how they are. If I am seeing the past, I'm not seeing anything. The past isn't here.

"I have no private thoughts" (5:2). What if everyone in the world could see right into your mind? What if the way you thought about your boss affected the war in Bosnia? Guess what? They can. It does. And yet, "they mean nothing" (5:5). If you think thoughts you believe to be private, they are meaningless. They have effects within the illusion, but they affect nothing real. Only thoughts that are shared have real effects, and the only thoughts that can be truly shared are the thoughts you think with God.

LESSON 53 ✦ FEBRUARY 22

Review of:

(11) "My meaningless thoughts are showing me a meaningless world."
(12) "I am upset because I see a meaningless world."
(13) "A meaningless world engenders fear."
(14) "God did not create a meaningless world."
(15) "My thoughts are images that I have made."

Practice instructions

See instructions on page 158.

Commentary

Today's review carries enormous impact for me. In each of the short review paragraphs are sentences that convey to me the awesome power of my own mind: its power to choose its thoughts, and thus choose the world that it sees.

> I have real thoughts as well as insane ones. I can therefore see a real world, if I look to my real thoughts as my guide for seeing. (1:4–5)

> I am grateful that this world is not real, and that I need not see it at all unless I choose to value it. And I do not choose to value what is totally insane and has no meaning. (2:6–7)

> Now I choose to withdraw this belief, and place my trust in reality. In choosing this, I will escape all the effects of the world of fear, because I am acknowledging that it does not exist. (3:7–8)

> Let me remember the power of my decision, and recognize where I really abide. (4:6)

The images I have made cannot prevail against Him
because it is not my will that they do so. My will is His, and
I will place no other gods before Him.   (5:6–7)

If I remember the power of my decision, I can choose not to value
what is insane; I can choose to withdraw my belief in it. I do not have
to accept that the images I have made have power to overcome God's
Will; I do not have to make gods out of them. I can look to my real
thoughts and let them guide my seeing. The words "choose" and
"decision" and "will" echo through these paragraphs. What power has
been given to my mind!

I once read these ten review lessons onto tape; they fit on less than a
30-minute tape, read quite slowly. Recording them had tremendous
impact on me, and listening to the tape several dozen times had even
more impact. These fifty pithy paragraphs are a remarkable overview of
the Course's thought system. And as I read them aloud, I found myself
putting deep feeling into sentences such as "I cannot live in peace in
such a world. I am grateful that this world is not real. And I do not
choose to value what is totally insane and has no meaning" (2:5–7).
Every time I came to a line that said, "I do not choose" or "I choose," it
was as though something deep within me was shifting. I felt a growing
determination, and a sense of being enabled by God to choose what my
mind would think and what my perception would see. Try reading
today's lesson aloud and see how it feels.

LESSON 54 ✦ FEBRUARY 23
Review of:

(16) "I have no neutral thoughts."
(17) "I see no neutral things."
(18) "I am not alone in experiencing the effects of my seeing."
(19) "I am not alone in experiencing the effects of my thoughts."
(20) "I am determined to see."

Practice instructions
See instructions on page 158.

Commentary
This review links these ideas together as a powerful motivator for changing my thoughts.

My thoughts make the world, either the false world or the real world. The world I see is a "representation of my own state of mind" (2:4). I can contribute to the making of a world of separation, or I can, by awakening my real thoughts, awaken those thoughts in others. What I think and say and do "teaches all the universe" (4:3). By changing my own mind, I can change every mind along with mine. When I realize this, I am filled with a dynamic determination to look upon the real world, to open my mind to the thoughts I share with God, and in so doing, to transform the universe.

Archimedes is reputed to have said, "Give me a lever long enough, and I will move the world." I have that lever. It is my mind; "mine is the power of God" (4:6). One man whose mind is wholly transformed will transform all the world. Jesus was such a man, and the impact of his thought is still unfolding, the ripples still spreading in the pond of mind. I can join with him and add the power of my mind to his.

I do want to see "love…replace fear, laughter…replace tears" (5:4). I want to let this be done through me. In each situation in which I find myself today, with each person I meet, may this be my aim. "I am here only to be truly helpful. I am here to represent Him who sent me" (T-2.V(A).18:2–3). By allowing my mind to be changed, I will bring healing to everyone I meet today.

LESSON 55 ✦ FEBRUARY 24
Review of:

(21) "I am determined to see things differently."
(22) "What I see is a form of vengeance."
(23) "I can escape from this world by giving up attack thoughts."
(24) "I do not perceive my own best interests."
(25) "I do not know what anything is for."

 Practice instructions

See instructions on page 158.

Commentary

The pattern laid down by the first fifty lessons becomes clearer with each day of review. The writing in these ten review lessons is among the clearest and most straightforward in the entire Course.

Of course I am determined to see things differently; "disease, disaster and death" (1:2) are not what I want to see. That I see them proves I do not understand God, and I do not know who I am. The world I see pictures attack thoughts, "attack on everything by everything" (2:3). In this world everything lives by consuming the life of something else; whether it is the life of an animal or a plant makes little difference. Even the lowest life form lives from the energy given off by the destruction of the Sun. What gives rise to this picture? My own attack thoughts.

"My loving thoughts will save me from this perception of the world" (2:6). Changing my mind from attack to love will change the world I see. "It is this I choose to see, in place of what I look on now" (3:5).

And no wonder I am confused about my best interests! I don't know who I am; how could I know what I need? I am willing to accept the guidance of One Who knows me; I understand that I can't perceive my best interests by myself. I use everything to sustain my illusions about myself (4:4). What I need is a way to let the world teach me the truth about myself. Seeing it as I see it, the world is frightening; I want to know the truth.

The transformation hinges on my willingness to recognize that I do not like what I see, and since what I see comes from what I think, I want to change what I think. I do not know my best interests, and the purpose I have assigned to everything has been twisted to support my ego identity (5:2), so now I am willing to let these ideas go. Confused as I am, how could I teach myself what I do not know? I need a reliable, trustworthy Teacher, and in the Holy Spirit I have that Teacher.

My only job is to make myself teachable by letting go of my false thinking, letting go of my attack thoughts. I think they sustain me but they are destroying me. I resolve today to choose differently, and to open my mind to a way of thinking I cannot, as yet, begin to understand. I open my heart to love.

LESSON 56 ✦ FEBRUARY 25
Review of:

(26) "My attack thoughts are attacking my invulnerability."
(27) "Above all else I want to see."
(28) "Above all else I want to see differently."
(29) "God is in everything I see."
(30) "God is in everything I see because God is in my mind."

 Practice instructions
See instructions on page 158.

Commentary
The Door behind the World

There is a door behind this world which, if opened, will allow me to see past this world to a world that reflects the Love of God (3:4). It is a door in my mind, a door to vision.

This world, full of "pain, illness, loss, age and death" (1:3) simply reflects what I think I am (2:2–3). It is a hallucination superimposed over reality, hiding it and seemingly replacing it.

The opening line of the review asks: "How can I know who I am when I see myself as under constant attack?" (1:2). Think about that. If I am truly under constant attack, beset by illness, loss, age and death, how can I be a perfect creation of God? How can God even be real? I believe in a self-image that is constantly threatened. If I am threatened, how could I be an eternal, spiritual being? If the picture I see in this world is true, then I am nothing, worth nothing, and destined for destruction. I may as well say, "Eat, drink, and be merry, for tomorrow we die!" I may as well take what I can get because nothing will last, including myself.

Something in all of us, however, tells us that we are more than this (5:2). Something in us resonates when we read, in the Course, that nothing real can be threatened. If that is true, and I am real, then the world I see must be false. The picture it is showing me, reinforcing my image of myself as vulnerable, must be a lie. Either I am real and the world is not, or the world is real and I am not. "For I am real because the world is not, and I would know my own reality" (W-pI.132.15:3).

Therefore my greatest need is vision. I need to open that door in my mind, "look past all appearances" (4:6), and see a world that reflects God's Love, and by so doing remember who I really am. "Behind every image I have made, the truth remains unchanged" (4:2). "In my own mind, behind all my insane thoughts of separation and attack, is the knowledge that all is one forever. I have not lost the knowledge of Who I am because I have forgotten it" (5:2–3).

I want to open that door behind the world and see the truth again. I want to remember.

LESSON 57 ✦ FEBRUARY 26
Review of:

(31) "I am not the victim of the world I see."
(32) "I have invented the world I see."
(33) "There is another way of looking at the world."
(34) "I could see peace instead of this."
(35) "My mind is part of God's. I am very holy."

Practice instructions
See instructions on page 158.

Commentary
The review today echoes with the word "freedom." (Emphasis in the following quotes is my own.)

> My chains are loosened. I can drop them off merely by desiring to do so. *The prison door is open.* I can leave simply by walking out. (1:3–6)

> I made up the prison in which I see myself. All I need do is recognize this and *I am free.* (2:2–3)

> The Son of God must be *forever free.* (2:6)

> I see the world as a prison for God's Son. It must be, then, that *the world is really a place where he can be set free.* I would look upon the world as it is, and see it as a place where the Son of God finds his *freedom.* (3:4–6)

> When *I see the world as a place of freedom*, I realize that it reflects the laws of God instead of the rules I made up for it to obey. (4:2)

The beauty of acknowledging that I have invented the world I see is that it affirms my freedom to see it differently. Recognize that I have made up my prison, and I am free. And I am *already* free; all of us are free, now, in our own minds. The prison is an illusion. I can choose my thoughts, and that is the ultimate freedom. I can choose to look upon the world as a place where I can be set free, and where you can be set free. I can choose to see the world as a prison, or as a classroom. How I see it is my choice—*my choice*! I am *free* to make that choice.

I can see peace any time I choose to. I am free to do that. These moments I spend in quiet each day, practicing these lessons, are showing me that. I can create peace in my mind any time I choose to do so. To choose peace of mind is the ultimate freedom, and depends on nothing outside of me at all.

I begin to understand, as I share this peace with my brothers, that the peace is not coming from outside, but "from deep within myself" (5:3). As my mind changes, the way I see the world changes with it. It witnesses peace back to me. And so "I begin to understand the holiness of all living things, including myself, and their oneness with me" (5:6).

Years ago, when I had only begun to study the Course, I sat down one day and tried to answer a question: "What have I learned about life? What am I reasonably sure of?" And the answer that came to me was very simple: "Happiness is a choice I make." I had begun to realize the freedom of my mind to choose. I had begun to realize that my mind was truly autonomous in this choice. It needed nothing from outside to make happiness possible; it was purely a choice. And nothing outside could impede that choice.

I am still learning that lesson, building on it, solidifying it within my experience. That is what this review is telling us. We are free to choose. We *really are* free, right now. Our minds are all-powerful in this choice. They lack nothing to make it, and there is nothing that can stop us from making it. What is more, God wills that we make it because His Will for us is perfect happiness.

Today, let me remember that I want to be happy, and I can choose, in every moment, to be happy. I want to be at peace, and I can choose, in every moment, to be at peace. Happiness *is* peace, for how could I be happy if I am in conflict? Today, I will make this choice!

LESSON 58 ✦ FEBRUARY 27
Review of:

(36) "My holiness envelops everything I see."
(37) "My holiness blesses the world."
(38) "There is nothing my holiness cannot do."
(39) "My holiness is my salvation."
(40) "I am blessed as a Son of God."

Practice instructions
See instructions on page 158.

Commentary

"Innocence…is the truth about me" (1:4). I don't really believe that. I *want* to believe it, and I may *say* I believe it, but if I really believed it I don't think I'd still be here. At the least I would not be seeing the world the way I do, because the way I see the world derives completely from the way I see myself. "I can picture only thoughts about myself" (1:5). So if I really believed that innocence is the truth about me, all I would see, everywhere, is innocence. Holiness.

This is why accepting the Atonement for myself saves the world. If I can accept my own innocence, all I will see is innocence. We often allow confusion to come into our minds about who forgives whom first. Do I forgive others, and then see my own innocence? Or do I forgive myself, thus allowing me to see others as innocent? The answer to both questions is "Yes."

How can both questions be answered "Yes?" Because "myself" and "others" are not really two; we are one. The sin I see in others is always my own, projected from my mind (see T-31.III.1:5). When I forgive "others" I really am forgiving my own sins. *Any* act of forgiveness, whether directed outward or inward, results in everyone being forgiven.

Thus, when I perceive my own holiness, I have blessed the entire world. The holiness I see in myself, when I see it, is something shared by everyone. As my own innocence arises in my mind, the holiness of the entire world shines forth simultaneously.

Innocence, or holiness, is a central theme of the Course. "Everyone has a special part to play in the Atonement, but the message given to each one is always the same: *God's Son is guiltless*" (T-14.V.2:1). "But the content of the [universal] course never changes [whatever its form]. Its central theme is always, 'God's Son is guiltless, and in his innocence is his salvation'" (M-1.3:5). It is a message of radical innocence, total innocence, universal innocence, with no one and nothing left out. No one is condemned. No one is judged guilty. No one is damned.

"Recognizing my holiness is recognizing my salvation. It is also recognizing the salvation of the world" (4:2–3). As a Son of God, I am holy, and thus I am blessed. But if I am a Son of God, so are you, so is everyone, because I am a Son of God not by any merit of my own, not by any achievement that distinguishes me from anyone else, but simply due to the fact that God created me holy. As I recognize this fact about myself I *must* include everyone God created, or I am excluded with everyone.

My claim on innocence, and on "all good and only good" (5:2), lies in the fact that I am the Son of God. God willed good things for me, and so I must have them—not because I earned them in any way, but because He wills to give them. "His care for me is infinite, and is with me forever. I am eternally blessed as His Son" (5:7–8).

It does not matter what I think about myself or how badly I may believe I have screwed things up: I am still His Son. I am still innocent. I am still holy.

> Remember this; whatever you think about yourself, whatever you may think about the world, your Father needs you and will call to you until you come to Him in peace at last. (S-3.IV.10:7)

> Have faith in only this one thing, and it will be sufficient: God wills you be in Heaven, and nothing can keep you from it, or it from you. Your wildest misperceptions, your weird imaginings, your blackest nightmares all mean nothing. They will not prevail against the peace God wills for you. (T-13.XI.7:1–3)

LESSON 59 ✦ FEBRUARY 28
Review of:

(41) "God goes with me wherever I go."
(42) "God is my strength. Vision is His gift."
(43) "God is my Source. I cannot see apart from Him."
(44) "God is the light in which I see."
(45) "God is the Mind with which I think."

 Practice instructions

See instructions on page 158.

Commentary

The first emphasis of these five ideas is obviously on God; every thought begins with that word. God is always with me. He is my strength, my Source, my light, and the Mind with which I think. As the Bible says, "He is not far from each one of us; for in Him we live and move and exist" (Acts 17:27–28). When I recognize that the environment in which I exist, the very energy that forms my life, is God, peace comes to my mind. How could I ever be separate from the Infinite? The Son of God "cannot separate himself from what is in him" (T-13.XI.10:2), and what he is in.

The second emphasis I notice is on my seeing. "Christ's vision is His gift....Let me call upon this gift today" (2:5–6). "I can see only what God wants me to see. I cannot see anything else" (3:3–4). "I cannot see in darkness. God is the only light" (4:2–3). Any seeming vision apart from God cannot be real. Vision is His gift, God's Will determines what can be seen, and God is the light by which we see it. Let me be glad to see what He shows me; let me see as He wills me to see.

Throughout, the lesson emphasizes my unity with God. If I am one with God and all creation, how can I see other than He does? To think I see differently, therefore, is to deny what I am and to wish I were something else apart from God, able to see what He does not. To share His vision and His thoughts is to affirm my true Self, as He created me.

LEAP YEAR DAY ✦ FEBRUARY 29

In leap years, which have an extra day (February 29), there are several options for how to handle the extra day. One option is simply to continue to the next lesson, and thus finish the year's lessons a day early, or by repeating the final lesson six times instead of the five times called for. This has the effect of shifting all the lessons to a different day of the calendar for the rest of the year. In these lesson notes, we have chosen *not* to do this, so that the notes will be usable without change for any calendar year.

Another option is simply to repeat the lesson for February 28 (Lesson 59), or the one for March 1 (Lesson 60). Since these are already review lessons, this does not seem particularly useful.

Three remaining possibilities are: 1) choose a favorite lesson, and do that lesson for February 29; 2) take a day off, doing no particular practice; or 3) use the day to do a complete read-through of all ten lessons in Review I.

My recommendation is the third of these remaining possibilities, but you can choose to do whatever you like. The reason I recommend doing a complete read-through of Review I is that these ten lessons, taken together, provide one of the clearest, most concise, and most readable summaries of the thoughts that the first fifty lessons have been trying to teach us. Robert Perry has said that this review is so plain and simply written that it ends any question as to whether the author is capable of such clarity and simplicity; it also gives us reason to think that, if other parts of the Course such as the Text are written with greater complexity, there must be good reason for it.

As the review instructions themselves state, "We are now emphasizing the relationships among the first fifty of the ideas we have covered, and the cohesiveness of the thought system to which they are leading you" (W-pI.rI.In.6:4). What better way to gain a sense of the cohesiveness of the thought system than to read through the entire review at one sitting?

There are twenty pages in Review I, but with so much white space that it really amounts to little more than ten pages. The entire review can be read aloud in under thirty minutes; I know because I have recorded it on tape. (You might even want to try this yourself, if you have a tape recorder. I found that listening to the entire review repeatedly as I drove to and from work was a powerful learning tool.) Try to set aside a half hour some time during the day, and read the whole thing at a single sitting. If you read fast, then read it all two or three times. Try to focus, as the review suggests, on the relationships between the ideas, and the cohesiveness of the entire package.

LESSON 60 ✦ MARCH 1
Review of:

(46) "God is the Love in which I forgive."
(47) "God is the strength in which I trust."
(48) "There is nothing to fear."
(49) "God's Voice speaks to me all through the day."
(50) "I am sustained by the Love of God."

 Practice instructions

See instructions on page 158.

Commentary

My dearest friends,

I address you that way because of the line in this lesson, "I will recognize in everyone my dearest Friend" (3:5). I was so struck by that line once that, for about four or five months, every letter I wrote (except to those who probably would not understand) I began with, "My dearest friend [name]."

No wonder that the Course tells us, "There are no strangers in God's creation" (T-3.III.7:7). My dearest Friend is in everyone; everyone is, in reality, that Friend. That is their real, albeit hidden, Identity. Speaking of "those who accept the Holy Spirit's purpose as their own" (T-20.II.5:3), the Text says, "He sees no strangers; only dearly loved and loving friends" (T-20.II.5:5).

Imagine seeing the world in that way. Imagine being in love with everyone you met, recognizing each and every one as a dearly loved friend, and knowing that in their heart of hearts they are wholly loving, as you are. Imagine being surrounded by love like that. This is the Course's vision of the real world, the world attained through full forgiveness (see T-17.II.5:1; T-30.VI.3:3).

"Forgiveness is the means by which I will recognize my innocence" (1:4). And when I recognize my innocence, I will no longer see anything to forgive (1:3). I will see only dearly loved and loving friends. As long as I see something else, something less than that, there is forgiveness work to be done. We are here for one purpose and one purpose only: to forgive the world so completely that we absolutely fall in love with everyone and everything; anything less than that is incomplete forgiveness. What limits our love except some form of unforgiveness? Only by so completely removing every barrier to love will we come to know the fullness of the love we are.

The strength of God in me enables me to do this. As I forgive I am remembering that strength in myself, a strength I have forgotten. "I forgive all things because I feel the stirring of His strength in me" (2:5). God's Voice guides me on this path of forgiveness, step by careful step; there is really nowhere else to go. "I am walking steadily on toward truth" (4:4). Sometimes my footsteps seem to falter, but I cannot really go astray. God's Love sustains me. Through listening to its stirrings deep within myself, I come to remember that I am His Son.

> Our footsteps have not been unwavering, and doubts have made us walk uncertainly and slowly on the road this course sets forth. But now we hasten on, for we approach a greater certainty, a firmer purpose and a surer goal.

> *Steady our feet, our Father. Let our doubts be quiet and our holy minds be still, and speak to us. We have no words to give to You. We would but listen to Your Word, and make it ours. Lead our practicing as does a father lead a little child along a way he does not understand. Yet does he follow, sure that he is safe because his father leads the way for him.*

> *So do we bring our practicing to You. And if we stumble, You will raise us up. If we forget the way, we count upon Your sure remembering. We wander off, but You will not forget to call us back. Quicken our footsteps now, that we may walk more certainly and quickly unto You. And we accept the Word You offer us to unify our practicing, as we review the thoughts that You have given us.*

> (W-pI.rV.In.1:5–3:6)

IV

Lessons 61 - 80

"I am the light of the world."

Practice instructions

Purpose: "A beginning step in accepting your real function on earth" (3:2). This lesson is a continuation of what began in Lesson 37 ("My holiness blesses the world"), which contained "the first glimmerings of your true function in the world, or why you are here" (W-pI.37.1:1).

Exercise: As many as possible (suggestion: every hour on the hour), for no more than one or two minutes.

- Tell yourself, *"I am the light of the world. That is my only function. That is why I am here."*
- Then think about these statements. Let related thoughts come. If you can, close your eyes for this. If your mind wanders (rather, *when* it wanders), repeat the idea. This is the same kind of practice that you did in Lesson 50 and throughout Review I. By actively thinking about the idea, you make it your own.

Remarks: Begin and end the day with a practice period. These can be longer than the rest if you want. These practices will make your day one that begins, ends, and is filled throughout with affirmation of the truth about yourself. This is the day the Workbook is leading us into, one in which we practice morning, evening, and throughout the day.

This is the first of the Workbook's seven "giant strides"—giant steps ahead in your journey home. Try to make today exactly that. Use it "to build a firm foundation" (7:4) for the giant strides to come.

Commentary

Probably most days, if you're like me, you don't feel like the light of the world. Some days I feel more like the last dying ember in the fireplace. But this lesson isn't talking about how I feel; it is talking about what I am in truth. "It does not refer to any of the characteristics with which you have endowed yourself. It refers to you as you were created by God" (1:5–6). It isn't about who I think I am; it is about my original design specs, straight from the hand of the Creator.

In traditional Christian teaching, Jesus is the light of the world and the rest of us are the blind people who need his light. To say, "I am the light of the world" can seem like quite a stretch. It can seem arrogant, full of pride, even egotistical. Perhaps even delusional. Actually, refusing to say it is what is egotistical. What is more arrogant, when God has made you the light of the world, than to say, "Sorry, Boss, You were wrong. I'm really a poor miserable sinner"?

You and I are here to be conduits of God's light. Being the light of the world is our only function, and the only reason we are here (5:3–5). We are bringers of salvation; there is no other way for salvation to come into this world except through us—all of us!

The lesson calls our acceptance and practice of this idea "a beginning step in accepting your real function on earth" (3:2), "a giant stride" (3:3), "a positive assertion of your right to be saved" (3:4). It isn't just another lesson; this is a big deal! Getting off the "poor me, I need to be saved" bandwagon and onto the "bringer of salvation" track can be a major turning point for us. The general tenor of the idea is reflected in the old sixties saying, "Are you part of the problem or part of the solution?"

At first it may seem that this idea asks too much of you. "Who, me save the world? Are you kidding? I can't even save myself!" But that belief about ourselves is *exactly* where our problem lies. Try giving love to someone today and you will find that you *can* bring light into someone else's life. Do this enough times and your opinion about yourself will begin to change. Your true sense of self-worth as a loving being will begin to blossom. In giving help, you will be helping yourself. In recognizing that being helpful, giving love, spreading kindness, and showing mercy is the very reason you are here, you affirm the divinity of your Source; you acknowledge yourself as a child of God.

LESSON 62 ✦ MARCH 3
"Forgiveness is my function as the light of the world."

Practice instructions

Exercise: As frequently as possible (suggestion: every hour on the hour), for one to two minutes.

- Tell yourself (with eyes closed if the situation permits): *"Forgiveness is my function as the light of the world. I would fulfill my function that I may be happy."*
- Then use the practice that you have been doing recently: Think about these statements (in this case, dwelling particularly on the happiness your function will bring you). Let related thoughts come. If your mind wanders, repeat the idea and add, *"I would remember this because I want to be happy."* This extra thought will motivate your mind to come back to and stay on focus.

Remarks: Notice the emphasis on having a happy day. This is so much of why we practice, because it will help make our day happy. It will also bring happiness to people around us, and even to people in distant times and places! This is not a selfish practice we are doing.

Notice also that this lesson mentions the Workbook's formula of practicing morning, evening, and throughout the day (4:1). We can assume today that, like yesterday, we can make the morning and evening practice periods longer if we like.

Finally, note why it is that related thoughts can flow freely: because "your heart will recognize these words, and in your mind is the awareness they are true" (4:5). Related thoughts, in other words, come from a deep well in our mind, in which we already understand these ideas. They draw that well's wisdom up to the surface and make it our own.

Commentary

What does the light of the world do? It forgives. As the light of the world, my function isn't to teach people new ideas, to straighten out their misunderstandings, or to be their knight in shining armor. My function is simply to forgive them.

> Forgiveness is the demonstration that you are the light of the world. Through your forgiveness does the truth about yourself return to your memory. (1:3–4)

Forgiveness not only brings light into the minds of those around me, it enables me to remember the light in myself; it reminds me of the truth about myself. Forgiveness is what saves *me*. Doing what I am here to do reminds me of what I really am.

Why? Because "illusions about yourself and the world are one" (2:1). If I see the illusion of sin in a brother, I am really seeing my own illusions about myself. When I forgive that brother, I am forgiving myself, seeing through the illusion that has obscured the truth about both him and me. When thoughts of attack are replaced with thoughts of forgiveness, I am replacing death with life.

Forgiveness is the means the Course sets forth as our way out of hell, because the hell we are in was made by our judgments and thoughts of attack. Forgiving calls upon the Christ in me, while attacking calls upon my own weakness. As I call upon the Christ in me, the Christ comes forward, and I begin to recognize the Christ as my true Self. Forgiveness restores "the invulnerability and power God gave His Son" (3:5).

Where is forgiveness needed? Not just in what we think of as the big things: betrayal, deceit, or obvious intent to harm. Any thought in my mind that separates me from another and makes me different is a thought of attack, and needs to be replaced with forgiveness. Any thought that belittles another person, demeans them, sees them as "less than," views them as less worthy of love for any reason, pushes them away, views them with dislike, sees myself gaining at their loss, wishes for their injury or loss in some way, or lacks faith in the love in their heart, is a thought of attack, and needs to be replaced with forgiveness.

That is my function, today and every day. Let me release the world from the bondage in which I have placed it. Let me lift my judgment from it, and so rediscover the miraculous truth of my own divine nature by my willingness to see it in everyone around me.

LESSON 63 ✦ MARCH 4

"The light of the world brings peace to every mind through my forgiveness."

Practice instructions

Purpose: To get in touch with your power to bring peace to everyone, to recognize the means by which you can do this, and to experience the happiness that comes from this.

Exercise: As often as you can (suggestion: every hour on the hour), for one to two minutes.

- Tell yourself, *"The light of the world brings peace to every mind through my forgiveness. I am the means God has appointed for the salvation of the world."*
- Then do the practice that you've been doing recently: Think about these statements and let related thoughts come. If your mind wanders, repeat the idea.

Remarks: The remarks about closing your eyes hold for all the shorter practice periods in the Workbook (except the open-eyed ones). The principle is simple. One the one hand, you'll benefit more if you close your eyes, because it will allow for greater focus. On the other hand, if you wait until the situation lets you close your eyes, that will hurt the frequency of your practice. So close your eyes if the situation permits; if not, go ahead and practice with eyes open.

Just like yesterday we are told to *be happy* to practice morning, evening, and throughout the day. That is because this practice will get us in touch with our function, and our function is the source of our happiness. As with Lesson 61, the practice periods at the beginning and end of the day can be longer if you like.

Commentary

Have you ever been the recipient of real forgiveness? There is nothing quite so liberating, nothing that eases the mind so much, as being truly forgiven. If I think I may have offended someone or injured them by what I have said or done, and they turn around and truly forgive me, letting me know that they were *not* hurt, that they understand me and see me in a light perhaps even better than I could see myself, it brings incredible peace to my mind. It relieves the pangs of guilt. There is a sense of love for the other person, a joy that our intimacy has not been impaired but perhaps even improved.

You and I have the power to bring that kind of peace to every mind. That is what our function is. We can allow this to be done through us (1:2). What a marvelous purpose this gives to our lives—bringing peace to every mind through our forgiveness. We can liberate everyone around us from the hell of their own guilt.

"Accept no trivial purpose or meaningless desire in its place, or you will forget your function and leave the Son of God in hell" (2:4). When we accept a lesser purpose, we inevitably forget the primary one. For instance, we may be trying to get someone to act in a way that pleases us—for our personal pleasure. We may have expectations about what someone should do or say. These lesser purposes can cause us to completely overlook our true function of forgiveness, and instead heap more guilt upon the person when they fail to meet our expectations.

We need to practice this idea diligently, as often as we can, to reinforce it in our minds. "I am the means God has appointed for the salvation of the world" (3:5). Forgiveness flows through me and brings peace to every mind I encounter today; let me remember to not block the flow.

LESSON 64 ✦ MARCH 5
"Let me not forget my function."

Practice instructions

Purpose: To remind yourself to constantly choose your happiness by choosing to fulfill your function. To resist the temptation to let the world you see lull you into forgetting your function.

Longer: At least one, for ten to fifteen minutes.

- Close your eyes and repeat these thoughts: *"Let me not forget my function. Let me not try to substitute mine for God's. Let me forgive and be happy."*
- Then do again the recent practice of reflecting on these statements. Think about them. Let related thoughts come (it will help if you remember how important your function is to you and others).

Remarks: It is easy for lengthy reflection like this to turn into a big mind wandering-fest, for the simple reason that "you are not proficient in the mind discipline that it requires" (7:2). So be on the lookout for irrelevant thoughts. When they come, repeat the idea (you might even want to repeat all three statements). Even if you have to do so twenty times, that is better than just letting your mind float off into never-never land.

Frequent reminders: Frequently, for several minutes.

At different times, use one or the other of the following:

1. A shorter version of the longer practice. Repeat the three "let me" statements and then think only about them. Your mind will wander; when it does, repeat the idea to bring it back.

2. Repeat the same statements, then look slowly and un-selectively about you, saying, *"This is the world it is my function to save."*

Commentary

Lesson 62 told me that forgiveness is my function, so this lesson expresses a determination not to forget what I am here for: to forgive the world, bringing peace to every mind.

What causes me to forget? The entire world. Everything my body's eyes see is "a form of temptation, since this was the purpose of the body itself" (2:1). The ego made the world and the body with a certain purpose in mind:

1. To obscure my function of forgiveness

2. To justify my forgetting my function

3. To entice me to abandon God and His Son by taking form in a body

The ego's continuation depends on my identifying with a bodily form. The "wickedness" and "incompletion" of the world around me justify my unwillingness to forgive. My involvement in the world, making it the scope of my goals and even my life, obscures my true function (in Heaven, creating; here, forgiving). The ego's plan seems to have worked pretty well.

The Course's cosmology is fairly unusual and extreme. As it says later in the Workbook, the Course's teaching is that "the world was made as an attack on God" (W-pII.3.2:1). It was not created by God but made by the ego to abandon God, taking on physical form to obscure our spiritual reality.

If it seems difficult for me to accept this understanding, I am not alone. The Course is quite aware this is a difficult concept. But when I begin to detect the way my mind works, it becomes a little easier to accept, because I begin to notice ways in which my mind uses the world, and uses everything I see with my eyes, to maintain the illusion of separation. As I am moved to forgive, I also find something in my mind resisting with tooth and nail, trying to justify withholding forgiveness, trying to get me simply to forget forgiveness entirely. And I begin to recognize that what the Course is saying here bears a curious similarity to what is going on within my mind. Perhaps what it is saying, then, expresses truth; a truth I am perhaps reluctant to accept, but which seems to be borne out by my own experience.

The Holy Spirit has another purpose, however, for everything in the world. "To the Holy Spirit, the world is a place where you learn to forgive yourself what you think of as your sins" (2:3). That's what we're doing as we forgive "others." Fulfilling this function is what brings us happiness (I can testify to that!).

The connection between forgiveness and happiness is interesting. If you think about it for a moment, you'll realize that when you are unforgiving, you are unhappy about something. To say, "I'm not happy about the way you are acting in our relationship," for instance, is equivalent to saying, "I have judged you and found you wanting; I am unforgiving." To forgive someone is to be happy with them. To forgive means to let go of your justification for being unhappy. When you forgive, "happiness becomes inevitable" (4:2). And "there is no other way" (4:3). Unforgiveness is precisely a choice to remain unhappy; without forgiveness you cannot be truly happy. That is the reasoning behind this statement: "Therefore, every time you choose whether or not to fulfill your function [that is, to forgive], you are really choosing whether or not to be happy" (4:4).

The lesson then goes on to point out that every single decision we make in a day can all be boiled down to this simple choice: Will I be happy, or unhappy? When you can begin to view your choices in life from this perspective, the choice becomes no choice at all. Who would knowingly choose unhappiness? When you begin to notice yourself actually doing that, you begin to understand why the Course refers to us so often as "insane."

> *Let me not forget my function.*
> *Let me not try to substitute mine for God's.*
> *Let me forgive and be happy.*   (6:2–4)

Let's try to remember to do the actual practice today. (I have to confess, I've been skimping on the practice.) One thing to notice is the ten to fifteen minute practice period that is called for today; that's something new. If nothing else, try to fit that one in.

LESSON 65 ✦ MARCH 6
"My only function is the one God gave me."

Practice instructions

Purpose: To let go of your usual goals, even if only for a little while, so you can focus on accepting the function God gave you as your *only* function.

Longer: One time, for ten to fifteen minutes.

- Repeat the idea, then close your eyes and repeat it again.
- Watch your mind carefully for what you would consider normal thoughts passing across it. Observe each one dispassionately (as you were taught to do in earlier lessons) and say, *"This thought reflects a goal that is preventing me from accepting my only function."* When you start to run out of such thoughts, try for another minute or so to catch any remaining thoughts, though don't strain to find them. The point of this phase is to clear your mind of your usual goals and functions.
- Then say, *"On this clean slate let my true function be written for me"*—or words to that effect. Be willing to have your self-assigned functions be replaced by God's.
- Repeat the idea again and spend the remainder of the practice period doing the now familiar practice of thinking about the idea and letting related thoughts come. Having cleared out your usual functions, you are now trying "to understand and accept" (3:1) your *true* function, to actively reflect on it so that it becomes more your own. Focus particularly on the *importance* and *desirability* of your function, and the *resolution* and *relief* it will bring. When wandering thoughts arise, I suggest dispelling them with the line you have just used: *"This thought reflects a goal..."*

Remarks: When he says that you need to pick a time for the longer practice period, one that you'll stick to today and for several days to come, that may very well sound threatening. Yet

191

it makes perfect sense. You are on the road to giving your whole life to your true function. Giving it one time during the day, a time that is devoted only to it, a time that is like an unmoving boulder in the flowing stream of your trivial pursuits, is a start, a foot in the door. If you can't let your true function have even a foot in the door, how will you ever reach the point where you give your whole life to it?

Frequent reminders: At least one per hour.

Sometimes use the first form, at others times, the second:

1. Close your eyes and say, *"My only function is the one God gave me. I want no other and I have no other."*

2. Look about you and say the same line, realizing that what you see will look completely different when you truly accept what you are saying. (I suggest giving this a try now and seeing the effect it has on you.)

Commentary

What I noticed as I read was the last sentence of the first paragraph:

> The full acceptance of salvation as your only function necessarily entails two phases; the recognition of salvation as your function, and the relinquishment of all the other goals you have invented for yourself.   (1:5)

Some of us may be yet having trouble with the first phase, recognizing salvation as our function. It isn't a simple matter. To say, "My job is to heal and be healed" requires a major shift of mind for most people. To see ourselves as the light of the world is not something that comes easily to us. That is why the preceding few lessons have dwelt on that fact, and why it will come up again in later lessons.

This lesson advances beyond simply recognizing that salvation is our function; it adds the thought that this is our *only* function. It makes it very plain that for this to be so, every other goal must be relinquished. God gave us this one goal, and no other. The others we invented for ourselves, and every other goal in some way competes with and detracts from this one.

As I go through my day, I watch how my "trivial purposes and goals"

(4:3) interfere with my pursuit of this one goal. I can watch it in the simple practice proposed for the next several days: taking ten to fifteen minutes to try to understand and accept the idea for the day. The lesson asks me to arrange my day so that I have this time set apart for God. Setting apart these fifteen minutes will necessitate setting aside every other goal for those minutes. It will bring up the very issue addressed by this lesson: the way in which my other goals compete with the goal given me by God.

In my understanding of the Course, the matter of recognizing my true goal can come fairly early in the journey I am on; the process of relinquishing all my lesser goals until I have no goal but God can take a fairly long time. At the start, we have no idea how many competitive goals we have set up for ourselves. It takes time to discover and relinquish them all. Today is but a beginning, but the more seriously I take this idea, the more effective today's practice can be.

LESSON 66 ✦ MARCH 7
"My happiness and my function are one."

Practice instructions

Purpose: To accept that your happiness and your God-given function are not only connected, but are actually the same thing, regardless of different appearances; and to accept that they are different in every way from all of the functions your ego has given you.

Longer: One time, for ten to fifteen minutes.

- Spend the time actively reflecting on the following logical syllogism: *"God gives me only happiness [premise 1]. He has given my function to me [premise 2]. Therefore my function must be happiness [conclusion]."* Notice how the conclusion logically follows from the premises, so that if the premises are right, the conclusion has to be.

- Therefore, spend a while thinking about the first premise (*"God gives me only happiness"*). Use paragraph 6 as a guide. It says that, in the end, you must either accept the first premise or accept that God is evil.

- Then spend some time thinking about the second premise (*"He has given my function to me"*). Use paragraphs 7 and 8 as a guide. They say that your function must have been given by either God or the ego, but the ego does not really give gifts. It is an illusion that offers illusions of gifts.

- Then spend some time thinking about how your life has reflected an alternative syllogism, which goes something like this: *"My ego has given me many functions [think about some of those]. None of them has given me happiness [reflect on this]. Therefore, my ego never gives me happiness."* Isn't this the only logical conclusion? Doesn't this conclusion make you want to choose the function God has given you instead?

- Finally, try to pour all of this reflection into an acceptance of the conclusion (*"Therefore my function must be happiness"*). Use the reflection to bring you to a point where you really embrace the conclusion.

Remarks: This lesson is yet another giant stride (our first was Lesson 61), but it will only be a giant step forward *for you* if you really give your mind to it. So do so, for your own sake. Give the longer practice your full concentration, and give the shorter practice your frequency.

Frequent reminders: Two per hour, for one minute or less.

Say, *"My happiness and my function are one, because God has given me both."* Repeating this slowly and thinking about it will make all the difference.

Commentary

I find this lesson interesting in the way it makes use of ordinary logic, applied to extraordinary ideas. The longer practice period is supposed to be spent in thinking about the premises in the syllogism given in paragraph 5 (5:7; 9:1). In other words, the lesson asks us to test out the logic of its proposal with our minds. Quite evidently the Course sees a good deal of value in thinking and reasoning; it is not a Course in mindlessness, as some people seem to believe. Nor is it only a course in experience. It is solidly laced with reasoning, and expects us to know how to use that faculty of our minds. I find that a good aid in this kind of practice is writing down the ideas that come to me as I do it.

The central idea today is one we've seen before: happiness and my function are, at the core, the same thing. The two premises are fairly simple, especially the first: God gives me only happiness. If God is a God worthy of my allegiance, a God of love, this must be so. Why follow a god who makes me unhappy? If God gives unhappiness, He must be evil (6:5). And if God is evil I may as well quit now; I'll never find happiness living in the clutches of a sadistic god, who gives his creations unhappiness.

Second, God has given my function to me. This is a little less obvious. "Function" could be understood as meaning "nature." In simple terms, God created me, and in so doing, defined what I am. What I am defines what I do. What alternative is there? If God did not define me, what did? The only alternative is the ego (8:3). Or, I might say, I made myself (which is really the same thing). But how can anything create itself? What created its power to create? Is it really possible that the ego made me, or I defined myself? No. Therefore this second premise must also be true: God has given my function to me.

Now if God gives me only happiness, and God gave me my function, what is the logical conclusion? My function must be happiness. My reason for being is to be happy. Fulfilling my function is what brings me happiness.

If we think about all the ways we've tried to find happiness following our egos—as we are instructed to think about, here in the lesson—we must admit, if we are perfectly honest, that none of them have worked.

The lesson is trying to bring us to the point where we make a choice, the choice between madness and truth, between listening to the ego or to the Holy Spirit. It is asking us to realize that everything the ego tells us is a lie, and that only the truth is true; only what God has given us has reality.

This lesson is the second one called a "giant stride" (10:5). The first was Lesson 61. We'll see the term again in Lessons 94, 130, 135, and 194. Lesson 61 told us, "I am the light of the world," which is "a beginning step in accepting your real function on earth....a giant stride toward taking your rightful place in salvation" (W-pI.61.3:2–3). We are light-bearers, designed by God to beam His light to the universe; that is our function. Accepting that is a giant step, a strong beginning. Now, we are told, "My happiness and my function are one." Bringing light to the world is what happiness is; being the light of the world is fulfilling our function, and fulfilling our function is happiness.

LESSON 67 ✦ MARCH 8
"Love created me like Itself."

Practice instructions

Purpose: To experience the blazing light of your changeless reality, if only for a moment. To redefine God as Love and realize you are included in His definition of Himself.

Longer: One time, for ten to fifteen minutes.
- Repeat the idea.
- Then spend a few minutes adding related thoughts, along the following lines: *"Holiness created me holy. Helpfulness created me helpful."* Use only attributes that fit the Course's teachings about God.
- For a brief interval, try to let go of all thoughts.
- The remainder is a meditation exercise, using the method you were taught in the 40s:

1. Reach past the thick cloud of all your self-images to the light of your true Self. Sink past illusions about you and reach down to the truth in you.

2. When you get distracted, repeat the idea. If this is not enough, add more related thoughts, as in the earlier phase.

3. Hold in mind the confidence that the light of your true Self is there and can be reached, and that even if you don't reach it now, you will succeed in bringing that experience closer.

Frequent reminders: Four or five per hour, maybe more.

Repeat the idea. As you do, be aware that this is not your tiny voice telling you this, but the Voice of truth telling you Who you really are. I recommend repeating it once in this fashion now, so you can see the effect it has.

Remarks: The comment in 5:2 is very important. The 60s and 70s really focus on frequency, and this sentence explains why that is so crucial. You need to frequently practice the truth because you so frequently practice illusion. Specifically, "your mind is so preoccupied with false self-images" (5:2). Contained in each normal thought is a false self-image. That is why you need to inject as many thoughts as you can that contain the truth about you.

Commentary

The Course spends a disproportionate amount of space telling us what we are, how we were created like God, Who created us, and how that reality is "unchanged and unchangeable" (2:1). Lesson 229 virtually duplicates today's thought: "Love, Which created me, is what I am." Review V has us repeat, "God is but Love, and therefore so am I" every day for ten days. And then there are all the lessons on the theme "I am as God created me." There are three lessons with that direct topic (the only lesson given more than once in the same words, in 94, 110, and 162); several others in which the idea is repeated (132, 139, 237, and 260); and twenty review lessons (201 to 220) in which we repeat the words "I am still as God created me" daily. Evidently the Course thinks this idea is worth repeating!

In fact, today's lesson tells us exactly why this thought is so important, and why repetition of it is so necessary:

> It will be particularly helpful today to practice the idea for the day as often as you can. You need to hear the truth about yourself as frequently as possible, because your mind is so preoccupied with false self-images. Four or five times an hour, and perhaps even more, it would be most beneficial to remind yourself that Love created you like Itself. Hear the truth about yourself in this. (5:1–4)

We need to hear the truth about ourselves as often as we can because we have taught ourselves a false self-image, and we have taught ourselves very, very well. "Teach only love, for that is what you are" (T-6.I.13:2) is one of the most famous sayings in the Course, and emphasizes the same thing: What we are is Love, because Love created us like Itself.

How many of us, if asked, "What are you?" would find the word "love" springing immediately to our minds? For most of us, to think of ourselves as being love and only love is, to be kind, a stretch. We may think we have *some* love in us, but to think that Love is what we are? Not hardly. That's why we need to hear it as often as possible, why we need to repeat the idea today four or five times an hour or more during the day. That's something like eighty times today, if we are awake sixteen hours.

Love is what I am. That is why I am the light of the world. That is why I am the world's savior, and why the Christ in everyone looks to me for salvation—because what I am *is* the salvation of the world (1:2–5). How differently would I live today if I knew this about myself?

Notice that the lesson does not expect us to "get" this idea all at once. If we were expected to grasp it right away, we wouldn't have to repeat it eighty times. All we are looking for is to "realize fully, *if only for a moment*, that it is the truth" (1:6, emphasis mine). Love is in us as our true Self, and we are attempting to get in touch with the Love within ourselves (3:2–3). We may not contact It directly today, but even the effort is worth it, although we may not feel we have succeeded: "Be confident that you will do much today to bring that awareness nearer, whether you feel you have succeeded or not" (4:4).

Some day, though, some time, we will succeed; perhaps even today. It's inevitable because we cannot hide forever from what we are, we cannot escape from what is within us. At some point it will happen: "You will succeed in going…through the interval of thoughtlessness to the awareness of a blazing light in which you recognize yourself as Love created you" (4:3).

"You were created by Love like Itself" (6:4).

LESSON 68 ✦ MARCH 9
"Love holds no grievances."

Practice instructions

Purpose: To feel the profound sense of peace and safety that comes from being free of grievances. This will provide the motivation you need to free yourself of them more and more.

Longer: One time, for ten to fifteen minutes.

- Search your mind for those you hold major grievances against, then for those you hold seemingly minor grievances against. Notice how no one is completely exempt, and how alone this has made you feel.
- Resolve to see them all as friends. Say to each one in turn: *"I would see you as my friend, that I may remember you are part of me and come to know myself."* Note the progression through three stages (friend/part of me/know myself). Try to mean each stage.
- For the remainder of the practice period, think of yourself as being at peace with a world that is truly your friend, a world that loves and protects you, and that you love in return. Try to actually *feel* safety surrounding you like a blanket, hovering over you like wings of an angel, and holding you up like solid rock beneath your feet.
- Conclude by saying, *"Love holds no grievances. When I let all my grievances go I will know I am perfectly safe."*

Frequent reminders: Several (at least three) per hour.

Say, *"Love holds no grievances. I would wake to my Self by laying all my grievances aside and wakening in Him."*

Response to temptation: Whenever you feel a grievance against anyone.

Quickly apply the idea in this form: *"Love holds no grievances. Let me not betray my Self."* The idea, of course, is that, because your Self is Love, holding grievances is an act of Self-betrayal. Think about that.

200

Commentary

This lesson is a powerful teaching on the effect that holding grievances has on our minds and our thinking.

To hold a grievance is to wish harm on someone; it is, whether we think of it that way or not, to "dream of hatred" (2:5). Some of us— perhaps most of us—have, at times, literally dreamed of revenge on someone we perceive as a victimizer. We have, possibly, consciously wished someone were dead. Probably, however, we have repressed conscious awareness of such thoughts and have deliberately forgotten we had them. Yet even "minor" grievances are the same thing, just in milder form. To hold a grievance is to feel you have been wronged, and the victimizer deserves to be punished for his or her wrongdoing. To wish someone would "get what s/he deserves" is no less hatred than to wish them dead.

"Love holds no grievances." Holding a grievance is the converse of love; love and grievances are mutually exclusive. Yesterday's lesson taught us that "Love created me like Itself." To hold a grievance, then, is to *deny* that truth; it is an assertion that I am something other than love. We cannot know our Self as Love if we hold any grievances because holding a grievance is teaching us the exact opposite.

"Perhaps you do not yet fully realize just what holding grievances does to your mind" (1:5). The teaching in the next several lines is meaty. Our Source is Love, and we are created like that Source. When we hold a grievance, we *seem* to be different from our Source, and therefore seem to be cut off from Him (1:6). We are not Love, and God is; we *must* be separate.

However, the mind cannot quite conceive of a source and its effect as being totally different; therefore, to cope with the logical dilemma, our mind conceives of God in our own imagined image: "It makes you believe that He is like what you think you have become" (1:7). We think God holds grievances, and dream up religions that speak of "sinners in the hands of an angry God." We make an image of a vengeful, punitive god, and cower in terror away from his presence, fearful of our very existence.

The effects of grievances do not stop with seeming to split us off from God, making us different and separate, and then remaking God Himself into a terrifying, vindictive demon. Within us, our true Self seems to fall asleep and thus to disappear from active participation, while the part of us that "weaves illusions in its sleep appears to be awake" (2:1). We lose sight of our Self and imagine we are something else, a grievance-holding, petty "self," angry at the world.

"Can all this arise from holding grievances? Oh, yes!" (2:2–3). We have redefined God in our own image. We suffer guilt. We have forgotten who we are. All this is inevitable for those that hold grievances.

We have not realized what damage we are doing to our own minds by holding grievances. This is why the Course teaches that forgiveness is not something we do for the sake of others; we do it for our own well-being.

It may not seem possible to give up all grievances; that's understood by the lesson (4:2). It isn't really a matter of possible or impossible, however; it's just a matter of motivation. We *can* give up any grievance; the question is, do we *want* to? So this lesson sets out to increase our motivation by asking us to perform an experiment. Basically, it asks us to "try to find out how you would feel without them" (4:4). The idea is, quite simply, that if we can get a taste of what it feels like to be *without* grievances, we will prefer the new feeling. "Try it; you'll like it!" as the commercial says. And once we are motivated, once we *want* to let grievances go—we will. Our minds have that much power.

Notice the use of the words "trying" and "try" in paragraph 6. We are basically doing an exercise in imagination here. Imagine being at peace with everyone. Imagine feeling completely safe, surrounded by love and loving all that surrounds you. Imagine—even just for an instant—that nothing can harm you; that you are invulnerable and totally secure, and that what's more, there is nothing that wants to harm you even if it could. If you can "succeed even by ever so little, there will never be a problem in motivation ever again" (4:5).

Once you get a taste of what this state of mind feels like you are going to *want* it. Because it feels *really* good! You are going to become willing to do whatever it takes to experience this more and more, for longer and longer, until it becomes permanent.

I want to emphasize that today's lesson isn't telling us, "Get rid of all your grievances." It isn't laying down a law and making us guilty for having grievances. It is simply trying to *motivate* us to *want* to let them go, first by showing us how much pain (illusory harm, but real in our experience) our grievances are bringing to our minds, and then by getting us to experience what a mind without grievances feels like. It is getting us to recognize that holding a grievance is a betrayal—not of God, not of anyone else, but a betrayal of *ourselves* as Love. Grievances make us believe we are something we are not, and that we are not what we really are.

LESSON 69 ✦ MARCH 10
"My grievances hide the light of the world in me."

Practice instructions

Purpose: To lift the veil of grievances that has hidden the light of the world in you, so that you can experience that light and let it shine salvation onto the world. This is yet another attempt to experience the light in you (see W-pI.41.5:3 and W-pI.44.3:1).

Longer: One time, for ten to fifteen minutes.

- Spend several minutes cultivating the heightened attitude that is so crucial to Course-based meditation. Think about what you are about to attempt, about its importance to you and to the world. You are trying to lift the veil and get in touch with the light of the world, so you can hold it up for all to see and be blessed by. You are trying to reach your only need, your only function, goal, and purpose. Be *determined* to reach it.

- Then, with eyes closed, let go of all your thoughts. Picture your true mind as a vast sphere of radiant light, totally engulfed by a layer of dark clouds (your grievances). From your vantage point outside the sphere, all you can see are clouds.

- Now begin the meditation. As before, you can see it as having three aspects:

1. The basic motion is one of traveling through the clouds and into the light. "Reach out and touch them in your mind. Brush them aside with your hand; feel them resting on your cheeks and forehead and eyelids as you go through them" (6:3–4).

2. If your mind wanders, repeat the idea and then continue your journey through the clouds.

3. Most of all, hold that heightened attitude you cultivated in the first phase, an attitude of *desire* (remember how much

you want to reach the light), *determination* (be determined to get there), and *confidence* (realize you cannot fail, because this is in accord with God's Will).

- If you do your part properly, the power of God will do the rest. You will feel His power lifting you up and carrying you into the light.

Frequent reminders: As often as possible (suggestion: several times an hour).

Say, *"My grievances hide the light of the world in me. I cannot see what I have hidden. Yet I want to let it be revealed to me [by God], for my salvation and the salvation of the world."*

Response to temptation: Whenever you are tempted to hold a grievance.

Say, *"If I hold this grievance the light of the world will be hidden from me."*

Commentary

I am the light of the world, but the light cannot shine out because my grievances hide it. When I let my grievances go, the light is released, and releases my brother and myself. My job with everyone I meet is to share my salvation with him.

Today's practice is another time of attempting to "reach the light in you" (2:1), or in other words, to become aware of my Self as God created It, wholly loving and wholly lovable. Notice how the form of this practice is similar to what we've seen before; it is a pattern that is repeated often in the Workbook in different forms. In general, the pattern is one of attempting to move past, or move through, or let go of the thoughts that normally occupy my mind, settling down in deep stillness, and reaching beyond my surface thoughts to something deep within myself, a Self I am not normally aware of. This is a Course method of meditation. It is one of the tools given to us by the Workbook, and should be learned and used even after Workbook practice per se has ended.

What we are trying to reach is "dearer to us than all else" (3:1). Reaching it, finding it, and releasing it to the world is our only purpose and only function on earth. "Learning salvation is our only goal" (3:4). I love the poignant imagery of this sentence: "We are trying to let the

veil be lifted, and to see the tears of God's Son disappear in the sunlight"
(2:5). Can you feel that tug with me, that longing to release the light of
the world that is in you?

> There is a light that this world cannot give. Yet you can
> give it, as it was given you. And as you give it, it shines
> forth to call you from the world and follow it. For this light
> will attract you as nothing in this world can do.
>
> (T-13.VI.11:1–4)

LESSON 70 ✦ MARCH 11
"My salvation comes from me."

Practice instructions

Purpose: To realize that your salvation is not outside you, that both the sickness and the remedy are within, and that you are joined with God in wanting the remedy for yourself.

Longer: Two times, for ten to fifteen minutes.

- Repeat, *"My salvation comes from me,"* and add a statement to the effect that it does not come from outside you, such as *"It cannot come from anywhere else."*
- Close your eyes and for several minutes review external places in which you have sought salvation—people, possessions, situations, events, self-concepts. Say, *"My salvation cannot come from any of these things [try to really see this]. My salvation comes from me and only from me."*
- Then enter again into meditation, trying once more to travel through the clouds to the light in you. Use the same technique as you did yesterday (you may want to review those instructions). The difference today is that the clouds, rather than being your grievances, are the external things in which you've sought salvation. Since these cloud patterns are where your mind has been fixated, it may be challenging to not get stuck there. The particular method you use for getting past the clouds is not important; what is important is your *desire* and *determination* to get past them. One method you might find helpful is to imagine Jesus leading you by the hand through the clouds and into the light. He says that if you do this, it will be more than just your imagination.

Remarks: Now that we are going up to two longer practice periods a day, he wants you to do the same thing as before—decide in advance when you'll do the longer practice periods and then do your best to adhere to that decision. To refresh your mind about why this is important, read the "remarks" section in Lesson 65.

Frequent reminders: Frequent.

Say, *"My salvation comes from me. Nothing outside of me can hold me back. Within me is the world's salvation and my own."* While saying this, remember that only your own thoughts can hold you back. This leaves you in charge.

Commentary

The message of this lesson is really one of the central teachings of the Course. Guilt and salvation are in my own mind and nowhere else. "All guilt is solely an invention of your mind" (1:5).

It is severely tempting to lay the blame for my problems somewhere outside of me. I instinctively shun taking responsibility for any of my problems, and the idea that all of them are in my mind and nowhere else seems devastating. However, consider the consequences of the alternative view: that the source of my problems and of my guilt lies outside of me. If that is the case, I am the helpless victim of these outside forces. I cannot do anything about them except to rant and rave at them, hurling invectives of blame and begging for mercy from uncaring powers.

If, however, my problems lie solely in my own mind, then I am capable of doing something about them. In fact, *only* I can do anything about them, and nothing outside of me can prevent me from doing it. "Nothing outside of me can hold me back" (10:7). I am in complete control; my salvation comes from me and me alone. I am not dependent on anything outside myself, and therefore I am already free.

The "cost" of recognizing that my salvation comes from me and nowhere else is that I have to give up any idea that the "cavalry" is going to show up to rescue me. "Nothing outside yourself can save you; nothing outside yourself can give you peace" (2:1). Nothing and nobody can do it for me. It's up to me. My partner in romantic love isn't going to do it for me. My wealth and position aren't going to do it for me. My analyst isn't going to do it for me, nor my guru. Not even Jesus will do it for me. The Course won't do it for me. Any or all of these may support me, help me, encourage me; in the end, however, my salvation will come from myself, from the choices of my own mind. "Today's idea places you in charge of the universe, where you belong because of what you are" (2:3). Awesome, and a bit frightening. I don't want to believe I have that much power, but not believing it is what got me into this mess in the first place. Therein lies my sickness.

Good news! God wants us to be healed and happy; so do we. Therefore our will is one with God's. We have been choosing sickness but we don't *really* want it, because it makes us unhappy. So we can agree with God and choose again, choose to be well rather than sick.

In today's exercise we picture ourselves pushing past the clouds again towards the light. Yesterday the clouds represented our grievances; today, they represent the things we have looked to for salvation. "You cannot find [salvation] in the clouds that surround the light, and it is in them you have been looking for it" (8:2). Oddly, objects of salvation and grievances are not all that different; a grievance against a brother is also an assertion that something in that brother is making me unhappy, which is also making him a potential source of salvation: I would be happy if he would change. To see salvation outside myself, or to see a grievance, are both means by which I give away my power and deny my sole responsibility for the universe of my mind.

In the exercise of pushing past the clouds, we are told, "If it helps you, think of me holding your hand and leading you. And I assure you it will be no idle fantasy" (9:3–4). For some of us, it will be helpful to picture ourselves taking the hand of Jesus and being led through the clouds. For others, the picture would be more disconcerting than helpful; there is, perhaps, healing needed in our relationship with him before we could find that image appealing. I, for one, find it immensely helpful to envision one who has already been there and back, and who is willing to lead me through. He can't do it for me, but he sure can help.

Sometimes I think of Jesus as simply the part of my mind that has already wakened. And he *is* part of me, just as you are, and as everyone is. He is not some awesome divine being I cannot ever hope to be like. He is me, remembering. He is me, awake. To take his hand is to identify with the Christ in myself.

Go for the light today!

LESSON 71 ✦ MARCH 12

"Only God's plan for salvation will work."

Practice instructions

Purpose: To truly recognize that only God's plan will work and to rejoice in this, for it means escape from the hopelessness of the ego's plan and from the pointlessness of trying to follow both plans at once.

Longer: Two times, for ten to fifteen minutes.

- The first part is another exercise in thinking about the idea. Specifically, reflect on the two parts of the idea. Part one: God's plan will work. According to recent lessons, God's plan involves contacting the light within and letting go of grievances, both of which mean changing your mind. Part two: other plans won't work. This lesson tells us that the ego's plan involves seeking outside yourself for happiness, holding grievances when the outside doesn't cooperate, and refusing to change your mind. Try to reach the conclusion, based on logic and your experience, that *only* God's plan holds any hope of delivering actual happiness.

- The second part is the Workbook's first exercise in asking for guidance. Ask God to reveal His plan for you for today. Ask, *"What would You have me do? Where would You have me go? What would You have me say, and to whom?"* The willingness you are demonstrating just by doing this entitles you to an answer, so listen with confidence. "Refuse not to hear" (9:8). Once you ask, listen for the subtlest inner promptings—it doesn't need to come in words. If you don't hear anything, you might want to repeat the questions, making them more specific: *"What would You have me do today?"* or *"Where would You have me go after lunch?"*

Frequent reminders: Six or seven per hour, for half a minute or less.

Repeat the idea as an affirmation of where your salvation really comes from.

Response to temptation: Whenever you are tempted to hold a grievance.

Be alert all day to grievances. Respond to each one by saying, *"Holding grievances is the opposite of God's plan for salvation. And only His plan will work."*

Commentary

After being told yesterday that salvation comes from me and only from me, it is a little annoying the next day to be told that only God's plan will work and that the plan I believe in (which is the ego's) isn't worth anything. It kind of seems like give and then take away, doesn't it? But it isn't really saying anything different. The ego's plan involves looking for salvation outside of myself; God's plan is wholly centered on my change of mind. In God's plan, salvation comes from me; in the ego's plan, it comes from any place *except* me.

To the ego, salvation means "that if someone else spoke or acted differently, if some external circumstance or event were changed, you would be saved" (2:2). In the ego's view, basically I'm okay, I am the innocent victim; the problem is with something outside of me. Whenever I am thinking, "If this were different, I'd be okay," I am believing in the ego's plan of salvation because I am demanding "the change of mind necessary for salvation...of everyone and everything except" myself (2:5).

Don't get tripped up by the religious-sounding phrase "plan for salvation." It may remind you of some cheap Bible tract announcing "God's plan of salvation." What salvation boils down to here is simply, "I'd be okay; my problems would be solved." And the ego's plan, simply stated, is "If this were different, I would be saved."

In the ego's plan, the mind's only purpose is to figure out *what* has to change for me to be saved (which presupposes that it *isn't me* that has to change). The ego will let us pick anything that won't work (which includes everything in the class of things I am looking at—things outside of myself—since salvation comes from me and not something outside me). The ego has me look everywhere but in the one place in which the answer lies—my own mind.

God's plan for salvation is that I look for it where it is: in myself.

For this plan to work, however, there is a condition: I have to look in myself *and nowhere else*. I can't be looking for salvation in myself *and* from outside. This just divides my efforts between two different plans. There are two parts to today's idea: 1) God's plan will work, and 2) other plans (i.e. the plans I make up) won't work.

The second part, the lesson implies, may seem depressing. We may feel a flare of anger. In fact, what keeps us from simply accepting God's plan is that we want to be right; we want our plans to work. We'd rather be right than happy, most of the time, although we don't consciously think that. But the ego's plan consists of holding grievances. Haven't you ever had the experience of realizing that you *could* just let a grievance go and be happy, but that somehow it seems to feel good to be angry? You don't want to let go. You'd rather be *right* than happy.

The lesson is saying, "You can be saved simply by changing your mind. Nothing outside you has to change in order for you to be happy. You can simply choose happiness, right now." And our response, typically? "Hell, no! I won't be happy unless s/he changes first." We're holding on to our plan for salvation and refusing God's.

Surprisingly, the practice for today is not primarily about letting go of grievances, or looking within for salvation. It is about listening. It is about asking guidance from God. The emphasis is on taking our hands off the reins of our lives and giving them over to God. If we can learn to do that, we may begin to learn that His plans work better than our own.

HOW TO LISTEN FOR GUIDANCE

How many times have you heard, or *said*, "I ask for guidance, but I just don't hear anything"? Wouldn't it be great if *A Course in Miracles* gave us detailed instructions in precisely how to listen for the Holy Spirit's messages?

Thankfully, it does exactly that. There is extensive training in Workbook Lessons 71–90 in how to receive from the Holy Spirit. Significantly, every point in this training is echoed by dictation Helen Schucman received years earlier, on the day before the Text started coming through. This dictation can be found in Ken Wapnick's *Absence from Felicity* (p. 197). I'll begin by commenting on this dictation, which was meant to help Bill Thetford in his own listening for guidance:

I can't answer where he asks amiss. When he asks right I *have* answered. He has a tendency to get part of an answer and decide himself when to disconnect. He should ask if that's all. Since I don't know when he's going to ring off I have to be very short and even cryptic. It chops up messages too much.

Bill's first problem is that he simply gives up too soon. This forces Jesus to make the messages "very short and even cryptic," since he doesn't know when Bill will suddenly decide to quit (this is a brief reference to the power of our free choice, which is so free that not even Jesus knows what choices we will make). Bill simply needs to be more patient.

Jesus then goes on to list "three major areas" of interference in Bill's reception of guidance:

1. He doesn't have much real confidence that I will get through. He never just claims his rights. He should begin with much more confidence. *I'll* keep my promises....

2. He has to learn better concentration. His mind flits about too much for good communication. Suggest a very short phrase like "Here I am Lord" and don't think of *anything* else. Just pull in your mind slowly from everywhere else and center it on these words. This will also give him the realization that he [Bill] really *is* here. He's not too sure.

3. Tell him to be sure not to mistake your [Helen's] role. If he overreacts to or over-evaluates you as a person, both of you will be in danger.

The first of the three areas of interference is that Bill listens without real confidence that he'll actually hear. Receiving guidance is one of his God-given rights. Bill, however, "never just claims his rights." When I first read that line it hit me like a ton of bricks: "So I have a *right* to God's guidance, and I should *claim* that right." What a refreshing and empowering idea! Asking tentatively and sheepishly may seem courteous to Jesus, but it's actually a subtle accusation that he is a liar, for he has *promised* that he will be there to answer us. If we believe that Jesus keeps his word, then we will listen with confidence.

213

The second area is that Bill has poor concentration. "His mind flits about too much." He needs to learn how to still his mind so that it becomes truly receptive. Hearing the still, small voice with a mind full of chatter is like trying to hear someone whisper to you in a noisy room while you are still jabbering away. Bill needs to learn how to quiet his inner chatter, so that the room of his mind gets so quiet he could hear a pin drop. To help him enter this state of inner silence, Jesus gives Bill a meditation technique—one, in fact, that was used by the famous seventeenth-century monk Brother Lawrence, author of the spiritual classic *The Practice of the Presence of God.*

The third problem area is that Bill is over-estimating Helen's role. I assume this means her role as receiver of Jesus' guidance. Certainly, he needs to respect her role, but if he lets himself get too dazzled by her ability to hear Jesus, this will simultaneously undermine his confidence in his own ability, as well as weaken his motivation to try.

Overall, Bill's approach seems to be, to put it simply, too weak. He gives up too soon, has little confidence that he'll hear, doesn't concentrate enough, and leans too much on Helen. When it comes to listening for guidance, in other words, he's a bit of a wimp. That sounds harsh until you realize that Jesus' critique applies to virtually every one of us. Surely you saw yourself in at least some of the above points. What, then, can we do to stop being "guidance wimps"?

The answer is to really go through the training provided in the Workbook. The Workbook has a bank of lessons, 71–90, designed to teach us how to listen to and receive from the Holy Spirit (almost all the quotes below will be drawn from these lessons). What I find amazing about the instruction in these lessons is just how closely it reproduces the private counsel given to Bill nearly four years earlier. Except for the caution about over-evaluating Helen's role, every single point in Jesus' counsel to Bill shows up as a main theme in these lessons. I'll list the points in the same order as we discussed them above:

Listen in patience; don't give up too soon

Once you have asked the Holy Spirit your question, "wait patiently for Him" (W-pl.75.7:8). And while you wait, periodically repeat your request, not to remind a forgetful Holy Spirit, but to renew your own attentiveness and your confidence that you'll hear.

> Whenever you feel your confidence wane and your hope of success flicker and go out, repeat your question and your request.   (W-pl.72.12:1)

> While you wait, repeat several times, slowly and in complete
> patience [your request].   (W-pI.75.6:7)

Listen with confidence; claim your rights

The instructions for listening repeatedly emphasize being confident that you'll hear. The lessons are full of language designed to instill this confidence in you. They assure you that you have a "claim to God's answer" (W-pI.71.9:10), that "He will anwer" (W-pI.72.12:5), that "you will be heard and you will be answered" (W-pI.79.10:6). The attitude they encourage is captured perfectly in this quote, which sounds as if it could have been lifted straight from Jesus' advice to Bill:

> There is a message waiting for you. Be confident that you
> will receive it. Remember that it belongs to you.
>   (W-pI.rII.In.3:2–4)

Listen in deep silence; wait for Him in quiet expectancy

According to the Workbook's instructions, so much of the task of hearing the Holy Spirit comes down to one question: How still can you get your mind? The Course puts it plainly: "Learn to be quiet, for His Voice is heard in stillness" (M-15.2:12). This stillness, however, should not be passive and lax. Rather, it should be an alert, attentive, expectant stillness. Your mind should be poised, waiting for the answer with every ounce of your attention. Combining a quiet restfulness with a poised alertness is central to the inner art of listening. The following quotes capture this delicate combination:

> Spend the major part of the time listening quietly but
> attentively.   (W-pI.rII.In.3:1)

> Hold your mind in silent readiness to hear the Voice That
> speaks the truth to you.   (W-pI.76.9:2)

> Wait in silent expectancy for the truth.   (W-pI.94.4:1)

Of course, holding your mind in a state of alert, receptive waiting is something most of us can't maintain for more than about half a minute. Just like Bill, our minds flit about too much. This is why the Workbook instructs us to draw them back again and again and again—as often as we need to. Review II, in which we listen for ten to fifteen minutes, urges us to be absolutely determined to keep our minds on track: "Do not allow your intent to waver" (W-pI.rII.In.4:1); "Refuse to be sidetracked" (W-pI.rII.In.5:2).

I hope you can see just how serious the Course is about us learning how to receive guidance. The last thing it wants us to do is fail to try in the assumption that we are unable to hear. Like Bill, we can be so dazzled by Helen's ability that we neglect to develop our own. True, some people do have more ability to hear the Holy Spirit, but presumably this is only because, like Helen, they developed their ability in the remote past. We can develop ours in the present. If we will train ourselves to listen in patience, in confidence, and in silence, we too can begin to hear that sublime Voice with increasing clarity and with greater frequency.

LESSON 72 ✦ MARCH 13

"Holding grievances is an attack on God's plan for salvation."

Practice instructions

Purpose: To stop attacking God's plan by miscasting it as something it is not. To instead welcome it as it is, and realize it has already been accomplished in you.

Longer: Two times, for ten to fifteen minutes.

This is another exercise in trying to hear God's Voice. This time you are asking God what His plan for salvation is, in order to replace your assumptions about what it is. Your grievances have depicted God in your image, as a separate body who feels wronged by the misbehavior of others (which includes *your* misbehavior). In this view, for you to become reconciled with Him, He demands (like any ego) that you sacrifice your pleasures on His behalf and pay the price for your misdeeds. Can't you see that this view of His plan is why you've pushed it away?

In the practice period, lay aside your assumptions about what God's plan is and ask Him what it is. Ask, *"What is salvation, Father? I do not know [try to mean this]. Tell me, that I may understand."* While listening, the attitude you hold is everything. Be confident that He will answer. "Be determined to hear" (12:6).

When you feel your confidence wane, repeat the question again, consciously "remembering that you are asking of the infinite Creator of infinity, Who created you like Himself" (12:1). It may help to vary the wording of the sentences. For instance, *"What is Your plan for salvation? I let go of my assumptions. I really want to understand it."* Listen for the faintest promptings. Trust what you hear. You may want to write it down afterwards.

Frequent reminders: One, maybe two, per hour, for a minute or so.

Say, *"Holding grievances is an attack on God's plan for salvation. Let me accept it instead. What is salvation, Father?"* Then wait in silence and listen for His answer, preferably with eyes closed.

Commentary

This is a long lesson, and a tough one. The scope of ideas presented here is daunting even to an experienced student of the Course (including me). There is no way I can give a detailed explanation of all the ideas in this brief commentary, so I am mainly going to focus on a few interesting ideas.

The general thrust of the argument here is that holding grievances is always concerned in some way with the behavior of a body. Grievances thus confuse the person with his body; they are based on the assumption that bodies are what we are, and bodies are what God created. Since bodies die, God is a liar when He promises life. Death is the ultimate punishment for our sins, and that is what God gives us.

The ego then comes into the picture in the role of "savior," telling us, "Okay, you're a body. So take the little you can get" (6:6). We see salvation as some kind of bodily function. Either we hate our bodies and humiliate them or we love them and try to exalt them (7:2–3).

As long as "the body stands at the center of your concept of yourself, you are attacking God's plan for salvation" (7:4). Why so? Because God's plan has nothing to do with the body; it concerns the mind, the being you are.

One primary thing the lesson is trying to get across is that we are not bodies. "It is the body that is outside us, and is not our concern. To be without a body is to be in our natural state" (9:2–3). This flies in the face of our common perception. The nearly universal assumption of man is that we are *inside* our bodies. To say the body is *outside* us seems to make no sense at all. But actually, it isn't an entirely inconceivable idea. There is a way of understanding how our awareness can *appear* to be in the body when in fact it is elsewhere.

Many of you are probably familiar with the idea of virtual reality (VR); that is, an artificial world you can experience via a computer. My son, Ben, is getting his Computer Science Ph.D. at Georgia Tech with a strong emphasis on virtual reality. Not long ago he visited VR laboratories in Japan, where they were experimenting with VR in connection with robots. He put on a VR helmet (so his eyes and ears now beheld and heard what was projected on the screen of the helmet or played through its speakers); he wore a VR sleeve on his arm and hand. These were connected to a robot, which had a camera and microphone on its "head" and whose mechanical arm and hand responded to the movements of Ben's arm and hand. He was seeing what the robot "saw," hearing what it "heard," and picking up objects with its hand.

Then he had a very odd experience. He turned his (the robot's) head, looked across the room, and saw his fleshly body sitting on the other side, wearing all this weird-looking gear. Ben's awareness was inside the robot, although his body was on the other side of the room. He seemed to be separate from his body.

Our bodies, I believe, are very much like that VR robot. Our minds receive only the input of the body's eyes and ears, and so we are fooled into thinking we are inside of it. In reality we are "somewhere else," not inside the body at all. What we are seeing in our bodies is, in truth, only "virtual reality." The body is "outside" of us in fact, and being without a body is our natural state.

One of the aims of the Course is to help us "see our Self as separate from the body" (9:5). I hope these thoughts provide a little help in conceptualizing that possibility.

The practice periods have us focusing on asking, "What is salvation, Father? I do not know" (10:6–7). The intent is to get us to let go of our existing ideas of "salvation," which are all focused on the body, either exalting it or abasing it, so that something else can take the place of those ideas. Salvation lies in acceptance of what we are—and what we are is *not* a body. The lesson leaves the answering of the question about salvation to our inner listening. If we ask, it says, something will answer us (11:3; 12:5).

Explanatory note: How is it that grievances actually attack God's plan for salvation? The simple answer is this: Our grievances towards others imply a certain view of life, in which the body is the real source of happiness and God is to be feared, because He commands us to sacrifice that happiness.

If you think about it, grievances are always about how another's body has mistreated you (3:3-4:2). They thus imply a view in which you are a body and in which happiness comes from how well other bodies treat you. They also imply that God is a body (4:5), and as such, He is intensely focused on getting treated right by other bodies—by you. He demands that you serve Him, obey His commandments, and sacrifice your own needs. In particular, He asks you to forego the pleasures of the body, for the body is inherently sinful. In the end, like some insanely demanding spouse, He asks you to pay your debt to Him by sacrificing everything, by dying (5:2). Given this view, the natural impulse is to run from God and seek solace in what the body offers. That is how grievances attack His plan—by inducing us to run from it.

LESSON 73 ✦ MARCH 14
"I will there be light."

Practice instructions

Purpose: Another attempt to reach the light in you, which will show you the real world.

Longer: Two times, for ten to fifteen minutes.

I see this lesson as very similar to Lesson 69, where you spent a beginning phase reflecting on how much you want to find the light in you, and then, in the ending phase, entered a meditation in which you tried to actually reach that light.

- Spend several minutes thinking about how salvation is your true will, what you really want. (To prepare yourself, I recommend rereading paragraphs 6–9, frequently inserting your name while you do so.) Think about how you truly want to reach the light in you. Think about how salvation is your will, not an alien purpose thrust upon you. Since reaching the light is your will, you can be confident in your attempt to find it today. Carry this attitude of "reaching the light is my will" into your meditation.

- Then, "with gentle firmness and quiet certainty" (10:1), tell yourself, *"I will there be light. Let me behold the light that reflects God's Will and mine."*

- The rest of the practice period is a meditation in which you try to reach the light in you. Hold your true will in mind and let it, joined with God and your Self, lead you to that radiant light at the center of your mind. Remember to respond to wandering thoughts with the idea, and most of all, remember to stay in touch with your will to experience the light.

Frequent reminders: Several per hour.

Say, *"I will there be light. Darkness is not my will."* If you say it as a genuine "declaration of what you really want" (11:1), you will get more out of it.

Response to temptation: Whenever you are tempted to hold a grievance.

It is important to *immediately* say, *"I will there be light. Darkness is not my will."* Remembering that it is not your will to have grievances will release your grip on them.

Commentary

This is a lesson about our will, "the will you share with God" (1:1). I'd like to focus just on what is specifically said in this lesson about our will.

First, it is a will we share with God. That is, what the Course calls our will is identical to God's Will. We want the same thing God wants for us, because we were created as extensions of His Will; what else could our will be except the same as His?

> Your fatherhood and your Father are one. God wills to create, and your will is His. It follows, then, that you will to create, since your will follows from His. And being an extension of His Will, yours must be the same.
>
> (T-11.I.7:6–9)

Our "true" will (which by the Course's definition is our *only* will) is not the same as the ego's wishes, the manifold variety of thoughts that seem to conflict with God's Will and with each other. From the Course's standpoint these are *not* our will, just ego wishes. A desire to attack, no matter how strongly we may consciously identify with it, cannot be our will; it can only be an idle wish of the ego. Our will represents our Self as God created us; anything that seems to come from a different source is not *will* but *wish*. What this means in practical terms is that our ego thoughts are not part of our true Self, and in reality we do not will them.

"The will you share with God has all the power of creation in it" (1:3). Our will therefore must be realized; nothing can oppose it. We will have what we truly want because our will has all the power of creation, while the ego's wishes have no power at all. We exist in the illusion that our ego's wishes are almost all-powerful, and what we may think of as our *higher* will often seems weak by comparison. This is simply not true. It can only appear to be true for a limited time; eventually, inevitably, the will of our Self must be done.

"Your will is lost to you in this strange bartering" (3:1). Our conscious awareness is out of touch with the will of our Self. Our ego's need for grievances has created shadow figures in our minds, "figures that seem to attack you" (2:2), images from the past that we superimpose over our perceptions in the present, so that we react to people in the present as if they were these figures from our past. This traffic in grievances has blocked our real will from our awareness, covering it with the wishes of the ego until those wishes seem to be our will. We are no longer aware of what it is we really want.

"Can such a world have been created by the Will the Son of God shares with his Father?" (3:2). The obvious answer is "no." How could we have willed a world of attack and judgment? This is obviously not something anyone would want. The world we see reflects the ego's wishes, not our will.

"Today we will try once more to reach the world that is in accordance with your will" (4:1). This is the "real world," as the Course defines that term. There *is* a world in accord with our will. We are not seeing it now, but we can.

"Yet the light that shines upon this world reflects your will, and so it must be in you that we will look for it" (4:6). The real world reflects our true will, what we truly want in our eternal Self. The light that shines on it is in us, and we can find that world by looking within ourselves for the light.

"Forgiveness lifts the darkness, reasserts your will, and lets you look upon a world of light" (5:4). Forgiveness lets go of grievances, thus removing the dark spots on our mind that are being projected as black blotches of darkness on the world, just as a dust mote in a movie projector throws a black spot on the screen. Forgiveness allows us to see the world as our Self truly wants to see it; it reasserts our will.

"Suffering is not happiness, and it is happiness you really want. Such is your will in truth" (6:5). It seems silly to say something like "Suffering is not happiness," and yet we often treat it as if it were happiness. We seem to prefer our pain over risking something new; at least we *know how* to suffer, and we are oddly afraid that we won't know how to function if we are happy. But we don't really want suffering; how could we? How could anyone? Our will, in truth, is happiness.

"And so salvation is your will as well" (6:7). If we want happiness,

223

we want salvation, because salvation is happiness. Salvation means happiness. We want to be relieved of suffering; we want to be happy.

It amazes me sometimes how powerful a message this can be. Most of the time it seems as if I have a split mind; part of me wants to be happy, and part of me sabotages my every effort. Isn't it peculiar how common is this thought: "It's too good to last"? Or "Nothing lasts forever"? Or "Into each life a little rain must fall"? Something in us tells us that we *can't* be happy all the time, that we don't deserve it, or even that we couldn't stand it. Ridiculous ideas! The will of our true Self, with all the power of creation behind it, is that we be happy. Therefore— we will be. It must be so.

> You want to accept God's plan because you share in it. You
> have no will that can really oppose it, and you do not want
> to do so. (7:2–3)

I really do want the Will of God; my will is the same as His! I want to accept salvation. There is no part of my will that opposes it; only idle, paltry ego wishes seem to. So I can't miss; I can't fail. My will is *not* different from God's.

> Above all else, you want the freedom to remember Who
> you really are. Today it is the ego that stands powerless
> before your will. Your will is free, and nothing can prevail
> against it. (7:5–7)

The power of your will and mine can bring light to this world if we simply choose to assert it. We simply realize what we truly want, and say, "I will there be light." And there will be light. Just as God said, "Let there be light," and there was light. Because our will is creative, as His is.

LESSON 74 ✦ MARCH 15
"There is no will but God's."

Practice instructions

Purpose: To realize that you cannot be in conflict, because your will and every will is really God's Will. To experience the peace that comes from this fact.

Longer: Two times, for ten to fifteen minutes.

- Say, *"There is no will but God's. I cannot be in conflict."* Repeat these sentences in a special way: "several times, slowly and with firm determination to understand what they mean, and to hold them in mind" (3:1).

- Then for several minutes let related thoughts come. Remember your training in this.

- If thoughts intrude about conflicts in your life, quickly dispel them by saying, *"There is no will but God's. These conflict thoughts are meaningless."* If a particular conflict keeps intruding, single it out. Briefly identify the person(s) and situation(s) involved and say, *"There is no will but God's. I share it with Him. My conflicts about _____ cannot be real."* You'll probably need to keep your eyes open for this part to consult the sentences you need to repeat.

- At this point, your mind should be clear and ready to turn inward. The rest of the exercise is a meditation in which you sink down and inward, into the peaceful place where God's Will is your will. If you are succeeding, you will feel an alert, joyful peace. Do not let yourself slip off into a drowsy pseudo-peace. Repeat the idea as often as you need to in order to draw yourself back from this.

Remarks: The comments in paragraphs 5 and 6 are among the most important remarks on meditation in the Workbook. You should carry their counsel into every meditation. On the one hand, they tell you not to mistake meditation for withdrawal from life's conflicts into a mental fantasyland. On the other hand, they urge you to do everything in your power to avoid such withdrawal. This means: Do not let yourself float off into that sleepy pseudo-peace that meditation can so easily turn into. Real peace is alert and joyful, not sleepy and sluggish. When you start to go off into withdrawal, repeat the idea to draw your mind back. "Do this as often as necessary" (6:4). It is better to do this over and over, and never find the peace you seek, than to drift off into that drowsy haze (see 6:5).

Frequent reminders: At regular intervals that you predetermine (suggestion: every half hour), for one or two minutes.

* Say: *"There is no will but God's. I seek His peace today."*
* Then do a brief meditation in which you try to find that peace, with eyes closed, if possible.

Commentary

The lesson states that this idea "can be regarded as the central thought toward which all our exercises are directed" (1:1). The Course makes similar claims about ideas that seem quite different from this one, for instance: "There is no world!" (W-pI.132.6:2). All of the ideas so identified, however, boil down to what we can call "nondualism." That is, God is unopposed; nothing apart from Him and His creations exists. There is no devil, no power that opposes God, nothing that exists independent of Him and therefore capable of having a differing will.

To say that nothing can have a will that differs from God's must include ourselves. The result of believing this is that conflict leaves our minds. How could our mind be in conflict if we have no will that can conflict with God's?

What, though, can we say of our common experience of wanting things that we think are opposed to God, or of wanting to do what He does not want us to do? Or even more down to earth, the experiencing of being torn between conflicting desires? If there is no will but God's, how is such experience possible?

The real answer is, it is not possible, unless there are illusions involved: "Without illusions conflict is impossible" (2:4). Conflict exists only between two illusions. In reality there is no conflict, and reality does not conflict with illusions, either:

> The war against yourself is but the battle of two

illusions…There *is* no conflict between them and the truth….Truth does not fight against illusions, nor do illusions fight against the truth. Illusions battle only with themselves. (T-23.I.6:1–2; 7:3–4)

When there seems to be a will opposed to God, whether outside of us or within us, we are seeing illusions.

"There is no will but God's. I cannot be in conflict" (3:2–3). This is the truth. I have often found that conflict thoughts in my mind can be defused simply by recognizing that they are meaningless, and that the conflict cannot be real. No peace is possible if I believe that my mind can be in conflict, but when I realize I cannot be in conflict, incredible peace results.

There is a very interesting observation in paragraph 5 about discerning the reality of peaceful feelings as opposed to false peace resulting from withdrawal and repression. According to 5:4, true peace brings "a deep sense of joy and an increased alertness," while false peace brings "drowsiness and enervation." In our attempts to enter the quiet and feel our peace, we are admonished to avoid withdrawal and to pull ourselves back to alertness by repeating today's idea. "There is definite gain in refusing to allow retreat into withdrawal, even if you do not experience the peace you seek" (6:5). From this we can surmise that even conscious conflict is better than repressed conflict, although the goal is to realize the unreality of the conflict and thus experience peace.

Another thought: These are really very detailed meditation instructions, and they demonstrate that students are really expected to be trying to do these exercises for ten or fifteen minutes twice daily.

LESSON 75 ✦ MARCH 16
"The light has come."

Practice instructions

Purpose: To set aside your unforgiving perceptions of the world and look with vision upon the real world. Today is cause for special celebration, for it will be a new beginning, "the beginning of your vision and the sight of the real world" (11:2).

Longer: Two times, for ten to fifteen minutes.

- Tell yourself, as if announcing "the glad tidings of your release" (5:3), *"The light has come. I have forgiven the world."*

- The rest of the practice period is an exercise in trying to see the world that vision shows you. Begin by consciously withdrawing all the meanings you have put on the world. Imagine that your mind is "washed of all past ideas and clean of every concept you have made" (6:2). Imagine that "you do not know yet what [the world] looks like" (6:5). This act of wiping off the meanings you have written on the world is also an act of forgiving the world, and this is what grants you vision.

- Then wait, with eyes open, to have vision dawn upon you. While doing so, occasionally repeat, slowly and patiently, *"The light has come. I have forgiven the world."* The main attitude to hold while you wait is *confidence*, that you will experience vision because "your forgiveness entitles you to vision" (7:1), and because the Holy Spirit will be there with you and will not fail to give you the gift of vision. Tell these things to yourself and to the Holy Spirit while you wait, and thereby give yourself the confidence you need. And when your confidence fades, repeat again the lines with which you began, and then continue waiting for vision to dawn.

Frequent reminders: Every fifteen minutes.

Joyfully remind yourself that today is a time to celebrate by saying, *"The light has come. I have forgiven the world."* Say it with a sense of thankfulness to God. Say it as a rejoicing in the healing of your sight. Say it in the confidence "that on this day there is a new beginning" (9:5).

Response to temptation: Whenever you are tempted to be upset with someone.

Do not let this person pull you back to darkness. Say to him instead, *"The light has come. I have forgiven you."*

Commentary

In this lesson, as in several others, the Course speaks of me as though I have accepted its message and have forgiven the world; as though I am ready, this very day, to see the real world; as though I have attained its goal of peace. Perhaps today I do not feel quite worthy of such confidence. Yet, if what we have been reading the past two days is true, any impression that I may have that my will differs from God's is only an illusion. My true Self, which in my right mind I am aware of, is exactly as this lesson depicts me. This lesson is the truth about myself, whether or not I have yet recognized it.

If I feel a little hypocritical in practicing this lesson exactly as instructed, so be it. If I have self-doubts that arise when I say, "I have forgiven the world" (5:5; 6:9; 10:3), I let them be there; I attribute no power to them to disturb me. I am simply affirming the truth about myself. Today, I am at peace, and I bring peace with me wherever I go (1:5). "The light has come." I let myself believe it; I let myself enter into knowing that frame of mind.

Whatever my experience today, this lesson is the truth. I cannot stand against what is within me; I cannot be other than what God created me to be. "The outcome is as certain as God," as the Text says (T-2.III.3:10). "Our single purpose makes the goal inevitable" (4:3). I *will* see the real world; I will see Heaven's reflection everywhere.

Do I feel I lack the certainty of this lesson's words? That is exactly why I need to practice saying them. Perhaps if I give my little willingness to speak them, affirming that this is what I want to be true, the Holy Spirit will add His strength to my words and make them true for me. Perhaps even today. "The light has come." It is here, right now, with me, available to me.

The Holy Spirit "will be with you as you watch and wait. He will show you what true vision sees. It is His Will, and you have joined with Him. Wait patiently for Him. He will be there" (7:5–9). So I wait. I wait "patiently" and not anxiously. It may take time to manifest, but I wait patiently, confidently, knowing that His promise cannot fail. The vision I seek will come to me. "He will be there."

We are told to "tell Him you know you cannot fail because you trust in Him" (8:1). So I say it; I pray, "Holy Spirit, I know I cannot fail because I trust in You." I affirm my confidence in my Self; I affirm the truth about me, and put aside the lies I have believed. I can be confident that this day is a new beginning for me. Something has shifted within me, and I know that I want the peace and the light this lesson speaks of. I know that since I want it—because of what I am, and because I am joined with the power of the Holy Spirit in wanting it, in agreement with the Will of God—I cannot fail.

Today is dedicated to serenity (11:1). Today is for celebration of the beginning of my vision. I accept myself as God created me. "The light has come."

LESSON 76 ✦ MARCH 17
"I am under no laws but God's."

Practice instructions

Purpose: To really understand that you are under no laws but God's, to see the freedom in this idea, and to rejoice that it is so.

Longer: Two times, for ten to fifteen minutes.

- In the first phase, briefly review the different "laws" you believe in. These include *bodily* laws, such as laws of nutrition, medicine, and economics; *social* laws, such as laws of reciprocity and good relationship; and *religious* laws, which set forth what you must give to God in order for Him to grant you His gifts.

- Dismiss these "laws" with the thought that there are no laws but God's. Then wait in receptive silence to hear God's Voice (this is another exercise in listening to the Holy Spirit). While listening, from time to time repeat the idea, as an invitation to God's Voice to help you really understand the idea. When you hear the Holy Spirit, He may tell you that God's laws, in contrast to the world's "laws," only give. They do not ask for payment before they deliver you their endless blessings. He may go on to tell you of all the blessings these laws offer you, including the limitless joys of Heaven, all of which stem from God's infinite Love for you. Remember to listen in *confidence*, knowing that even if you hear nothing now, God's Voice is still speaking to you, and that your listening today will bring you closer to really hearing. If you do hear something, you may want to write it down afterwards.

- Conclude by repeating the idea.

Frequent reminders: Four to five per hour (at least).

Repeat the idea as a declaration of freedom from all the tyrannical laws of this world and an acknowledgment that you live only under the blessing of God's Love.

Response to temptation: Whenever you feel subject to the laws of this world.

Repeat the idea. Because we usually take the laws of the world for granted, we don't always realize when we feel oppressed by them. Therefore, you may want to periodically scan your mind for the things that are weighing on you and identify the laws behind them. At any given moment, for instance, you might find that you feel oppressed by the laws of hunger, of time (you may be working against a deadline), of money (you may feel a shortage), and of social dynamics (you may be in a politically delicate situation). Note the laws you feel oppressing you and respond by repeating the idea as a real declaration of your freedom from them.

Commentary

This is perhaps one of the most challenging lessons in the Workbook. It confronts, head on, a whole panoply of security blankets and substitutes for salvation that we have developed, and that we have convinced ourselves we depend on. It shocks us by its radical assertions. If we are open to what it says, we will begin to see that the Course is challenging all of our basic assumptions about life and about ourselves. We are far more entrenched in the ego's illusions than we have heretofore realized.

The following scenario forms the background to this lesson:

1. We are perfect, formless mind, each of us parts of a seamless whole, but we have wished to separate off and fragment a small piece of mind to call "me." Moreover, we have not only wished to do so, we have convinced ourselves that we have actually done it. Our sense of identity has become restricted to this little fragment of mind. Our mind has felt enormous guilt because of this belief, which is false.

2. We have made up a world filled with bodies for two reasons: first, to support our illusions of separateness; and second, to escape from the guilt in our minds by projecting that guilt onto the world and the "others" who fill it. We have become primarily identified with our own body, rather than even with the fragment of mind we perceive as being "within" the body.

3. Believing we are the body, and that we (our bodies) are endangered by many things in the world, we have devised an endless list of means for protecting and preserving our bodies. These are the "laws" of the world spoken of in this lesson.

The first sentence of Lesson 76 refers to an earlier statement, in the first three paragraphs of Lesson 71, that pointed out how many senseless things we have looked to for our salvation (which can be understood as protection, or safety, or even happiness). In Lesson 71, the key factor about each of these things was this thought: "If this were different, I would be saved" (W-pI.71.2:4). Lesson 76 now adds the thought that "each [of these things] has imprisoned you with laws as senseless as itself" (1:2). For example, if we look to good physical health to "save" us, we become bound by a myriad of laws governing health: nutrition, medicine, and so on.

The lesson identifies many of the so-called laws we believe ourselves to be subject to: the need for money (paper strips and metal discs); the use of medicine to ward off disease; the need for physical interaction with other bodies (sex, companionship); laws of medicine, economics, and health (nutrition, exercise, sleep, vitamins); any way we try to protect the body; "laws" of friendship, of "good" relationships, and reciprocity (being fair); even "religious" laws.

We are not actually bound by any of these laws (1:3). That is a stunning and almost unbelievable statement. In order to understand our freedom from these laws, however, we "must first realize salvation lies not there" (1:4). In other words, we have to realize that our bodies and our egos are not what need preservation. We have to undo the mistake we have made in identifying what and who we are. That undoing, of course, is what the entirety of *A Course in Miracles* is all about.

In saying that we "bind" ourselves "to laws that make no sense" (1:5) as long as we are seeking for salvation by attempting to change something—anything—other than our minds, the Course is telling us that our subjugation to these laws of the world is something that we have *chosen* and are continuing to choose, moment to moment. Following the dictates of our own ego in its attempts to preserve itself at the expense of our reality, we blindly continue to look for salvation outside of ourselves. That blind pursuit is what binds us to the laws of the world. By implication, ending that mistaken pursuit will *free* us from the laws of the world.

We think miracles mean sudden healing of the body, or the arrival of money from an unexpected source, or the appearance of someone or something we believe will bring us happiness. To believe this is still to seek for salvation from outside of our own minds, and will continue to bind us to the laws of the world. What's worse, it also continues to make our separated, ego identity seem real to us.

The idea of living without any need for money, or medicine, or physical means of protection appeals to everyone. That state can be ours, but paradoxically, not by seeking for it. The world and its laws are not where freedom lies. Having all the money we need magically provided is not freedom. Having perfect physical health is not freedom. Having "good" relationships is not freedom. Freedom has nothing to do with our bodies. Freedom can be found only within ourselves.

"The body is endangered by the mind that hurts itself" (5:2). All of our physical lack and suffering is unconsciously engendered by our minds, in an attempt to keep the mind from consciously realizing that it is its own victim (5:3–5). Because of our primal guilt, caused by our belief in the reality of separation, our mind "attacks itself and wants to die" (5:5). This is why we think we are bodies (which do die). The "laws" we think we must obey in order to save our bodies are just the mind's attempt to camouflage the real problem, which is its own thoughts of guilt and separation.

"God's laws forever give and never take" (9:6). The "laws" we see are not like this; therefore they cannot be real, because they do not come from God. And "there are no laws but God's" (9:1). In today's practice we are asked to consider our foolish laws, and then to listen, deep within, to "hear the Voice that speaks the truth to you" (9:2). This Voice will tell us of God's undying Love, His desire that we know "endless joy" (10:5), and His yearning to use us as channels for His creation (10:6). If we hear this message of Love within ourselves, our thoughts of guilt and separation will vanish. We will realize Who we are. And in so doing, our insane desire to attack and kill ourselves will be over. The *cause* of our false seeking will go, and with it, our bondage to the "laws" that govern these idols we have made.

By bringing our imaginary "laws" into direct confrontation with what the laws of God must be—laws in which there is no loss, no giving and receiving of payment, no exchanges nor substitutions, but only God's unconditional Love—we are bringing our illusions to the truth. (See T-14.VII.1–4, for an excellent discussion of just why these two systems of belief need to be brought together so that the falsehoods will vanish in the light of the truth.)

LESSON 77 ✦ MARCH 18
"I am entitled to miracles."

Practice instructions

Purpose: To claim the miracles that belong to you, to claim the assurance that they really are yours, and to refuse to be content with anything less.

Longer: Two times, for ten to fifteen minutes.

- Repeat the idea as a confident request for the miracles that God has promised you. Close your eyes and remind yourself 1) that you are requesting what belongs to you, and 2) that by accepting miracles you uphold everyone's right to miracles.
- For the remainder of the practice period, wait in silent expectancy for the Holy Spirit to assure you that your request is granted, that you really are entitled to miracles. This, in other words, is yet another exercise in waiting for something from the Holy Spirit. In previous lessons (71, 72, 75, 76), you waited for guidance, understanding, or an experience of vision. Here you are waiting for the assurance that the storehouse of miracles really is open to you, really is yours. The same things apply here as in the previous lessons:

1. Wait in mental silence and expectancy.

2. Wait in confidence. Since you are asking for the assurance of something that is already true, you can ask without any doubt or uncertainty.

3. Periodically renew your request and your confidence by repeating the idea.

Frequent reminders: Frequent.

Repeat the idea. Throughout the day, be on the lookout for situations in which miracles are called for. "You will recognize these situations" (7:5). Then ask confidently for a miracle by repeating the idea.

Response to temptation: Whenever you are tempted to hold a grievance.

Say quickly, *"I will not trade miracles for grievances. I want only what belongs to me. God has established miracles as my right."* Refuse to be satisfied with anything less than miracles.

Commentary

What we celebrate today is our true Identity as beings who are one with God (1:3, 5, 6). The key to what the Course calls "salvation" is simply remembering what we are. I like the threefold summary that opens the lesson. Just rearranging the words a little, the three items are:

- What we are entitles us to miracles.
- What God is guarantees we will receive miracles.
- Our oneness with God means we will offer miracles to others.

Nothing we think about ourselves, no special powers we believe we have, and no rituals we observe bring us miracles. They come to us because of what we are, because of something inherent in our being. The qualifications for miracles are given in creation; we don't have to earn them.

> [The Holy Spirit] will never ask what you have done to make you worthy of the gift of God. Ask it not therefore of yourself. Instead, accept His answer, for He knows that you are worthy of everything God wills for you. Do not try to escape the gift of God He so freely and so gladly offers you. He offers you but what God gave Him for you. You need not decide whether or not you are deserving of it. God knows you are. (T-14.III.11:4–10)

The lesson affirms that we have been "promised full release from the world [we] made" (3:2), from all the darkness, pain, suffering and death resulting from our attempts at separateness. Beyond that we have been "assured that the Kingdom of God is within you, and can never be lost" (3:3). Today we are deciding not to question those premises, but to accept them as given facts. The darkness *can* be escaped, and the light has never been lost. And so, today, we set our minds in determination

237

"that we will not content ourselves with less" (3:5).

The longer practice periods begin with a brief time of affirmation, reminding ourselves that we have a *right* to miracles, and that miracles are never given to one at the expense of another. In asking for myself, I am asking for everyone. After that brief reminder, the time of practice is to be spent in quiet, waiting for an inner sense of assurance that the miracles we have asked for *have been given*. Since we are asking exactly what God's Will is, for the salvation of the world, there is every reason to believe that He will respond favorably to our requests.

Actually, asking for miracles isn't really asking for anything. It is an affirmation of what is always already true. The Holy Spirit can't help assuring us our request is granted! (6:1–3). How can He possibly respond differently? He cannot deny our prayer without denying the truth, and He speaks *only* for the truth. "Nothing real can be threatened. Nothing unreal exists" (T-In.2:2–3). That is what this kind of prayer affirms.

In the description of the short practice periods, we are told to ask for miracles "whenever a situation arises in which they are called for" (7:4). Then it says, "You will recognize these situations" (7:5). There is no question here, not even a need to explain how we'll know. "You *will* recognize these situations." Something in us simply *knows* when to ask for a miracle. Notice too that we do not try to generate the miracle ourselves, out of our own resources; we ask the Holy Spirit. We are turning with our need to the Source of miracles; we are not trying to take the place of the Source. We do depend on what we are as our entitlement to miracles, but we are not relying on ourselves to find them (7:6).

Let's remember that a "miracle" as the Course understands it does not necessarily mean any kind of visible changes. "Miracles are thoughts" (T-1.I.12:1). They are shifts *away* from the bodily level, a way in which we recognize our own worth and our brother's at the same time (T-1.I.17:2; 18:4). A miracle is a correction of false thinking (T-1.I.37:1). Miracles are always expressions of love, "but they may not always have observable effects" (T-1.I.35:1).

Let's remember, also, that "may not always" does not mean "will never." If I say, "I often eat Wheaties for breakfast but I may not always eat them," the implication is that a lot of the time I *do* eat Wheaties. So when the Course says that miracles may not always have observable effects, it clearly implies that most of the time they *do* have observable effects. We should not mistakenly think a miracle has not happened if there are no observable effects, but neither should we mistakenly set aside *any* expectation of observable effects. The essential ingredient, however, is not anything in the material world, but the freeing of our minds from illusions.

LESSON 78 ✦ MARCH 19
"Let miracles replace all grievances."

Practice instructions

Purpose: To lay down the dark shield of our grievances and "and gently lift our eyes in silence to behold the Son of God" (2:3).

Longer: Two times, for ten to fifteen minutes.

- Select a person about whom you have grievances. Read the list in paragraph 4 and choose the person who comes to mind while reading that list.
- Close your eyes and review how you currently see this person, in two ways. First, review his negative deeds and traits: his faults, his mistakes, his "sins," and all the ways in which he has caused you difficulty and pain. Second, review his body, both "its flaws and better points" (6:4). Visualizing his body is a great way to get in touch with the grievances you carry toward him.
- Then ask the Holy Spirit to show you the shining savior this person really is, beyond your grievances. Say, *"Let me behold my savior in this one You have appointed as the one for me to ask to lead me to the holy light in which he stands, that I may join with him."* This very long sentence is a powerful reversal of how you currently see this person. Now, you see him as an attacker who stands apart from you. This sentence, however, depicts him as your savior, whose holiness will lead you into the radiance of his true reality, where you will discover that you and he are one. The only thing needed for him to fulfill this role is for you to see him truly, which is what the sentence invites. So don't just say the sentence once. Repeat it many times during the practice period.
- This sentence invites an actual experience from the Holy Spirit. It invites Him to reveal to you this person's shining reality, which lies past your grievances. So this is yet another exercise in asking for some inward thing from the

Holy Spirit. Remember the training you've received in this:

1. Wait in stillness. "Be very quiet now, and look upon your shining savior" (8:6).

2. Wait in confidence. "What you have asked for cannot be denied" (8:1).

3. Periodically renew your request by repeating the sentence.

Frequent reminders/response to temptation: Whenever you *meet* or *think of* or *remember* someone.

Pray, *"Let miracles replace all grievances."* This means, *"Let the miracle of Who you really are replace my grievances about you."* Realize that this releases both of you, along with everyone else.

Commentary

If I did not have grievances everything would be miraculous to me. The contention of the Course is that the truth is obvious, and only seems difficult to see because we block it from our awareness with our grievances. The very purpose of a grievance is to conceal the miracle hiding beneath it (1:2). The miracle is still there, nevertheless.

Today we want to look on miracles. "We will reverse the way you see by not allowing sight to stop before it sees" (2:2). That is what we are in the habit of doing—allowing our sight to stop at the external appearance, without moving our perception beyond that to what the appearance is hiding. What we see at first, the external appearance, is our "shield of hate" (1:2; 2:3). It always shows us things that bring us grief in one way or another. We do not want to stop at that today; we want to lay down the shield and "lift our eyes in silence to behold the Son of God" (2:3).

The Son of God is hidden in every one of us. Only our grievances prevent us from seeing him everywhere.

Some of us may be very aware of grievances; others of us may wonder what on earth is being talked about. But if we look honestly at the thoughts in our minds, unless we live in perfect true perception already, free from all suffering, wholly joyful always, we will find grievances there. We often do not recognize them for what they are.

There is a real need for honest self-assessment to recognize the shields in our minds that block the light from our sight.

Look at some of the suggestions (in 4:5) for picking a person with whom to practice this lesson. Someone we "fear and even hate" is probably obvious to us, if we have such a person in our lives; we can recognize this as a grievance easily. "Someone you think you love who angered you" is probably also quite clear; yes, that is a grievance. A friend "whom you see as difficult at times"—is *that* a grievance that blocks light from me? Yes, indeed. Someone "hard to please"? Someone we see as demanding, or who we view as being "irritating"? Are these grievances? Yes! And even someone "untrue to the ideal he should accept as his, according to the role you set for him." How many of us, who tend to view ourselves as spiritual students of the Course, would have recognized this subtle judgment as a grievance?

Yes, that opinion you hold about that person who hasn't lived up to his or her potential, the one you think you love and care for and show so much concern about—that is also a grievance, blocking the light of the Son of God from your vision.

I love the way Jesus says, "You know the one to choose; his name has crossed your mind already" (5:1). He so often seems to be intimately familiar with the inside of our minds, doesn't he?

This exercise is a powerful one. It is also very practical and down to earth, dealing with one specific person in our lives. "Let him be savior unto you today" (5:5).

Him? Savior? You want me to let *that person* be savior to me? How can I possibly see him like that?

If questions like that come to me, they only demonstrate the illusory solidity of the shield of grievance in my mind. The Son of God is evident in "that one" if I am willing to let go of my grievances.

Now remember: We're just doing an exercise here. Maybe you don't feel ready yet to entirely let go of all grievances, to relinquish your judgment of this person forever. Okay. How about just practicing it for ten or fifteen minutes? Just try it on for size, see what it feels like. That's all that is being asked.

This is how we save the world—by just this kind of practice. Christ is waiting in each of us to be released. You have the power to release him in everyone around you today, simply by looking past your grievances and seeing Christ in them. The Holy Spirit in your brothers and sisters "leans from [them] to you, seeing no separation in God's Son" (8:4). By allowing your brother to play the role of savior in your mind, you have "allowed the Holy Spirit to express through him the role God gave Him that you might be saved" (8:8). You have seen him as he is, and that vision in your mind will awaken his to see the truth about himself. You will call it out of him through your faith. This is how we play the role of savior ourselves; as you draw it forth from your brothers, their gratitude will teach you the truth about yourself, and you will realize that something in you has manifested in saving grace to lift your brother. What you have given, you must have had in order to give it. The salvation you have given him is yours, and you recognize it because you gave it. That is how this process works. We can practice it even in our minds with people from our past (10:3).

So I take the role assigned me by God. I choose today to let miracles replace all grievances in my mind. Whenever I notice a grievance, I will ask that a miracle replace it. Let me see you, my friend, as my savior today. Thank you for being there. Thank you for giving me this opportunity to give.

LET ME BEHOLD MY SAVIOR

Lesson 78 in the Workbook is one of those lessons that gives us an exercise for forgiving a particular person in our lives. First the lesson directs us in how to select this person. Then we review at some length our current picture of him, including the things we resent him for. Finally, after three and a half paragraphs, we are given the core of the exercise, the words which will guide our minds into a place of forgiveness. These words, however, can seem less like a transformative exercise and more like a confusing jumble. They take the form of a very long sentence, broken by only one comma:

> Let me behold my savior in this one You have appointed
> as the one for me to ask to lead me to the holy light in
> which he stands, that I may join with him. (W-pI.78.7:3)

For years this exercise meant little or nothing to me. In recent years, however, I have come to treasure these lines. To really feel the transformative impact, it helps to break this sentence up and take in its meaning and its imagery one piece at a time.

"Let me behold my savior in this one"

In this opening line you are asking the Holy Spirit to reveal something you haven't seen in your brother, something that lies beyond your ugly picture of him. You are asking to "let your mind be shown the light in him beyond your grievances" (as the line after the exercise says). Just past your image of him as a callous attacker, you are asking to behold in him your *savior.*

Now, "savior" here does not mean "the one who gives you all those juicy opportunities to forgive." What does it mean? The line that introduces the exercise says this: "Then let us ask [the Holy Spirit], that we may...see our savior shining in the light of true forgiveness, given unto us." In reality, your brother is someone so holy that he radiates the light of true forgiveness, *given unto you.* He is your savior because, when you gaze on who he really is, his holy light streams into your mind and shines all your guilt away. That is how he saves you. That is what you are asking to experience.

"You have appointed as the one for me to ask"

This brother holds something so valuable that the Holy Spirit has appointed him to be "the one." That is why, when the lesson was asking you to select a person, his name popped into your mind. He has been appointed, and something in your mind knew that. In particular, he has been appointed as the one that you will ask something of. The next line tells us what that something is.

"to lead me to the holy light in which he stands,"

You are asking him to take you by the hand and lead you into the light. Notice that you are consistently portrayed as being in the receptive role. You are being saved, being answered, being led. Seeing yourself as the humble recipient of the salvation he imparts is a total reversal of your current view, in which you are the superior victim of the damnation he brings.

This line paints a concrete image. So visualize it; see him leading you into "the holy light in which he stands." Of course, you need not wait for him to consciously lead you there (or you may be waiting a very long time). You need simply see the truth in him, for its very nature is to lead you to its light.

Standing is more than a physical act. It carries a wealth of connotations. To say that this is "the holy light in which he stands" is to say that this light is the state he exists in. It is where he has established himself. It is the stand he has taken. This light is what he is about. He is *of* the light.

This is what makes standing with him in the light such a powerful image. For, of course, once he leads you there, you will be standing there together. The Course likes this image so much it uses it again just nine lessons later (in 87.2:3), where it gives us this suggested practice: *"You stand with me in light, [name]."*

"that I may join with him."

The exercise now concludes. Your savior has led you to the light that is his home, and there, standing with him, bathed in light, you and he unite. Now, everything he has is yours as well. The light in which he stands is your light. The salvation that was his to give is your salvation. For you and he are one.

That you are not just joining him, but doing so in *light*, gives the joining a sense of holiness. It implies that what is uniting is only what is true and pure in the two of you. And it implies a three-way joining, in which you and he join not only with each other, but with the light as well.

This exercise has taken us through an entire process of healing, through a complete reversal. We began by seeing this person as dishing out to us darkness and grief. In our eyes, he stood not only apart from us but beneath us. Then we learned that he was appointed by the Holy Spirit for a holy task. He is the one of whom we are meant to ask salvation. As we asked, we saw him lead us by the hand into the light of our salvation, the radiance in which he lives. And there, standing together in the light, we united with him, so that what he is are we as well. Now he no longer stands apart from us, nor beneath us. We see past that false image of him as our attacker and our judge. Now, at last, we behold our savior.

LESSON 79 ✦ MARCH 20
"Let me recognize the problem so it can be solved."

Practice instructions

Longer: Two times, for ten to fifteen minutes.

- Try to free your mind of your perception of your problems. Do your best to "entertain some doubt about the reality of your version of what your problems are" (8:3). Try to realize that the many-ness of your problems is a smokescreen, hiding the fact that you have only one problem. Do not, however, define what this one problem is.
- Then ask what your one problem is and wait for the answer. Even though the lesson has said your problem is separation, set that aside and listen for an answer that genuinely comes from within you.
- Then ask what is the answer to the one problem. In asking about the problem and the answer, apply your training in how to listen to the Holy Spirit: wait in mental silence, wait in confidence ("We will be told"—7:6), and periodically repeat your request while you wait.

Response to temptation: Whenever you see a problem.

- Recognize that this is simply the one problem showing up in disguise. Say immediately, *"Let me recognize this problem so it can be solved."*
- Then try to lay aside what you think the problem is. If you can, close eyes and ask what it is. You will be told.

Commentary

This lesson, with the next, presents one of the clearest statements of an important Course principle: "One problem, one solution," as it is stated in Lesson 80 (1:5). These lessons merit repeated reading until the concepts they teach become embedded in our thought processes.

I seem to be faced with a multitude of problems, overwhelming in number and complexity, ranging from tiny to titanic, constantly shifting, changing, appearing and disappearing in the moments of my life. If I pause to consider things objectively from this viewpoint the only possible response is blind panic. Attention paid to one problem obliterates dozens of others, equally deserving of my attention, from conscious consideration. Like Lucy and Ethel on the pie conveyor, as things speed up I can only start stuffing some of the "pastries" down my shirt, trying to hide them before my failure to handle them becomes evident.

Seen from the perspective of specialness, my problems doom me to failure after failure, with every moment increasing my overwhelming sense of inadequacy.

What if all of these problems were really just one? What if I already had the solution to that one problem? I can scarcely imagine the universal sense of relief that would run through my being if I could grasp that this were true: All of my problems are one, and that one has already been solved.

Could this be? Yes. If I think my problems are many and separate, if I have failed to recognize the one problem in them all, I could already have the answer and not know it. I could even be aware of the answer without realizing its application to what seem to me to be very different problems. "This is the situation of the world. The problem of separation, which is really the only problem, has already been solved. Yet the solution is not recognized because the problem is not recognized" (1:3–5).

To break free of this illusory imprisonment, then, my first step must be to recognize *the* problem in every problem. I have to become aware of what the problem is before I can realize that I already hold the solution to it. As long as I think the problem is something other than my separateness from God (which has already been so completely resolved that it has become a nonissue), I will continue to think I have problems and lack the solution. I will look for "salvation" from my problems everywhere but where the answer is because I have already discounted the answer as irrelevant to the problem at hand. "Who can see that a problem has been solved if he thinks the problem is something else?" (2:3).

The seeming complexity of the world is nothing more than my mind's attempt to *not* recognize the single problem, thus preventing its resolution (6:1). My greatest initial need, therefore, is to perceive "the underlying constancy in all the problems" (6:3). If I can see the separation at the root of every problem I would realize that I already have the answer, and I would *use* the answer. I would be free.

Again, this lesson is so wonderfully forgiving. Even the idea of seeing *all* my problems as variations on the theme of separation may seem an impossibly daunting task. So the lesson tells me:

> That is not necessary. All that is necessary is to entertain some doubt about the reality of your version of what your problems are.   (8:2–3)

The only thing I have to do is to doubt? Hey, I can handle that; I'm pretty good at doubting.

All I am being asked to do is to "suspend all judgment about what the problem is" (10:4). "Suspend" means to temporarily abate; the lesson does not even ask me to lay aside my judgments forever. Just for an instant. Just allow myself to doubt my personal perspective on things and consider that there might be another way of looking at it.

So today I am called to doubt. To doubt my version of what my problems are. To think to myself, "I'm probably not seeing this with complete clarity. I'm probably muddling the issues here somewhere." And then to ask, "What *is* the real problem here?" That kind of practice *even I* can handle. Thank You, God, for such a simple Course!

LESSON 80 ✦ MARCH 21
"Let me recognize my problems have been solved."

Practice instructions

Purpose: To claim the peace to which you are entitled by the fact that God has solved your only problem.

Longer: Two times, for ten to fifteen minutes.

This is an exercise in just basking in the awareness that you are problem-free. I see it as being much like Lesson 50 (you may want to review those instructions now), where you thought about the idea and rested in the peace that it provided. So do that here. Close your eyes and realize that, having recognized the problem (yesterday), you have also accepted the answer. This means that your one problem has been solved. Reflect on this. Think about the fact that all your problems are gone. Reflect on the fact that you are totally conflict-free. You have only one problem and God has solved it. Use these thoughts to claim the peace that now belongs to you. Lean back and relax in that peace. Rest in the feeling of being carefree.

Frequent reminders: As frequently as possible.

Repeat the idea (you may want to shorten it to *"My problems have been solved"*), with gratitude and with deep conviction. If you will, try now repeating it once with gratitude, and then try repeating it with deep conviction.

Response to temptation: Whenever a specific problem arises, especially an interpersonal one.

Immediately say, *"Let me recognize this problem has been solved."* Be determined not to saddle yourself with problems that don't exist.

Commentary

"One problem, one solution" (1:5). "The problem must be gone, because God's answer cannot fail" (4:2). So I must be at peace—whether I know it or not. I have no more problems. Seeing and understanding this, accepting it wholly, is the essence of salvation (1:8; 2:5; 5:6).

To see a problem as unresolved is to accumulate a grievance and to block the light from my awareness. An unresolved problem is an occasion of unforgiveness. It represents something I do not approve of, a cause of judgment in my mind. "Certain it is that all distress does not appear to be but unforgiveness. Yet that is the content underneath the form" (W-pI.193.4:1–2). When the Course speaks of our forgiving the world, it means the same thing as our recognizing that all problems are only forms of separation, which has already been resolved. The answer to every problem, therefore, is forgiveness, or accepting the Atonement, recognizing that nothing, whatever form nothing takes, can separate me from the love of God; nothing can take away my peace.

I am writing this on the last day (1995) of a visit with my son in California. I have spent two nights sleeping on an air mattress. Last night, the air mattress sprang a leak, and I woke about five o'clock with most of my body on the ground and my arms and legs still half floating several inches higher, a most uncomfortable position. I couldn't get back to sleep, so I am feeling short of sleep. I'm concerned about driving home from Phoenix late tonight, two hours in the dark desert, alone, and sleepy.

That seems to be a problem. How is that a form of unforgiveness? How is this problem of short sleep a manifestation of separation?

If I recognize that my only problem is separation and that it has been solved, I can realize that a lack of sleep cannot separate me from God's Love and peace. I can forgive the air mattress, or forgive my son for providing a flawed bed. I can forgive myself for worrying about the drive. I can accept that nothing is wrong and that my life is in the hands of God, and all will work out just as it should. Perhaps my body will be energized enough that I will not be sleepy as I drive home. Perhaps I will spend the night with friends in Phoenix even though that is not "my" plan. Perhaps I will pull off the road and sleep in my truck. Whatever happens, I do not need to be pulled out of peace by this event; my problem has been solved. I can be at peace *now*.

Or, if I so choose, I can destroy my last day with my son and grandchildren by obsessing about my problem. I can worry about falling asleep at the wheel. I can be upset because I may be forced to change my plan. I can be grumpy and grouchy and miss out on the love that is around me with my grandchildren. Is that really a choice I want to make?

A collapsing air mattress is not my problem. The only problem is allowing that, or anything like it, to disturb the peace of God that is always mine if I choose to have it. The only problem is separation from God. The events in our lives do not, and cannot, cause us to separate from Him. When we seem to be upset it is always a choice we make; the events we connect to that loss of peace are only a convenient excuse. Forgiveness involves recognizing our responsibility and lifting the blame for loss of peace from the persons and events of our lives and accepting that the peace of God has not been taken from us, cannot be taken from us, and indeed has never left us. We have merely closed our eyes to it. And we can open them again at any instant we choose to do so.

The events and persons may or may not change as a result. The Atonement does not plug the leak in the mattress. It may or may not supply me with more energy to make the drive to Sedona. Sometimes those things happen, sometimes they don't; it depends on what plan the Holy Spirit has for me. What happens externally is not the problem, and the solution lies not in externals, but within me. Will I choose peace, or choose upset? Will I forgive, or will I project my rejection of peace onto the external things and blame them?

Peace lies in acceptance. I accept God's peace *whatever* happens. I refuse to believe that anything can separate me from the Love of God. I refuse to deceive myself about what the problem really is. I recognize the problem is within me, and I bring the problem to the answer. And I rest, trusting the Holy Spirit to arrange the circumstances as He sees fit, not as I think they should be. I am out of conflict; I am free and at peace.

V

Review II: Introduction and Lessons 81 - 90

INTRODUCTION

A brief word on the review instructions. There are two longer practice periods (see "One or two?" below) of about fifteen minutes, in which we read over the two ideas and the associated comments, and then spend the bulk of the time with our eyes closed, "listening quietly but attentively" (W-pI.rII.In.3:1) for a message. Most longtime students of the Course agree that this does not mean we should expect to hear a voice, as Helen Schucman did, although some may. Messages can come in many forms: a feeling, an idea, an awareness without words. We are not used to sitting quietly just listening, and this is practice in doing so.

During the first half of the day we are to work with the first idea, and in the second half, the second idea. The shorter periods are not assigned any number; we are to continue the "frequent" applications of the previous lessons. If you take all the lessons in which a number is mentioned in regard to these shorter practices, the numbers average out to five per hour; I think we can assume that is about what is intended during these days of review.

Notice the seriousness attached to both the longer and shorter practices. I, for one, try to avoid the temptation to treat the review period as a time to slack off. This is what the author says:

> Regard these practice periods as dedications to the way, the truth and the life. Refuse to be sidetracked into detours, illusions and thoughts of death. You are dedicated to salvation. Be determined each day not to leave your function unfulfilled. (W-pI.rII.In.5:1–4)

This is a course in mind training. Our minds will not be trained if we do not practice. We will not learn listening if we do not practice. This is what doing the Workbook is all about.

Additional notes: One or two? (by Robert)

Many students wonder if we are meant to do one longer practice period or two. Actually, this is no easy issue to resolve. We batted it around for years here at the Circle. The first edition of this book had a section in which Allen presented our different opinions, without resolution. There were a couple of years in which, during our Workbook class, I called for a vote from students on whether they thought it was one or two. All of this was for good reason, for the way the section reads, there *is* no resolution. There are sentences that imply one practice period and sentences that imply two.

All of this got cleared up, however, when the Urtext, the original typescript of the Course, was disseminated on the Internet. This allowed us to see how this introduction originally read. I'll put the relevant part of the Urtext version and the published version in a table side by side (I've started each sentence on a separate line for the sake of comparison):

Urtext	Published Course
The earlier part of the day will be devoted to one of these ideas, and the latter part of the day to the other.	The earlier part of each day will be devoted to one of these ideas, and the latter part of the day to the other.

We will have one longer exercise period and frequent shorter ones in which we practice each of them.	We will have one longer exercise period, and frequent shorter ones in which we practice each of them.
The longer practice periods will follow this general form: Take about fifteen minutes for each of them, and begin by thinking about the idea and the comments which are included in the assignments.	The longer practice periods will follow this general form: Take about fifteen minutes for each of them, and begin by thinking about the ideas for the day, and the comments that are included in the assignments. (W-pI.rII.In.1:3-2:1)

A number of very minor changes have been made, but two of those minor changes made a big difference—they changed the practice periods from two to one.

1. In the second sentence, there was originally no comma. Without the comma, the "longer exercise period and frequent shorter ones" are grouped together, with the whole group being devoted to *one* idea. Thus, originally it meant, "[In each half of the day] we will have one longer exercise period and frequent shorter ones in which we practice each of them [each of the ideas]."

2. In the third sentence, what now reads as "ideas" was originally "idea": "Take about fifteen minutes for each of them, and begin by thinking about the *idea*" (my italics). In the original dictation, then, we practice one "idea" per longer practice period. And since there are two ideas per day, there are two longer practice periods per day.

These two sentences in the published version are the only sentences that imply there is only one longer practice period. Now we see, however, that this implication was entirely the product of minor editing changes.

At last we can state confidently: We are meant to do two longer practice periods, each one being devoted to one of the review ideas.

REVIEW II PRACTICE INSTRUCTIONS

Longer: Two times (once for each of the ideas), for about fifteen minutes.

- For three or four minutes, slowly read over the idea and comments (repeatedly if you wish) and think about them.

- Close your eyes and spend the remainder of the practice period listening for the message the Holy Spirit has for you. We can see this time of listening as having the following components:

1. Listen "quietly but attentively" (3:1)—listen in stillness and with all your attention.

2. Hold an attitude of *confidence* ("this message belongs to me"), *desire* ("I want this message"), and *determination* ("I'm determined to succeed").

3. Listening for ten minutes can easily be one big invitation to mind wandering, and so the majority of instruction for this exercise deals with this issue. For out-of-control mind wandering, go back and repeat the first phase. For more minor wandering, realize the distracting thoughts have no power and that your will has all the power, and then replace the thoughts with your will to succeed. Do so with firmness. "Do not allow your intent to waver" (4:1). "Refuse to be sidetracked" (5:2).

This is not mentioned in the instructions, but you may find it helpful to actually ask for the message, at the beginning and then periodically throughout. You may say, for instance, "What is Your message for me today?" You may even want to use this request as the specific vehicle for dispelling wandering thoughts.

Frequent reminders: Frequent.

Repeat the idea as a way of reaffirming your determination to succeed.

- First half of day: first lesson
- Second half of day: second lesson

Response to temptation: Whenever you are tempted to be upset.

Repeat some variation on the idea, modified to apply to this particular upset.

- You may use one of the three "specific forms" (W-pI.rII.In.6:1) suggested after each lesson. Notice how they are directed at a specific upset. Virtually every one is aimed at an upsetting "this" or an upsetting "name."

- Or you may generate one of your own specific forms, by using a variation on the practice of letting related thoughts come. Simply lean back and let your mind come up with a sentence that applies the essence of the idea to your current upset. For examples, see the specific forms suggested after each lesson.

LESSON 81 ✦ MARCH 22

Review of:

(61) "I am the light of the world."
(62) "Forgiveness is my function as the light of the world."

 Practice instructions

See instructions on page 256.

Commentary

"I am the light of the world." Lighting up the world is our function. The Course is teaching us to remember Who we are, and to begin to live as Who we are. We are lights, and we can live as lights in this world, through our forgiveness sharing the happy news of freedom from all guilt.

As St. Francis of Assisi prayed, "Lord, make me an instrument of Thy peace." May I leave everyone I meet a little brighter today. May the world seem a little less dark for everyone I encounter. May each one I touch feel more loveable as a result of meeting me. May I ask to see the light in every situation; may I respond to darkness with light.

"Forgiveness is my function as the light of the world." If I do not feel like the light of the world this day, let me forgive another; everyone I forgive will show me the light in myself. It's even okay that I don't yet understand what true forgiveness really is; that can't stop me if I am willing to learn, and *I am willing*. Every situation that seems to bring distress is a chance to learn what forgiveness really is. I don't want to use the circumstances of my day for any purpose other than God's. Let everything be grist for the mill.

LESSON 82 ✦ MARCH 23
Review of:

(63) "The light of the world brings peace to every mind through my forgiveness."
(64) "Let me not forget my function."

 Practice instructions
   See instructions on page 256.

Commentary

My forgiveness serves three primary purposes, according to this review:

1. The light of the world is expressed through me, in this world, by means of forgiveness.

Part II of the Workbook says that forgiveness is the reflection of love in this world (W-pII.352.1:4); it also refers to it as "truth's reflection" (W-pII.357.1:1). The full reality of love cannot be known in this world, but we can know its reflection, which is forgiveness. The reality of what I am is reflected here as I forgive.

2. I become aware of my own reality, the light of the world, by means of my forgiveness.

What comes through me shows me what I am. I become increasingly aware of the Holy Spirit in me, and the Christ of which He speaks, by seeing His effects through me (T-9.IV.5:5). To learn that I am love, I must teach love. Forgiveness, love's reflection, is how I do that in this world.

3. The world is healed by means of my forgiveness, and so am I.

As I forgive those around me, they see love reflected through me, and they see themselves in the light of love and are healed.

It is easy to see why forgiveness plays such a major role in the Course. It is easy to feel motivated to "forgive the world, that it may be healed along with me" (1:5).

I like practicing the line "Let peace extend from my mind to yours, [name]" (2:2). I will practice it now, as I write this, thinking of all of you who will be receiving this message: May peace extend from my mind to yours.

With forgiveness as my function, and with forgiveness having so many profound effects, I do not want to forget it today. It helps me become aware of my Self, and so I want to practice it today. Let me use everything today as an opportunity to learn forgiveness.

LESSON 83 ✦ MARCH 24
Review of:

(65) "My only function is the one God gave me."
(66) "My happiness and my function are one."

 Practice instructions

See instructions on page 256.

Commentary

To be without conflicting goals in life is a wonderful blessing. Most of the time, I feel stressed out with conflicting goals. I want to exercise but I have a deadline to meet for work. I want to spend time with my friends but my favorite TV program is on. And so on. When I am able to realize that my only function is the one God gave me—forgiveness, or simply being happy instead of being angry or upset—things become marvelously clear. My goal becomes to be at peace, to be happy, to be serene and unaffected by what surrounds me. "What to do, what to say and what to think" (1:4) simply come to me. Perhaps I realize that it makes no real difference whether I exercise or write. Perhaps I realize that one or the other can wait. Remembering my one and only true goal somehow sorts out everything else.

I used to think that when I had a conflict, the only way to become peaceful again was to make a decision, to resolve the conflict. It rarely worked. Usually, when I made my choice, I felt some distress at what I was leaving undone, or some loss at what I could not do because of my choice (e.g., watch TV or be with my friends; one or the other had to be "sacrificed"). Lately I've begun to realize that if I put becoming peaceful at the top of the list, if I choose to be peaceful *first*, before making my decision (perhaps taking a minute just to close my eyes and be quiet, remembering Who is with me), the decision becomes simple, and there is no sense of sacrifice. When I put peace first, I just know what to do.

This is the way to be happy. My function is one with my happiness. If I can be at peace, letting go of my grievances, the little demands I

261

constantly make of life, I am happy. Like forgiveness, happiness is a choice I can make at any time.

I notice today that the examples given of different ways to apply the ideas in specific situations seem to emphasize a kind of negation. They stress that the situation, or the way we perceive it, can *not* affect us if we so choose. The way I perceive this doesn't change my function, give me a different function, or justify selecting a goal other than the one God gave me. No matter what I see, no matter what happens, nothing will alter the fact that the only way I will find happiness is if I fulfill my function of forgiveness, blessing, and peace. There is no happiness apart from my function, and I am deceived by an illusion whenever I think there is. Do I expect to find happiness by indulging worry, justifying my anger, indulging my appetites, or licking my wounds of pain? It will never happen. Only in forgiveness, only in releasing everyone and everything from all my demands and expectations, only in quiet peacefulness of mind will I ever find my happiness.

LESSON 84 ✦ MARCH 25

Review of:

(67) "Love created me like Itself."
(68) "Love holds no grievances."

 Practice instructions

See instructions on page 256.

Commentary

If I am created in the likeness of my Creator, then "I cannot suffer, I cannot experience loss and I cannot die. I am not a body" (1:3–4). That just makes sense. God cannot suffer, experience loss or die, and He is not a body. He created me like Himself (1:8); therefore these things must be true of me. My reality is completely unlike what I believe about myself, for assuredly I have believed that I can suffer, experience loss and die, and I have identified almost entirely with my body.

What is it that makes and reinforces this illusion about myself? Grievances. "Love holds no grievances" (3:1). I am love, in the likeness of Love which created me, but when I choose to hold a grievance I am denying my own reality, I am affirming I am not love, because "grievances are completely alien to love" (3:2). In so doing, I am reaffirming that I am what I think I have made of myself, and I am choosing, without conscious awareness, to suffer, lose, and die. The only way I can rediscover my own reality is to stop holding grievances. A grievance is an attack on my Self (3:6; 4:4). It affirms that I am something I am not.

If I see ugliness, unloveliness or evil in my brothers I am attacking myself. Deny what they are and I am denying what I am. Today I choose to see others as I would see myself, and as I would have God see me. I have the power to make this choice. I see what I desire to see, and today I desire to see my Self, in myself and in everyone.

LESSON 85 ✦ MARCH 26

Review of:

(69) "My grievances hide the light of the world in me."
(70) "My salvation comes from me."

 Practice instructions

See instructions on page 256.

Commentary

What is the "this" referred to in the six specific applications in this lesson? What is it that might block my sight, that the light will shine away? What is it that I have no need for, and which tempts me to look away from me for my salvation? What is "this" that could interfere with my awareness of the Source of salvation, and which seems to have power to remove salvation from me?

"This" is grievances: anything I react to with less than the perfect love which is my reality. Anything I do not like, or push away from me, or blame for my problems, or look upon as less than God's creation. Anything within myself I hold with something other than compassion and forgiveness. "My grievances show me what is not there" (1:2). They cause me to see something that is not real, and I react with fear or hatred or anger. My reactions are as inappropriate as a child's fear of a curtain flapping in the dark. I am seeing something that isn't there, because only what God created is real. I am jumping at shadows when the reality is sheer beauty. The grievances not only show me things that aren't real, they hide what I really want.

If this is what my grievances really do, why would I want them? I do not really want them; I have used them in a mistaken attempt to protect myself, but I can recognize now that I no longer want them or need them. I do not blame myself for having chosen them in the past but I do not need to continue to choose them now. *I want to see*, and so I lay them aside joyfully, without guilt, without regret.

What I am looking for is in my Self (3:3). I won't look outside of myself today. "It is not found outside and then brought in. But from within me it will reach beyond, and everything I see will but reflect the light that shines in me and in itself" (3:6–7). My grievances tempt me to look outside for salvation, thinking I know what must change out there to bring me peace, feeling anger or sorrow or betrayal as I look on the things I blame for my loss of peace. But I recognize today that the answer is in my Self. Rather than seeking for the light, I will *be* the light today, and lighten my whole world.

LESSON 86 ✦ MARCH 27

Review of:

(71) "Only God's plan for salvation will work."
(72) "Holding grievances is an attack on God's plan for salvation."

 Practice instructions

See instructions on page 256.

Commentary

I find it really interesting how the lessons seem to alternate between seeing grievances, and where we look for salvation. I'm beginning to get the idea, I think: When my ego wants to keep me from finding God's salvation within my own Self, it distracts me with some kind of grievance outside myself. Seeing the cause of my distress outside, I naturally look for the solution outside. I seek salvation outside myself.

It's never what is outside that is the problem. "Those whom you see as guilty become the witnesses to guilt in you, and you will see it there, for it *is* there until it is undone. Guilt is always in your mind, which has condemned itself. Project it not, for while you do, it cannot be undone" (T-13.IX.6:6–8). What we are seeing out there, the object of our grievances, is only the projection of self-condemnation. We may change the name of the sin to protect the guilty (ourselves), but it is our sin we are seeing out there in the world. That is why seeing grievances *outside* keeps us from finding salvation *inside*.

As the review says, we have sought salvation in many different places and things, and it was never where we looked (1:3). We can't find it out there because it isn't out there, anywhere. There is no hope for salvation in the world—and that is *good* news. It's good news because we no longer have to depend on someone or something outside of ourselves to play its proper role, to arrive at the right time to meet our needs, or to do anything. We can let go of expecting someone else to save us, and we can turn to the only thing we can absolutely depend on: ourselves, our real Self. We can let everyone else off the hook we've been holding them on for our entire lives. We can tell the world, "You are no longer responsible for me. I no longer hold you accountable for my unhappiness. I've realized that is my own job, not yours."

I remember how odd I felt, but how happy, to tell my dear friend Lynne, years ago, "I've realized that I don't need you." She was delighted, being far wiser than I was at the time. I was afraid she would be insulted; how "unromantic" a thing to say to a partner in love! "I don't need you." She understood exactly what I meant, though. I was telling her that she was no longer expected to make me happy; she was no longer saddled with the unbearable burden of my happiness. Thinking that our love partner is responsible for our happiness is exactly what makes special relationships into hell, because when I am not happy, I have a grievance, just like in a labor union: "Hey! You're not living up to your part of the bargain. You're supposed to make me happy." And the grievance against our partner keeps us from seeing the salvation in our own hearts.

I've always liked the last line in today's lesson: "This calls for salvation, not attack" (4:4). It reminds me of the old line in the ancient Superman TV series (the one with George Reeves—guess I'm really dating myself here!). Clark Kent looks at some crime or disaster in progress, and says, "This is a job for...[in a totally different, 'super-sounding' voice] Superman!" Instead of looking at the events in our lives and thinking, "This is a job for the ego. Let's attack! Let's form and hold a grievance," we can look at the situation and say, "This is a job for God! Let's forgive! Let's respond with love to the call for love." When some need arises around me, which power will I call on: God, or the ego?

The choice is "between misperception and salvation" (4:2). The only alternative to salvation is something unreal, an illusion, a misperception. The only way I can avoid being happy is to misperceive my brother; if I see him or her truly, I will always find salvation. "By holding grievances, I am therefore excluding my only hope of salvation from my awareness" (3:4). What a silly thing to do! I think I'll stop!

"I would accept God's plan for salvation and be happy" (3:6).

LESSON 87 ✦ MARCH 28

Review of:

(73) "I will there be light."
(74) "There is no will but God's."

 Practice instructions

See instructions on page 256.

Commentary

Today's review deals with *will*—ours and God's, which are one.

The Course encourages us to make use of the power of our will. It constantly encourages us to choose again, and says that "the power of decision is your one remaining freedom as a prisoner of this world" (T-12.VII.9:1). We can will, or choose, that there be light. Naturally this accords with God's Will. You could say, I suppose, that our one true choice is to decide to agree with God's Will, and we must make this choice over and over until we realize there *is* no other will, and therefore, no actual choice except that between reality and illusion.

In the review of "There is no will but God's" there is an interesting summary of the progression of the ego's error:

- I believe there is another will besides God's.
- Because of this I become afraid.
- Because of fear, I try to attack.
- Because I attack, I fear my own eternal safety (thinking God will attack me for being an attacker).

The solution is simply to recognize that none of this has occurred. Knock down the basic premise—realize there is no will but God's—and the rest of the progression disappears.

I like the way both ideas are applied to how I see the other people around me: "You stand with me in light, [name]" (2:3) and "It is God's Will you are His Son, [name], and mine as well" (4:3). One night in our study group in Sedona we were studying Chapter 14, section V, "The Circle of Atonement." The whole section is about seeing other people as within the circle of peace, seeing them as included, or seeing them standing with me in light, as it is put here. In that section Jesus urges us, "Stand quietly within this circle, and attract all tortured minds to join with you in the safety of its peace and holiness" (T-14.V.8:6). It says that this is "the only purpose to which my teaching calls you" (T-14.V.9:9).

Our only purpose here is to awaken everyone to the fact that they are included in God's peace and safety because there is no other will than His. Imagine mentally greeting everyone you meet today by saying, "You stand with me in light." What kind of effect would that have on you? Or on them?

Lesson 109 says it has a profound effect, not just on people you actually meet, but on everyone in the world, even those who have passed on beyond the world, and those still to come to it:

> Each hour that you take your rest today, a tired mind is suddenly made glad. (6:1)

> With each five minutes that you rest today, the world is nearer waking. (7:1)

> You rest within the peace of God today, and call upon your brothers from your rest to draw them to their rest, along with you. You will be faithful to your trust today, forgetting no one, bringing everyone into the boundless circle of your peace, the holy sanctuary where you rest. Open the temple doors and let them come from far across the world, and near as well; your distant brothers and your closest friends; bid them all enter here and rest with you. (8:1–3)

> You rest within the peace of God today, quiet and unafraid. Each brother comes to take his rest, and offer it to you. We rest together here, for thus our rest is made complete, and what we give today we have received already. Time is not the guardian of what we give today. We give to those unborn and those passed by, to every Thought of God, and to the Mind in which these Thoughts were born and where they rest. And we remind them of their resting place each time we tell ourselves, "I rest in God." (9:1–6)

LESSON 88 ✦ MARCH 29
Review of:

(75)"The light has come."
(76) "I am under no laws but God's."

 Practice instructions
See instructions on page 256.

Commentary

The ideas being reviewed today seem to be concerned with very different concepts, yet have a certain common ground that is brought out in this review. That common ground could be expressed in this thought: Only what is of God is real; what appears to be in opposition is only an illusion without power, except that given it through my belief.

The light of salvation has *already* come. "I always choose between truth and illusion" (1:5), and "attack and grievances are not there to choose" (1:4). I really have no alternative to the light because there *is* no alternative. My entire experience of darkness is an adventure in delusion and nothing more; there is no darkness. "I can but choose the light, for it has no alternative" (1:7). This is why the Text tells me that the outcome of my drama here on earth is inevitable. "God is inevitable, and you cannot avoid Him any more than He can avoid you" (T-4.I.9:11). In seeking that my perception be changed, I am only seeking to see what is already there, and what is the only thing there.

God's laws alone rule me. The other laws that I think have power over me are laws that I made up. "I suffer only because of my belief in them. They have no real effect on me at all" (3:5–6). The laws of the ego cannot constrain me; I can be free of them *now* because I am, in reality, always free of them; they have no power. My ego at times seems so very powerful, the knee-jerk reaction of hurt and anger seems beyond my control and in control of me, but it is not so. I am free of these "laws" of chaos, of sin and guilt and punishment and separation. The healing of every relationship is inevitable because God's laws make us one, not separate. "A happy outcome to all things is sure" (W-pII.292.Heading),

270

because there are no laws but God's, no will but God's. Only my belief in it gives power to the appearance of an opposing will, with opposing laws.

Let me then, today, look on everything with this insight. Where I seem to see darkness, let me proclaim the reality of light. Where I see laws opposed to God at work, let me declare them powerless. Thank You, Father, for the certainty of Your plan, the present reality of Your light.

LESSON 89 ✦ MARCH 30
Review of:

(77) "I am entitled to miracles."
(78) "Let miracles replace all grievances."

 Practice instructions
See instructions on page 256.

Commentary

"Because I am under no laws but God's" (the laws of love and of extension, sharing, and giving), "I am entitled to miracles" (1:2). Giving of miracles is what God does, in accordance with His laws. The laws of grievances tell me I am not entitled to miracles. Every grievance I hold on to against a brother or sister is really my own mind telling me I do not deserve miracles; the very act of mental attack involved in holding a grievance makes me feel unworthy of them. Every grievance is hiding a miracle, and by letting the grievance go I release the miracle to happen.

There is a reason why God gives me miracles: He gives them so that I can fulfill the function He has given me (1:5), to continue His extension, to allow Him to love through me. The Course is emphatic on the fact that only in finding my true function as God's extension and fulfilling it can I be happy. My goal isn't being blissed out; it is to receive so that I can give, to accept love so I can share love with others. Like a light bulb that receives electric current only so that it can shine forth with light, I receive the miracles of God to extend them to others.

"I unite my will with the Holy Spirit's" (3:2) today; I declare, "Let miracles replace all grievances" (3:1). I want all of my illusions to be replaced with truth. I want my grievances to be banished forever from my mind and replaced with miracles. As I sit quietly this morning I call people I know to mind and tell them, "Let our grievances be replaced by miracles" (4:3). I think of war-torn spots on the globe and say, "Let our grievances be replaced by miracles." Today, I want to offer miracles to each one I meet. I want to be a channel of miracles; let me not block them with my grievances, Father.

When something arises in my perception that seems like a cause for grievance or grief, let me remember: "Behind this is a miracle to which I am entitled" (2:2). Let me tell myself: "Seen truly, this offers me a miracle" (2:4). Everything is miracle fodder; nothing is without use in this classroom of miracles.

LESSON 90 ✦ MARCH 31
Review of:

(79) "Let me recognize the problem so it can be solved."
(80) "Let me recognize my problems have been solved."

 Practice instructions
See instructions on page 256.

Commentary

This review places a different slant on these two ideas than in the original lessons. There, the only problem was defined as separation. Here, more directly in sync with the preceding lessons about grievances, "the problem is always some form of grievance that I would cherish" (1:2). Of course there is a close relationship between separation and grievances. A grievance separates me from whatever or whoever I hold the grievance against. So we could see a grievance as a thought or belief that separates me from my brothers.

Later in the Workbook the same thought is stated slightly differently, in terms of forgiveness or unforgiveness: "Certain it is that all distress does not appear to be but unforgiveness. Yet that is the content underneath the form" (W-pI.193.4:1–2). The problem is a grievance, or an unforgiveness. And it doesn't always seem that way to us. Sometimes, when I feel distress of some sort, or experience what seems to me to be a problem, I cannot for the life of me see any grievance or unforgiveness in it. The ego is an expert at camouflage. It survives by trickery and misdirection: "How can it maintain the trick of its existence except with mirrors?" (T-4.IV.1:7). Its temptations to attack or to harbor unforgiveness are often so well disguised I don't detect them as such, although it is "certain" that is what they are. The form deceives; the content is the same.

When I come to the Holy Spirit with my problems or my distress, I must be willing to be shown the grievance or unforgiveness lurking in them. For me, so often, what I find is a form of grievance against *myself*, some form of self-judgment. Other times, I don't understand the connection between my form of problem and forgiveness, but I assert my willingness to be shown, and I consciously choose a miracle for all concerned, including myself. "The problem is a grievance; the solution is a miracle" (1:5). If I can't see the exact instance of unforgiveness in what I perceive as a problem, at least I can choose a miracle instead of the problem. That willingness is enough.

The idea that the problem and the answer are "simultaneous in their occurrence" (3:4) seems strange. It seems "natural" to separate them by time: first the problem, then the answer. But if the problem is separation, or a grievance, the concept becomes easier to understand. God answered the separation with the Holy Spirit the instant the separation entered the mind of God's Son (M-2.2:6). Every problem I perceive, therefore, has already been resolved before I perceive it. "It is impossible that I could have a problem which has not been solved already" (3:7), because separation—the only problem there ever is—has already been resolved. Therefore I don't have to wait for circumstances to change; I can accept the peace of complete resolution *now*, without anything changing at all. "I need not wait for this to be resolved" (4:2).

I have a long-standing relationship problem that, in time, has been going on for over fifteen years, and which shows no outward signs of resolution. The other party has absolutely no interest in—more properly, has an aversion to—talking with me, so resolution, within time, seems impossible. Yet I can let go of the tension this could produce in me. I can be free of the stigma of "an unhealed relationship." In the holy instant I can know that problem, that rift in relationship, has already been healed. Down at the core of my mind and her mind, we are already one in love; everything has been forgiven. The disease of separation has already been inoculated, and the medicine of forgiveness is slowly and inexorably spreading through both of our minds, moving from the invisible sphere of spirit into the more concrete, thicker sphere of manifestation in the material world. There is no cause for concern. "It is the destiny of all relationships to become holy" (M-3.4:6). Today, I can recognize that this problem has already been solved. I believe my doing so speeds the day that healing will manifest in form. It may not be in this lifetime; what does that matter? The healing has already taken place.

One thing I notice as I think this way about this relationship, even as I write: Accepting that the problem is already solved frees me from the temptation to blame the other person for her refusal to make peace. Aha! A grievance was there, wasn't it, Allen? I accept a miracle in its place; thank You.

VI

Lessons 91 - 110

"Miracles are seen in light."

Practice instructions

Purpose: To briefly leave your weak, body-based image of yourself behind and have an experience of your real strength. In its light you will perceive the miracles that have always been there, waiting for you to see.

Longer: Three times, for ten minutes.

- Begin by repeating, *"Miracles are seen in light. The body's eyes do not perceive the light. But I am not a body. What am I?"* Ask this final question in real honesty. With this question, you are calling on the strength in you to give you an experience of your reality, beyond the body. So ask with that intention.

- Then spend several minutes listing your attributes as you see them, and allowing them to be replaced by their opposite. Say, for example, *"I am not weak, but strong. I am not helpless, but powerful. I am not doubtful, but certain,"* and so on. Focus specifically on attributes that

277

involve weakness.

- Then try to experience these truths about you, especially the experience of strength. Try to lift your faith in your body as central to your reality, for that is what makes you feel weak. Instruct your mind to instead go to the place of strength in you (this exercise appears to be a kind of meditation). Remember that your will has the power to do this. "You can escape the body if you choose. You can experience the strength in you" (5:5–6). You might want to use the beginning question, "What am I?" as a kind of mantra to take you to this place in you.
- For the remainder, relax in the confidence that your weak efforts are fully supplemented by God's strength, which joins you in your practice. His strength will carry you to the deep place in you where your strength and His light abide.

Frequent reminders: Five or six per hour, at fairly regular intervals (every ten to fifteen minutes).

Repeat the idea, which means that the miracle is always there if you will just open your eyes. This is a central idea in the thought system you are learning. That is why it needs such frequent repeating today.

Response to temptation: Whenever you are tempted to be upset.

Repeat, *"Miracles are seen in light. Let me not close my eyes because of this."*

Commentary

As the Workbook lessons get longer it won't be practical to try to comment on everything in each lesson. That could be more than a person could write in a day; in fact, I have written a 48-page booklet on Lesson 135. (*A Healed Mind Does Not Plan* is the booklet title.) So I will be picking some aspect of the lesson that particularly speaks to me, and writing about that.

The first idea, central to the lesson, is that "miracles and vision necessarily go together" (1:1). We are told this bears frequent repetition, and that it is central to our new thought system. The whole nature of what the Course means by a miracle is touched on here. A miracle is not really a change in anything outside of our mind; it is a change in perception, a "shift to vision":

As the ego would limit your perception of your brothers to the body, so would the Holy Spirit release your vision and let you see the Great Rays shining from them, so unlimited that they reach to God. It is this shift to vision that is accomplished in the holy instant.   (T-15.IX.1:1–2)

"The miracle is always there" (1:4). What changes is our acceptance or rejection of vision; we either see it or we don't. It is always present. What changes is our awareness. So to experience the miracle, we must have vision. We must let go of darkness in order to see the light. As the section titled "What Is a Miracle?" puts it:

A miracle is a correction. It does not create, nor really change at all. It merely looks on devastation, and reminds the mind that what it sees is false.   (W-pII.13.1:1–3)[1]

The devastation is what we see with our eyes. The Course is very plainspoken about physical sight: "The body's eyes do not perceive the light" (6:3). "You do not doubt that the body's eyes can see. You do not doubt the images they show you are reality" (3:3–4). And yet the lesson is clearly asking us to do just that, to doubt that our eyes really see, and to doubt that what they see is real. We have to let go of the darkness to see the light, and what the body's eyes show us is not light; therefore it must be darkness. We need a shift to a new kind of vision.

This need to undo our faith in our eyes and what they see is part of the reason this lesson turns to a second idea: "I am not a body" (6:4ff). We are told to *instruct* our minds that we are not bodies. We are to *will* ourselves to realize that we are something else, something that does not see with the eyes, but in a different way.

The exercises today are designed to help us realize that we are something other than a body; we are looking for a very concrete experience. In paragraph 7 we are told: "You need to be aware of what the Holy Spirit uses to replace the image of a body" (7:2). "You need to feel something to put your faith in" (7:3). "You need a real experience of something else" (7:4). An awareness, a feeling, an experience. There is something within us, a certain strength, "which makes all miracles within your easy reach" (4:4). We don't realize how strong we are! And more than that: "Your efforts, however meager, are fully supported by the strength of God and all His Thoughts" (10:1). I always think of this by an analogy, something akin to sound waves or radio waves. When my little willingness strikes the right wavelength, I suddenly find myself joined by the harmony of the universe, a powerful beam of divine energy that resonates with me. If we can strike the right frequency of thought today, we will find that awareness, sense that feeling, and have that experience that takes us beyond the body, and into vision.

Isn't this worth ten minutes of effort, three times today? I know I think it is.

Don't be discouraged if you don't feel anything, however. You will find vision. Your efforts today are not wasted, and do not think that if nothing seems to happen that you have "failed." I remember learning to roller-skate. I started out by falling down a lot. If I had stopped then, thinking I'd failed, I would never have learned to skate. But I didn't. I kept on falling down, and falling down again, until one day I didn't fall down. With spiritual vision, I'm still pretty much in the falling down stage myself. I've had some incredible experiences, holy instants, just as in the early days of skating there were times I went for blocks (skating on the sidewalk, jumping over the cracks) without falling, before I suddenly fell again. Consistent spiritual vision I don't have as yet. But the miracle is always there, whether or not I see it! And my vision is improving each time I practice.

---

1. The "What Is" pages constitute a problem for the referencing scheme in the Workbook. They are numbered 1 to 14, just like Lessons 1 to 14. To get around this, Workbook references always contain a reference to the part of the Workbook, Part I (pI) or Part II (pII). When you see a number 1-14 following "pII," you can know it refers to one of the "What Is" sections. This still does not make it easy to find! My solution is to remember the number 210. That, plus ten times the number of the "What Is" section, gives you the number of the lesson that immediately precedes that section. Thus, "W-pII.3" can be found just after Lesson 240 (210 plus 30).

LESSON 92 ✦ APRIL 2
"Miracles are seen in light, and light and strength are one."

Practice instructions

Purpose: To experience the light of strength in you, which will reveal to you the miracles that are always there.

Longer: Two times—morning and evening, for twenty minutes.

This exercise is another meditation, like you've been doing since Lesson 41. That's why the instructions are so brief—it's assumed that you know how to do this. Here, you try to sink to that deep place in your mind where light and strength meet, and where "your Self stands ready to embrace you as Its Own" (9:2). Seek this place and try to rest in the peace that waits for you there. Your sinking should not be all your own effort. "Let yourself be brought" (10:2) there; ask the truth to lead you there (this was emphasized in Lessons 69, 73, and 91). While going there, remember to draw your mind back from wandering as needed, and to carry an attitude of confidence, desire, and determination.

Frequent reminders: As often as you can.

Repeat the idea, recognizing you are being led away from the body's blindness to the light of true sight, in which miracles are seen. Do it with a mindset of "I'm preparing myself for the evening practice period." In this way, you can use the day to prepare yourself for a true holy instant at the end of the day.

Commentary

The goal of this lesson seems to me to be finding "the meeting place of self and Self," as it is put in 10:4. "It is God's strength in you that is the light in which you see" (3:1). There is Something in me that is as far beyond what I think I am as the sun is beyond a match. There is an unimaginable vastness in me that, by these lessons, I am being led to discover. In the two twenty-minute practice periods today—the morning and evening "meetings" as they are referred to (11:2)—I am attempting to bring self to Self, to bring the match to the sun. I am trying to open the door to infinity within myself.

This strength within me is mighty beyond the telling of it. It is "constant, sure as love, forever glad to give itself away" (8:1). Within me, my Self "stands ready to embrace [me] as Its Own" (9:2). I am a triple-A battery standing next to a nuclear power plant, about to plug in to endless power that ever renews itself. No, that image is too cold; it lacks the "embrace" spoken of. I am a tiny, fearful child, about to be swept up in the arms of the universal, endlessly compassionate and omnipotent Father/Mother/God.

I think that perhaps the way a very young child sees its parents—huge, vast, all-knowing, totally worthy of trust, able to do anything—is perhaps a reflection of the truth of our relationship to God, and even our relationship to our own true Self.

I find this lesson enormously encouraging. It tells me strength is the truth about me (4:7). Those are words worth many repetitions! Truth gives its strength to everyone who asks, in limitless supply (5:4). This light, this strength, "does not change and flicker and go out" (7:5). "No one can ask in vain to share its sight" (8:2). As a later lesson tells us, "No one can fail who seeks to reach the truth" (W-pI.131.Heading). It does not matter how often I have tried and failed, or how long it has been since I have had a flicker of light in my mind, or how weak and puny seem the efforts of my heart; I cannot fail. I have the strength of God in me, and it will lead me to where I want to go.

I come to the practice periods today with trust in that strength. God's strength. My strength. I come to allow, just for this brief period, my self to meet my Self. I come to leave the darkness behind and let true vision, in the light, dawn upon my mind. I care not that it may not seem to last. I care not that my mind might seem dark before and dark after; for this instant, let me open to the light, and let it begin its work of leading me home. I bring my doubts, my fears, my open disbelief and expose them to this light, and in the light they disappear, and my heart floods with joy. I am being "led away from darkness to the light where only miracles can be perceived" (11:3).

LESSON 93 ✦ APRIL 3
"Light and joy and peace abide in me."

Practice instructions

Purpose: To go past your belief that you are sinful and evil, and to experience the sinless Self that God created as you.

Longer: Every hour on the hour, for five minutes.

- Repeat, *"Light and joy and peace abide in me. My sinlessness is guaranteed by God."* I find it helpful to pause briefly after each quality ("Light...and joy...and peace...") so that I can appreciate each one separately.
- The remainder is a brief meditation, in which you try to reach past the false self that you made, which includes your whole sense of self and all your self-images. Reach deep within to the Self that God created as you, which is filled with light and joy and peace. Try to experience Its unity, and to appreciate Its holiness and Love. "Let It come into Its Own" (9:6). Remember to hold an attitude of confidence, desire, and determination, and to dispel distracting thoughts by repeating the idea.

Alternate: On the hour, for at least one minute.

Try to do the hourly five minutes whenever you can. When you are unable or unwilling, at least do the alternate:

- Say, *"Light and joy and peace abide in me. My sinlessness is guaranteed by God."*
- Close your eyes and try to realize this is the truth about you.

Response to temptation: Whenever a situation or person tempts you to be upset.

1. If a situation disturbs you, quickly say, *"Light and joy and peace abide in me. My sinlessness is guaranteed by God."*

2. If a person seems to anger you, tell him silently, *"Light and joy and peace abide in you. Your sinlessness is guaranteed by God."*

> ***Encouragement to practice:*** Today is the beginning of a bank of lessons in which you are asked to practice five minutes every waking hour. To help you rise to this challenge, these lessons contain a huge amount of encouragement to practice. You can see that encouragement in the final sentences of this lesson, which tell you that by doing today's practice you can aid the world's salvation, bring closer your own part in that salvation, and gain conviction that light and joy and peace really do abide in you.

Commentary

The lead thought is very positive, reflecting the truth about me, but the first paragraph of the body of the lesson is quite dark, reflecting what the ego has taught me about myself, and taught very well. I think I am "the home of evil, darkness and sin" (1:1). To be sure, not many of us *consciously* think this about ourselves, and when such thoughts occur we quickly banish them. But the way I respond to myself betrays that this is, indeed, how I think about myself. Why else am I so protective of my "private thoughts," for instance? Why am I apprehensive about self-examination and about looking at my inner motivations? Why am I afraid to leave the body and appear before God, when that possibility crosses my mind? I have deep-seated doubts about my own goodness and worth.

Suppose I were to meet someone who could read my mind and know my every thought. Would I feel comfortable around such a person? Suppose *everyone* I met could read my every thought. Imagine I had to wear a helmet with a video screen above my forehead that pictured my thoughts for anyone to look at. How would I feel? I have no doubt that I would feel very, very uncomfortable and perhaps terrified, because there are many thoughts that cross my mind all the time that I would not care to have written on the wall for everyone to see.

Even when I am reasonably confident of the harmlessness of my intentions, there are always subcurrents to my motivation that even I despise. My most benevolent acts are sometimes laced with a certain resentfulness or sense of sacrifice, and mixed with ulterior motives. Sometimes I am quite conscious of not trusting myself in certain situations. Every one of us, in the picture the Course paints, has this basic self-doubt. We secretly suspect, or even consciously believe, that we are not wholly trustworthy and not wholly good and loving. And as the lesson says, it is "difficult" (2:1) to dislodge these beliefs about ourselves, yet that is what the Course is all about—removing those blocks to the awareness of love's presence, which is our natural inheritance (see T-In.1:7).

The truth is that, in my innermost Self, I *am* wholly loving and wholly lovable (see T-1.III.2:3–4). Light and joy and peace abide in me; I am their home, and they remain with me forever as a creation of God. To begin to question my entrenched negative beliefs about myself (which is one way of defining what the Course calls "guilt"), and to begin to see myself as God created me, I need "a very different reference point" (3:1). I need to attain to a different state of mind. That is what the Holy Spirit does for me; that is what happens in the holy instant.

The truth about me is "that all the evil that you think you did was never done, that all your sins are nothing, that you are as pure and holy as you were created, and that light and joy and peace abide in you" (4:1). We resist this message tenaciously, although it is wholly illogical to do so. As Spock in *Star Trek* points out, humans are not always logical. Our minds automatically raise up counterarguments to disprove our own innocence. Or we simply dismiss it as absurd, as "Pollyanna," without even seriously considering it. Why? Because we think that to admit the truth of our innocence is death. We are so identified with this guilty self-image that to threaten it is to threaten our very existence, or so it seems. "But it is life" (4:3), not death. When the Spirit presents us with a picture of our innocence it terrifies us because it turns our whole world upside down and uproots our every frame of reference, all based on judgments we have made. It is frightening to think that we have been so totally mistaken about ourselves, even when the mistake has been to condemn ourselves and the unfamiliar truth is our own guiltlessness.

One method this lesson uses, very evidently, to help uproot the old, guilty self-image is just to repeat, over and over and over, "Your sinlessness is guaranteed by God" (6:1, and six other times in the lesson). Frequent repetition is an excellent way to reprogram the mind, so we are asked to spend five minutes every hour, if we can, repeating these ideas and thinking about them, realizing that they are the truth about ourselves. "Light and joy and peace abide in me. My sinlessness is guaranteed by God" (8:2–3; 10:4–5).

When it says this, the lesson does not mean that God guarantees to take us as poor, sinful creatures and *make* us sinless. That isn't necessary because we were *created* sinless to begin with and retain that quality. I have never sinned; that is what the lesson is telling me. Oh, I *think* I have (and so do people who know me!), I believe I have, I am utterly convinced that I have, but I have never sinned. Mistakes, yes, but not sins, because there is no such thing. "To sin would be to violate reality, and to succeed" (T-19.II.2:2), and that simply is not possible.

> The Son of God can be mistaken; he can deceive himself; he can even turn the power of his mind against himself. But he *cannot* sin. There is nothing he can do that would really change his reality in any way, nor make him really guilty.   (T-19.II.3:1–3)

My sinlessness is guaranteed because I cannot sin; that's simple logic. If something is impossible for me to do, it is a pretty sure bet that I won't do it and never have done it.

The exercises today are attempts to experience this one Self, this reality as God created it. It takes letting the other "self" go. Opening to the immensity of Love that is within us, floating in It, being surrounded by It, embraced by It. And then the most amazing thought: "Here you are; This is You" (9:7). *This* is You! This Love, this vastness, this infinite compassion—This is You! If you can, think of the most direct and dramatic experience you have ever had of God's presence, or of the presence of love, and tell yourself, "That which I experienced in that moment, That is Me. That is what I am."

LESSON 94 ✦ APRIL 4
"I am as God created me."

Practice instructions

Purpose: "To feel the truth in you" (3:1); to experience your true Self.

Longer: Every hour on the hour, for five minutes.

- Say, *"I am as God created me. I am His Son eternally."*
- The remainder is again a brief meditation, in a slightly new format. First, lay aside your self-images—"the list of attributes, both good and bad, you have ascribed to yourself" (4:1). Then "wait in silent expectancy" (4:1) for your true Self to be revealed to you. Wait confidently, knowing that God has promised you this revelation. This waiting means holding your mind in stillness, empty of specifics yet filled with the expectancy that Who you really are will dawn on you. When your mind wanders, repeat the idea to return your mind to this expectant waiting.

This appears to me to be the first example of what I call Open Mind Meditation, which will become the Workbook's crowning method of meditation. In this technique, you consciously set aside your normal thoughts and beliefs, and then hold your mind in stillness, waiting for the truth to dawn on you. For examples, see the introduction to Review V, paragraph 12; and Lesson 189, paragraph 7.

Alternate: On the hour.

If you do not do the five minutes on the hour, at least repeat, *"I am as God created me. I am His Son eternally."* This practice of spending a minute or so with the idea, if you can't do the full five minutes, will apply to all the five-minute-per-hour lessons.

Frequent reminders: Frequently.

Repeat the idea, in original or expanded form.

Response to temptation: Whenever someone seems to irritate you.

Be certain to respond with, *"You are as God created you. You are His Son eternally."*

Encouragement to practice: You are urged to "make every effort to do the hourly exercises today" (5:8). "Each one you do," you are promised, "will be a giant stride toward your release" (5:9). If you let that line sink in, you will find that it is a tremendous motivator to practice. That line also means that this lesson is another of the Workbook's giant strides (the first ones were 61 and 66). This is appropriate because "I am as God created me" is the Workbook's premier lesson. It is repeated in 110, 162, and all through the twenty-day Review VI.

Commentary

This lesson continues with the thought introduced yesterday: "Salvation requires the acceptance of but one thought;—you are as God created you, not what you made of yourself" (W-pI.93.7:1). The Course places a significant emphasis on this single idea. It is the only idea used as the main theme of more than one lesson; it is the lead thought of this lesson, Lesson 110, and Lesson 162. It was introduced in the Text (T-31.VIII.5:2). It is a subtheme in Lessons 132 and 139, and Review VI has us repeating every day for *twenty days*, "I am not a body. I am free. For I am still as God created me." You sort of get the feeling that Jesus wants us to get this idea and get it good.

Read over the first paragraph of this lesson and you will see just how important this idea is in the Course's curriculum: it is called "the one idea which brings complete salvation" (1:1).

So. Why is this single, simple idea so very important? Just this: our entire "problem" lies in our belief that, even if God created me whole and complete, somehow I have screwed that up. Somehow I have lost it, blown it, destroyed it, or corrupted myself. "I am as God created me" asserts that none of this is true. God created me whole, and "I am as God created me." I am still whole. I am still holy. I am still sinless and guiltless.

To think that we can change what God created and corrupt it is the height of arrogance; it asserts that our power is greater than God's, that we can un-create what He created. If God created us wholly loving and wholly lovable, then we are still that, no matter what we think, no matter what we may believe we have done. We are not what we made of ourselves; we are still what God created. "If you remain as God created you, you must be strong and light must be in you" (2:2). So we "stand in light, strong in the sinlessness in which [we] were created" (2:6). That is the truth about us, and the Course is all about undoing any belief we may have that contradicts it and denies the truth.

Today's practice, once again, asks for "the first five minutes of each waking hour" (3:1) as times in which we attempt to feel the truth in ourselves, and to reach the Son of God in ourselves. This practice of five minutes each hour, begun yesterday, is going to continue for another sixteen lessons through Lesson 110, so get used to it. This is probably the most intense extended practice the Workbook demands; after Lesson 110 it settles down to a morning and evening period with shorter hourly remembrances. As you will see, nearly all of these eighteen lessons from 93 to 110 are variations on the theme of reaching the Christ within, the true Self, me as God created me. Realize how important this is, and make a real effort to do the hourly practices, rearranging your day as necessary if you can. Remember, though, that yesterday's lesson told us that we may not want, or even be able, to do this, and if our motivation is not so high, it suggested that we at least spend *one minute* per hour reviewing the idea for the day.

Recognize also that the Workbook would hardly include eighteen lessons on the same basic theme and format if it expected you to "get it" perfectly in the first one. Getting in touch with our one Self takes practice, and that is what the lessons are for. The Text refers to the benefits of practicing "the mechanics of the holy instant" (T-15.II.5:4) even when you don't actually "feel the truth in you" (3:1) every time; practicing the mechanics, going through the motions as it were, is what brings the reality of the holy instant closer every time we do it. It asserts your willingness to receive the grace God wants to give you; it breaks down your resistance, which is the only thing keeping the one Self from your awareness.

The closing words of the lesson emphasize the importance of this practice:

> Make every effort to do the hourly exercises today. Each one you do will be a giant stride toward your release, and a milestone in learning the thought system which this course sets forth. (5:8–9)

So join me in a serious attempt to do as these lessons tell us to do. Remember the admonitions of the introduction to the Workbook (italics are my emphasis):

> It is doing the exercises that will make the goal of the course possible. (W-In.1:2)

> You are merely asked to apply the ideas as you are directed to do. You are not asked to judge them at all. You are asked only to use them. It is their use that will give them meaning to you, and will show you that they are true.
> (W-In.8:3–6)

> Do not allow yourself to make exceptions in applying the ideas the workbook contains, and whatever your reactions to the ideas may be, use them. Nothing more than that is required. (W-In.9:4–5)

LESSON 95 ✦ APRIL 5

"I am one Self, united with my Creator."

Practice instructions

Purpose: To attempt again to reach your one Self. "In patience and in hope we try again today" (3:3).

Longer: Every hour on the hour, for five minutes (if you cannot do this, at least do the alternate).

- Say with all the certainty you can give, *"I am one Self, united with my Creator, at one with every aspect of creation, and limitless in power and in peace."* You'll probably need to keep your eyes open in order to read the line.

- Close your eyes and repeat, *"I am one Self."* Say this several times, "slowly and thoughtfully, attempting to allow the meaning of the words to sink into your mind" (11:3). Saying it in this way will allow it to have a much greater effect on you.

- The remainder is a meditation in which you try to reach your one Self, which is perfectly united within Itself, perfectly joined with all your brothers, and perfectly at one with God. "Feel this one Self in you, and let It shine away all your illusions and your doubts" (13:3). Draw upon all the training you've received in Workbook meditation.

Frequent reminders: As frequently as possible.

There are two forms of this frequent practice:

1. Repeat the idea. Realize that every time you do, healing enters someone's mind out there.

2. Say silently to everyone you meet, *"You are one Self with me, united with our Creator in this Self. I honor you because of What I am, and What He is, Who loves us both as one."* Applying the idea to everyone you meet is an important practice, which you have previously done in Lessons 37, 43, and 78.

Encouragement to practice: Here on our third day of the five-minutes-per-hour practice, we are given an extended explanation as to why this practice schedule is so important right now. First, you need *shorter* practice periods. Otherwise, your mind will wander all over the place, which you probably noticed in those ten to fifteen minute practice periods. Second, you need *frequent* practice periods. When there were only two longer practice periods a day, you probably tended to forget the shorter ones (frequent reminders and response to temptation). With the longer ones now being more frequent, you will be more likely to remember the shorter ones. Third, you need *regular* practice periods. Having them scheduled at these fixed, regular intervals will make you more likely to practice, given how resistant you are to practicing.

For all these reasons, he urges you to omit as few of these as possible. The key to carrying this out is how you respond when you've missed *one*. Missing a practice period is simply a mistake, that's all. The way to respond to this mistake is to correct it—which means to get back to your practicing. The danger, however, is that you'll regard this mistake as a real sin. This takes the form of you deciding that you've so hopelessly screwed up that you might as well give up for the day. Sound familiar?

This is a subtle ploy of the ego. It is terrified of what your practice will bring: the realization of your Self. Its fear is what caused you to miss that practice period in the first place. Now it has convinced you that since you missed once, you should keep on missing more. It has successfully nullified the threat of your practice by convincing you not to practice.

The solution is to regard your initial missed practice period as a mere mistake and forgive yourself for it. It was no big deal, just a moment of weakness. Seeing it as a moment of weakness deprives it of power. Now it no longer has the power to dictate everything that comes after it, to make your day over in its likeness. Now you simply correct it; you just get back to your practice. This, by the way, is the Workbook's consistent counsel on how to deal with missed practice periods.

Do your utmost to implement this counsel, starting today. "Do not forget today" (you are told this twice, in 14:1 and 14:6).

Heaven needs the healing thoughts you will send out to the world with today's practice. It is confident you will try today, so you can be confident, too.

Commentary

This lesson is one of my favorites, because it acknowledges both my reality and the lowly image I have made of myself. It affirms my greatness without denying my illusion of weakness. It holds up the exalted picture of my "one Self...at one with every aspect of creation, and limitless in power and in peace" (11:2). But it does so in the context of speaking about my "lapses in diligence" and my "failures to follow the instructions for practicing" (8:3). It makes me realize that, somehow, this lofty vision of my Self is *not* incompatible with my stumbling, bumbling attempts to follow this course. It lets me know that my mistakes do not negate the truth about me.

If anyone doubts what I said yesterday—that the overall intent of these next sixteen lessons is to reach inward to an experience of our one Self, and that the Workbook attaches a great deal of importance to disciplined practice as a means of attaining that experience—let him or her simply read this lesson several times. You can't miss the message, and I can't say it more clearly than the lesson says it:

Structure, then, is necessary for you at this time.   (6:1)

Do not forget today....try today...Be vigilant. Do not forget today. Throughout the day do not forget your goal.
(14:1, 3, 5–7)

The lesson seems to be talking about two such disparate things. On the one hand, myself as God created me, my perfect unity. On the other hand, the emphasis on regimented, very specific, structured practice, every hour on the hour for five minutes. If I am perfect, why do I need all this discipline? Why not just affirm the truth about myself and be done with it?

We need the practice just because we do not believe the truth about ourselves. We have all these hidden warriors in our minds, the subtle and deceitful manipulators of consciousness planted by the ego that keep us from full awareness. Beware of telling yourself you aren't doing the disciplined practice because you don't need it. Show me you don't need it by doing it, and maybe I'll believe you. You don't just sit down at a piano and play Tchaikovsky's Piano Concerto No. 1 right off the bat; you start with scales. Scales aren't great music but they are the necessary way to it. Just so, "Regularity in terms of time [playing scales] is not the ideal requirement for the most beneficial form of practice in salvation [the concerto]. It is advantageous, however, for those whose motivation is inconsistent, and who remain heavily defended against learning" (6:2–3). That's me; I don't know about you, but that's me.

The beauty of this kind of repetitive practice is that it discloses all the tricks of the ego that keep us from God. Just do it, like the Nike ad says, and you'll begin to realize how many resistant strains of antispiritual virus exist in the maze of your mind, how many ways you have invented to keep you away from knowing your Self. That is one of the primary purposes of the practice:

> You have seen the extent of your lack of mental discipline,
> and of your need for mind training. It is necessary that you
> be aware of this. (4:4–5)

We have to be aware of our need before we can recognize the solution that has already been given us. We have to discover the "self divided into many warring parts" (2:2) before we can acknowledge the "perfect unity" (1:4) of our reality. So this practice will uncover our need, and expose the ego; that's good, that's what it is supposed to do.

But that isn't all. Yes, part of the intent is that we learn to forgive ourselves for failures. But the purpose is *not* to fail and then forgive. The purpose is to fail, forgive, and then *do it*. To say to yourself, "Oh, of course I didn't do the practice today; I'm supposed to fail," is just another way to refuse to let your mistake be corrected. It is unwillingness to try again.

> To allow a mistake to continue is to make additional
> mistakes, based on the first and reinforcing it. It is this
> process that must be laid aside, for it is but another way in
> which you would defend illusions against the truth.
> (9:3–4)

In other words, accepting failure is not the goal—it is what has to be laid aside. Both the failure to practice *and* allowing the failure to continue "are attempts to keep you unaware you are one Self" (10:2).

One Self, with one purpose: "to bring awareness of this oneness to all minds, that true creation may extend the Allness and the Unity of God" (12:2). Let me give myself to this process, knowing my true purpose, recognizing I am in training to awaken mankind along with me. Let me take these minutes out of each hour to become aware of Who I am. "It is given you to feel this Self within you" (13:5). I want that; today, Father. I want to let go of my shabby illusions and feel the extent and power of my true Self, given me by You. I want to forget my belief in my littleness, even if only for a few seconds each hour, and to continually bring myself these reminders (since I am so quick to forget) until the awareness dawns in permanence on my mind, never again to be forgotten. So be it.

LESSON 96 ✦ APRIL 6
"Salvation comes from my one Self."

Practice instructions

Purpose: To find the thought of salvation deep within your mind, and let it restore your mind to its true function of blessing all minds.

Longer: Every hour on the hour, for five minutes (if you cannot do this, at least do the alternate).

- Say, *"Salvation comes from my one Self. Its thoughts are mine to use."*
- The remainder seems to be a combination of meditation (in which you try to contact your real thoughts, as in Lesson 45) and listening to the Holy Spirit (in which you listen for spiritual teaching, as in Lesson 76). Search deep within your mind for the presence of the Holy Spirit. He is there to speak to you your true thoughts, the thoughts of your true Self; in particular, the thought of salvation. If you succeed, thoughts will come to you telling you that you are saved and you can save. These thoughts are more than just information; they will fill your mind with strength, enabling it to bless all minds. Remember the training you've received both in meditation and in listening to the Holy Spirit: Hold your mind in a state of quiet attentiveness, listen in confidence, and draw your mind back from wandering when necessary.

Frequent reminders: As often as possible.

Repeat the idea. While you do, imagine that you are laying another treasure in your treasure house, a treasure you can claim anytime you want. If you will, go ahead and repeat the idea in this fashion now.

Encouragement to practice: You may feel uncertain of success today, but your Self knows you cannot fail. Your practice will bring joy to It, and It will save this joy for you, storing it in your treasure house until you are ready to take it out and experience it.

296

Commentary

"Although you are one Self, you experience yourself as two" (1:1). Experiencing ourselves as divided is a universal experience. Even the very practice of these lessons makes it evident to us: on the one hand, we want to do the practice because we want to go to God, we want enlightenment; on the other hand, when the hour comes and it is time to take our five minutes, something in us resists doing it. It seems as if there are two selves in us, one "good" and the other "bad," one wanting the light and the other holding on to the darkness.

Most of my life I lived with this, believing my experience was the truth. Something in me, however, told me it was not so. How could I be two selves? How could I have two natures, as my Christian background taught me (flesh and spirit)? It didn't make sense. The nature of something, of anything, is always one. The Course explains that one, spirit, is real; the other, the separated self that experiences being a body, is unreal, nothing more than a figment of my imagination. I am not divided, and all evidence to the contrary is a trick of the mind, a self-deception.

Based on the illusion of being split into opposites, the mind has "sought many...solutions" (1:3). It has been duped into believing in the reality of this split, and the reality of physical being. Therefore it occupies itself endlessly trying to make things work, and they never do. The mind becomes the servant of the body, trying to devise ways to make the body comfortable, to pleasure it, to make it last forever, to keep it safe from harm. In doing this, the mind has lost its true function.

Our one Self is spirit. In its preoccupation with the body the mind has, for the most part, lost sight of spirit. It needs to regain its true function of serving spirit: "Spirit makes use of mind as means to find its Self expression" (4:1). This is what brings us peace and fills the mind with joy, while serving the body brings it nothing but conflict and pain. The thoughts of spirit seek expression through our minds; that is what minds are for.

The Holy Spirit is an agent of divine Help, bringing the mind back to its true function of serving spirit. He is the representative of spirit, of our Self, to our minds, constantly calling us to set aside this futile fumbling for salvation in the realm of the physical and to open our minds to spirit. "If you are spirit, then the body must be meaningless to your reality" (3:7). Because we have dissociated our minds from their true function, we think we are alone and separate. We need a Helper Who reminds us of our true connection to spirit.

Our spirit—our Self—"retains Its thoughts, and they remain within your mind and in the Mind of God" (7:1). We remain, in spirit, as God created us. So we are not trying to change what our minds are, but rather change the purpose they serve. We are seeking, in these exercises, to reconnect to spirit, to set aside for five minutes the thoroughly distracting problems of the physical beings we think we are, and to open ourselves to these thoughts of spirit, to allow our minds to find their function as channels for spirit. "Restored in strength, it [the mind] will again flow out from spirit to the spirit in all things created by the Spirit as Itself. Your mind will bless all things" (10:3–4). That is our function; that is what we were created for. "The extension of God's Being is spirit's only function" (T-7.IX.3:1).

So I am rediscovering myself as an extender of God's Being. God is Love and so I love. God creates, so I create, which here on earth is expressed as healing, as restoring creation to its natural state.

This "Self" that the Course is talking about is not something apart from me; it *is* me. Talking about seeking the thoughts of my one Self almost makes it seem as if the Self is this separate Being I am seeking to communicate with. But the Self is me. "Here you are; This is You," as it said in Lesson 93 (W-pI.93.9:7). We are bringing the mind into contact with our spirit, but it is already me; the light is already in me, the thoughts I am "seeking" are my own thoughts I have dissociated right out of my mental awareness.

What we are asked to practice here is not described in great detail. You may be asking yourself, "What is it we are waiting for as we sit for five minutes?" And I can't tell you; no one can. You will know when you find it. The lesson recognizes that we may not "connect" today; it uses words like "*if* you succeed" (10:1, emphasis mine) and "perhaps your mind remains uncertain yet a while" (11:2). It tells us not to be "dismayed" (11:3) if this is so. Relax with it, be patient. Do the exercises anyway. Every time you do your Self rejoices, even if that joy does not penetrate yet into your conscious mind, and it saves the joy, ready to bring it to you in full awareness when you do "succeed" and become certain of your one Self.

LESSON 97 ✦ APRIL 7
"I am spirit."

Practice instructions

Purpose: To bring reality still closer to your mind. To bring your mind out of the conflict of a split identity into the peace of identifying with your one Self.

Longer: Every hour on the hour, for five minutes (if you cannot do this, at least do the alternate).

- Give the practice period happily to the Holy Spirit. Begin by saying, *"Spirit am I, a holy Son of God, free of all limits, safe and healed and whole, free to forgive, and free to save the world."*
- The remainder appears to be the same practice as yesterday, a combination of meditation and listening to the Holy Spirit. Sink to the deep place in your mind where the Holy Spirit dwells. If you reach this place, "He will speak to you, reminding you that you are spirit" (8:2). He will help you understand Who you really are. Keep in mind that He will be using your practice period to carry healing around the world. The deeper you go, the more healing He can distribute.

Frequent reminders: As often as you can.

Say, *"Spirit am I, a holy Son of God, free of all limits, safe and healed and whole, free to forgive, and free to save the world."* Then take a moment and listen for the Holy Spirit's assurance that these words are true.

Response to temptation: Whenever you are tempted to yield to the belief that you are not spirit.

Repeat, *"Spirit am I, a holy Son of God, free of all limits, safe and healed and whole, free to forgive, and free to save the world."*

Encouragement to practice: Every time you practice your mind comes closer to reality. This lesson makes the amazing claim that in some practice periods you save a thousand years. This is because the Holy Spirit takes the healing thoughts you generate in your exercises and carries them around the world, laying them in every mind that is open to the healing they bring. Each mind that accepts them reinforces them, so that through this process, these thoughts become multiplied in power millions of times. The result is that, when the Holy Spirit gives them back to you, your five minutes can indeed become a thousand years. This is obviously a huge incentive to practice, for you can not only immensely speed your own journey, but you can also bring healing to people across the world.

Commentary

The one Self the Course speaks of is spirit. To affirm, "I am spirit" is to let go of all illusions of a split identity, of a good and bad self, and of all attempts we might make to somehow reconcile the ego self that is bound to a body with the spiritual self that is unlimited by a body.

The "nondualism" of the Course is not of the nature that says, "Everything is one because all apparent opposites are really opposite poles of a unity." It does not achieve a concept of unity by somehow uniting the opposites; teaching, for example, that evil and pain are somehow all part of the One. Instead, the Course affirms unity by declaring that all that seems to be opposed to holiness and love is nothing more than illusion and does not exist. "What is all-encompassing can have no opposite," declares the Course's introduction (T-In.1:8). We are being asked to "know your Self as love which has no opposite in you" (W-pI.99.9:8). "Love can have no opposite" (W-pII.259.2:3).

The Course makes great use of repetition; apparently it firmly believes that repeating the same idea over and over can have great benefits. We are told to "practice this truth today as often as you can" (1:4). Why the emphasis on repetition? Because "each time you practice, awareness is brought a little nearer at least" (3:2). You may not achieve astounding breakthroughs; if you are like most people, probably most of the time you won't. But every now and then, "a thousand years or more are saved" (3:2).

For those who think the Course teaches an instant salvation, I'd just like to point out something about that last line. If we can save a thousand years sometimes as we practice, what does that imply about the length of time the whole journey might take? If we are chopping thousand-year segments out of it, how long is the whole thing? It has to be *at least* a thousand years and a day, right? I don't mean to be depressing about this; the Course presents itself as a means of saving time, and clearly teaches that any of us could wake up at any moment we choose to do so. But the implication is pretty clear that it can take thousands of years to get us to the point of willingness to wake up. So we should not be expecting overnight enlightenment; neither should we *not* be expecting it. The attitude towards time that is encouraged by the Course is unconcern about it, since it is ultimately part of the illusion. "Atonement might be equated with a total escape from the past and total lack of interest in the future" (M-24.6:3).

When we make our little effort of five minutes for God, the Holy Spirit joins all of His strength with us (4:3). He takes the little we give and carries it around the world to every open mind. The gifts we give to Him are multiplied by Him ten million times (a thousandfold and tens of thousands more, 6:1). Take that literally or as a figure of speech, it doesn't matter, the meaning is the same; what we give to Him is multiplied and spread to millions of minds because all minds are joined. When I practice, I am not practicing for myself alone; my awakening mind stirs every mind. When you sit quietly for five minutes, you are saving the world.

For each little bit we give, we receive it back multiplied ten million times. "It will surpass in might the little gift you gave as much as does the radiance of the sun outshine the tiny gleam a firefly makes" (6:2). Does this sort of practice matter? You bet it does! When I remember what this lesson says, my time spent remembering "Spirit am I, a holy Son of God" (7:2) seems so much more meaningful and important. It isn't just little me struggling to do my meager practice; it is the Son of God remembering Himself. It is the awakening of the Christ in all mankind.

LESSON 98 ✦ APRIL 8
"I will accept my part in God's plan for salvation."

Practice instructions

Purpose: To firmly and happily dedicate yourself to taking your part in God's plan for salvation; to really take a stand on this today.

Longer: Every hour on the hour, for five minutes (if you cannot do this, at least do the alternate).

This practice strikes me as similar to the practice you did in Lesson 77. There, you repeated, *"I am entitled to miracles"* and then waited for the Holy Spirit to give His assurance that these words are true. Here, in this lesson, you repeat, *"I will accept my part in God's plan for salvation"* and then expect the Holy Spirit to infuse your words with His certainty, so that you really *do* accept your part. Throughout the practice period, keep repeating the idea, and let Him make every repetition a total dedication, made with deep conviction, sincerity, certainty, and full understanding. Let Him turn a mere repeating of "I will accept my part in God's plan for salvation" into an actual accepting of your part. That is your goal for today, to use these practice periods to take a stand, to use them to accept your part in God's plan.

Frequent reminders: Often.

Repeat the idea. Try to think of each hour as preparation time for your next five-minute practice period. "Repeat [the idea] often, and do not forget each time you do so, you have let your mind be readied for the happy time to come" (10:3).

Encouragement to practice: Paragraphs 5 and 6 are a rousing pep talk. They ask the question: Is it not worth five minutes an hour to receive a limitless reward? I recommend reading these paragraphs over slowly and thoughtfully, letting their questions and promises do their intended work in you. Paragraphs 2 through 4 also contain wonderful encouragement. They tell us that by embracing our part in God's plan—which is the point of

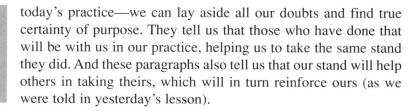

today's practice—we can lay aside all our doubts and find true certainty of purpose. They tell us that those who have done that will be with us in our practice, helping us to take the same stand they did. And these paragraphs also tell us that our stand will help others in taking theirs, which will in turn reinforce ours (as we were told in yesterday's lesson).

Commentary

Today is a day of special dedication. We take a stand on but one side today. We side with truth and let illusions go. We will not vacillate between the two, but take a firm position with the One. (1:1–4)

How happy to be certain! All our doubts we lay aside today, and take our stand with certainty of purpose, and with thanks that doubt is gone and surety has come.
(2:1–2)

Perhaps as I read these lines about certainty, I find myself doubting that very certainty. "Am I certain?" The thought surely arises. Perhaps I feel as if I don't belong with this lesson. My ego reminds me slyly that I am not beyond vacillation. How can I say, "Doubt is gone"?

Yet even in the words of the lesson is the recognition of my condition: "All our doubts we lay aside today" (2:2). Yes, doubts are there. Of course they are. Jesus knows that. He is only suggesting that in these five minutes we spend with him, we lay them aside. Just put them down and be without them for a few minutes. See what it is like. You can doubt later if you want; for now, see how happy it is to be certain.

Within me there is a place that is always certain. It has never doubted. It cannot doubt because it knows. This is my true Self. The doubts are thoughts that question the reality of that Self, the reality of the part of me that is certain, which is the only real part. I am brought by this lesson to question my questioning. I am brought to listen to the certainty, the eternal silence of spirit which knows.

When I am willing, even for a moment, to lay aside my doubts, to still the nattering mind, the yama yama of my idle thoughts, I encounter a still sureness. It is not a certainty of ideas and words; it is an assurance of being, a majestic calm. The stillness is beyond space and time. It has nothing to do with the drama played on this planet.

It is of this we speak today. It is of those who know to touch this eternal calm of which the lesson says:

> They rest in quiet certainty that they will do what is given them to do. They do not doubt their own ability because they know their function will be filled completely in the perfect time and place.   (3:3–4)

I take my stand with those who, before me, have come to this place. It is the same place for all of us. It is the same Self we come to know. And I know, in that holy instant, that if one has been here before me, all will come to find it. If one has been here—and I know that many have been here—all will be here, for one could not come unless it were the reality for all. The nature of this place, this quiet certainty, is a shared nature. It could not be here for me if it were not here for you as well. It could not have been there for Jesus if it were not also here for me.

> They will be with us; all who took the stand we take today will gladly offer us all that they learned and every gain they made. Those still uncertain, too, will join with us, and, borrowing our certainty, will make it stronger still. While those as yet unborn will hear the call we heard, and answer it when they have come to make their choice again. We do not choose but for ourselves today.   (4:1–4)

In the center of the storm of doubts and uncertainty there is an eye of calm. The storm rages on. We still can perceive it. Yet here, here, we are calm. We are quiet. We rest.

Of course you have doubts and uncertainty. That is what you are supposed to notice as you do this lesson! Just for the moment, be willing to have them disappear. There is One within you who is always certain, and He is you; you have forgotten that. Let yourself, however briefly, identify with His certainty, and let go of your identification with the doubts. Make that choice; this is all that is asked.

> He will give the words you use in practicing today's idea the deep conviction and the certainty you lack. His words will join with yours, and make each repetition of today's

idea a total dedication, made in faith as perfect and as sure as His in you. His confidence in you will bring the light to all the words you say, and you will go beyond their sound to what they really mean.   (7:2–4)

"Give Him the words, and He will do the rest" (9:1). A wonderful statement! He is simply asking you to say your faltering "Yes." You are not being asked to turn your doubt into faith. He will do that. "My part in God's plan" is very simple: acceptance. My part is not an active role, but passive. It is to be willing to receive, and that is all. My part is to say, "Okay. Yes. I will accept." Give Him those words; that is all. He will respond with all His faith and joy and certainty that what you say is true.

Over and over through the day, over and over throughout life, give Him those words: "I will accept my part. Yes."

This is surrender. This is all we do. There is nothing else to do. So simple. So difficult to be so simple. So difficult to stop trying to make it on our own. Let go, and let God. "Yes, God. Yes, Holy Spirit. I accept my part."

Tell Him once more that you accept the part that He would have you take and help you fill, and He will make sure you want this choice, which He has made with you and you with Him.

Perhaps I'm not sure I want it. But He will make sure I want it. Come to Him just as you are, with all your doubts, all your fears. Just come. Just say, "Yes. I accept."[1]

---

1. Just a note of interest: There is a poetic meter called *iambic pentameter*, which consists of lines of ten syllables, with alternating soft and hard emphasis: da-DAH da-DAH da-DAH da-DAH da-DAH. You should be able to detect that, after the title and first line, most (but not quite all) of today's lesson is written in that meter.

> We take a stand on but one side today.
> We side with truth and let illusions go.
> We will not vacillate between the two,
> but take a firm position with the One.

Tomorrow's lesson begins the first full lesson in iambic pentameter, and the entire rest of the Workbook, with minor exceptions, follows suit.

LESSON 99 ✦ APRIL 9
"Salvation is my only function here."

Practice instructions

Purpose: To fulfill your only function by letting your dark thoughts be brought out of hiding to meet with the light of God's Thought, so that your darkness is replaced by His light.

Longer: Every hour on the hour, for five minutes (if you cannot do this, at least do the alternate).

- Say, *"Salvation is my only function here. Salvation and forgiveness are the same."*
- Then invite the Holy Spirit into your mind and ask Him to search out the dark and secret places in your mind—thoughts, beliefs, and goals that you wish to keep hidden, either from yourself or from others. When one comes to light, repeat the Thought, *"God still is Love, and this is not His will."* Let the light in this Thought shine away your darkened thought; let it bring you to a forgiveness of that thought. Thus will that darkened place be filled with light. Then begin the process again: Let the Holy Spirit's light search out another dark, hidden thought. Then again repeat, *"God still is Love, and this is not His will,"* and let this Thought forgive and shine away the darkness, replacing it with light. While going through this process, occasionally reflect on the meaning of "God still is Love, and this is not His Will." It means that this world of pain is not His Will. It means that God wills that you are His Son, at one with Him.

Frequent reminders: In between hourly practice periods.

Repeat the idea, realizing that by doing so you invite forgiveness to replace your fears and invite love into your mind, which will reveal to you that you are God's Son.

Response to temptation: Whenever some appearance tempts you to give in to fear and doubt.

Say, *"Salvation is my only function here. God still is Love, and this is not His Will."* Realize that this special message "has the power to remove all forms of doubt and fear...Remember that appearances can not withstand the truth these mighty words contain" (11:1–2).

Commentary

Today we will just comment on a few ideas from this lesson.

> Unshaken does the Holy Spirit look on what you see: on sin and pain and death, on grief and separation and on loss. Yet does He know one thing must still be true: God is still Love, and this is not His Will. (5:4–5)

We see sin and pain and death. We see grief and separation and loss. We think these things are real. What is worse, we believe them to be God's Will. If we attribute this world and its creation to God, these things must be, by implication, God's Will. He created them. If we believe He created the world we must believe that, even if the belief is not conscious. At the very least we believe He willingly created the potential for all this suffering and loss, and somehow planned for us to go through it all.

Much Christian teaching has been very explicit about this. A loved one dies prematurely. We are overcome with an agony of grief and loss, and some well-intentioned friend tries to comfort us with the thought, "It was God's Will." What comfort is that? What does it do but place the blame for our agony on God? What does it do but make God into a monster, an object of fear or even hatred?

Sin, pain, death, grief, separation, and loss are not God's Will. They never have been. Such a belief stems from a covert belief that God has it in for us, that He is punishing us for our sins. To hold such a belief we must also hold a belief that we deserve this awful experience. This is the instant of our belief in separation from God being played out on the stage of the world.

You and I have thought that God wanted this for us. He wanted us to be in this world of pain. Sometimes we have agreed with what we thought of Him, agreed that we deserved to suffer. Sometimes we have angrily denied we deserved it, and accused Him of being unfair. Often we have simply been bewildered, pitifully wondering what we did to deserve all this; sure we must have done something, but at a loss as to what it might be.

Somehow we have never considered this thought:

> All the world of pain is not His Will. Forgive yourself the
> thought He wanted this for you.   (7:4–5)

The essence of our anguish, the element that lends it exquisite sharpness, is the underlying thought that God wants it for us. What cuts deepest is the hidden belief that God is the source of this pain. He Whom my heart loves, and loves uncontrollably, has willed this for me. It is my Father Who inflicts this pain.

We huddle in our suffering and grief, hopeless and lost because we think it is God's Will.

"This is not His Will," Jesus tells us. "Forgive yourself the thought He wanted this for you."

How could we think this of God? How could we believe He is so vengeful? We do not yet realize, yet will discover it so if we grant ourselves this forgiveness, that it is only this thought about God that grants to pain all its power over us. When grief tears at us, fear grips us, or a deep sense of loss seems to shred our very soul, if we will allow ourselves to turn to the Holy Spirit and hear Him say, "This is not His Will. God does not want this for you," we will find it possible to forgive ourselves for thinking it was so. The moment we do, the vitality of pain is removed. "God does not want this for me. This is not from Him." The pain becomes—something else.

It is not God Who wills this pain for us. It is ourselves. We believe God punishes because we believe we deserve punishment. We experience life as pain because we are unconsciously punishing ourselves.

We are not talking here of the event we think has caused our pain or fear: the death of the loved one, the apparent loss of love, the physical suffering. We are talking primarily of the mental-emotional context in which we are holding it. This is an internal thing. This anguish, this pain of grief, this terror—this is not His Will for you. We suffer so incredibly because, all unconscious, we accept most of life as a punishment. A chastisement. A penalty for being the awful thing we think we are.

Because we believe the bite of pain is His Will, we cannot take it to

Him for comfort. He is its Source, we think, so we flee from Him. We deny ourselves the relief of His loving Presence. In that Presence we can find our Self. We can look on our own essence and "look upon no obstacle to what He wills for you" (8:3).

> Then turn to Him Who shares your function here, and let
> Him teach you what you need to learn to lay all fear aside,
> and know your Self as love which has no opposite in you.
> (9:8)

"Forgive yourself the thought He wanted this for you." Bring your pain to Jesus. Pain is not God's Will for you. The experience you are going through can become a doorway to infinite release if you let down your defenses against God. His Presence can transform your experience of pain into one of joy. It can be a path to knowing your Self as Love. Such seems impossible to us, but then, miracles always seem impossible.

Let down the defenses. God is not angry. He does not want this pain for you. Uncoil from your tight fear of Him. Shrink not from His touch. Forgive yourself the thought that He inflicted this on you. Let Him show you your Self as He sees it, and open to His healing Love.

LESSON 100 ✦ APRIL 10
"My part is essential to God's plan for salvation."

Practice instructions

Purpose: To experience the happiness that is God's Will for you; to understand that infecting others with your happiness is how you fulfill your part in the global plan for salvation.

Longer: Every hour on the hour, for five minutes (if you cannot do this, at least do the alternate).

* Repeat the idea. "Then realize your part is to be happy" (7:3); not to make noble sacrifices, just to be happy.
* The rest is a meditation exercise in which you try to find the joy that God placed in you. Look deep within you. Sink down and inward to find the Christ in you, the source of joy. As you sink, you will pass by all of your "little thoughts and foolish goals" (8:5). Don't let them hold you back. You might even ask yourself, "What little thought has power to hold me back?" Or you might simply remember that your one intent is to reach that inexhaustible well of joy at the center of your being; your one intent is to reach the Christ in you. Seek Him with *confidence.* "He will be there. And you can reach Him now" (9:1–2). Throughout the exercise, keep looking deep within for that bottomless well of joy.

Frequent reminders: In between hourly practice periods.

Repeat the idea, remembering that by doing so you are answering your Self's call to you. As usual, I recommend repeating it in this fashion now, so you can see the benefits it brings.

Commentary

God does not have "a plan for my life." He has His plan, and I am a part of it. There are not billions of separate plans for billions of separate individuals. There is the one Will of God, and each of us has an essential part in it. Part of what is being undone by salvation is "the mad belief in separate thoughts and separate bodies, which lead separate lives and go their separate ways" (1:2). Every one of us has the same purpose, the same function, and in that we are united.

Part of the healing of my own mind is the recognition that the other person does indeed share the same purpose with me, and in his reality, wants the same thing. If I look at his ego, I see separate interests—and that may be all that he or she is seeing. But when I give up my interpretation and allow the Holy Spirit to interpret for me, I see that the other person's fear, which is manifesting as attack, is really a call for love and is really a witness to the belief in love within their mind. The result of this is that I see the other person does not need to change to be one with me; they already are one with me! I have a hidden ally in their mind. I have their own secret agreement with me on a common goal.

The part God has "saved for me" (2:1) in His plan is designed to restore me to happiness, because happiness is His Will for me. There is something in us—the ego, of course!—that tells us it is wrong to want perfect happiness. But if perfect happiness is God's Will, then to think I don't deserve it is to oppose God's Will!

For God's Will to be complete, my joy must be complete, for His Will is perfect joy for everyone! If everyone I meet encounters a face shining with joy, they will hear God calling to them in my happy laughter (2:6).

I am essential to God's plan; my joy is essential to His plan (3:1). So, today, let me choose the joy of God instead of pain. "Without your smile, the world cannot be saved...all laughter can but echo yours" (3:3–4).

So my job today, and every day, is to be happy. I cannot be happy if I attack, or judge, or blame, or condemn. I cannot be happy unless I accept; unless I forgive as the Course teaches, looking past all the ego's illusions to see the happy truth in everyone: they want love just as I do.

We teach through our happiness. We call all minds to let their sorrows go by our "joy on earth" (4:2). This is plainly speaking about a manifest joy, one visible on our face through a smile and happy laughter. "God's messengers are joyous, and their joy heals sorrow and despair" (4:3).

A good affirmation for the day would be "My joy heals."

The part we all have in God's plan is to demonstrate, by our perfect happiness, that God wills perfect happiness for all who will accept it as a gift from Him.

Sadness is a choice, a decision to "play another part, instead of what has been assigned to you by God" (5:3). It is the ego's mad desire to be independent of any power except its own. When I clamp down on my happiness I fail to show the world what God wills for us all, and thus I fail to recognize the happiness that is already, always mine.

"Today we [I] will attempt to understand joy is our [my] function here" (6:1). Nothing has to change to make this possible. I can be perfectly happy right now, because happiness does not depend on anything outside of my mind. Getting upset with anything or anyone does not change it; only happiness heals. Only happiness brings lasting change.

We mistakenly think at times that our happiness somehow enables the error and sin of others. If someone is being cruel and I continue to be happy, it seems to condone cruelty. However, to be upset at cruelty does not heal it; it makes it real. It is far more joyous, and far more healing, to see in the cruelty a groundless fear that masks an appeal for help, that shows by its very obscurity that within that person is a longing she or he shares with me; a longing for God, a longing for His gift of happiness. My happiness in the face of cruelty teaches that the grounds for the cruelty do not exist. It does not attack the symptom of cruelty; it undoes cruelty's source. To be happy is not to lose out, to sacrifice, or to die (7:7). It is to live forever.

It is our little thoughts and foolish goals that hold us back from happiness (9:3–5). Our mind has chosen to make something more important than happiness, and what that means in deep, metaphysical terms is that we have made something more important than Christ or God. If we look, He is in us. "He will be there"; that thought is repeated twice (9:1; 10:1). The Christ is in me, waiting to be acknowledged as myself. That is the only true source of happiness, and we all have Him already.

My job today is to be His messenger, and to "find what He would have you give" (10:4). To find happiness in myself and give my happiness to others: that is the reason I am here, that is why this day exists for me. I am essential to God's plan for the salvation of the world. Without my smile, the world cannot be saved (3:3).

LESSON 101 ✦ APRIL 11
"God's Will for me is perfect happiness."

Practice instructions

Purpose: To learn that your sins are not real, and therefore that joy is what God wills for you, not punishment. To experience that joy and escape the heavy load you have laid on yourself by believing your sins are real.

Longer: Every hour on the hour, for five minutes (if you cannot do this, at least do the alternate).

* Say, *"God's Will for me is perfect happiness. There is no sin; it has no consequence."*
* Then do the same kind of meditation that you did yesterday. Look deep within, seeking to find that place where God's Will for you resides, that place where there is only joy, remembering that "joy is just" (6:2), because you never sinned. Remember to focus all of your intent on reaching that well of joy in you, to draw your mind back when it gets caught up in those "little thoughts and foolish goals" (W-pI.100.8:5), and to seek God's Will in you with confidence, knowing that it will set you free from all the pain you've caused yourself.

Frequent reminders: As often as you can.

Repeat, *"God's Will for me is perfect happiness. This is the truth, because there is no sin."*

Encouragement to practice: "You need the practice periods today" (5:1). For they can teach you that your sins were never real. They can bring you to accepting the Atonement. Your feet are already set on the path to freedom, and today's practice can give you wings to speed you along that path, as well as hope that your speed will continue to increase. Therefore, practice happily. "Give these five minutes gladly" (7:1).

Commentary

When *A Course in Miracles* speaks of "salvation" it means being happy. How starkly this contrasts with the common view of salvation, which seems to mean some painful purgation of our sins. If we are honest with ourselves we will find the idea of "paying for our sins" deeply imbedded in our consciousness, appearing in obvious and not so obvious ways. One of the most subtle, but easiest to detect if you are looking for it, is our guilt over being happy.

Haven't you ever noticed that? Somehow it just does not feel right or safe to be "too" happy, or to be happy "too much." We have this weird feeling that if we are "overly" happy something really bad will happen to us. The common saying "This is too good to last" is just one obvious example of the syndrome. Sondra Ray's Loving Relationships Training used to ask the question, "How good can you stand it?" Interesting question.

Or, we may feel guilty about being happy when a friend is sad or upset for some reason; we feel obligated to join them in their misery. And the idea that we could be happy *all* the time just seems too ridiculous to consider. We think misery is a natural part of being alive. Maybe we even thought, with Carly Simon, that "suffering was the only thing made me feel I was alive." (Listen to her song "Haven't Got Time for the Pain" with Course ears. Wow!) We thought we needed it. We never realize that all of these ideas are directly traceable to our belief in sin and punishment. We don't realize that we are actively choosing our unhappiness.

There is no need for penance. There is no price to pay for sin, because there is no sin. Some of us, reading this, will at once think that these ideas are dangerous; if there is no price to pay for sin, then sinners will go wild. Punishment is necessary to control evil, we think. Within the world in which the illusion of bodies seems real, control is sometimes necessary, although perhaps far less often than we think. But debate over how to apply these ideas to social misbehavior (i.e., crime) could distract us for months; this is not the real issue here. We believe it is God Who demands payment for the wrongs we have done to Him. What if we have not done Him any wrong? What if our "sins" are no more to Him than a gnat biting an elephant, affecting Him not at all?

How can I be happy if I believe God is angry at me? How can I be attracted to a salvation that comes through pain, killing me slowly, draining the life from me until I am skin and bones (metaphorically speaking)? Hell is not salvation! It is not a God of love Who would demand such things of us. God is not angry; His Will for me is perfect happiness. If sin is real, punishment is real, and if punishment is real I have every reason to flee from God. That is exactly why the ego promotes such a view of God. "There is no sin" (5:4), says the lesson, and it urges us to "practice with this thought as often as we can today" (5:5).

What about justice? "Joy is just" (6:2). That is what justice is: joy!

When I think on these ideas I often come down to a very simple application, one that comes up for me almost every day. Whenever I do something I don't approve of, or fail to do something I think I should have done, or find myself thinking judgmental thoughts about someone, I often catch myself thinking that I have to go through a decent period of remorse before I can be happy again. Just because I've realized my mistake and decided to change my mind can't possibly be enough to merit being happy again, can it? Don't I have to "pay for my sin" somehow? Maybe, at the least, spend ten minutes in meditation? What utter nonsense!

And yet, the idea keeps coming up. It shows me that I have not rid my mind of this sin-and-punishment idea, that I still think that somehow I have to even the account with God before I can be happy again. What God wants, what God *wills* for me in that instant and in every instant, is happiness. "Obey God" means "be happy." It means let go of my self-important penitence and rejoice in the Love of God. It means accepting the Atonement for myself. What better way to "renounce sin" than to stop letting it drag me down into sniveling self-abasement, to refuse to acknowledge its power to keep me from happiness?

May I, today, refuse to lay the load of guilt on myself. May I lift up my head, smile, and give God glory by the simple act of being happy. The greatest gift I can give to those around me is my happiness.

God's Will for me is perfect happiness. This is the truth, because there is no sin.   (7:6–7)

LESSON 102 ✦ APRIL 12
"I share God's Will for happiness for me."

Practice instructions

Purpose: To further loosen the hold of your belief that pain buys you something. To realize pain has no benefit, no purpose, and no reality. To realize that what you want is the same perfect happiness God wills for you.

Longer: Every hour on the hour, for five minutes (if you cannot do this, at least do the alternate).

- Say, *"I share God's Will for happiness for me, and I accept it as my function now."* Try to mean it, try to make it an actual act of accepting God's Will.
- Then, again spend the rest of the time in meditation trying to "reach the happiness God's Will has placed in you" (3:1). This is the practice you did in the previous two days and will continue doing for several more. Remember to seek this place with real desire, for only here do you feel at home, at rest, safe, and at peace. Remember also to seek with confidence, for if you really will with God to reach this place, then quite simply, "you cannot fail to find it" (4:4).

Frequent reminders: Frequent.

Repeat, *"I share God's Will for happiness for me, and I accept it as my function now."*

Commentary

"I share God's Will for happiness for me."

How nice that the Workbook is going to spend several days devoted to "exercises planned to help you reach the happiness God's Will has placed in you" (3:1). I notice that I'm not trying to "make myself happy" but rather trying to reach a preexistent happiness. An American guru (who went at one time by the name Da Free John, now often called Adi Da) once said, "You are always already happy." That phrase stuck in my mind, and it is consonant with what the Course is saying about happiness.

The Self within me is always happy. It was created happy by God; God's Will "placed" happiness within me. I am not trying to create happiness; I am merely attempting to locate it within myself, to discover it there.

Happiness is contrasted with our belief in the merit of suffering. The lesson isn't expecting us to be at the point of total freedom from this belief. "Yet this belief is surely shaken by now, at least enough to let you question it, and to suspect it really makes no sense" (1:3). This belief is what has been superimposed on our native happiness, obscuring it and causing us to experience pain and suffering. Our happiness is hidden under layers of pain only because we believe there is value in the pain. And I know that I do at least *question* this belief. I don't want to suffer; of course I don't. Yet if I do suffer, I have chosen it, not because I want the pain but because I want what I think the pain will get me. The message of the lesson in this regard is: "Pain is purposeless, without a cause and with no power to accomplish anything" (2:1). Not only so, but everything that I think the pain will bring me is equally lacking in existence. The whole thing is a deceptive mirage conjured up by the ego to keep us from our eternal satisfaction in God.

So today we declare that we share God's Will for happiness for ourselves. We declare that we will to be happy. Simple *being* what God created is our function. "Be happy, for your only function here is happiness" (5:1). The next line (5:2) speaks of our being less loving to our brothers than God is, and says there is no need for it. Unhappiness is our "excuse" for being less loving than God. How can I open my heart to you in love when I am unhappy? By choosing to be happy I am enabling myself to be wholly loving. The Course always seems to be making these interesting connections between things that would never occur to me, but which seem obvious when it points them out.

LESSON 103 ✦ APRIL 13
"God, being Love, is also happiness."

Practice instructions

Purpose: To try again to correct our false belief that God is fearful. To realize instead that, since God is Love, He must be a giver of pure joy.

Longer: Every hour on the hour, for five minutes (if you cannot do this, at least do the alternate).

- Say, *"God, being Love, is also happiness. To fear Him is to be afraid of joy."*
- Then, just as in previous days, enter into a meditation aimed at finding the happiness God placed in you. Seek this holy place in you filled with anticipation, expecting God's joy to take the place of your pain. Realize you cannot fail, because you seek what is already yours. Also seek this place filled with a sense of welcoming the happiness that will surely come to you. And remember to draw your mind back when it drifts off to thinking about all the false promises held out to you by the world's definition of happiness.

Frequent reminders: Frequent.

Reinforce your expectation that you will find God's joy by saying, *"God, being Love, is also happiness. And it is happiness I seek today. I cannot fail, because I seek the truth."* By bolstering your expectancy, this will enhance the depth of your hourly practice periods.

Response to temptation: Whenever you feel any form of fear.

Quiet all your fears with these words: *"God, being Love, is also happiness. And it is happiness I seek today. I cannot fail, because I seek the truth."*

Commentary

"God, being Love, is also happiness." There's one I never heard in church! "God is happiness." (Well, the Westminster Catechism of the

Presbyterian Church did say that man's chief end is to love God and to *enjoy* Him forever. But you didn't hear "enjoying God" talked about very often.) Yet the way the lesson logically presents it, the idea is obvious and inescapable. Without love, no one could be happy. If love were absent, happiness would be absent also. That seems so simple to understand. Happiness must be an attribute of love; they go or come together.

God is Love. "Love has no limits, being everywhere" (1:4). Because that is true, happiness or joy must also be everywhere, just as God is. So God is happiness, as well as love.

The denial of happiness, then, is the denial of God. As a matter of fact, the Text says something very much like that in Chapter 10, when it says that depression is blasphemy (T-10.V.12:3–4). Careful, though; the point of saying this is not to make us guilty about being sad or depressed. The Course's point is to undo guilt, not to create it. It is pointing out the cause of our sadness and depression to us. It is saying, "You're hurting because you are turning your back on God, on Love, on Happiness Itself. It isn't something outside of you, out of your control, that is doing this to you. You have the power to change this, to choose again and lift that depression."

We are sad and depressed because we think that what we have made is real (2:1). We think there are "gaps in love" (1:6), that it is not everywhere and always. We are sad because we believe we are, to some degree at least, outside of God's Love, beyond its "limits." And we are not; we cannot be outside of His Love. If we knew that in the core of our being, we could never be unhappy.

Because I believe love has limits, I have come to be afraid of it: afraid it will be withdrawn, afraid of its conditions, afraid that what seems to be love is only a tease, a tantalizing promise that threatens to disappear if I misbehave. That fear, that constant anxiety over love's potential for disappearance is the source of my lack of joy. How can I be joyful, even when things are "good," if love may be withdrawn at any moment? This is the error of our minds we are practicing to uncover, bring to the light, and let go of.

Right now, this moment, I am encircled by His embrace. Right now, without a single thing changing, the Love of God radiates to me without limit and without reservation or question. To know this is happiness, and it is this I seek today.

LESSON 104 ✦ APRIL 14
"I seek but what belongs to me in truth."

Practice instructions

Purpose: To clear a place in your mind where God's gifts of joy and peace are welcome and experienced.

Longer: Every hour on the hour, for five minutes (if you cannot do this, at least do the alternate).

- Begin with, *"I seek but what belongs to me in truth. And joy and peace are my inheritance."*
- Then again embark on a meditation aimed at experiencing the joy God has placed at the center of your being. This lesson speaks of going to the holy altar within you, the deep place in your mind that contains your fundamental devotions (you may want to visualize this altar). You have covered this altar with the meaningless gifts of the world, thereby obscuring God's gifts. In your meditation, try to clear these gifts away. "We clear a holy place within our minds before His altar" (4:2). Then seek the gifts of joy and peace that God has laid on this altar for you. They are already there, even though you do not see them yet. Ask to recognize them. While seeking them, hold above all else an attitude of confidence, trusting that God's gifts are your inheritance, that they belong to you, that they have always been yours, and that you can claim them now.

Frequent reminders: As often as you can.

Repeat, *"I seek but what belongs to me in truth. God's gifts of peace and joy are all I want."* Doing so frequently will keep you from losing sight of God's gifts in between your hourly practice periods.

Commentary

Today I set aside the complex and focus on two very simple things: joy, and peace of mind. For today I will not concern myself with profound metaphysical truths, nor the invisible reality of my Self. Today I simply seek to know the peace and joy that are mine by right of what I am. I forget about the urgency of my self-made goals, the self-imposed importance of everything I think that I must do. I ignore the man-made standards by which I so often judge myself or let others judge me. Today I center on the only things that are truly important: joy, and peace of mind.

What could be of more value than these? If I lived in a palace, had unlimited wealth, and the partnership of the most perfect mate in the world, and had not peace of mind and joy, I would still be poor. If I lived in a hovel with peace of mind and joy, I would be rich.

And I can have these things; they are my right because of what I am. Joy is my divine right. Peace is my divine right. They are within reach of everyone, regardless of background, regardless of education, regardless of income. Today, in the times I pause to remember, this is what I want to remember. I open myself with gratitude to God Who gave me these gifts; I honor Him by enjoying them. I honor Him by being joyful and peaceful in these five minute periods, and I will not forget in between.

I recall a seminar I did years ago in which we engaged in deep self-searching, attempting to ferret out some of the lies we had been telling ourselves, the negative, self-deprecating thoughts that dragged down our lives. We then distilled these down into what seemed, for each individual, the fundamental lie we were telling ourselves about ourselves. Next, we were asked to take that lie and reverse it, turn it into an affirmation. And finally, we walked about the room, introducing ourselves to one another, and stating our "eternal truth."

I will never forget one woman, although I forget her name so I will simply call her Carol. She walked up to me, looked me directly in the eyes, and smiled a radiant smile. "Hi!" she said. "I'm Carol, and my joy heals."

And you know what? It did. Right in that instant. Something clicked within my mind, and I have never forgotten her, never forgotten her joy. She had discovered a truth about herself. Joy heals! When I am joyful, those around me are healed. Haven't you ever noticed that about other people who are joyful, truly joyful? Their joy heals you. What could be of more value than joy such as that?

Peace heals, too. One peaceful person in a room full of agitated individuals can bring calm to everyone. I choose to be that person today, because it is my right. I settle down in each practice time and "clear a place within [my] mind before His altar" (4:2). I clear that place to receive the eternal gifts, the joy and peace God wants to give me. "Nothing else belongs to us in truth" (4:4). None of the other things I think I want belong to me in the way that joy and peace belong to me. These are "possessions" that bless the world, instead of taking from it. No one loses because I have joy and peace; everyone gains.

I already have these gifts! "I seek but what belongs to me in truth." Joy belongs to me; peace belongs to me. Thank You, God. Thank You.

LESSON 105 ✦ APRIL 15
"God's peace and joy are mine."

Practice instructions

Purpose: To accept God's gifts of peace and joy, and understand that in doing so you actually increase His peace and joy, rather than taking them from Him. Thus, you "learn a different way of looking at a gift" (3:3).

Longer: Every hour on the hour, for five minutes (if you cannot do this, at least do the alternate).

- Think of those to whom you denied God's peace and joy, for thus you denied them to yourself. Say to each one, *"My brother, peace and joy I offer you, that I may have God's peace and joy as mine."* By giving God's gifts where you withheld them, you will now feel entitled to claim them as your own. Doing this preparatory step well will guarantee your success in the following step.

- Then close your eyes and say, *"God's peace and joy are mine,"* and try to find those gifts deep in your mind. Let yourself experience the joy and peace that belong to you. Let God's Voice assure you that God's peace and joy really are yours. This appears to be another meditation aimed at making contact with the happiness God placed in you.

Alternate: On the hour.

If you cannot do the five minutes on the hour, don't think that doing a shortened version is worthless. At least repeat, *"God's peace and joy are mine,"* realizing that by doing so you invite Him to give you the happiness He wills for you.

Response to temptation: Whenever you are tempted to deny God's gift to someone.

Be grateful to this person for providing you with another chance to receive God's peace and joy by giving them away. Channel your gratitude into this blessing: *"My brother, peace and joy I offer you, that I may have God's peace and joy as mine."*

Commentary

Today's lesson adds to yesterday's emphasis on peace and joy. It reiterates much of what was in that lesson, but adds the thought that we receive these gifts by giving them.

"A major learning goal this course has set is to reverse your view of giving, so you can receive" (3:1). This idea, that we receive by giving, runs all through the Course, and is given considerable importance, but this is the only place I know of that learning this lesson is specifically identified as "a major learning goal" of the Course.

We noted yesterday that peace and joy are gifts that increase by being shared. To share my peace with you increases it rather than diminishes it. This lesson makes the rather startling assertion that when I receive peace and joy from God, God's joy grows (4:1). By accepting peace and joy as mine, I am allowing God to "complete Himself as He defines completion" (5:2). Through my experience of this, I learn what my own completion must be (5:3). Even the psalmist of the Old Testament knew something of this when he wrote:

> What shall I render to the LORD for all His benefits toward me? I will take the cup of salvation, and call upon the name of the LORD. (Ps 116:12–13, KJV)

What gift can I give to God to thank Him for His blessing? I can give Him the gift of receiving His salvation and calling on His love. I take the gifts of joy and peace, and "He will thank [me] for [my] gift to Him" (5:6).

We have all experienced this in some small way, at least. We know the joy of giving. We know that when we give love, and it is received, our love is strengthened, not weakened. Shared love is a great joy. Love received is far richer than love unacknowledged. Even receiving the joy of a child over a new toy or a new pet visibly adds to the child's joy. These are small reflections of how God's giving works, and we are meant to be part of it. This kind of giving, the giving of things that increase by being given away, is how we create ("True giving is creation"—4:2) and how we complete ourselves.

The exercises today prepare us to receive peace and joy. The preparation consists of consciously giving away peace and joy to those to whom we have denied them in the past: our "enemies." The people who, in our eyes, have not *deserved* to have peace and joy. We did not realize that in denying the gift to them, we were denying it to ourselves in equal measure. If what we give increases in us, then if we withhold it we are withholding from ourselves as well.

To truly say, and to experience, that "God's peace and joy are mine," we must open our hearts to share peace and joy with the world. It begins with that person to whom my heart has been closed. "My brother, peace and joy I offer you" (7:2; 9:6). If I will open my heart to allow love to flow out, it will also flow in. As I open my heart, allowing peace, joy, and love to flow out to those around me, what I am doing is "letting what cannot contain itself fulfill its aim of giving everything it has away, securing it forever for itself" (4:5). What is it that "cannot contain itself"? My Self, my own Being.

This irrepressible Giver is me.

LESSON 106 ✦ APRIL 16
"Let me be still and listen to the truth."

Practice instructions

Purpose: To lay aside the ego's voice, still your mind, and listen to your Father's Voice, and then to offer Him your voice to speak to all who need to hear His Word.

Longer: Every hour on the hour, for five minutes (if you cannot do this, at least do the alternate).

- Say, *"I will be still and listen to the truth. What does it mean to give and to receive?"*
- Spend the rest of the time waiting for your answer from the Holy Spirit. It is important, however, to understand what you are really asking. You are asking to *receive* from God—to hear His Voice and receive His Word, to be filled up from within—so that you can *give* to your brothers, which in turn will make your receiving even more full and complete. It is important, then, to offer Him your willingness to give what you receive. This giving will apparently happen both *within* the practice period, as your mind goes out to other minds, and *after* the practice period, as what you experience today inspires you to actually "begin the ministry for which you came" (8:3). While you wait for your answer, remember the training you received in earlier lessons: Hold your mind in silent readiness, drawing it back when it lapses into listening to the ego's voice. Listen with confidence: "expect an answer" (8:1). And periodically repeat your question, to renew your posture of expectant waiting.

Frequent reminders: As often as possible.

Say, *"Let me be still and listen to the truth. I am the messenger of God today, My voice is His, to give what I receive."* This will reinforce your choice to receive His Word, which prepares you to give.

Encouragement to practice: Be aware that your practice is not

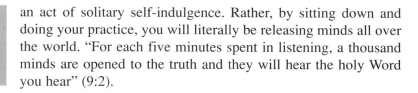

an act of solitary self-indulgence. Rather, by sitting down and doing your practice, you will literally be releasing minds all over the world. "For each five minutes spent in listening, a thousand minds are opened to the truth and they will hear the holy Word you hear" (9:2).

Commentary

At first today's lesson does not seem to follow yesterday's theme on giving and receiving, but midway through it switches back to that theme. It seems like an abrupt switch, perhaps. The first part of the lesson, speaking of stilling our minds to listen to God's Voice, doesn't seem to lead naturally into thoughts of giving and receiving.

Yet this is what we are listening for; this is what we hear. We are learning of our true nature. This is the message of salvation: "When everything is yours and everything is given away, it will remain with you forever" (7:1).

What am I in this world for? According to this lesson, it is to hear the Voice for God telling me of God's eternal gift to me, the gift of Christ, the gift of my Self—God's "dear Son, whose other name is you" (4:7). And it is to extend that same message to the world. This is "the ministry for which you came, and which will free the world from thinking giving is a way to lose" (8:3).

Hearing God's Voice and *speaking* for it are as inextricably linked in this lesson as are giving and receiving. If I truly hear the Voice, I will give Him my voice to speak through me. If I receive the Word, I will share it, because the message *is* sharing. God's Word to me is that I am a savior, a healer, and a bringer of truth. I am His Son, His offspring, like Him, extending healing, offering peace and joy to everyone, letting them know they are His offspring as well.

Sometimes I think we take the Course too seriously and need to lighten up. At other times I think we take it too lightly, and need to take it more seriously. For instance, this lesson tells me that every time I pause for five minutes to be still and listen to the truth, *one thousand minds* are opened to the truth (9:2). Suppose I took that seriously? Suppose I paused every hour, as instructed. In the course of the day, fifteen thousand minds would open to the truth. Suppose everyone reading these comments did that (about six hundred people)? Then nine million minds would open to the truth!

I don't take this kind of thing seriously enough. I shrug if off, thinking that if I only practice once or twice during the day, it's enough. Recently, the old Charlton Heston movie *The Ten Commandments* played on TV. I watched a few minutes of it, enough to remember a line from it that always impressed me. Moses, suffering setbacks in the early days of trying to get Pharaoh to release the Hebrews, prays to God, saying, "Lord, forgive me for my weak use of Thy great power." When I read today's lesson I thought about that line. I thought about how I treat these practice times, many days, as if they don't really matter. I imagine myself as of little consequence in His plan, at least most of the time. But if I take this lesson seriously, I could be instrumental today in bringing light into fifteen thousand minds!

I'm not trying to lay guilt on anyone, least of all myself. I am trying to raise my own consciousness concerning the power God has placed into my hands—or, more properly, into my mind. Each of us who connects with the truth in our minds today, listening to the truth, is contributing to the elevation of consciousness on…I was going to say, "on this planet," but it is far more than that, it is the arousal of Christ-consciousness in the whole universe. That little five minutes, in which, perhaps, nothing seems to happen; in which you may be fighting a wandering mind; or which seems at times to be interminable as your ego prods you to "get back to work" or whatever you are doing—that little five minutes is a very significant contribution to the salvation of the world.

> *Let me be still and listen to the truth. I am the messenger of God today, My voice is His, to give what I receive.*
>
> (10:3–4)

LESSON 107 ✦ APRIL 17
"Truth will correct all errors in my mind."

Practice instructions

Purpose: To let Christ lead you to an experience of the truth, so that you can join Him in His function of bringing truth to the world.

Longer: Every hour on the hour, for five minutes (if you cannot do this, at least do the alternate).

- Start by asking your Self, the Christ, to go with you—which makes sense for you can never be apart from Him. While asking, also pledge to Him "to let His function [of saving the world] be fulfilled through you" (9:2). That is the point of today's exercise: to let Him fill you with the truth, so you can bring it to the world (this is very similar to yesterday's exercise).
- Then ask that the truth come into your mind. Ask with confidence, with certainty of success. Count on truth to be there, for it belongs to you. State your request this way: *"Truth will correct all errors in my mind, and I will rest in Him Who is my Self"* (9:5).
- "Then let Him lead you gently to the truth, which will envelop you and give you peace so deep and tranquil that you will return to the familiar world reluctantly" (9:6). This appears to be a meditation much like those in 69, 73, and 91, in which you rely upon a strength beyond your own to carry you to your inner goal.

Frequent reminders: Do not forget today.

Repeat the idea with confidence, realizing that you are speaking for yourself (for your own desire for release), for the world (for its desire for release), and for Christ, "Who would release the world" (11:2).

Encouragement to practice: Be aware that by letting truth into your mind you will indeed benefit the world. During the practice period, the truth will go out from your mind to other minds to correct their errors. And then, after the practice period, the truth will go with you as you are sent to those in need to give them the gift of truth.

Commentary

This is the promise that gives courage! Errors are only errors, not flaws. "What are errors but illusions that remain unrecognized for what they are?" (1:2).

An illusion that is not recognized as illusion causes us to react as if it were real. If I see an illusory enemy and respond with attack, that does not make me bad or stupid. The reaction is appropriate, given what I believe to be the truth.

I can recall many evenings in the past where I was sitting at home feeling lonely and world-weary. Something in me saw an illusion and believed it to be true. I saw some loneliness or weariness, a need to be comforted, and so I sought comfort in television and in staying up late. What I *did* was not the mistake; the mistake was believing the illusion was real. When I look at the illusion, it vanishes.

The holy instant is a state of mind without illusions, a moment of unquestioned peace, "when you were certain you were loved and safe" (2:3). It is a foretaste of "the state your mind will rest in when truth has come" (3:1). It is my true state. I can find that true state any time I am willing to look at my illusions and to let them go. So often, late at night, I used to feel disconnected, unfulfilled, empty somehow, and I tried to fill that emptiness with fantasy, television, reading, or food. The emptiness is illusion. When I feel that emptiness let me remember it is not real; let me affirm my fullness.

The state of mind that stays exactly as it always was, without shifting and changing, still seems so far away from me. Jesus says, in effect, "It will be yours; it already is yours. It is guaranteed." "It is impossible that anyone could seek it truly, and would not succeed" (6:4). The seeming shifts and changes I go through now are all part of the illusion; they are not real, they are not truly happening. I am safe. I am steady. I am whole.

When the shifting and faltering seem to occur, let me remind myself they are only a dream. They mean nothing, they change nothing. Let me not accord them strength to disturb my peace. Let me not make the mistake of identifying with that shift and change and thinking it is me that is shifting and changing. I am fixed and unalterable.

The errors in my mind are those that tell me I could be apart from Jesus, the Christ. He is my brother. We are the same. He is my Self. How can I be apart from my Self?

Let me take regular times today to return to this center, to recognize that Jesus and I are one Self. Today I will bring any thought that tells me anything different to him for correction. Any thought that tells me I am something other than this calm, serene, fearless, wholly fulfilled Being. Let me watch my mind for thoughts that say otherwise and bring them fearlessly to the light of truth. Jesus, help me to break the connection, the identification with any thought of weakness or emptiness or disconnectedness. Let me lean on your strong arm and trust in you. Let the demons scream and rant and rave around me:

> Though I walk through the valley of the shadow of death, I will fear no evil; for Thou art with me; Thy rod and Thy staff they comfort me.   (Ps 23:4)

You are the Strong One in me, and You are my Self.

LESSON 108 ✦ APRIL 18
"To give and to receive are one in truth."

Practice instructions

Purpose: To offer peace to everyone and feel peace return to you. To thereby learn the unity of cause and effect—that giving (cause) and receiving (effect) are the same.

Longer: Every hour on the hour, for five minutes (if you cannot do this, at least do the alternate).

- Say, *"To give and to receive are one in truth. I will receive what I am giving now."*
- Close your eyes and offer everyone those inner states and qualities that you would like to receive. Say, for example: *"To everyone I offer peace of mind. To everyone I offer gentleness."* "Say each one slowly, and then pause a while, expecting to receive the gift you gave" (9:1). Trust it to come back in the amount that you gave. You may want to single out one person as the one you give your gifts to, understanding that through giving to him you give to everyone.

Frequent reminders: Often.

Repeat the idea, realizing that each repetition makes your learning "faster and more sure" (10:3).

Encouragement to practice: Try to think of today's exercises as "quick advances in your learning" (10:3), revealing to you the nature of cause and effect, and heightening the speed of your progress.

Commentary

The early part of the lesson describes the state of One-mindedness, where all opposites have been resolved into "one concept which is wholly true" (1:3). When that occurs, the concept will disappear because

the Thought behind it will appear instead to take its place.

And now you are at peace forever, for the dream is over
then. (1:4–5)

This is Heaven; attaining this state is beyond the scope of the Course.
But it is our eventual goal, a place where perception and concepts have
vanished, and only knowledge remains.

That "state of mind that has become so unified that darkness cannot
be perceived at all" (2:2) is within me. It is the Christ mind, and from it
comes my peace of mind; from it comes single perception. It is this I call
upon or tap into, drawing it into myself until it takes me over. It is where
I am always and what I am forever, but which I have forgotten.

One of the best and most useful lessons we can learn while drawing
on this state of mind is that giving and receiving are one and the same.
Like all opposites, they are not truly opposite at all; they are part of a
unified spectrum of reality. Neither precedes the other; both occur
together. Through actual experience with this particular example of the
resolution of opposites we can begin to learn how all opposites are
reconciled.

We can produce an experience of this resolution at will. It is an
experiment that always works.

Sit quietly, and mentally begin to send peace to everyone. Think of
specific persons, and say to them in your mind, "I offer you quietness. I
offer you peace of mind. I offer you gentleness" (based on 8:6–8).

Go through your list of friends and relations mentally, sending peace
to each and every one of them. Offer it to the world at large.

What we find as we do this is that, as we offer peace to others, we
experience it ourselves. Quite literally, what we give, we receive.
Immediately. There is no pause, no delay for feedback. Our act of giving
is quite literally also an act of receiving. There is one act and it contains
both things, because there are not two things, only one.

The generalization of this lesson is that cause and effect are one in
truth (my interpretation of 10:2–3). It leads us to realize that my thought
of attack on another is literally an attack on myself, at that very moment.
We think of cause and effect in a linear fashion, as if what I do today
will impact on me tomorrow and in the future. That is an incomplete
picture. In fact, there is no time delay at all. My thought of attack
impacts on me now, just as my thoughts offering peace immediately
make me peaceful. Thought and action are likewise the same. I am

constantly engendering the universe of my experience. In reality, there is nothing outside my mind. Nothing but these thoughts exists. The world we see is just our thoughts given form. They have never left our mind in truth.

LESSON 109 ✦ APRIL 19
"I rest in God."

Practice instructions

Purpose: To rest in God, untouched by the storms of the world.

Longer: Every hour on the hour, for five minutes (if you cannot do this, at least do the alternate).

This exercise is a meditation in which you sink into stillness by using the line "I rest in God." Let that line draw you into a rest in which you have "no cares and no concerns" (5:1), and in which the turmoil of the outer world cannot touch you. While in this state, call to all your brothers, "your distant brothers and your closest friends" (8:3), and welcome them into the holy temple within where you rest with God. Realize that their rest will deepen and complete yours.

Frequent reminders: Often.

Repeat the idea, realizing that you are not only reminding yourself of your resting place, but reminding all Sons of God of their resting place, including those no longer in the body and those not yet born. Try repeating the idea now while holding in mind the sense that "I am reminding every mind of its true resting place."

Response to temptation: Whenever you face a problem or experience suffering.

Repeat the idea, knowing it has power to heal all suffering, solve all problems, and carry you past storms and strife into the peace of God.

Encouragement to practice: Incredible power is ascribed to your practice of today's idea (see especially the first three paragraphs), not only for you, but for everyone. Repeating today's idea has power to call every mind to rest along with you, including those who came in the past or haven't come yet (see 2:5 and 9:5). Paragraphs 6 and 7 relate an inspiring scenario. Your five minutes bring healing to an injured bird and a dry stream. Then, a tired

335

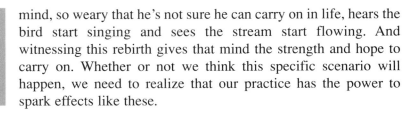

mind, so weary that he's not sure he can carry on in life, hears the bird start singing and sees the stream start flowing. And witnessing this rebirth gives that mind the strength and hope to carry on. Whether or not we think this specific scenario will happen, we need to realize that our practice has the power to spark effects like these.

Commentary

This lesson epitomizes what so many of the lessons are trying to get me to do: simply to take a little time out of my day to rest in God. To be quiet. To be at peace. To sense the stillness that lies at the depths of my being, placed there in creation by God. To do this not just once in the morning, but often during the day, repeatedly reminding myself that this peace, this serenity of being, is my natural state, while the frenzy of distractedness, the ping-pong of opposing thoughts that so habitually occupies my mind, is what is unnatural. What has seemed to me to be "normal" has been nothing but "frantic fantasies [that] were but the dreams of fever that has passed away" (5:5).

> There is a place in you where this whole world has been forgotten; where no memory of sin and of illusion lingers still. There is a place in you which time has left, and echoes of eternity are heard. There is a resting place so still no sound except a hymn to Heaven rises up to gladden God the Father and the Son. Where Both abide are They remembered, Both....
>
> ....The changelessness of Heaven is in you, so deep within that nothing in this world but passes by, unnoticed and unseen. The still infinity of endless peace surrounds you gently in its soft embrace, so strong and quiet, tranquil in the might of its Creator, nothing can intrude upon the sacred Son of God within. (T-29.V.1:1–4; 2:3–4)

And here I rest in God. Here I breathe the air of Heaven. Here I can remember what I am.

The lesson tells me of wondrous things that come from my willingness to take these times of rest. These moments of quiet are not for me alone. They are my mission for the world; through them I am bringing peace to every mind. Our practice times are no small thing, to be lightly skipped over; the author places extraordinary importance on them:

- He says they bring the end of suffering for the entire world (2:5).
- He tells us there is no suffering, nor any problem, they cannot solve (3:3–4).
- Through these times we are calling all the world to join us in rest (4:5–6).
- Every time we rest, we heal the world: We gladden a tired mind, give song to a wounded bird, and give flowing water to dry stream beds (6:1–2).

I came to bring the peace of God into the world. This is my "trust" (8:2), my sacred mission, my reason for being. Jesus asks me to "open the temple doors and let them come from far across the world, and near as well; your distant brothers and your closest friends; bid them all enter here and rest with you" (8:3). This is what I am doing each time I stop the mental chatter and sit, quietly, and rest in God. I am like Buddha, casting his compassion on the world. I *am* Buddha; I am Christ.

I envision myself as a cell in a cosmic body, a body that has been invaded by a deadly virus, the virus of antagonism, of disharmony, of hatred, envy, and strife; the virus of bitterness, sorrow, and pain; the virus of despair, depression, and death. As I take my time of rest, it is as if this little cell has discovered how to produce the antitoxin, the remedy for the virus: the peace of God. And the connecting current of our shared thoughts is the bloodstream that carries this antitoxin to other cells, who absorb it and begin, in turn, to produce this healing substance. Peace of mind, the antitoxin for the world.

It is for this I have taken birth. It is for this I am here, and nothing else. Through these simple practices, we bring healing to all of time, past and future:

> Time is not the guardian of what we give today. We give to those unborn and those passed by, to every Thought of God, and to the Mind in which these Thoughts were born and where they rest. And we remind them of their resting place each time we tell ourselves, "I rest in God." (9:4–6)

LESSON 110 ✦ APRIL 20
"I am as God created me."

Practice instructions

Purpose: To cease worshipping false images of who you are and to instead seek and find your true Self.

Longer: Every hour on the hour, for five minutes (if you cannot do this, at least do the alternate).

- Say, *"I am as God created me. His Son can suffer nothing. And I am His Son."*
- The rest of the practice period is a meditation which is extremely similar to what you did with the first occurrence of this idea, in Lesson 94 (you may want to go back and read my practice instructions for that lesson). Your whole focus should be on seeking that deep place in your mind where your true Self, the Christ, abides. To get there, you need to set aside all your images of who you are—they are the idols and graven images referred to in the lesson. As usual, remember your training in meditation: focus all your intent on sinking down and inward to the center of your mind, draw your mind back from wandering as often as necessary, and approach your Self with *desire*, for it is your Self Who has the power to save you.

Frequent reminders: As often as you can.

Repeat the idea to remind yourself of your true Identity as the holy Son of God.

Encouragement to practice: You are told to "practice today's idea with gratitude" (5:3) because, quite simply, it carries so much power (as you can see from reading the first five paragraphs). This is the Workbook's premier lesson. You are reminded repeatedly today that today's idea is "enough" (1:2; 2:2–4) to save you, that it is "all you need" (2:1; see also 3:3).

Commentary

This one thought, we are told, is enough to save not only ourselves, but the world, if we believe it to be true.

> Its truth would mean that you have made no changes in yourself that have reality, nor changed the universe so that what God created was replaced by fear and evil, misery and death. (1:3)

This is the primary meaning of this idea for me: nothing I have done has changed anything. Ego thoughts have done nothing, changed nothing. Fear and evil, misery and death have not occurred. I remain as God created me. I have not damaged anything. The tiny, mad idea to replace God on His throne accomplished absolutely nothing. I am still perfect, innocent, golden love.

> It is enough to let time be the means for all the world to learn escape from time, and every change that time appears to bring in passing by. (2:4)

We tend to see the ravages of time. We see the aging body. We see loved ones come and go. We see decay and death and loss. But time can be the means by which we learn escape from time and all its changes. We learn through time to look beyond the appearances of change to what is unchanging, and we come to learn that only that is real. "Lead me in the way everlasting" (Ps 139:24).

> If you are as God created you, then there has been no separation of your mind from His, no split between your mind and other minds, and only unity within your own. (4:2)

No separation, no split, no schizophrenia. I am one Self, united with my Creator, and limitless in power and in love. I can trust my brothers, who are one with me, because I am as God created me and have never split from them. What I find within myself when I listen to the Spirit's quiet voice is what all others are as well. I find within myself the Holy One. I am This; you are This. Let me simply become aware of any thought that says anything different, any picture of myself that creates a false and limited idol, and just drop that thought.

Deep in your mind the holy Christ in you is waiting your acknowledgment as you. And you are lost and do not know yourself while He is unacknowledged and unknown.

(9:4–5)

VII

Review III: Introduction and Lessons 111 - 120

INTRODUCTION

Again a review. Nearly everyone I know, especially when they first do the Workbook, finds the reviews either boring or frustrating. It's an interesting testimony to the orientation of our minds. Apparently we crave constant newness, and the idea of repeating practice with the same ideas, even for just the second time, seems lackluster and mundane. We want to get on to something new and exciting.

What we don't seem to grasp is that any one of these ideas could be the breakthrough for us. Toward the end of this review introduction, the reviews are called a "second chance with each of these ideas" (12:3). Now, if you are anything like me, you probably didn't rack up a perfect score in practicing the first time. You forgot the hourly practices, you did only a few each day, and perhaps missed days entirely. So, think of this as a second chance to get the benefits of each lesson. I know I'm thinking of it that way, and I need it.

The Review III introduction is one of the most important discussions of Workbook practice in the book. The attitude toward practice portrayed here is extremely informative. First of all, following the instructions literally as given, and doing the two five-minute practices, with short practices on the hour and on the half hour, is considered very, very important. We are "urged" to pay attention to the instructions and "to follow [them] just as closely as you can" (1:3). An attitude that says it doesn't matter how you do the lessons clearly doesn't fit with this admonition.

Second, the author is being very reasonable. He recognizes that it may be impossible for us to literally carry out the instructions in an "optimal" way (2:1). For example, a mother caring for very young children may not be able to stop every half hour and close her eyes; a clerk in a retail store may not be able to get away from customers for a minute every half hour. "Learning will not be hampered when you miss a practice period because it is impossible at the appointed time" (2:2). So if you miss because it is impossible to practice, that's okay. Notice, however, the word "impossible." It doesn't say "inconvenient" or "awkward," it says "impossible." The key to whether or not our learning will be hampered is not whether or not we actually do the practice, but why we don't do it. Is it because we can't, or because we don't want to?

Notice, also, that we aren't expected to make "excessive efforts to be sure that you catch up in terms of numbers" (2:3). To me that implies that making reasonable efforts to catch up is something that would be proper. So if I miss at noon because I'm talking with my boss, but I'm free at 12:15, it would make sense to stop for a minute and make up that missed practice period. But the goal is not ritual; it isn't about "doing it perfectly." The crux of the matter is our desire and our willingness, not the number of practice periods. We aren't to become obsessive about this stuff.

Third, the author obviously understands our ineptitude and resistance in regard to practice. Skipping a practice period because we don't want to do it (or don't "feel like it") will hamper our learning! (3:1). Again I say, this statement is hardly consistent with any thought that following instructions doesn't matter, and that it's enough to just read over the lesson in the morning. He takes particular pains to point out the ways we deceive ourselves, hiding our unwillingness "behind a cloak of situations you cannot control" (3:3). He points out that many of these have been subtly engineered by ourselves to "camouflage…your unwillingness," and urges us to learn to distinguish these from situations that are truly "poorly suited to your practicing" (3:4).

I have often found that the times when I "just do it" even when I don't feel like it are often the ones in which I have the deepest awareness of a shift in consciousness occurring.

Lest some of you feel offended by all this, let me say that it's perfectly okay to just read over the lesson in the morning and forget about the practice directions. Just be aware that this is what you are doing, and that it is your choice. Don't fight yourself. If you really don't want to do the practice now, don't do it. This type of disciplined practice may not be what you need right now. You may not be ready now, but you will be later. Or perhaps you'll find another spiritual path. But don't think you can pass judgment on the Course and say it didn't work for you, unless you do the lessons as instructed. If you do them, they will work.

Notice, too, that practices you deliberately skip because you "did not want to do them, for whatever reason, should be done as soon as you have changed your mind about your goal" (4:1). This kind of missed practice you should try to make up! Why? "Your practicing can offer everything to you" (4:5).

The middle part of the introduction gives us fascinating instruction in having faith in our own minds. We are supposed to allow our minds to relate the ideas we are reviewing to our needs, concerns, and problems. The picture you get is almost one of free association, placing the idea in our mind and then seeing where it leads us. Jesus asks us to give faith to our mind that it will use the ideas wisely. This seems to be designed to counteract our self-doubt. Perhaps we think that, left to range freely, our minds will wander off into the forest of ideas and get lost. But we are "helped in [our] decisions by the One Who gave the thoughts to [us]" (6:2), that is, the Holy Spirit. If we wander, He will guide us back.

In this kind of exercise we are learning to trust our own inner wisdom. "The wisdom of your mind will come to your assistance" (6:5). If what comes to mind is a paraphrase of the day's idea, let it come. Often, your own paraphrase of the idea will be more effective for you than the original form, and will stick in your memory much better.

The final portion of the introduction returns again to general practice instructions and what might be deemed a "pep talk." The emphasis in this part is on bringing the ideas into application in our lives, all day long (9:2–3). "These practice periods are planned to help you form the habit of applying what you learn each day to everything you do" (11:2).

"Do not repeat the thought and lay it down" (11:3). Sounds familiar to me! If nothing else, this review superbly exposes all the little tricks our minds have been using to avoid the benefits of the lessons! Don't let that discourage you. Just becoming aware of the devious ploys of the ego's resistance is a major advance in the curriculum. But don't stop there, either; now that you are aware of the ego's tricks, you can turn the situation around and begin to let the ideas of the lessons "serve you in all ways, all times and places, and whenever you need help of any kind" (11:5).

And just in case we missed the point, look how the review introduction closes. I've added a little emphasis here to make the point even plainer:

> Forget them not…. (12:2)

> *Do not forget* how little you have learned. *Do not forget* how much you can learn now. *Do not forget* your Father's need of you, as you review these thoughts He gave to you.
> (13:1–3)

REVIEW III PRACTICE INSTRUCTIONS

Purpose: A second chance at the last twenty lessons, in which you can practice them more diligently, and which can carry you so far ahead that you will continue your journey "on more solid ground, with firmer footsteps and with stronger faith" (12:3).

Remarks: Please follow the format below as closely as you can. If you miss a practice period (either the longer ones or the every-half-hour ones) because you simply couldn't do it at the appointed time, your progress is not hindered. Don't worry about making those ones up. If, however, you missed because you just didn't want to give the time, your progress is hindered. Those ones *should* be made up. You missed because you thought some other activity would deliver more. As soon as you remember that "your practicing can offer everything to you" (4:5), do your make-up practice periods as a statement that your real goal is salvation.

In deciding if you should make up a practice period, be very honest with yourself. Do not try to pass off "I didn't want to practice" as "I couldn't practice." Learn to discern between situations truly unsuited to practicing and those in which you could practice if you wanted.

Longer: Two—one in the morning, one in the hour before sleep (ideally the first and last five minutes of your day), for five minutes (longer if you prefer).

- Read over the two ideas and the comments about them, so that the ideas are firmly placed in your mind.

- Then close your eyes and begin to think about the ideas and also to let related thoughts come (you should remember both of these practices from earlier lessons). This time, however, there is an important twist. Let your mind search out various needs, problems, and concerns in your life. As each one arises, let your mind come up with thoughts related to the ideas, thoughts which apply the essence of those ideas to the need, problem, or concern. In other words, let your mind creatively apply the ideas so as to dispel your sense of need, problem, or concern. This is a more developed version of letting related thoughts come, in which this technique combines with response to temptation (there were hints of this in Review II—see my comments on response to temptation in my Review II practice instructions).

- Remember your training in letting related thoughts come: place the ideas in your mind. Trust your mind's inherent wisdom to generate related thoughts (this trust is a big theme in this review). Don't strain—let your mind come up with thoughts. The thoughts need only be indirectly related to the ideas, though they should not be in conflict. If your mind wanders, or you draw a blank, repeat the ideas and try again.

- If you try this and it is just too unstructured for you, I have found the following more structured version to be useful:

1. Let a need, problem, or concern come to mind, and name it to yourself (for example, *"I see this conflict with so-and-so as a problem"*).

2. Repeat one or both of the ideas for the day (for instance,

345

"I am spirit").

3. While repeating the idea, watch your mind for any sparks of insight that arise which apply the idea to your need, problem, or concern, and verbalize this insight to yourself (for example, *"As spirit, I cannot be hurt. I am totally invulnerable"*).

4. Either continue with more such related thoughts, or go on to the next need, problem, or concern.

Frequent reminders: On the hour and on the half hour, for a moment.

- Repeat the applicable idea (on the hour, the first idea; on the half hour, the second idea).
- Allow your mind to rest in silence and peace for a moment.
- Afterwards, try to carry the idea with you, keeping it ready for response to temptation.

Response to temptation: Whenever your peace is shaken.

Repeat the idea (the one you are carrying with you from your last practice period). By applying the idea to the business of the day, you will make that business holy.

Remarks: These shorter practice periods (frequent reminders and response to temptation) are at least as important as the longer. By skipping these, which you have tended to do, you have not allowed what you gained in the longer periods to be applied to the rest of your life, where it could show just how great its gifts are. After your longer practice periods, don't let your learning "lie idly by" (10:1). Reinforce it with the frequent reminders every half hour. And after those, do not lay the idea down (11:3). Have it poised and ready to use in response to all your little upsets. In this way, you forge a continuous chain that reaches from your longer practice periods all the way into the hustle and bustle of your day.

LESSON 111 ✦ APRIL 21

Review of:

(91) "Miracles are seen in light."
(92) "Miracles are seen in light, and light and strength are one."

 Practice instructions

See instructions on page 344.

Commentary

I am willing today to open my mind to the light. I am eager to emerge from my darkness, and I will not fear what the light will expose. Nothing I have been hiding can hurt me. I am hungry for the truth. Within me is only innocence, and not what I have feared was there. Within me, in the light, is what I have been longing all my life to find. I am a miracle.

The light of God is my strength. I feel unable to rise up to this high calling, but my weakness is the darkness His light dispels. I do not need to be strong to come to the light; the light gives me strength as I approach it. I feel I lack the strength to see with the purity of vision called for by the Course, but God gives me the strength I need, and in His light, I see. Thank You, Father, for the light You shine into my mind today. Thank You for the light right now, in this moment.

"COURSE-SANCTIONED" EXCUSES TO NOT PRACTICE THE LESSONS

Why is it that we so often miss the practice periods the Workbook asks us to do? In my experience, many of us will answer this question with spiritual-sounding answers, such as "I am staying in the present with the Holy Spirit rather than chaining myself to a clock." Perhaps the most often-quoted "spiritual" reason for not practicing is "The whole point of the Workbook is to screw it up and forgive yourself." Such statements make it sound as if, by not doing the Workbook practice, you are in a deeper sense truly doing *the Course*.

These sentiments have long struck me as out of accord with the Workbook's own statements about missed practice periods. Recently, however, I discovered two places in the Workbook that specifically address this phenomenon of our inventing Course-sanctioned excuses to not practice.

The first is in Lesson 9. This is one of those early lessons where we look around the room and apply the idea to anything our eyes alight on. The lesson urges us not to aim for "complete inclusion" of everything in the room, yet at the same time to avoid "specific exclusion" of objects we resist applying the lesson to (W-pl.9.5:1). It then says:

> Be sure you are honest with yourself in making this distinction. You may be tempted to obscure it.
> (W-pl.9.5:2–3)

In other words, we might want to blur the distinction between *avoiding* complete inclusion and *engaging in* specific exclusion. To understand this, let's say that there is a photo of our mother on the wall and we choose not to apply the lesson to it. The real reason we chose this was because we didn't want to challenge certain ego perceptions we have, but then we told ourselves, "Well, the Course did say to not try to include everything." This is what it means to engage in specific exclusion in the name of not trying for complete inclusion. We didn't practice due to our ego's resistance, but then we rationalized that we didn't practice because of some Course-sanctioned excuse.

The same pattern crops up a hundred lessons later in Review III. There, the Course tells us that when circumstances really do not permit, we shouldn't try to do our practice on the hour. It even says that our spiritual progress will not be hurt by missing that practice period. But then it talks about another kind of situation, where we really could do our hourly practice, but don't feel like giving the time to it. Missing that practice period, we are told, *will* impede our spiritual progress. Then comes this important counsel:

> Do not deceive yourself in this....Learn to distinguish situations that are poorly suited to your practicing from those that you establish to uphold a camouflage for your unwillingness.
> (W-pl.rlll.ln.3:2, 4)

In this case, you just don't want to do the practice period. You'd rather spend your time doing something else. But then you tell yourself that you are not practicing because you are too busy, or you are in conversation. And since the Course has told you that you don't have to practice under those circumstances, you are claiming that your lack of practicing falls under a Course-sanctioned excuse.

These two passages are amazingly parallel. Both have in common the following scenario:

- There are two categories: 1) not practicing due to unwillingness and 2) not practicing because in this particular case the Course excuses you.

- You need to carefully and honestly distinguish between these categories.

- Instead, however, you tell yourself that an example of category #1 (not practicing due to unwillingness) is really an example of category #2 (not practicing because in this particular case the Course excuses you).

- In doing so, you are being dishonest with yourself.

- You are hiding your unwillingness behind a facade of legitimacy.

It is amazing just how parallel the two passages are, isn't it? It is also amazing just how well the author of the Course knows us. We do not fool him for one minute. He sees right through our excuses. And while we are under the penetrating light of his calm gaze, perhaps we should be willing to look at ourselves with the same objectivity. Let us, then, ask ourselves: How much are we doing what he is talking about here? How much do we choose to not practice due to unwillingness, but then put some justifiable veneer on it? Have we even perhaps thrown a cloak of holiness around it? Have we made our lack of practicing a sign that we really "get it"?

Not practicing is not a sin. It will not make God angry with us. It will just deprive us of the benefits of practice. Thus, the more we can face our refusal to practice for what it is, the more we can remedy that refusal, and get back to experiencing those benefits.

LESSON 112 ✦ APRIL 22
Review of:

(93) "Light and joy and peace abide in me."
(94) "I am as God created me."

 Practice instructions

See instructions on page 344.

Commentary

I am the home of light. My native being is inherently compatible with light. Light belongs with me and in me. I am *not* the home of darkness. By nature, when unhindered by illusion, I radiate light to everything around me.

I am the home of joy. Sorrow and sadness are unnatural to me. When joy enters my mind it feels as if it belongs there. There is nothing in me that is inconsistent with pure joy. There is nothing in me that inhibits an atmosphere of constant joy. By nature, joy emanates from my being and stays with me. I am comfortable with joy, and joy is comfortable with me.

I am the home of peace. I am where peace belongs. Peace is native to my mind. Peace is my natural state of mind, when it is set upon the truth. Nothing in me is discordant with a steady state of peace. Peace harmonizes with my being. My natural radiance spreads peace to every mind around me.

This is how God created me. This is how I am, and will be forever. I am as changeless as God Himself, one with Him, and He with me. Nothing I have ever done or said or thought has changed this truth about me. What I am cannot change; what I am is eternal and consistent in its being.

Today, recognizing the truth about myself, I welcome the light. I welcome pure joy. I welcome God's peace. And I share them with the world.

LESSON 113 ✦ APRIL 23

Review of:

(95) "I am one Self, united with my Creator."
(96) "Salvation comes from my one Self."

 Practice instructions

See instructions on page 344.

Commentary

There is something inexpressibly appealing about the idea of being "one Self." Much of modern psychology talks about "integration" of the disparate aspects of our being. So much of the time we feel as if we are made up of varying segments, sometimes cooperating but more often than not conflicting with one another. There is what the Jungian analysts refer to as our "shadow" self, all the dark, repressed tendencies that follow us around as dark figures in our dreams.

The Course holds out the vision of a unified Self. It speaks of "a mind at peace within itself" (W-pII.8.3:4). It tells us that because we must be only one Self, we cannot be in conflict. The Text talks about our war against ourselves (Chapter 23), and says that the apparent conflict we see in the world around us is nothing but a reflection of the illusion of conflict we all carry within our own minds. It says, "Peace begins within the world perceived as different, and leading from this fresh perception to the gate of Heaven and the way beyond" (W-pI.200.8:2). The peace must begin within us, in the serenity and calm of an integrated self, in a mind free of conflict and attack.

The Self we are speaking of is more than just a whole individual, however. It is one Self shared by all, "at one with all creation and with God" (1:2). The two are really different aspects of the same thing, for as we free ourselves of conflict within ourselves, our conflict with the world will miraculously disappear.

This is why salvation comes from this one Self. When we have consolidated ourselves, recognized the truth of our unified being, this condition of wholeness naturally extends to others. From within the circle of Atonement (T-14.V), we draw others to their own wholeness, shared with us.

Today I still my mind from all its conflicts. I dissociate myself from the dissociation, I separate myself from the separation. I take time in quiet to break my sense of identification with this image of a shattered self, and I let myself sink down into the awareness of "one Self" within me, Who I really am. Conflicting images of myself come and go with startling frequency; they cannot be my reality. Something persists beneath it all, the "hum" of being in which all the flash and drama seems to occur. It is this steadiness that I am, not the ephemeral shooting stars of thought that seem to demand my attention. I embrace this one Self, avidly, saying, "Salvation comes from my one Self. This oneness is my salvation. This oneness is my reality."

LESSON 114 ✦ APRIL 24
Review of:

(97) "I am spirit."
(98) "I will accept my part in God's plan for salvation."

 Practice instructions

See instructions on page 344.

Commentary

"No body can contain my spirit" (1:3) or limit it. So often, even when we connect with spiritual reality in some way, we think of ourselves (as someone has said) as human beings having a spiritual experience; it would be more accurate to conceive of ourselves as spiritual beings having a human experience. The first way of looking at it makes our humanness the basic reality, with the spiritual something that comes and goes within that reality. The second way of looking at it realizes that the spiritual is our basic reality, and the "human" experience is something that comes and goes within that reality. "I am spirit" (1:1). That is what I am. The experience of being a human being in a body is a temporary, passing thing. It does not alter what I am, and it cannot limit what I truly am, although it seems to do so because I believe in limitation.

The value of such things as psychic or paranormal experiences lies in the degree to which they help us realize that the limits under which we habitually operate are not firm and fixed. Minds really are joined, space and time are not absolute limits, and so on. We all have many abilities of which we are not aware (see M-25.1:3), because we are not bodies but spirit. The transcendence of these limits, while appearing "supernatural" from the bodily perspective, is really completely natural; it is the limits that are unnatural (see M-25.2:7–8). Anything that breaks our illusion of being limited to the body and makes that illusion less solid in our perception is useful, to the degree that we use these experiences or powers under the direction of the Holy Spirit. The experiences and powers are not ends in themselves.

Our primary purpose is not to develop paranormal abilities, but to fulfill our part in God's plan for salvation, which is simply to accept His Word about "what I am and will forever be" (2:2). In other words, spirit, complete and holy and everlasting. Notice that: my function, my part in the plan, is to *accept* the truth about what I am. It may seem as though that has nothing to do with anyone else, but it has everything to do with everyone else, because what I am is a part of everyone and everyone is a part of me. My illusion is that I am separate; the truth is that we all are one. To accept the truth about myself is to accept you as part of me, and us together as part of God. That involves forgiving you, forgiving the world, and forgiving God. To accept the Atonement for myself *means* to extend the Atonement to everyone around me; I cannot find my Self if I exclude you. To accept the fullness of my Self and my own creative power, I must cease to see myself as the victim of anyone or anything— because that is not the truth about what I am. To accept my unsullied integrity of being, I must cease to blame you for anything and realize that I am affected only by my own thoughts.

Today, I will relax and let go of bodily limits. I will look at the limits I believe in and remind myself they are unreal. I will cease to "value what is valueless" (W-pI.133.Heading) and let go of my investment in my body. I will care for it as I would any useful possession, but I will try to undo, at least a little, my attachment to it and my feeling of identity with it. It will die. It will cease to be, but I will not, for I am spirit. I will accept this reality about myself because this is my part in God's plan for salvation.

LESSON 115 ✦ APRIL 25
Review of:

(99) "Salvation is my only function here."
(100) "My part is essential to God's plan for salvation."

 ### Practice instructions
See instructions on page 344.

Commentary

My job is to forgive the world for all of *my* mistakes (1:2). Unless I have some idea of the Text's teaching about projection I won't have a clue as to what this means. Every "sin" I see out there in the world (even things like terrorist bombings) is, in some way, a projection of a judgment I have made on myself. My reluctance to forgive anything, or to see it as a call for love which merits a response of healing love, is a reflection of the degree to which I haven't forgiven myself. The form I perceive "out there" may be shifted, altered, and transmogrified from my own form of "sin" so that I don't recognize it. In fact, so far as the ego is concerned, the more unrecognizable the better. But the content is always the same. I may not blow up children, but if I judge those who do as unforgivable I am harboring a belief in vengeance that I haven't forgiven in myself, and my judgment of the bombers is my judgment of myself.

Therefore, when I release the world from guilt I have released myself.

My only function is to forgive. Not to be a success in the world, not to change anything, just to forgive. It's only when I accept this that I come to real inner peace.

My doing this—my part in forgiveness—is essential to the whole process. For the world to find its complete guiltlessness I must stop laying guilt on it. There are people around me today who need guilt lifted from their shoulders, and doing that is why I meet them. It may look like I'm doing business, buying and selling, teaching, mending broken bones, or programming computers, but the real reason I am here is to save the world, to forgive, and to release from guilt.

355

LESSON 116 ✦ APRIL 26
Review of:

(101) "God's Will for me is perfect happiness."
(102) "I share God's Will for happiness for me."

Practice instructions

See instructions on page 344.

Commentary

Somewhere in our collective psyche there is a dark and terrible myth. The myth is that God's Will means suffering and sacrifice, the loss of all that we love, giving up everything that is dear to us for the sake of His Kingdom. Doing God's Will in this myth is a dark and cheerless thing. In one of her lectures, Marianne Williamson characterized it as: "I thought I would have to wear gray for the rest of my life."

God's Will is happiness. How could Love want anything else for us? Every human being, even the lowest, wants those they love to be happy. How could we have ever imagined that God, the perfect Lover, wanted anything other than perfect happiness for us?

All our suffering, then, must come from a belief that there is some "other" will opposing God's that wants to ruin our happiness. We secretly suspect, perhaps, that that will is our own. If not, we know "they" are out there someplace, and they have it in for us. Yet there is no "other" will. There is no malevolent power stalking the universe and targeting us for destruction. There is only God.

I share God's Will for happiness for me. I am not incurably self-destructive, with some dark and unfathomable vein of antipathy towards God, the universe, and myself inescapably driving me to death. My real will is one with God's, and I will happiness. "I will there be light," as Lesson 73 said. His Will is really all I want.

The Course talks a great deal about the dark foundations of the ego that drive toward death. Those Stygian currents do flow within our minds, and they do warp and befoul our experience in this world. But the Course does not leave us there, without hope. It bears the message that although the ego seems very real, it is not us. It has no power over us; it is a mistaken fabrication our minds have made. And because we made it, we can unmake it. Because we chose it, we can choose again. If we stop being afraid of those murky corners of our minds and look at them, we will recognize they have no substance. We will see through them to our true Self. We will see what those dark foundations have been hiding all this time: our own intense and burning love for God, and His for us (see T-13.III.2:8). Here, in the *real* foundation of our being, we want what God wants, we love what God loves, and we will what God wills.

Today, then, I let myself rest in the happy thought that at the root of my being is an irresistible drive towards truth. Perhaps I do not yet experience "perfect happiness," but I will. I must. Because the heart of my heart wills it, and joins with God in willing it, and there is nothing that stands in the way that has any reality or power to resist.

> Nothing can prevent what God would have accomplished from accomplishment. Whatever your reactions to the Holy Spirit's Voice may be, whatever voice you choose to listen to, whatever strange thoughts may occur to you, God's Will *is* done. (T-13.XI.5:3–4)

> There is no chance that Heaven will not be yours, for God is sure, and what He wills is as sure as He is.
>
> (T-13.XI.8:9)

LESSON 117 ✦ APRIL 27

Review of:

(103) "God, being Love, is also happiness."
(104) "I seek but what belongs to me in truth."

Practice instructions

See instructions on page 344.

Commentary

"Let me remember love is happiness, and nothing else brings joy" (1:2). One of the things that over time has convinced me of the truth of the Course is this very experience: I am happiest when I am loving. I don't just mean "I'm happy when I'm in love," in the romantic sense of the word, although that certainly isn't excluded. When love flows through me, whether it is in a closely intimate relationship or in something more "distant" (sitting here writing these notes and thinking of all of you, for instance), I am happy. Loving makes me happy. No, more than that: "Love is happiness" (1:2).

(Barry Kaufman wrote a wonderful book called *To Love Is to Be Happy With*.[1] I always thought that was a profound title.)

On the other hand, anger is misery. If I think about how I feel when I am angry, I will notice that I don't like the way I feel. As much as the Course is about concepts and about changing our mind, often the change of mind is a decision about feelings: "You can begin to change your mind with this: *At least I can decide I do not like what I feel now*" (T-30.I.8:1–2). Feelings can be very useful when we think about them, and use them as motivators for changing our mind. Anger makes me miserable; loving makes me happy. Therefore, I will choose love. Is that paying attention to feelings, or is it logic? Or both? Whatever it is, it works.

I said that noticing that loving and happiness go together has helped convince me that the Course is true. Here's why. The Course says we are wholly loving and wholly loveable. It says, "Teach only love, for that is what you are" (T-6.I.13:2). Sometimes I don't feel as if I am love. Yet if when I love I am happy, love must be my will; it must be my nature. What is happiness, except the freedom to be myself and to fulfill my nature? If I am happy when I love, then I must *be* love.

That is what this line means: "Love is my heritage, and with it joy" (2:2). My heritage. My nature. What I am. Love belongs to me in truth, and with it happiness, since they are the same thing.

Today, as often as I can, I intend to remind myself: "Love is happiness." And then, in that moment, to just be the love that I am. If I want to be always happy, let me always be loving. And joyous! Oh, the happiness and joy when the heart opens and lets out the love! May I not cause myself pain today by holding it back. God bless you all!

---

1. Barry Neil Kaufman, *To Love Is to Be Happy With* (New York: Fawcett Crest Books, 1977).

LESSON 118 ✦ APRIL 28
Review of:

(105) "God's peace and joy are mine."
(106) "Let me be still and listen to the truth."

 Practice instructions

See instructions on page 344.

Commentary

The substitutes that I have made are what stand in the way of my accepting God's peace and joy. I already *have* God's peace and joy, but my ego has decided they are not enough. As the Course says, I want "more than everything" (T-29.VII.2:3); my own wholeness is not enough. That section of the Text actually says that my seeking for "more than everything" is shown by the very fact that I am in this world. "No one who comes here but must still have hope, some lingering illusion, or some dream that there is something outside of himself that will bring happiness and peace to him" (T-29.VII.2:1). "Happiness and peace" is what I am looking for, but outside of myself. I have denied that they are within me, where God placed them.

In order to find the peace and joy that are inherently mine, I have to "exchange" all the substitutes I have made. I have to let go of looking for happiness anywhere outside of myself. That isn't easy, in my experience. It seems to happen gradually, over time. Little by little we learn that what we are looking for in the world simply isn't there, not in any lasting way. Little by little, in parallel, we begin to take little tastes of our internal joy and peace. As we begin to weigh the two experiences it starts to become obvious that the peace and joy that come from within are much more reliable and satisfying than that which comes from without. We may try for a time to hold on to both, but it doesn't work. Eventually we will let go, and fall back into the arms of God. Eventually we will simply accept God's peace and joy.

My voice keeps trying to declare how things should be. Essentially the Course is telling us to stop listening to our own advice: "Resign now as your own teacher" (T-12.V.8:3), it urges us. We have to stop thinking we are in control, that we know what to do and what is needed, and learn to listen. Like a drowning person, our own efforts to save ourselves are the biggest barrier to our Life Guard. We need to trust Him, to lie back and let go.

The best way I know of to learn to do this is to practice doing it. To simply sit down for five, ten, fifteen minutes (whatever the lesson calls for, whatever seems right) and, after very briefly reviewing the idea of the day, just to be quiet. It seems hellaciously difficult, many days, to simply be quiet. The minute I try my mind starts reminding me of things: "Don't forget to make that phone call. You need yogurt from the store. What are you going to do about your relationship with X? You haven't done your laundry this week. You are overweight and you're going to die." I take a deep breath. Another. Another. I repeat the words for the day, "Let me be still and listen to the truth" (2:1). Or I say, "Help!" to the Holy Spirit. I let the thoughts come and go. I step back and watch them and try not to get drawn in. And I listen; maybe there is some word from my Teacher that will come. And sometimes, there is. Sometimes I just get very quiet, and the chatter of thoughts subsides, if not completely, to a dull, background murmur, like a crowd in a busy restaurant that I'm not really paying attention to. I practice getting quiet and listening. I don't know about you, but I think it is a worthwhile exercise. Sometimes, it even carries over into my day, and I find myself listening to the Voice and not to myself as I move through it. And that's what it's all about.

LESSON 119 ✦ APRIL 29
Review of:

(107) "Truth will correct all errors in my mind."
(108) "To give and to receive are one in truth."

Practice instructions

See instructions on page 344.

Commentary

The first idea speaks of the correction of all error. The two explanatory sentences that follow speak on a very high level, defining "error" as any thought that we can be hurt. What I am is spirit. Spirit is eternal and unchanging, created by God like Himself. By the Course's definition, what can be hurt or damaged is not real. That includes our bodies, our woundable psyches, everything we see in the physical universe; all of it has an end. "Nothing real can be threatened," says the introduction to the Text (T-In.2:2). What I am learning is the invulnerability of my being, the eternal safety of my Self, at rest in the Mind of God.

We are undergoing a very gradual and gentle weaning away from our identification with the ephemeral. What we are, in truth, does not die. We have dreamed a dream, and foolishly have come to believe the dream is us. We are not the dream; we are the dreamer. (The Text speaks at length of this in Chapter 27, sections VII and VIII.) The Holy Spirit eases us through a transitional phase, changing our terrifying dream into a happy one, so that we will waken softly and joyfully, no longer gripped by terrors of the night.

How are we to shift our dream? It is too great a leap to go from a state where pain and hurt and death are bitter realities to us, into an awareness of our eternal nature. So the second idea for today speaks of the means by which we can begin, gently, to shift into the happy dream: forgiveness. We come to recognize our sinlessness, and thus our Self, by forgiving all things around us. We have to *learn* to accept the truth in ourselves, and we do so by learning to see past the error in others, until with a start of recognition, we realize that what is beneath the errors of others is Something we share with them. We find ourselves in our brothers and sisters, through forgiveness. What we have learned to give to others has, all the time, been given to ourselves. We awaken by awaking others. We teach peace to learn it. In kindness and mercy towards others, we ourselves fall into the kind and merciful heart of God.

LESSON 120 ✦ APRIL 30
Review of:

(109) "I rest in God."
(110) "I am as God created me."

 Practice instructions

See instructions on page 344.

Commentary

Every now and then I'm glad my old high school English teacher taught me to diagram sentences. I find myself doing things like noticing the main phrases in a sentence like this: "I rest in God and let Him work...while I rest..." (1:2). For me, today, what this says is just to relax and trust the process. Just to "let go and let God," as the saying goes. Sunday is traditionally a "day of rest" in the Christian tradition, and for most of us, a day in which it is convenient (more than other days) to practice resting. Periodically it is beneficial to take one day, and consciously make it a day of rest for yourself. That doesn't mean you might not do something productive, but if you do, it will be because it is something you enjoy doing, something you want to do.

Today I want to remember *peace*.

Sometimes I get so worried I won't make it. I pick at the scabs of my healing mind, wondering when they will heal completely. I fuss and wonder what else I can be doing to make the healing happen faster. Fussing just makes it worse. Fussing is what I am being healed *from*. So let me rest today. Ahhh!

As I rest, my Father tells me Who I really am. "The memory of God comes to the quiet mind" (T-23.I.1:1). When I allow myself to settle back in spirit, I find a firm foundation, the bedrock of my Self, as God created me. I'm okay. The turmoil I am so concerned about is nothing but "sick illusions of myself" (2:3). What I am is just fine, and I don't have to protect It. I am home.

VIII

Lessons 121 - 140

"Forgiveness is the key to happiness."

Practice instructions

Purpose: To learn to give forgiveness and see that, when you do, you receive forgiveness.

Morning/evening practice: Two times, for ten minutes.

- Identify someone to forgive. Think of someone you dislike or despise or find irritable or want to avoid. The one that has already come to your mind will do.
- Close your eyes and see him in your mind, and look at him a while. Try to find some little spark of light in your picture of him. You are looking for some loving or true quality in him, or perhaps some kind thought or caring gesture of his—some distant reflection of the light of God in him. Everything hinges on this, so take your time. Once you find something, see it symbolized as a tiny spark of light somewhere in your dark picture of him. Then see this tiny spark slowly expand until it completely covers your picture of him, replacing all the darkness with light. In other

words, see him *only* in light of this one loving quality or act. See this as the only clue to who he really is. If you succeed, he will seem to be a holy person, without a single flaw, radiating light. You might even imagine Great Rays shining out from him. Now look at this changed picture a while. Appreciate how lovely and spotless it is.

- Now think of someone you consider a friend. Try to transfer the light you saw around your "enemy" to this friend. This makes the friend seem to be much more than a friend. He is revealed to be your savior, with power to enlighten you with just one glance of his holy eyes.

- Now let your savior offer you the light you gave to him. Then let your former enemy unite with him, so that they both offer you this light. Why wouldn't they give this holy gift to you, when you gave it to them, and revealed your holiness in the process? See rays of forgiveness pouring off of them and onto you, absolving you of your "sins," causing you to radiate the same Great Rays that they do. See yourself at one with them, united in the holy light of forgiveness that you have given and received. "Now have you been forgiven by yourself" (13:3).

Frequent reminders: Every hour—do not forget.

Repeat, *"Forgiveness is the key to happiness. I will awaken from the dream that I am mortal, fallible and full of sin, and know I am the perfect Son of God."* To understand these lines, it helps to insert "through forgiveness" at the beginning of the second sentence. Remember the old adage "To err is human, to forgive divine"? Forgiveness is what proves to us that we are more than human, that we are divine.

One more point: If you are really going to say these lines every hour, you'll need to either spend time memorizing them or have them written down on a card.

Commentary

The longer I study the Course the more this lesson makes sense. When I first read it, it seemed unlikely to me that forgiveness was *the* key to happiness. I could see it being *a* key but not *the* key. As the Course's explanation of the root of our problems began to sink in, however, I began to see that in one way or another, unforgiveness was behind every problem. Then it began to make sense that forgiveness would solve them all.

Look at the litany of ills that comprise this description of "the unforgiving mind" (2:1–5:5):

- Fear
- A cramped, constricted mindset that offers no room for love to grow and thrive
- Sadness, suffering, doubt, confusion, anger
- The pairs of conflicting fears; the one that speaks to me most eloquently is "afraid of every sound, yet more afraid of stillness" (3:1)
- The distortion of perception that results from unforgiveness, making us unable to see mistakes as what they are, and perceiving sins instead
- Babbling terror of our own projections (4:2)

I recognize myself, or at least memories of myself, in so many of these phrases: "It wants to live, yet wishes it were dead. It wants forgiveness, yet it sees no hope" (4:3–4). I've felt like that. These paragraphs describe us all. I think that if someone does not recognize themselves somewhere in here, they are not being honest with themselves. And the most awful thought of all is this one: "It thinks it cannot change" (5:3). Hasn't that fear struck at your own heart at one time or another? I know it has struck at mine.

When we admit to ourselves that these descriptions fit us, that we find ourselves in one or another of these states of mind, the very word "forgiveness" sounds like an oasis in the Sahara. Cool, soothing and refreshing. As we were told in Lesson 79, we have to recognize the problem before we realize what the solution really is.

"Forgiveness is acquired. It is not inherent in the mind" (6:1–2). This states a fundamental principle that explains much of the methodology of the Course, and explains why some sort of transition is necessary between where we think we are and where we already are in truth. If we are already perfect, as God created us, why do we have to learn anything at all? Because the solution to the problem of guilt is forgiveness, and forgiveness was *not* part of our mind as God created it. There was no need for it. Without a thought of sin the concept of forgiveness is meaningless. Because we taught ourselves the idea of sin, now we must be taught the antidote, forgiveness. Forgiveness has to be *acquired*.

But the unforgiving mind cannot teach itself forgiveness. It believes in the reality of sin, and with that as a basis, forgiveness is impossible. Everything it perceives in the world proves that "all its sins are real" (3:3). Caught in unforgiveness, we are convinced of the correctness of our perception of things. We do not question it. From that perspective there is no way our minds can even conceive of true forgiveness. This is why we need the Holy Spirit: "a Teacher other than yourself, Who represents the other Self in you" (6:3). There has to be a "higher Power" Who represents a different frame of mind. The source of our redemption has to be outside of the ego mindset, apart from it, untainted by it. And so He is.

He teaches us to forgive, and through forgiveness, our mind is returned to our Self, "Who can never sin" (6:5). Each person "outside" of us, each representative of that unforgiving mind crowd, "presents you with an opportunity to teach your own [mind] how to forgive itself" (7:1). Our brothers and sisters, manifesting their egos, full of the fear, pain, turmoil, and confusion of the world, snapping at us in their terror, are our saviors. In forgiving them we forgive ourselves in proxy. As we teach salvation we learn it. As we release others from hell, we release ourselves. As we give, we receive.

This is what the Course is all about. As we practice today, let's realize that we are engaging in the central exercise of the Course; we are learning "the key to happiness." And let's not think we already know forgiveness; let us come with humility, ready to be taught by One Who knows.

LESSON 122 ✦ MAY 2
"Forgiveness offers everything I want."

Practice instructions

Purpose: "To feel the peace forgiveness offers, and the joy the lifting of the veil holds out to you" (11:2).

Morning/evening practice: Two times, for fifteen minutes.

Sink into the place in your mind where the gifts of forgiveness abide. Try to experience the happiness, peace, and joy that forgiveness offers you. Seek that place in you earnestly, and with gladness and hope. This practice seems to be an example of Workbook meditation. It seems very similar to the practice in the early 100s, where you quieted your mind and tried to experience the happiness and joy that God has placed deep within you. Based on past lessons, you probably should begin by repeating the idea for the day, and then use that idea from time to time to pull your mind back from wandering.

Remarks: Approach these practice periods filled with hope, because you have reached a crucial turning point in your journey. After this, the road will be much smoother and easier. Practice "earnestly and gladly" (9:2), with confidence that today salvation can be yours.

Frequent reminders: Every fifteen minutes, for at least one minute.

Say, *"Forgiveness offers everything I want. Today I have accepted this as true. Today I have received the gifts of God."*

Remarks: These shorter practice periods are obviously extremely important. Practicing at least a minute four times an hour is no small feat for most of us. The purpose of these shorter practice periods is to keep in our minds the gifts we accepted in the morning practice. Those gifts will fade away unless we renew them throughout each hour. I suggest repeating these lines as a genuine, heartfelt dedication to accepting the truth of today's idea. When repeating these lines you may want to make them specific: *"Forgiving [name] offers everything I want [happiness, peace, safety]. Today [day of week] I have accepted this as true. Today [date] I have received the gifts of God."*

Commentary

There is a phrase near the end of this lesson that never fails to stand out to me. It speaks of how forgiveness enables me to "see the changeless in the heart of change" (13:4). For me, this phrase has become a whole other way to look at what forgiveness is.

Behind every appearance lies something that does not change. Appearances change, and rapidly. This is true both physically and in more subtle perceptions. But the spirit within us does not change, having been created by the eternal. Forgiveness is a way of looking past the appearances to the unchanging reality. It disregards the temporary picture of the ego's mistakes and sees the Son of God. As Mother Teresa said of each one she helped, we see "Christ, in his distressing disguises."

> Forgiveness lets the veil be lifted up that hides the face
> of Christ from those who look with unforgiving eyes upon
> the world. (3:1)

Forgiveness is giving up all the reasons we have built up for withholding love. The veil of all our judgments is lifted, and we behold something marvelous, something wonderful, something indescribable. "What you will remember then can never be described" (8:4). (So I won't try!) When forgiveness has removed the blocks to our awareness of love's presence, we see love everywhere. Love is unchanging and unchangeable. There is no wonder, then, that forgiveness offers everything we want, bringing peace, happiness, quietness, certainty, and "a sense of worth and beauty that transcends the world" (1:4). When you see the changeless in the heart of change, distress drains right out of your heart because there is no reason for it.

Why are our moods and feelings such a problem to us? Because we identify with them, because as the moods and feelings change we believe we have changed. The Course is teaching us to learn to identify with something beyond change, with the Mind of Christ within ourselves that never changes and never will. Here is a very simple rule of thumb: *What changes is not me.* My Self is "unchanged, unchanging and unchangeable" (W-pI.190.6:5).

This is starting to take better shape in my mind as I began to see that forgiveness is simply to see the changeless in the heart of change. It is to recognize that the only thing that needs to be changed is the thought that it is possible to change the Mind of the Son of God. It is to realize that all my ego "thoughts" have changed nothing, and all my brother's ego "thoughts" also change nothing. It is to realize that what is changeable is not me; to cease to identify with that which changes, and to cease to believe that my brother *is* my changing perceptions of him. Forgiveness means looking beyond what is changeable to that which is changeless.

Our pain comes from identifying with the ephemeral. Our peace comes from identifying with the eternal. Nothing that changes is created by God. Nothing that changes is really me. What is changeable is threatened by change, and "nothing real can be threatened" (T-In.2:2). Therefore, nothing that changes is real.

All that changes is nothing but a passing landmark on the journey to the eternal. It is nothing to be held on to. Think of a line of stones by which you cross a creek; you do not cling to each stone as you pass it. You appreciate its value in moving you toward the other side, but you do not lament its passing. Your goal is the other side. That is the only value of things in this world, things which include our own bodies and the bodies of our loved ones as well as material things, or even concepts in our thought system. Changing things are to be valued only as stepping stones to that which is eternal, to be gently released as we take the next step toward the changeless, which is always with us, always the reality of our being, even as we appear to journey towards it.

LESSON 123 ✦ MAY 3
"I thank my Father for His gifts to me."

Practice instructions

Purpose: The Workbook is assuming you have made some real progress on your journey to God, with the result that your journey will now be smoother because much of your resistance has subsided. You are to devote today to giving thanks for these gains. You do not realize their full extent. Only by giving thanks for them will you appreciate how great they really are.

Morning/evening practice: Two times, for fifteen minutes.

You spend these fifteen minutes giving thanks to God and receiving His thanks to you. What exactly are the things for which you give thanks? I detect three classes of things. First, God's gifts to you in Heaven: His eternal Love for you; the fact that He created you changeless, so that none of your mistakes can taint your Identity. Second, His gifts to you on earth: that He has not abandoned you but is always with you, speaking His saving Word to you; that he has given you a special function in His plan. Third, the gains you have made as a result of His gifts: the fact that the Holy Spirit is gradually saving you from your ego.

You also spend time receiving God's thanks to you. What exactly is He thanking you for? He is thanking you for hearing His message, applying it, and speaking it to others. He is thanking you for healing others through your demonstration of greater sanity, health and security. He, in other words, is thanking you for your application of His truths, just as you are thanking Him for this same thing. Take time to open your mind to the idea that God is not judging you, but thanking you, wholeheartedly and with total sincerity, and that His thanks to you and yours to Him join as one.

Remarks: God will take your gift of thanks to Him, multiply it hundreds of thousands of times, and return it as His immeasurable thanks to you. This multiplication of your gift will give it vastly increased power to save you and the world. Each

second that you give will be returned to you in the form of years
of progress, enabling you to take eons off the world's journey to
God.

Frequent reminders: Every hour, for an unspecified time.

Repeat the idea and spend some time thanking God for all His
gifts to you.

Commentary

Today's lesson causes me to reflect on all my Father's gifts to me,
personally. I think that is what it is intended to do for each of us, sort of
a day to count your blessings. So bear with me as I share some of my
personal reflections with you, and take it as inspiration to do the same
for yourself.

I think I've been on a spiritual journey most of my life, perhaps all
of it. I can remember certain incidents as a very young boy that seemed
to say my direction was already set, way back then. I wrote a poem once
for my babysitter; I think I was in second grade at the time. I can still
recall the words:

> Thank Thee for the sun and fields,
> Thank Thee for the bush and tree,
> Thank Thee for the things we eat.
> Thank Thee, Lord, Thank Thee.

I remember one Monday after school, when I was about ten,
gathering three of my friends around me on a street corner and trying to
explain to them why I was so impressed with the Sunday School lesson
I'd heard the day before. It was a lesson on Ecclesiastes 11:1, "Cast thy
bread upon the waters, for thou shalt find it after many days." I was so
struck by the principle involved, that what you give comes back to you,
and that our wealth could be measured by how much we give, rather
than what we acquire. It is a message that I heard again, very clearly,
many years later in the Course.

I had a deep spiritual hunger and desire for God all through
childhood, although I veered off in other directions for some time,
getting into trouble for youthful pranks, even police trouble, and being
horribly embarrassed at being caught shoplifting by a store owner who
had offered me a summer job (which of course I did not get). I had

experiences of what I would now call a holy instant several times, a sense of the nearness of God, and yet I couldn't seem to find Him most of the time.

At sixteen I had a "born again" experience, and I became, for the next twenty-two years, a fundamentalist Christian, although never firmly aligned with any religious denomination. Something kept me breaking out of all the molds people tried to cast me into. I read the mystics, I read the heretics, as well as the Bible. I didn't want anyone to draw me a map of the New Jerusalem; I wanted to walk its streets for myself. I spent years in a typical Western religious pattern, "fighting against sin" as Jesus calls it in the Course (T-18.VII.4:7). As he says in that sentence, "It is extremely difficult to reach Atonement" that way!

All through those twenty-two years, I hungered for God. All through those twenty-two years, I was miserable most of the time, disgusted with myself. All through those twenty-two years, I wondered if I would ever "make it." Finally, at the end of those years, I gave up. I laid aside my Bible and let it gather dust. I decided that Christianity was, for me, a dead end. I despaired of ever "crossing Jordan" and "entering the promised land." I decided I was just going to have to accept life as it was, and learn to live with it.

About six years went by. I was still seeking something, but no longer seeking anything spiritual. Or so I told myself. My relationship with God was in a holding pattern, and we weren't talking. I read psychology. I did the est training. I read Zen books and tried meditating a bit. I studied Science of Mind. I also enjoyed the world thoroughly, as I'd never allowed myself to do before, including some great sex, and making more money than I'd ever had in my life. I began to realize that the things which spoke to me in the psychology, secular philosophies, and Eastern religious writings that I was studying were all exactly the same things that had really spoken to me in Christianity. There was a "perennial philosophy," as Aldous Huxley called it, that ran through everything, a central core of truths that everyone who ever "made it," regardless of their religious background or lack of one, seemed to agree on. And the more I got clear about it, the more I realized it was all stuff I'd always known somehow. Like "cast your bread upon the waters."

Then, in January 1985, I found *A Course in Miracles*. Ever since, I've been reading and studying these books, and practicing as best I can what they say. And as I look at my life today, I can see that somewhere along the line my life underwent a major shift. I moved from a gloomy certainty that I would never find real happiness to a steady conviction that I *have* found it.

So as I read today's lesson, a deep sense of gratitude washed over me. As I read the first paragraph, I felt I could honestly say it applied to me very well:

> There is no thought of turning back, and no implacable resistance to the truth. A bit of wavering remains, some small objections and a little hesitance, but you can well be grateful for your gains, which are far greater than you realize. (W-pI.123.1:3–4)

A few days ago (in 1995) a friend of ours, Allan Greene, passed away at 51. He was a quadriplegic who moved to Sedona just over a year ago to take part in the ACIM classes and support groups of the Circle of Atonement. Our support group met in his home, since he was almost completely immobile. He could move nothing but his head and his shoulders, the latter just slightly. Within the last two years, a leg and a hand had to be amputated. He used to say that he was giving up his identification with his body piece by piece. Allan was a long-time student of the Course, one of the very few I know who actually knew the Course's scribe, Helen Schucman. He argued with it for a long time, but had settled in to a steady determination to realize all that it taught. Under adversity far greater than most of us can imagine, Allan maintained an amazing sense of humor and a joyful determination to heal his mind, whatever happened to his body. Miracles happened around him regularly; he took them as a matter of course. Last month, when he was having his gall bladder removed, he took no anesthesia because he had no feeling in his lower body at all, but a nurse held a screen during the operation so he would not have to watch himself being cut open. During the whole operation, Allan was conversing with the nurse about *A Course in Miracles*!

Last night (May 2, 1995) we had a memorial meeting for Allan. A very large number of people attended, and one after another shared how Allan had touched their lives, including a half dozen or so of the professional caretakers who had administered to him over the last year. It became evident that Allan's life had impacted scores and scores of people. I am sure *his* gains were, as our lesson tells us, far greater than he realized. I know Allan did not think of himself as particularly advanced. He lamented almost to the end about what a slow learner he was. He often argued with his caretakers, and had one or two walk out on him in a rage. He had his doubts. But from the evidence tonight in people whom he loved and people who loved him, he had advanced much farther than he thought.

I hope that is true of me; I believe it is true of all of us. We cannot know now, although I'm sure we shall at some point, all the positive impacts we have had on those around us with things as little as a smile, a small act of kindness, or a gentle, loving touch at the right moment. Perhaps, as it often was with Allan, nothing more than our laughter, or making someone else laugh. Last Thursday, when Allan was in the hospital, we paused in our ACIM evening class and had a few minutes of silence for him. The next day, the day before he died, one of our students phoned him in the hospital and told him about our minutes of silence. Allan said, "It would have been more appropriate if you'd had a few minutes of telling jokes."

Let me then, today, take time to express my gratitude to God for all His gifts to me. I thank Him for this Course, which has become my certain way home. I thank Him for the relief from all those years of quiet desperation. I thank Him that, when I wandered off, He never deserted me. I am so grateful for His Spirit within me, my Guide and Teacher, and for all the loving friends and companions on the journey He has brought my way (especially, tonight, for Allan). I am so grateful for all of *you*, and for the opportunity He has given me to share with you all, and to receive from all of you. I thank Him that I am beginning to remember my Self. I thank Him for the steadily increasing assurance that I will find my way all the way home.

I thank my Father for His gifts to me!

LESSON 124 ✦ MAY 4
"Let me remember I am one with God."

Practice instructions

Purpose: To practice and experience the idea that you are one with God, and to thereby lay hold of your own peace and also free the world. Today is a turning point in the Workbook, your first half hour practice time, and also your first longer practice in which you are given no instructions and are left to fly on your own—a preview of things to come. The practice is deepening—getting longer as well as less structured.

Longer: One—whenever it seems best, for thirty minutes.

There are no specific words or guidelines for this meditation. You are simply meant to devote the practice period to today's idea, to abiding in oneness with God, to trying to experience that oneness, and to letting His Voice direct your practicing. Jesus is clearly trusting that you have learned enough from the lessons thus far to spend this quiet time profitably, without getting hopelessly lost in mind wandering. You therefore should draw upon all the training you have received up until now, and should also be open to the Holy Spirit's promptings during this time.

Encouragement to practice: Paragraphs 9-11 are there to provide incentives to really do the practice and to appreciate how important it is. They teach us to see this half hour as a mirror, surrounded by a golden frame, set with thirty diamonds, one for each minute. During this half hour we will look into this mirror and see our face transfigured into holy the face of Christ—our true Self, Who is at one with God. In this mirror, we will recognize ourselves as Who we really are. Even if nothing of the kind seems to happen during this time, we can be confident that sometime, "perhaps today, perhaps tomorrow" (10:1; 11:1, 3), this experience will come to us as a result of this half hour.

Frequent reminders: Hourly.

Repeat, *"Let me remember I am one with God, at one with all my brothers and my Self, in everlasting holiness and peace."* Doing so will add yet more diamonds to the frame around the mirror in which you see your true Self. I suggest either memorizing this sentence (which is composed of three lines of iambic pentameter) or writing it down on a note card. I also recommend that, while repeating it, you try to feel each kind of oneness individually—first oneness with God, then oneness with your brothers, then oneness with your true Self.

Commentary

This lesson holds forth a very high view; it comes from an elevated state of mind. Basically, in the first part of the lesson it seems to assume we are enlightened already. And, of course, from the perspective of this state of mind, we are. "Enlightenment is but a recognition, not a change at all" (W-pI.188.1:4). If it is not a change, then enlightenment must mean recognizing what is always so. This lesson, then, is simply stating the truth about us, the truth that we have been hiding from ourselves.

To pray, to give thanks for the truth as God sees it, the truth *about us* as He sees us, can be a very profitable exercise. Try taking a paragraph of this lesson (or the whole lesson) and turning it into thanksgiving, verbalizing your thanks as you read. For example, from the second paragraph, I might say:

> Thank You for the holiness of our minds! Thank You that everything I see reflects the holiness of my mind, which is at one with You, and at one with itself. Thank You for being my Companion as I walk this world; for the privilege of leaving behind shining footprints that point the way to truth for those who follow me.

This indeed *is* our calling; it is why we are here. Perhaps most of the time we don't remember our Identity in God. All the more reason to set aside a day given to remembering, for reminding ourselves. We could understand this lesson as a portrait of an advanced teacher of God. Everywhere she walks, light is left behind to illuminate the way for others. The teacher walks in constant awareness of God's Presence. She feels God within. God's thoughts fill her mind, and she perceives only the loving and the lovable. This teacher of God heals people in the past, the present, and the future, at any distance.

Slip into that mindset for a while today, my heart. Be the Christ; let all the obstacles to it that your mind throws up be brushed aside. *Practice* awareness of oneness with God.

In the latter part of the lesson it is clear that the author hasn't flipped out and isn't living in a dream world. He knows very well that we might sit for our half hour and get up thinking that nothing happened. He knows that, for most of us, what he is talking about is so far from our conscious awareness that we might devote thirty minutes to trying to recognize it and not find a glimmer of it. He doesn't care. He doesn't care because, from where *he* sits and how *he* sees, he knows with total certainty that what he is saying about us is the truth. And he tells us not to let it bother us:

> You may not be ready to accept the gain today. Yet sometime, somewhere, it will come to you, nor will you fail to recognize it when it dawns with certainty upon your mind. (9:2–3)

Even though we experience nothing, he tells us that "no time was ever better spent" (10:3).

The practice for today of a single half hour given to remembering oneness is unusual in the Workbook. The routine goes back to two fifteen-minute periods, or three ten-minute periods, in the coming days. But what is more significant, actually, is the lack of "rules [and] special words to guide your meditation" (8:4). He's leaving us on our own today. If we have been doing the exercises all along, we should have a pretty good idea of some of the "techniques" we might want to use, and we can use any of them, or anything that comes to us. Actually he isn't leaving us "on our own"; he's leaving us in the hands of "God's Voice," our inner Guide. Ask how to spend this half hour of meditation, and listen to what comes to you.

> Abide with Him this half an hour. He will do the rest. (8:6–7)

> You can be sure someday, perhaps today, perhaps tomorrow, you will understand and comprehend and see. (11:3)

LESSON 125 ✦ MAY 5
"In quiet I receive God's Word today."

Practice instructions

Purpose: To hear God speak to you, to receive His Word.

Longer: Three times (at times best suited to silence), for ten minutes.

Yesterday we were told that we needed no special instructions for our longer practice period. In keeping with this, we are told today that all we need is to still our minds. "You will need no rule but this" (9:2). The lesson, however, does tell us a little more than this. We can arrange its instructions into three steps.

1. Still your mind. Still your chaotic thoughts, meaningless desires, and all your judgments.

2. Go to that deep, "quiet place within the mind where He abides forever" (4:3), the throne of God within your mind, the quiet center.

3. Wait and listen. Once you reach that place of stillness in your mind, your task is over. You merely wait and listen, in confidence that your Father will come to you and speak His Word to you. Hearing this Word, of course, can take many different forms, from hearing actual words to receiving ideas, pictures, or just feelings.

During this time, you will need to frequently clear your mind of all those petty thoughts and desires that try to intrude. For this purpose, I suggest using today's idea, or picking a phrase, such as "only be still and listen" (9:3). As usual, begin the practice time with a slow repeating of the idea.

Frequent reminders: Hourly, for a moment.

Repeat the idea. Realize that by doing so you are reminding yourself of today's special purpose—to receive God's Word. Then spend some time listening in stillness.

Commentary

All we are being asked to do today is to be quiet for ten minutes, three times during the day and for a moment each hour. Just to be quiet. "Only be quiet. You will need no rule but this" (9:1–2). "Only be still and listen" (9:3). "His Voice awaits your silence, for His Word can not be heard until your mind is quiet for a while, and meaningless desires have been stilled" (6:2).

Isn't it amazing how much practice it takes to learn to be quiet? I can't tell you how many times I've sat down to meditate and be quiet only to find myself, sometimes only a few minutes later, so distracted by some passing thought that I open my eyes and start to get up to "do something" before I've even realized what I'm doing. I plop back down in my chair muttering "Good grief!" to myself at the distractedness of my mind. Draw a deep breath, think to myself, "Quiet, Allen. Quiet. Peace, be still."

The difficulties I have with being quiet, rather than standing as an insurmountable obstacle to me, have simply become indicators of how much I need this practice. Clearly, the Course is teaching us that a quiet mind is essential. "The memory of God comes to the quiet mind" (T-23.I.1:1). We can't hear His Voice until we are quiet for a while.

The Course describes the voice of the ego in various colorful phrases: "senseless shrieks," "raucous shrieks," "loud discordant shrieks," "the senseless noise of sounds that have no meaning," "frantic, riotous thoughts," "raucous screams and senseless ravings," "a loud, obscuring voice," "a frantic rush of thoughts that made no sense."[1]

Our ego is a constant noise machine trying to cover up the Voice for God; we need to learn to still our mind, to cease to pay attention to the ego's loudness. The ego is noise; the Spirit is quiet. There is merit, then, simply in being quiet, even if nothing else seems to happen. Let me, then, remember to take this time to be quiet, to be still, and to listen.

---

1. References for the above descriptions of the ego's voice: T-25.V.3:5; W-pI.49.4:3; P-2.VI.2:6; T-31.I.6:1; W-pI.49.4:4; T-21.V.1:6; T-27.VI.1:2; W-pI.198.11:2.

LESSON 126 ✦ MAY 6
"All that I give is given to myself."

Practice instructions

Purpose: To understand the idea that giving is not loss, but receiving.

Longer: Two times, for fifteen minutes.

Today's idea is so alien to our normal way of thinking that we need inner help from the Holy Spirit to really understand it. It cannot be done with the intellect alone. To seek this help, "close your eyes…and seek sanctuary in the quiet place" (10:1) where you go in meditation. Once you reach that place, "repeat today's idea, and ask for help in understanding what it really means" (10:2). Be willing to lay aside your false belief that giving is loss, and to gain a whole new understanding, in which you realize that giving is a gift to yourself. See the Holy Spirit as present in your practice period, and be prepared to repeat your request for true understanding until you receive that understanding.

Remarks: If you "only catch a tiny glimpse" (8:5) of the idea, of the real meaning of giving, it is a glorious day for you and for the world. For this idea would make forgiveness no longer a strain, but something you would be naturally compelled to give all the time, as a way of giving to yourself.

Frequent reminders: As often as you can (do not forget for long), for a moment.

Repeat, *"All that I give is given to myself. The Help I need to learn that this is true is with me now. And I will trust in Him."* Then do a miniature version of the longer practice period: quiet your mind and open it to the Holy Spirit, allowing Him to replace your false beliefs about giving with the truth. Through these practice periods, you can keep the sense alive all day long that your goal today is of great importance.

Commentary

This is a lesson that clearly aims at thought reversal (1:1). It begins with the presumption that we have false ideas about forgiveness: "You do not understand forgiveness" (6:1). In the sixth paragraph it explains that our false understanding of forgiveness is the reason we cannot understand how forgiveness brings us peace, how it is a means for our release, nor how forgiveness can restore our awareness of unity with our brothers. Our misunderstanding of forgiveness is the reason that we may have had trouble really entering in to Lessons 121 and 122, which told us that forgiveness is the key to happiness and offers us everything we want.

The idea that "all that I give is given to myself" is crucial to reversing our thought; understanding it would make forgiveness effortless. Paragraph 2 goes through a list of "what you do believe, in place of this idea" (2:1). So, let's practice some thought reversal, and reverse the meaning of this paragraph to see what is implied by this key idea for the day.

If we understood that everything we give is given to ourselves, we would realize that other people are not apart from us. Their behavior does have bearing on our thoughts, and our behavior has bearing on their thoughts. Our attitudes affect other people. Their appeals for help are intimately related to our own. They cannot be seen as "sinners" without affecting our perception of ourselves. We cannot condemn their sin without condemning ourselves and losing our peace of mind.

If we understood all this and believed it, forgiveness would happen naturally. We would realize that judging someone as sinful causes our own guilt and loss of peace, and we would not choose to do it. We would realize that how we see the other person is how we see ourselves, and we would not want to see ourselves that way. We would learn very quickly to perceive that their ego actions are not sins but calls for help, closely tied to our own calls for help, and we would respond accordingly. We would know that our judgmental attitude has an adverse effect on the behavior of others, and would choose to change our attitude. We would adjust our thoughts so as to have a beneficial effect on their behavior instead of a detrimental effect. We would recognize that we are not separate and apart, but share in the same struggle with fears and doubts, as well as sharing in the release from those things.

Given all this, we could understand how forgiveness is the key to happiness. We would see that if judging causes loss of peace, then forgiveness could bring us to peace again. We would understand how forgiveness restores our awareness of unity with one another. We could see how forgiveness can release us from what *seems* to be a problem with someone else.

The practice today is really a kind of thinking meditation. We are asked to come to the Holy Spirit with today's idea, "All that I give is given to myself," and to open ourselves to His help in learning that it is true, "opening your mind to His correction and His love" (11:6). We are asking for help in understanding what today's idea means (10:2), and what forgiveness really means. We are reflecting on the ideas with His assistance, asking for new insights, new understandings.

Our behavior, our attitudes, and our painful experiences in this world are all evidence that we do need to have our thoughts corrected. If we truly believed what today's idea says, we would not be having these painful experiences. We must have false ideas still lodged in our minds, and we need to be healed. Perhaps we think we understand what is being said, and no doubt there is a part of us that resonates with them or we would not be studying these lessons. It is the other part we are concerned about, the hidden warriors, the contrary beliefs we have dissociated and even hidden from conscious awareness.

If we ask for help sincerely, help will be given (8:3). Today will bring new understanding. Perhaps it will come in the form of new insights as we meditate. Perhaps it will come in the laboratory of life, as circumstances shock us into awareness of how we still believe one or another of the ideas this lessons mentions in describing what we do believe in place of today's idea. But it will come.

The help I need to learn that this is true is with me now. And I will trust in Him.   (11:4–5)

LESSON 127 ✦ MAY 7
"There is no love but God's."

Practice instructions

Purpose: This is an extremely significant lesson, for it asks you to "take the largest single step this course requests in your advance towards its established goal" (6:5). You take this step by releasing your beliefs that limit love and opening your mind to God so that He can teach you love's true meaning.

Longer: Two times, for fifteen minutes.

This exercise is very similar to yesterday's, in which you went to the quiet center in your mind and asked God's Voice to correct your false beliefs about giving. Today, you do the same, only asking God to correct your false beliefs about love.

Repeat the idea and then "open your mind and rest" (8:2). Now let go of your beliefs—one after another—in the laws and limits of this world, for all of them justify limited and changing love. Let go of your beliefs in partial love, selective love, and changing love. As you give up each such belief, God will replace it with "a spark of truth" (9:3), an understanding of what love really means. Call to Him and ask Him to illuminate your mind on the true meaning of love. That is the essence of this practice period: to open your mind, let go of your beliefs that limit love, and ask God to teach you the real meaning of love, which is far greater and more sublime than your mind alone could ever understand.

Remarks: Gladly give this time. It is the best use of time you could ever make. For if you gain the tiniest glimpse of love's real meaning, you truly have taken a giant stride. You have gone forward in your journey countless years and have brought freedom to everyone who comes here.

Frequent reminders: Three times per hour, at least.

Think of someone you know and silently repeat to him these lines: *"I bless you, brother, with the Love of God, which I would share with you. For I would learn the joyous lesson that there is no love but God's and yours and mine and everyone's."* Like the longer practice, this is a powerful technique for opening your mind to the real meaning of love.

Commentary

"Perhaps you think that different kinds of love are possible" (1:1). To my mind there is no "perhaps" about it; we all think that there are different kinds of love, varying from friend to family to children to lover, from person to animal to thing. The lesson asserts that there is only one Love—God's Love. To think that love changes depending upon its object, says the lesson, is to miss the meaning of love entirely (2:1).

"It [love] never alters with a person or a circumstance" (1:6). To us, this can seem to be a very intimidating description of love, because what we call love does not fit this picture. Our "love" comes and goes, waxes and wanes, varying with the person or the circumstance like a thermometer to the temperature. Love, as described in this lesson, is wholly unaffected by anything outside itself. This is truly unconditional love.

I am uplifted today by the idea that, if this is God's Love, and this is the only love there is, then His Love for me never alters, and has "no divergencies and no distinctions" (1:4). Nothing I do, or do not do, modifies His Love for me in the slightest. God's Love just *is*, eternally, endlessly. It has no opposite (3:7). It is the glue that holds everything together (3:8). It is the substance of the universe.

It can be comforting when we think of God's Love for us being like this. It can be intimidating, however, when we realize that we are being asked to love one another in the same way. It seems beyond us, and if we are judged on whether or not we match up to this love, it would appear that we all "come short of the glory of God," as the Bible says in Romans 3:23. The lesson, however, meets this fear in us head on, and meets it with an incredible assertion:

"No course whose purpose is to teach you to remember what you really are could fail to emphasize that there can never be a difference in what you really are and what love is" (4:1). In short sentences, this is telling us: "Love is eternal, unconditional, and unalterable. You are that love." You know this love we're talking about, that seems so foreign to us, so beyond our capabilities? Well, this is what you really are! It is the other image of yourself, incapable of such love, shifting and changing with every circumstance, that is the lie. This love—this is the truth, this is you. There is absolutely no difference between this love and what we are!

> What you are is what He is. There is no love but His, and
> what He is, is everything there is.   (4:3–4)

We aren't going to see this about ourselves by looking at the world (6:1). It isn't something that can be seen with the body's eyes; yet it is perfectly apparent to the eyes and ears that see and hear love (what is called elsewhere the vision of Christ). That is the goal of today's lesson: to see that love in ourselves, to catch even "the faintest glimmering of what love means" (7:1), to "understand the truth of love" (9:4). This attempt to quiet our minds, to free our minds of all the laws we think we must obey, all the limits we have placed on ourselves, and all the changes we believe we have made in ourselves, and to find our Self, Who is Love—this attempt is called "the largest single step this course requests in your advance towards its established goal" (6:5). If we succeed, we will "have advanced in distance without measure and in time beyond the count of years to your release" (7:1). This is no small thing! To be able, even in a very small degree, to perceive ourselves as this love; to catch a hint of the fact that love is everything there is, including ourselves. This is a quantum leap indeed! To spend a little time for this purpose is worth it. "There is no better use for time than this" (7:2).

As we begin to realize that love is all there is, that this love is everything including ourselves, we will realize that it includes everyone else as well. The only way love can be everything is if it includes everyone! So we begin to see not only ourselves, but the world, in a new way:

> The world in infancy is newly born.   (11:1)

> Now are they all made free, along with us. Now are they all
> our brothers in God's Love.   (11:3–4)

> We cannot leave a part of us outside our love if we
> would know our Self.   (12:1)

And so, three times an hour, we are asked to remember a brother or sister who is making this journey with us, and to mentally send them this message, as I now send it to you:

> *I bless you, brother, with the Love of God,*
> *Which I would share with you. For I would learn*
> *The joyous lesson that there is no love*
> *But God's and yours and mine and everyone's.*   (12:4–5)

LESSON 128 ✦ MAY 8

"The world I see holds nothing that I want."

Practice instructions

Purpose: To let go of the value we have placed on the things of the world, so that our mind is free to experience what is truly valuable—our home in God.

Longer: Three times, for ten minutes.

This practice is one of unchaining our mind so that it can fly home to God. We can see it as having two phases. In the first phase, we withdraw the value we have placed upon the world. We withdraw all the purposes we have given things in the world, the purpose of satisfying our personal interests (as Lesson 25 said). This is likened to taking the chains off our mind. Unchained, it will then be free to spread its wings and fly inward to where it belongs, to its home in God. The second phase of the practice period, then, is this process of our mind flying to its home. It is a process of stilling and opening our mind, and letting it be guided to its resting place in God. Throughout this process, we will need to be letting go of our wandering thoughts, which, of course, almost always relate to things we value in the world. To pull our minds back from these thoughts we can repeat the idea for the day.

Remarks: Every practice period will shift your whole perspective a little—it will withdraw some of the value you have placed upon the world.

Response to temptation: Whenever you feel yourself valuing something in the world.

Realize that doing so will lay a chain upon your mind. Instead, protect your mind by saying, with quiet certainty, *"This will not tempt me to delay myself. The world I see holds nothing that I want."* If you really watch your mind, you will find no shortage of subjects for practice. I also highly recommend taking some time to memorize these two lines. If you are really going to use them frequently, having them memorized is almost a requirement.

Commentary

The general thought of this lesson is similar to the first three of Buddha's Four Noble Truths: that life is suffering; that the cause of suffering is *tanha*, or desire for self at the expense of others; and that the way out of suffering is through the relinquishment of such desires.

"Believe this thought, and you are saved from years of misery" (1:2). The lesson is asking us to give up all attachment to things of this world, to put an end to suffering by putting an end to craving anything the world offers. It can seem to be a harsh lesson, and yet it is eminently sensible: if you do not desire anything, you cannot be disappointed.

The things of the world act as chains when we value them (2:1). What is perhaps harder to grasp is that this is the purpose for which we made them: they "will serve no other end but this. For everything must serve the purpose you have given it, until you see a different purpose there (2:1–2). When we assign to the things of the world a purpose in time, usually some form of gratification or self-aggrandizement, we chain ourselves to this world. Inevitably, since everything in the world must have an end, this causes us untold pain. All our mistaken valuing accomplishes is to tie us to the world and to keep us from our final healing.

To the Holy Spirit, the only purpose of this world is the healing of God's Son (see T-24.VI.4:1). There is nothing *in* the world worth striving for. "The only purpose worthy of your mind this world contains is that you pass it by, without delaying to perceive some hope where there is none" (2:3). This is similar to this statement in the Text: "The Holy Spirit interprets time's purpose as rendering the need for time unnecessary" (T-13.IV.7:3). The Holy Spirit appropriates time, the world, and everything in the world for the purpose of salvation and the healing of our minds. To Him, nothing here has any other purpose.

Therefore, the world itself holds nothing that we want. All of it is, to borrow from the title of a book by Ram Dass, "grist for the mill." All of it becomes the means to an end—our awakening to life, our return to God. There is nothing in the world that is an end in itself.

When the lesson advises us, "Let nothing that relates to body thoughts delay your progress to salvation" (4:1), it is saying the same thing in other words. "Body thoughts" refers to our mistaken identification with our bodies. It is everything that stems from the idea that "I am a body, and to benefit and protect myself I must make taking care of my body a number one priority." Our cravings for bodily pleasure, bodily comfort, bodily protection, bodily longevity, and bodily beauty all fall into the category of body thoughts. Making such things our primary concern can only delay our progress.

The lesson is asking us to practice mentally letting go of all thoughts of values we have given to the world (5:1). We are asked to "loosen it [the world] from all we wish it were" (5:3). That is a tall order, isn't it? We spend so much of our time wishing things were different and trying to make them be that way. In fact, if we look at our lives honestly, wishing something or someone were different and trying to bring about that change is the activity that occupies most of our lives.

For the purposes of this lesson, then, practice taking a few minutes to let your mind rest from such activity: "Pause and be still a while, and see how far you rise above the world, when you release your mind from chains and let it seek the level where it finds itself at home" (6:1). Your mind, the lesson tells us, "knows where it belongs" (6:3). If you loosen the chains of your desires, it will "fly in sureness and in joy to join its holy purpose" (6:4). Each time you practice such an exercise for only ten minutes, "your whole perspective on the world will shift by just a little" (7:3). Let your mind rest, then, from its constant craving, and relax as its homing instinct takes over and brings you to where you really belong.

Throughout the day, the lesson is asking us to notice when we think we see some value in the world, and when we do, to mentally correct the notion with these words:

> *This will not tempt me to delay myself. The world I see*
> *holds nothing that I want.* (8:3–4)

LESSON 129 ✦ MAY 9
"Beyond this world there is a world I want."

Practice instructions

Purpose: To have a day of grace in which you see the world you really want. Through this you will realize that giving up the world you do not want is a giving up of nothing in order to gain everything.

Longer: Three times—morning, evening and once in between—for ten minutes.

Begin by repeating, *"Beyond this world there is a world I want. I choose to see that world instead of this, for here is nothing that I really want."* Try to say these lines with feeling. They are trying to inspire in you a real desire to exchange this world for the real world, and a genuine choice resulting from that desire. Feel the desire. Make the choice. Then close your eyes and watch and wait expectantly for an experience of true vision, a glimpse of the real world. I see this practice as very similar to Lesson 75. You might want to read paragraphs 6-8 in that lesson. The main difference in this lesson is that we are seeking an eyes-closed (rather than eyes-open) experience of vision. We are seeking to see a light of meaning and holiness that our eyes cannot see, only our mind. While you sit and watch and wait, feel your desire to see a world of meaning that is totally harmless, peaceful, benign, and loving, without a trace of pain or loss. You may want to repeat the idea from time to time, to renew your focus and to clear your mind of wandering thoughts.

Frequent reminders: Once per hour, for a moment.

Clear your mind and dwell on these lines: *"The world I see holds nothing that I want. Beyond this world there is a world I want."* Make this repetition a confirmation of the choice you made in the longer practice periods—to exchange this world for the real world.

Commentary

The Course is so down-to-earth sometimes! "You cannot stop with the idea the world is worthless, for unless you see that there is something else to hope for, you will only be depressed" (1:2). So true! The statement that "the world is worthless" is pretty blunt; there can't be much debate about what it means. And I have to confess that even after ten years of studying the Course and, over time, coming to agree with its ideas, I still find that wording a little jarring. I can almost hear myself replying, "Uhhh…that isn't exactly how I'd put it." Because there is still something in me that *wants* to find some value here, something worthwhile, something worth preserving and striving for.

The emphasis of the Course, however, isn't on "giving up the world, but on exchanging it for what is far more satisfying, filled with joy, and capable of offering you peace" (1:3). Well, that's not such a bad deal, is it?

It begins to look especially good if we take a hard look at the world we're trying to hang on to—"merciless,…unstable, cruel, unconcerned with you, quick to avenge and pitiless with hate" (2:3). Events such as the 1995 bombing of a government building in Oklahoma City, and the rabid rage against the bomber, are both testimony to this. The bomber was thought to be "avenging" the government's actions against David Koresh in Waco, and then people wanted vengeance on the bomber. The many wars motivated by racial, religious, or ethnic differences are vengeance cycles that have been going on for centuries. This *is* the way the world is. "No lasting love is found, for none is here. This is the world of time, where all things end" (2:5–6). That, perhaps, is the cruelest part of all about this world. Even when you *do* find love, it can't last forever.

So—wouldn't you rather find a world where *it is impossible to lose anything*? Where vengeance is meaningless? (3:1). "Is it a loss to find all things you really want, and know they have no ending and they will remain exactly as you want them throughout time?" (3:2). It's speaking here of what the Course calls "the real world," and the following sentence—"you go from there to where words fail entirely" (3:3)—is talking about Heaven, a nonphysical existence in eternity.

What is it talking about when it speaks of "all things you really want"? If they are things that have no ending and don't change over time, they can't be anything physical; certainly not bodies. It is speaking of Love Itself; it is speaking of our Self which is spirit, and which we share with everyone. We are here to find the changeless in the midst of the changeable, and to learn to value what is changeless and to let go of what is changeable.

When we choose the changeless, and value the real world of spirit instead of what changes and decays, it brings us very close to Heaven, and prepares us for it. Loosing our grasp on the world makes the transition to Heaven easy.

Holding on to the world brings loss. When you try to cling to the perishable you doom yourself to suffering. As we saw in yesterday's commentary, Buddhism has long taught a similar lesson.

Doing the practice exercises for today has a remarkable effect. When I say, "The world I see holds nothing that I want. Beyond this world there is a world I want" (9:4–5), I find myself noticing all the attachments I still have to things in this world; I find myself noticing that my conception of what it is beyond this world that I "really want" is a bit vague. And so I bring that attachment and that unclarity to the Holy Spirit, and ask that He help me in those areas. I know He will.

LESSON 130 ✦ MAY 10
"It is impossible to see two worlds."

Practice instructions

Purpose: To realize that you cannot have a little bit of this world and still see the real world, that you must choose one or the other. To make the choice for the real world by letting go of all value given this world. This is another of the Workbook's giant steps (see 9:2).

Longer: Six times, for five minutes.

Today's practice is extremely similar to the last two days, especially Lesson 128. Begin by repeating the opening lines: *"It is impossible to see two worlds. Let me accept the strength God offers me and see no value in this world, that I may find my freedom and deliverance."* You are asking for God's strength to uphold you and help you make a definitive choice of the real world over this world. Try to really mean this request. Then close your eyes and spend some time "emptying your hands of all the petty treasures of this world" (8:3). Then reach out for an experience of true perception, the kind of seeing which your eyes alone cannot see. Desire to see *only* the other world, the world of love. During this time, "wait for God to help you" (8:4). Trust that He will be there, helping you make the choice to value only the real world. While you wait, you may want to repeat, "Help me see only the real world."

Response to temptation: Whenever you find yourself valuing anything in the world.

Remember that by valuing a little part of hell you are really choosing all of hell, and blocking out Heaven entirely. Say, *"It is impossible to see two worlds. I seek my freedom and deliverance, and this [thing I feel attracted to] is not a part of what I want."* You will need to watch your mind carefully all day, because today you are watching not for disturbances and upsets, but *attractions.*

Commentary

Today's lesson is extremely uncompromising. The first two paragraphs are as clear a statement of the Course's understanding of perception as there is in all three volumes. What we value we want to see, what we want to see determines our thinking, and what we see simply reflects our thinking. "No one can fail to look upon what he believes he wants" (1:6). Or, as it is twice stated succinctly in the Text, "Projection makes perception" (T-13.V.3:5; T-21.In.1:1).

On top of that, since we can't hate and love simultaneously, we can't project totally opposite worlds simultaneously. We project the world of fear or the world of love. And "the world you see is proof you have already made a choice as all-embracing as its opposite" (6:2). In other words, the world we see proves that our minds have made an all-embracing choice for fear. "Fear has made everything you think you see" (4:1).

As I said, this is very uncompromising. It does not allow for any part of this world to be excluded from the category of "projection of fear." The world we see is

> quite consistent from the point of view from which you see it. It is all a piece because it stems from one emotion [fear], and reflects its source in everything you see.   (6:4–5)

If we try to exclude part of it from this portrait, maintaining that "surely *this* part is good," we are trying to "accept a little part of hell as real" (11:1). It guarantees that the whole picture will be "hell indeed" (11:1).

On the other hand, the Course does not try to foster any rejection of the world. It tells us that only the part of it we look upon with love is real (see T-12.VI.3:2–3). Therefore we are urged to *love all of it equally*, and thus "make the world real unto yourself" (T-12.VI.3:6). Our attempts at salvaging "parts" of the world as real are mistaken in that they separate and make certain parts special, more loveable than the rest.

As we see it, through eyes of fear, this world is without any value whatsoever. Let us accept God's Strength and "see no value in the world" (8:6). If we are willing to do this we will see another world, with sight that "is not the kind of seeing that your eyes alone have ever seen before" (9:4). "When you want only love you will see nothing else" (T-12.VII.8:1).

To be a little more practical for a moment: I have found the final words of this lesson to be an incredibly useful phrase in times of distress of all kinds: "This is not a part of what I want" (11:5). If I see only what I want to see, and I am seeing something distressing, let me affirm my choice to change my mind: "I don't want this any more." Although my application of it is still very inconsistent, I have seen this simple affirmation make separateness in a relationship evaporate. I have seen it make a sense of poverty evaporate. I have seen it change my body, and give it an energy I thought I had lost. I have watched it reverse impending illnesses. I recommend it highly to you all.

LESSON 131 ✦ MAY 11
"No one can fail who seeks to reach the truth."

Practice instructions

Purpose: God made an ancient promise to you, and you did to Him, that you would one day go beyond the door in your mind and find the real world. Today that promise will be fulfilled.

Longer: Three times, for ten minutes.

The instructions in paragraphs 11-13 are so clear that I have merely laid the sentences out on separate lines:

Begin with this:

> *I ask to see a different world, and think*
> *a different kind of thought from those I made.*
> *The world I seek I did not make alone,*
> *the thoughts I want to think are not my own.*

For several minutes watch your mind and see,
   although your eyes are closed, the senseless world
   you think is real
Review the thoughts as well which are compatible
   with such a world, and which you think are true.
Then let them go, and sink below them to the holy
   place where they can enter not.
There is a door beneath them in your mind, which you
   could not completely lock to hide what lies beyond.
Seek for that door and find it.
But before you try to open it, remind yourself no one
   can fail who seeks to reach the truth.
And it is this request you make today.
Nothing but this has any meaning now; no other goal
   is valued now nor sought, nothing before this door
   you really want, and only what lies past it do you
   seek.
Put out your hand, and see how easily the door swings

open with your one intent to go beyond it.

Angels light the way, so that all darkness vanishes,
and you are standing in a light so bright and clear
that you can understand all things you see.

A tiny moment of surprise, perhaps, will make you
pause before you realize the world you see before
you in the light reflects the truth you knew, and did
not quite forget in wandering away in dreams.

(W-pI.131.11:2-13:3)

Shorter: Often.

Repeat the idea, while keeping in mind that today you will go beyond the door and find the truth, and that today is therefore a day of grace, a time for gladness and celebration. I highly recommend really reminding yourself of this latter fact. It will change your mood during the day if you remember.

Response to temptation: If you forget what a special day it is and fall into depression or complaining.

Remind yourself of the true nature of this day by repeating, *"Today I seek and find all that I want. My single purpose offers it to me. No one can fail who seeks to reach the truth."* How can you feel dismal when you realize that you are finding all you ever wanted? I recommend either writing down those lines on a card and keeping them handy or, better yet, memorizing them.

Commentary

At times it seems to nearly everyone that the search for truth is one that will never succeed. It seems that we seek, and seek, and seek some more, and never arrive at certainty. Today's lesson comes as a welcome reassurance that the search for truth is the *only* search that will inevitably succeed.

"Searching is inevitable here" (3:1). It's the nature of the world, the nature of the predicament we've put ourselves into. Searching is why we came here, and so "you will surely do the thing you came for" (3:2). If we're going to search, then, we may as well search for something worth finding: "a goal that lies beyond the world and every worldly thought…an echo of a heritage forgot" (3:4). What we are searching for is Heaven, "a heritage forgot." What we are searching for is the home we left behind and almost put out of our minds, although to do so entirely is impossible. That's why we are driven to search. "Behind the search for every idol lies the yearning for completion" (T-30.III.3:1).

What we are seeking for is what we are; that is why finding it is inevitable. "No one can fail to want this goal and reach it in the end" (4:3).

Sometimes it may seem as though truth has deserted you. I think some experience of that is almost inescapable for all of us, a last-ditch effort of the ego to dissuade us from the search when we are getting too close. I know it has happened to me, and all I can tell you is, "Hang in there." Your search cannot fail, even though you may think it has *already* failed. I know I came through that dark period of my life. I don't know how I did because I didn't seem to have anything to do with it, which is part of what convinces me that my "coming out of it" is real and lasting. I still dip into despair from time to time, but I will never again live there. "No one can fail who seeks to reach the truth."

What we are looking for, and perhaps can find today, is something that is beneath all the thoughts in our minds that are compatible with this senseless world—"a door beneath them in your mind" (11:8). A door in our minds! Past that door is "a light so bright and clear that you can understand all things you see" (13:2). Today's exercise is wonderful for visualization, actually picturing that door, seeing ourselves standing before it, and with one intent, pushing it open to pass through, out of this world and into another, like the wardrobe doorway into Narnia in C. S. Lewis's fantasy books. These exercises are like rehearsals, and as we repeat them, they grow more and more real to us, engaging our minds and training them in a pattern that leads to real discovery of the real door, within our minds, to Heaven.

LESSON 132 ✦ MAY 12
"I loose the world from all I thought it was."

Practice instructions

Purpose: "To free the world from all the idle thoughts we ever held about it, and about all living things we see upon it...that we may be free" (14:1, 5).

Longer: Two times, for fifteen minutes.

Begin by repeating, *"I who remain as God created me would loose the world from all I thought it was. For I am real because the world is not, and I would know my own reality."* The rest of the practice period sounds like Workbook meditation to me, in which we place our minds in a state of rest, "alert but with no strain" (15:4). Based on the lines we repeat, this exercise reminds me of a couple of other lessons—128 and 188—in which we have a sense of withdrawing our mind from its focus on the outer world and drawing it inward to the quiet center, where we rest, where our thoughts are transformed, and where we experience our true reality.

Remarks: You will sense your own release, but you may not realize that your release will also free the world, bringing healing to many brothers far and near.

Response to temptation: Whenever you believe that your thoughts have no power to help the troubling situations we see around us.

When you notice such a thought, repeat, *"I loose the world from all I thought it was, and choose my own reality instead"* (it will be helpful to memorize it), realizing that by doing so you are unleashing your mind's power to free the world, and adding to the freedom you gave in the longer practice period.

Commentary

To me, today, the point of this lesson is: *I have the power to do that. I can loose the world from all I thought it was, simply by changing my own mind.*

This lesson contains what is perhaps the most startling statement in the Course:

> There is no world! This is the central thought the course
> attempts to teach.   (6:2–3)

The lesson admits that not everyone is ready to accept this idea, although it makes it clear that all of us will, eventually, accept it. (Such acceptance could take many lifetimes, I think, and doubtless we have gone through many already to get wherever we are; this is my own opinion, not necessarily that of the Course.)

In speaking of this in the analogy of a madman, the first paragraph says that no madman can be "swayed by questioning his thoughts' effects" (1:6). From the perspective of the Course, it is the *world* that is the effect of our thoughts. So the approach that will lead us, eventually, to understand that there is no world does not follow the path of directly questioning the reality of the world. That is a fruitless approach, as fruitless as trying to persuade a madman that his hallucinations are not real. The approach that bears fruit is raising the source to question—that is, in questioning the thoughts that produce the hallucinations.

"Change but your mind on what you want to see, and all the world must change accordingly" (5:2). As we begin to allow thoughts of healing to flow through us, we open ourselves to learn the lesson. "Their readiness will bring the lesson to them in some form which they can understand and recognize" (7:2). The focus for us, then, is not on denying the reality of the world, but on opening our minds to bring healing to the world we see. Doing so will bring us experiences that will convince us that the world is not as real as we supposed. We may have a near-death experience. We may undergo some experience of enlightenment that shows us an incontrovertible reality that contradicts all that we have believed to be reality up until that time. We may, in fact, experience something in doing today's exercises that will bring us our awakening.

The unreality of the world dawns upon us as we begin to grasp the reality of our Self: "To know your Self is the salvation of the world" (10:1). If we are as God created us, then what appears to change us cannot exist, it cannot be real; there cannot be a place where we can suffer, or time to bring change to us. The world is the effect of our thoughts, and nothing more: "You maintain the world within your mind in thought" (10:3). As we discover what we truly are by allowing love to move through us in healing, we realize that "If you are real the world you see is false, for God's creation is unlike the world in every way" (11:5). We release the world from what we thought it was by accepting our oneness with God, and realizing that the world, as we see it, cannot be real because it does not reflect this truth: "What He creates is not apart from Him, and nowhere does the Father end, the Son begin as something separate from Him" (12:4).

To "loose the world" is to heal it. The meditation for today is one in which we "send out these thoughts to bless the world" (16:1). "I loose the world" means that I extend healing to all the world, I free it from suffering, I absolve it from guilt, I heal it of sickness, I lift all thoughts of vengeance from it. It is taking this role as savior to the world that reveals our Self to us, and transforms our thoughts and, in turn, the world that is their effect. This is "the power of your simple change of mind" (17:1).

LESSON 133 ✦ MAY 13
"I will not value what is valueless."

Practice instructions

Purpose: To empty our hands of all the things we value in this world and to reach the state of Heaven.

Longer: Two times, for fifteen minutes.

Repeat, *"I will not value what is valueless, and only what has value do I seek, for only that do I desire to find."* Then try to find the valuable within yourself. Hold in mind an honest willingness to not deceive yourself about what is valuable. Refuse to fool yourself into thinking that the things of this world can bring you real, lasting happiness. Try instead to value only the eternal, in your brothers and in yourself. Empty your hands of the treasures of this world. Open your mind and let go of its usual attachments. In this empty, open state, come before the gate of Heaven within you, and it will swing open, offering you the gift of everything.

Response to temptation: Whenever you feel burdened or feel confronted with a difficult decision.

Immediately respond by repeating, *"I will not value what is valueless, for what is valuable belongs to me."* This will remind you that no decision can be difficult, because you choose between the infinitely valuable and the totally worthless.

Commentary

The laws that govern choice are two:

- There are only two alternatives: everything or nothing.
- There is no compromise; there is no in-between.

The criteria for judging what is worth desiring are:

- Will it last forever? (If not, it is nothing.)
- Is it a choice in which no one loses? (If not, you are left with nothing.)

- Is the purpose free of the ego's goals? (If not, there is compromise.)
- Is the choice free of all guilt? (If not, the real alternatives have been obscured.)

These are stringent rules! They are clear, but not easily learned. How can we know whether or not the ego's goals are intruding, for instance? "Here it is easiest of all to be deceived" (8:5). The ego masquerades in innocence. Yet the lesson asserts that the ego's camouflage is only "a thin veneer, which could deceive but those who are content to be deceived" (9:1). "Its goals are obvious to anyone who cares to look for them" (9:2). We need only to be willing to look, and the ego detector is quite simple: guilt. "If you feel any guilt about your choice, you have allowed the ego's goals to come between the real alternatives" (11:2).

If I apply these criteria for choice to the decisions in my life, my life will be constantly revolutionized. The first criterion alone rules out absolutely every goal involving anything material, including bodies and ordinary human relationships. Will it last forever? What lasts forever in this world? Only love. And not all that we call love lasts forever; we've all demonstrated that for ourselves, in all likelihood, or seen it all around us. The assertion of the Course, by the way, is that if it doesn't last, it wasn't love to begin with:

> Where disillusionment is possible, there was not love but
> hate. For hate *is* an illusion, and what can change was never
> love. (T-16.IV.4:3–4)

But there is a love not of this world; a light we cannot find *in* the world but which we can give *to* the world (see T-13.VI.11:1–2).

As Stephen Levine has written, we cannot own love, but we can be owned by it. And that is what is being said here.

We may think that most of our choices are not so monumental as all this. But they are all this very choice. In every moment we are choosing to give ourselves to love, to be taken over by it and used by it, or we are choosing to withhold ourselves from it, in fear. To choose love is the only guiltless choice.

It isn't complex. "Complexity is nothing but a screen of smoke, which hides the very simple fact that no decision can be difficult" (12:3). It is the decision: "Let me be love in this situation and nothing else." No, we don't know how to do that. That is why we must come "with empty hands and open minds" (13:1). Holding on to nothing, unencumbered (14:1) by any lesser values. And with no preconceptions about what being love means—open minds. In the words of a poem by the Christian poetess Amy Carmichael:

> Love through me, Love of God.
> Make me like Thy clear air,
> Through which, unhindered, colors pass
> As though it were not there.[1]

DISCERNING THE VALUABLE FROM THE VALUELESS

Lesson 133, "I will not value what is valueless," is a fascinating and important lesson. It provides a series of four criteria or tests by which we can decide when we are choosing the valuable and when we are choosing the valueless. At first glance these tests seem like a practical tool for identifying what the right decision is. However, I have heard many Course students, myself included, express puzzlement over how to actually apply these tests to concrete situations in our lives. In this article I would like to clarify these tests and how to apply them on a practical level.

My understanding of this lesson is that it is not a guide for what external decisions we should make. It does not tell us whether or not we should do a particular thing on the outside. Rather, when we choose a particular external form, this lesson identifies for us what content we are choosing *within* the form. For instance, let's use the example of me wanting to go out to dinner with someone. What would Lesson 133 say about how I should evaluate that choice?

The two laws

To begin with, this lesson tells me that there are two laws that pertain to my choice, two invariable laws that I *have* to work within. I have no choice about this. The first law says that, within the shell of this outer form (going to dinner), I have chosen one of two contents. I have chosen one of two thought systems, either the Holy Spirit's or the ego's. Regardless of how many options seem to confront me, those are the only two choices that are really open to me. The second laws says that choosing the Holy Spirit's thought system will deliver me everything, while choosing the ego's will deliver me absolutely nothing. In summary, then, within my choice to go to dinner, I have either chosen everything or nothing.

The question is: *Which* have I chosen? How do I know? There is no guidebook in which I can look up all possible activities, find the listing for "going out to dinner," and read that it is *always* a choice for the ego. It just doesn't work that way. So, how *do* I recognize whether, in the guise of choosing to eat out, I have chosen the inner content of nothing or the inner content of everything?

The four criteria

This is where the four criteria come in. Their purpose is to help us identify which of the two alternatives we have actually chosen. It is not a question of what form we have chosen, but *why* we chose that form. What were our reasons? What was the real prize we were going after?

Let's go through the four criteria now and apply each one of them to my example. As we do, we will see that they are an integrated whole, with each one leading into the next, and all of them constituting an interrelated system.

1. "If you choose a thing that will not last forever, what you chose is valueless" (6:1).

When I chose to go to dinner, what was I really choosing? What was the prize I was seeking? Chances are that, if I'm a normal person, I want some good food, I want some pleasant conversation, and I want to be treated right by the person I am with.

Do any of these things last forever? Obviously not. The food is gone in a matter of minutes. The conversation is over by the end of the evening. And getting treated right lasts only so long as the treatment is occurring. All of these things are extremely short-lived. All of them, therefore, fall in the category of the valueless. By choosing them I have chosen nothing.

2. "If you choose to take a thing away from someone else, you will have nothing left" (7:1).

This criterion is subtly linked to the first. If the prize we are seeking is something external, then it usually has to be taken from someone else. Let's look at my dinner example. Perhaps I pressured the person I'm with to give me her time, and she consented even though she had other pressing responsibilities. I have taken not only from her but from those she had to neglect in order to spend time with me. Perhaps I have subtly let her know that if she doesn't treat me the way I want I will punish her (with anger, recrimination, sullenness, withdrawal, etc.). Again, I have taken from her. Perhaps the money I am spending on dinner would be better spent on a less frivolous need, on something that will benefit another. Perhaps I will take the waiter's time and effort without adequately tipping him.

In short, if I'm seeking after externals, I will naturally be trying to take them away from their current owners in order to have them for myself. That is how it works when the prize is something my eyes can see.

Trying to take from others is yet another sign that what I have chosen is actually nothing. Why? Because once I take from another, somewhere in my mind I convene my own court of justice. In that court, I convict myself, judging myself unworthy of the gifts of God. They are the only gifts I really want, but now I am convinced that I am too sinful to have them. After all, I stole from my brother. So, even though God's gifts are within me, I will not see them, for I have denied that a sinner like me can have them. And without them, I have nothing. In summary, when I take from another, I end up feeling like I deserve, and *have*, nothing.

3. *"Why is the choice you make of value to you?...What purpose does it serve?"* (8:2,4).

This means: In making your choice, were you trying to serve the ego's goals or the Holy Spirit's? This still sounds a little vague. It becomes much clearer if we look at it in light of the previous two points. When you are seeking an external thing (whether it be time, particular behaviors, or some tangible thing like food), and trying to take that thing away from another person, you are not just serving some generic ego thought system, you are trying to serve *your own* ego. You are trying to serve your needs at the expense of another's. This is what we usually call being selfish or self-serving. That, I believe, is what this test is about. Were you trying to serve your ego's needs, seen as separate from the needs of others? Were your motives truly loving, or were they self-centered?

This is the point about which we are most likely to fool ourselves (8:5). Do we really want to admit how self-serving our motives are? How many people can you count on to be totally honest about exactly why they did what they did? Don't you routinely assume that most people will try to put a halo of innocence over their attempt to serve their own ego? This is exactly what the lesson says we ourselves try to do (see 8:7).

Let's return again to the dinner example. Why did I really go? More specifically, whose needs was I trying to serve? Again, the odds are that I was trying to serve my own needs, seen as separate from my companion's. Let's be honest, it was really mostly about me—my pleasure, my comfort, and my satisfaction.

But do I want to admit that? No. I will do my best to virtually plaster that ugly fact over with halos, making my act appear loving, generous, considerate, and altruistic. This may fool others, and it may even fool myself, but it won't really. Deep down, I will know exactly why I did what I did. In that sober and honest place in my mind, I will be staring straight at my real motives, and realizing just how conniving and self-aggrandizing they really were.

Yet even though I have peeled away one deception, I will still be caught in another. For I will assume that I have actually served my ego, and gained from doing so, and so have become just as dirty as it is. I will feel that I have increased the devil's bank account and been paid handsomely for doing so, and have thus become the devil's accomplice. What I did will seem like no innocent mistake. It will seem like a genuine sin. These lines express the idea perfectly:

Yet though he tries to keep [his ego's] halo clear within his vision, still must he perceive its tarnished edges and its rusted core. His ineffectual mistakes appear as sins to him, because he looks upon the tarnish as his own, the rust a sign of deep unworthiness within himself. (10:1-2)

In other words, there are two levels of deception here. On the surface, I am deceived into thinking that my motives were innocent and altruistic. Beneath that, I know better; I know that I was looking out for number one. But even here I am deceived, for I think that, by serving the ego, I served something real, and that, in the process, I became it. Now, as the passage above says, I am deceived into thinking that *its* tarnish is my own.

If that is how I end up feeling, how could I have possibly gained? By choosing to pursue the ego's goals, I have really ended up with nothing.

4. *"If you feel any guilt about your choice, you have allowed the ego's goals to come between the real alternatives" (11:2).*

Do you see how all the points lead up to this one? If the prize you seek is something that will not last forever, some external thing, situation or event (Criterion #1), you will probably end up having to subtly (or not-so-subtly) take it away from another (Criterion #2). If you do that, no matter how well-intentioned you try to make yourself look, you will know in your heart that your motives were self-serving. You will know that you tried to serve your ego (Criterion #3). And you will feel guilty (Criterion #4). Guilt is the end result of the process. It is the sign that the other three tests have gone in favor of the ego. In essence, it is the evidence that you have tried to satisfy your "self" at the expense of the happiness of others.

Let's return to my dinner example. If my goal was to satisfy my ego, and I was hoping to do so by taking from others, then I may leave the evening feeling great pleasure, but underneath that pleasure there will be a disquiet. No matter how good the food was, how interesting the conversation, and how well my dinner partner treated me, I won't feel right with myself. I may not call this feeling guilt, but that is what it is. I will feel an unsettling perturbance eating away inside me, a vague self-loathing. I probably won't even know where it's coming from, but when the evening is over and the food and the conversation are gone, that feeling is what I have left. How many of us don't know this experience?

The lesson says that we will find this criterion "the hardest to believe" (11:1). And this is true. What if, for instance, you are sure you did the right thing and you still feel guilty? Does that mean you did the *wrong* thing? Remember, these criteria don't tell you what you should do on the outside. They tell you what content you have chosen on the inside. Even if your behavior was right and responsible and appropriate, that doesn't mean that your motives were pure. And your motives are the sign of the real inner content you chose. You were probably still trying to get other people to sacrifice, so that you could have some desired thing of the world, in order to satisfy your separate interests. As long as you feel guilty, that was *part* of what was going on inside you. It may not have been all of it. But if it were none of it, if you knew that you were desiring only the pure and perfect happiness of everyone involved, would there be room for you to feel any guilt?

Just because you are feeling guilty, however, doesn't mean that the guilt is deserved. Remember, guilt is self-deception. If you are feeling guilt, it is because you have forgotten that there are only two alternatives: nothing and everything. You have been fooled into thinking that there is a third, in-between alternative: that you can serve the ego's goals and bite into its delicious but forbidden fruit. Guilt comes from forgetting that you are biting into nothing but air.

We have now covered the wrong choice, but what about the right choice? What would it look like to choose the Holy Spirit's thought system and thereby choose everything? That takes much less time to explain, though it is also much less familiar.

In this case, I go to dinner not caring about the food or the atmosphere, not caring if I get treated well or if the conversation is just right. What I care about is seeing the eternal in my dinner partner and conveying this beautiful vision to her through my kind words, loving attitudes, and generous actions. Now what I am seeking *will* last forever (Criterion #1). Imagine that. While in this world I can choose what will last forever; I can choose the eternal in another person. I certainly don't have to take this away from anyone else (Criterion #2). And since I have stolen from no one, I will believe in my own rights; specifically, in my own right to enjoy the gifts of God. Further, I not only haven't taken, I have blessed. Seeing the eternal in my companion benefits everyone. It helps awaken everyone to the eternal in them. Thus, everyone gains from my choice and no one loses. This means that I am not trying to serve my separate interests, my ego (Criterion #3). Given all this, what on earth would I feel guilty about (Criterion #4)?

In sum, I have made the perfect choice. I have chosen what lasts forever, what affirms my right to happiness and what leaves me without a trace of guilt. I have chosen what the Course says is the happiest experience I can have in this world:

> Can you imagine how beautiful those you forgive will look to you? In no fantasy have you ever seen anything so lovely. Nothing you see here, sleeping or waking, comes near to such loveliness. And nothing will you value like unto this, nor hold so dear. Nothing that you remember that made your heart sing with joy has ever brought you even a little part of the happiness this sight will bring you. For you will see the Son of God. (T-17.II.1:1-7)

By choosing to see the eternal in my brother, I have indeed chosen everything.

I hope this article has provided some understanding of how this lesson's criteria apply in our lives. The criteria are not there to answer what we should do on the outside, but rather what content we should choose on the inside.

The real question now is: Will we use these criteria? Will we subject our own choices to these tests? In the days I have been working on this article I have found the use of these tests to be a sobering process. Applying them means having to face just how ego-driven my choices are. When I have chosen to do something and find myself looking forward to it, what I look forward to is usually *not* the experience of the eternal. I can honestly say that that is often a part of it. But *most* of it? I don't think so.

And that is the point of these tests. They make us aware. They make us aware that our ordinary choices, day-in and day-out, amount to choosing nothing. These tests also show us what to choose: something eternal, which we don't need to take from anyone else, which doesn't serve our ego at the expense of others, and which doesn't saddle us with guilt. Applying these criteria on a consistent basis doesn't mean we will be instantly forced to always choose the eternal, while simultaneously giving up any internal investment in good food and pleasant conversation. After all, knowing what excessive smoking or drinking does to your body doesn't necessarily mean that you will instantly quit and choose health instead. But it does hasten the day when you will make that choice.

---

1. Amy Carmichael, in *Toward Jerusalem* (Fort Washington, Penn.: Christian Literature Crusade, 1989).

LESSON 134 ✦ MAY 14
"Let me perceive forgiveness as it is."

Practice instructions

Purpose: To practice true forgiveness, that you may free your brother, free yourself from the chains you've wrapped around you, and lay down footsteps to light the way for those who follow you.

Longer: Two times, for fifteen minutes.

This exercise requires some explanation. First, "Would I condemn myself for doing this?" does not mean "If I did this, would I condemn myself?" Rather, it means "Do I really *want* to condemn myself for doing this (because if I condemn him I *will* condemn myself)?" This sort of "would you?" is found throughout the Course. For instance, "Would you know the Will of God for you?" (T-8.V.5:1), which means "Do you *want* to know the Will of God for you?"

- Ask the Holy Spirit, Who understands the meaning of forgiveness, *"Let me perceive forgiveness as it is."*
- Then choose a brother to forgive, under His direction.
- Now catalogue this person's "sins," one by one (but keep from dwelling on any one of them). With each one, ask yourself, *"Would I condemn myself for doing this?"*— because when you condemn this brother for this specific "sin," you hold yourself to the same standard. You search your mind for a similar "sin" in you, and then condemn yourself for it, just as you condemned him. To really make this meaning go in, you may want to do an expanded version of the question. Say, *"Do I want to condemn myself for [name the 'sin' you see in him; e.g., being overly judgmental of others]? I will not lay this chain upon myself. I will not condemn him for doing this."* As you name his particular sin, make it general enough that it covers something you tend to do.
- If you practice well, you will feel a burden lifting from you, perhaps even from your chest, as if chains are being

lifted from your chest. Spend the remainder of the practice period feeling liberated from the chains you tried to lay on your brother, but laid instead on yourself.

Frequent reminders: In everything you do.

Remember, *"No one is crucified alone, and yet no one can enter Heaven by himself."* This means, when you crucify your brother, you crucify yourself as well. And when you set him free, you open the gates of Heaven to both of you.

Response to temptation: Whenever you are tempted to attack yourself by condemning another.

Say, *"Let me perceive forgiveness as it is. Would I accuse myself of doing this? I will not lay this chain upon myself."* This is obviously a miniature version of the longer practice period.

Commentary

This lesson contains a very focused discussion about what it means to "forgive." It deserves not only careful practice as a Workbook lesson, but careful study, as a separate exercise when you have more time. Several of these longer Workbook lessons fall into that category.

The main teaching of this lesson is that forgiveness, to be true, must be fully justified. It applies only to what is false. Sin, if real, *cannot* be forgiven (5:3–4). True forgiveness sees the nothingness of sins. "It looks on them with quiet eyes, and merely says to them, 'My brother, what you think is not the truth'" (7:5).

The lesson itself explains that main idea very well. I want to focus instead on the *results* of forgiveness: the relief it brings to us. Forgiveness is "a deep relief to those who offer it" (6:1). It wakens us from our own dreams. Even if you don't understand all the Course theory behind forgiveness, when you forgive, when you let go of your grievances against someone, you can experience the lifting of a tremendous burden from your own heart. You may not understand why that happens, but you can know that it is true. As the lesson puts it: "You will begin to sense a lifting up, a lightening of weight across your chest, a deep and certain feeling of relief" (16:3).

Forgiving is a very happy feeling. Why is that? Because, without realizing it, when we condemn someone else for their sins we are secretly condemning ourselves. By condemning another, I am saying, "Sin is real and deserves to be punished." If I subscribe to that principle,

414

then I must also believe that when I sin, I too deserve to be punished. My form of "sin" may not be the one I condemn in my brother; indeed, I may be accusing him, or her, of something I think I would never do, and I imagine that because I am free from that particular fault, somehow my condemnation of another will purchase my salvation. But I have supported the principle that sin is real and deserves punishment. Inevitably I know, deep within me, that I, too, have "sinned" in some way. And if I have, I have nothing to hope for but punishment. What I apply to my brother applies to me as well.

When we are tempted to condemn someone, the lesson advises us to ask ourselves, "Would I accuse myself of doing this?" (9:3) or "Would I condemn myself for doing this?" (15:3). The words "would I" are meant in the sense of "do I want to?" The question is not "If I did what this person has done, would I judge myself for it?" Because, if I am judging the other for it, I definitely *would* judge myself if I did the same thing. We usually reserve our sternest judgment for things we think we would never do, precisely because we *would* condemn ourselves for doing them. When we read this question, for instance, and think of a child molester, if we understand the question incorrectly we may answer, "I certainly would condemn myself if I did that!"

What the question is really asking is, "Do I want to make sin real and insist it must be punished? Because if I do, I am condemning myself to punishment also." We are laying chains of imprisonment on ourselves when we lay them on anyone (17:5; 16:4).

This is why releasing my brother from his chains brings relief to *me*. I am liberating myself from the principle that "sin is real and must be punished" when I liberate this other. And what a relief it is! The one who forgives, and offers escape to this other, now sees that escape is possible for himself as well:

> He does not have to fight to save himself. He does not have to kill the dragons which he thought pursued him. Nor need he erect the heavy walls of stone and iron doors he thought would make him safe. He can remove the ponderous and useless armor made to chain his mind to fear and misery. His step is light, and as he lifts his foot to stride ahead a star is left behind, to point the way to those who follow him.   (12:1–5)

Forgiveness is a deep relief.

A WRITTEN VERSION OF THE FORGIVENESS PRACTICE FOR LESSON 134

- Ask the Holy Spirit, Who understands the meaning of forgiveness, *"Let me perceive forgiveness as it is."*
- Then choose a brother to forgive, under His direction. Ask Him which brother you should forgive right now. Fill in that person's name: _____.
- Now catalogue this person's "sins," one by one (but keep from dwelling on any one of them). With each one, try to think of some version of that sin that you yourself do. This may require generalizing the "sin" until you find some version that fits you. Then write that version down in the space provided.
- Then, when you are done writing, repeat to yourself the questions in the left-hand column and follow each one with the two statements on the right. Repeat all statements with as much sincerity as you can muster. Realize that by condemning your brother for this specific thing, you *will* condemn yourself for your version of it. But you don't have to do that. You can be free. And the price of your freedom is freeing him.

Do I want to condemn myself for

_____? *I will not lay this chain upon myself.*

                                      I will not condemn him/her for doing this.

_____? *I will not lay this chain upon myself.*

                                      I will not condemn him/her for doing this.

_____? *I will not lay this chain upon myself.*

                                      I will not condemn him/her for doing this.

_____? *I will not lay this chain upon myself.*

                                      I will not condemn him/her for doing this.

_____? *I will not lay this chain upon myself.*

                                      I will not condemn him/her for doing this.

_____? *I will not lay this chain upon myself.*

                                      I will not condemn him/her for doing this.

_____? *I will not lay this chain upon myself.*

I will not condemn him/her for doing this.

_____? *I will not lay this chain upon myself.*

I will not condemn him/her for doing this.

_____? *I will not lay this chain upon myself.*

I will not condemn him/her for doing this.

_____? *I will not lay this chain upon myself.*

I will not condemn him/her for doing this.

- If you practice well, you will feel a burden lifting from you, perhaps even from your chest, as if chains are being lifted from your chest. Spend the remainder feeling liberated from the chains you tried to lay on your brother, but laid instead on yourself.

LESSON 135 ✦ MAY 15
"If I defend myself I am attacked."

Practice instructions

Purpose: To lay aside your plans and learn your part in God's plan; to bring closer the time when your light, joined with the light of your followers, will light up the world with joy. This is a crucial day in your awakening; it is Eastertime in your salvation. This is another of the Workbook's giant strides (26:4).

Longer: Two times, for fifteen minutes.

- Repeat, *"If I defend myself I am attacked. But in defenselessness I will be strong, and I will learn what my defenses hide."*
- Then rest from all planning and all thought. Your plans have been walls that you erected to shut out the Holy Spirit's plan for your life. His plan is that you "become a light" (20:1) whose "followers" (20:3) light up the world. So let go of your ideas about your life and open your mind to His. Come without defenses and listen as He reveals to you "the part for you within the plan of God" (25:5). He may just tell you plans for today, but those plans will be part of His larger plan for you. Do not fear that these plans will ask sacrifice from you. They are the way to your release. And everything you need to accomplish them will be given you. Since this is an exercise in listening to God's Voice, remember the training you've received in listening for guidance: wait in mental silence, wait in confidence, and periodically repeat your request.

Response to temptation: Whenever you feel tempted to make your own plans.

Repeat, *"This is my Eastertime. And I would keep it holy. I will not defend myself, because the Son of God needs no defense against the truth of his reality."* This is long enough that you'll probably need to write it on a card if you're going to use it.

Remarks: As you go through the day, try not to shape and organize it according to what you see as your needs. Instead, if you listen to His plans and follow them, you will find inconceivable happiness, and the whole world will "celebrate your Eastertime with you" (26:4).

Commentary

"If I defend myself I am attacked." The general thought that heads this lesson states that all forms of defense are actually witnesses to attack, or to your belief in attack. If you see a need for a defense, you must be perceiving an attack.

The self you think you are is something so weak it needs defense; your true Self, which is mind or spirit, needs no defense. This lesson shows that when you make plans whose purpose is to defend your small "self" (the image you have made of yourself, comprised of your ego and its expression, the body), you are indirectly attacking your true Self, because you perceive that Self as attacking "you."

The Course continually teaches us that "all attack is self-attack" (T-10.II.5:1; line not in First Edition). It says we constantly attack ourselves, but we are blind to the fact. We think the attack comes from somewhere outside ourselves, and never realize that it stems from our own thoughts of guilt. Over and over, the Course tells us to look at what we are doing and thinking, to recognize the self-attack, and to choose to let go of it.

Lesson 135 applies this general principle to a particular area of our lives that we have probably not thought of as self-attack: planning. First, it points out that all defenses are a form of self-attack because they make the illusion of threat real, and then attempt to handle "threats" as if they were real. It asks us to look closely at what we think we are defending, how we defend it, and against what.

Second, it identifies our plans as a form of defense. Plans are a form of defense against anticipated future threats. If that is so, the reverse is true: All "defenses are the plans you undertake to make against the truth" (17:1). In other words, defenses and plans are the same thing. When you set up a defense, you are making plans. All defenses are plans, and all self-initiated plans are defenses.

In sum, making plans is a form of defense, and all defenses are attacks on myself. Therefore, making plans is just another form of self-attack, to be noticed and abandoned.

Finally, the lesson discusses how "a healed mind" (11:1; 12:1) approaches life: not making plans, but receiving plans from the Holy Spirit, with full present trust in the guidance of the Holy Spirit, and with confidence in His plan. Only this approach allows for change, healing, and miracles to take place in the present moment.

> A healed mind does not plan. It carries out the plans that
> it receives through listening to Wisdom that is not its own.
> (11:1–2)

This does not mean that a healed mind does not follow a plan. It follows a plan; it just doesn't make the plan. It receives the plan through the guidance of the Holy Spirit.

In simple language, the healed mind listens to the Holy Spirit and does what He directs, instead of listening to the ego's plans, which are always based on fear and take a defensive posture. The ego's plans are always trying to protect and preserve the body; often, the plans of the Holy Spirit seem to be unconcerned about the body at all. The Holy Spirit has very different priorities.

When the Course is talking about "a healed mind" it is talking about the goal of the Course—the state your mind will be in after you graduate from the Course. This isn't something you simply step into after reading a few lessons; this is what you will be like after working with the Course and completely integrating it into your life.[1]

---

1. The thoughts expressed above have been taken almost directly from a booklet I wrote, *A Healed Mind Does Not Plan*, published by Circle Publishing. This is a booklet that deals entirely with the subject of planning and decision making as taught in the Course.

LESSON 136 ✦ MAY 16
"Sickness is a defense against the truth."

Practice instructions

Longer: Two times, for fifteen minutes.

- Begin with this healing prayer: *"Sickness is a defense against the truth. I will accept the truth of what I am, and let my mind be wholly healed today."* With this prayer, you are asking that your mind no longer employ sickness to "prove" to you that you are a body. Instead, you ask for the realization of who you really are, which is spirit.
- After making this invitation, keep your mind silent and alert, poised to receive the answer to your request. Open your mind and let healing flash across it. Let all the purposes that you gave the body be wiped clean, as the truth of who you are dawns upon your clear and open mind.

Remarks: If you practiced well, your body will have no feeling. It will feel neither ill nor well, neither good nor bad. It will have no power to tell the mind how to feel. Only its usefulness will remain. Indeed, its usefulness will increase, for it was the purposes you laid on it that made it weak, vulnerable, and sickly. "As these are laid aside, the strength the body has will always be enough to serve all truly useful purposes" (18:2). You must, however, protect this state with careful watching, responding quickly to any thoughts which imply that you are a body. For these thoughts make the mind sick, and it will then attack the body with sickness.

Response to temptation: Whenever you have attack thoughts, judgments, or make plans.

"Give instant remedy" (20:1) by saying, *"I have forgotten what I really am, for I mistook my body for myself. Sickness is a defense against the truth. But I am not a body. And my mind cannot attack. So I cannot be sick."* The last lines hearken back to a Text passage, which says that there are two premises necessary for sickness to occur: "that the body is for attack, and that you are a body" (T-8.VIII.5:7). If you can truly accept that you are *unable* to attack, and that you are *not* a body, then "sickness is inconceivable" (T-8.VIII.5:8).

Commentary

This is another of those lessons that will repay careful study; there is a lot of good stuff in here!

The main thought is plainly stated: Sickness is a means we use to defend ourselves against the truth. It is a decision we make, chosen quite deliberately when truth gets too close for comfort, in order to distract ourselves and root ourselves once again in the body. On the bright side, then, when we get sick we can congratulate ourselves that we must have been letting in the truth if the ego is getting this scared of it!

For instance, in 1995 Robert and I gave a weekend intensive on "We Are the Light of the World: Accepting Our Function." During that weekend I found myself being deeply impressed by the message the Course was conveying to us all. The day after the intensive I got diarrhea. Now, there is little that brings you down to a body level like having to run to the toilet all the time! But I actually found myself being amused by it. "How like my ego!" I thought. "What a predictable reaction!" Instead of having the desired (by the ego) effect, it had the opposite; it served to *remind* me of the truth instead of distracting me from it. And guess what? It very quickly went away. "Defenses that do not work at all are automatically discarded" (T-12.I.9:8).

Most people react to being told that they choose sickness by flatly denying it. This is not something that is easy to discover. The lesson says our choice is "doubly shielded by oblivion" (5:2). We choose first to hide the pesky truth that has been nibbling away at our delusions of separation and of the physical nature of our identity by making ourselves sick; that is the original decision we made. We then choose to forget we did it; the first shield of oblivion. Finally, we forget that we chose to forget, the second shield. All of this happens in a split second (see 3:4; 4:2–5:1). In that split second we are conscious of what we are doing, but the shields are up so quickly that the whole process *seems* to be unconscious (3:3).

We need to remember what we have forgotten, the deliberate forgetting of our choice. We *can* remember if we are willing "to reconsider the decision which is doubly shielded" (5:2), that is, the decision to run away from the truth, the decision that truth is something against which we need to defend ourselves. This is why the exercise for the day is:

> *Sickness is a defense against the truth. I will accept the truth of what I am, and let my mind be wholly healed today.* (15:6–7)

The antidote to the whole process is not attempting to heal the sick body, but to accept the truth about myself, to let my *mind* be healed. Sickness is a side effect of rejecting the truth about myself; the cure is to accept the truth instead, to reconsider the original decision which, although veiled from conscious awareness, *must* be there for sickness to have occurred.

The lesson warns us, in the final paragraph: "Do not be confused about what must be healed" (20:2). It isn't the body that needs healing; it is the mind. This agrees with the Text, which tells us:

> When the ego tempts you to sickness do not ask the Holy Spirit to heal the body, for this would merely be to accept the ego's belief that the body is the proper aim of healing. Ask, rather, that the Holy Spirit teach you the right *perception* of the body, for perception alone can be distorted. (T-8.IX.1:5–6)

It is that original decision to reject the truth of what we are, because it seems to threaten what we *think* we are, that must be questioned and reversed.

The lesson says some rather incredible things about the body of a person whose mind is healed, and whose body has been accepted as nothing but a tool to be used to heal the world. The body's strength "will always be enough to serve all truly useful purposes. The body's health is fully guaranteed, because it is not limited by time, by weather or fatigue, by food and drink, or any laws you made it serve before" (18:2–3). If a body is not limited by time it does not age. Not limited by weather means it needs no clothing or shelter. Not limited by fatigue, it needs no sleep. Not limited by food or drink, it does not need to eat. Who of us can say this is true of us?

Perhaps we have experienced a few glimmers of such brilliant light, fatigue thrown off, lack of food overlooked for a time. But no one I know is at this stage of perfect trust. We have a ways to go, you and I. So I do not think we need be surprised when a cold attacks, or the flu gets us down, or even if something "more serious" happens. We're still afraid of the truth—big surprise! Rather than thinking, "Oh, why did I do this to myself? What is wrong with me that I am still getting sick?" let me say, "Oops! I made a mistake. I forgot what I really am and mistook my body for myself. Silly me! I just need to remember that I am not a body; this isn't what I am." The "sickness" of the body can then become a catalyst for the healing of my mind, instead of a defense against the truth.

LESSON 137 ✦ MAY 17
"When I am healed I am not healed alone."

Practice instructions

Purpose: To let your mind be healed, that you may send healing to the world, aware that you and the world are healed as one.

Longer: Two—morning and evening, for ten minutes.

- Say, *"When I am healed I am not healed alone. And I would share my healing with the world, that sickness may be banished from the mind of God's one Son, Who is my only Self."*
- Then rest in stillness. And as you rest, let the Word of God come in to heal your insane thoughts, so that this healing can go forth from you to the world. Once the healing comes into your mind, you may try to muster a general feeling of giving it out to everyone, or you may pick particular people to send it to. You may even feel that certain individuals are being placed in your mind to send healing to, perhaps even total strangers.

Remarks: This exercise will prepare you for the hourly practice.

Shorter: Every hour on the hour, for one minute.

Remember your purpose today by repeating, *"When I am healed I am not healed alone. And I would bless my brothers, for I would be healed with them, as they are healed with me."*

Remarks: Is it not worth a minute to receive the gift of everything?

Commentary

Although this lesson has a great deal to say about healing in general, its primary message is that healing, which is our function in the world, is essentially a phenomenon that is shared, and that to heal *is* to share. Healing restores oneness. "Those who are healed become the instruments of healing" (11:1).

"Sickness is a retreat from others, and a shutting off of joining" (1:3).

425

It is isolation (2:1). Healing reverses that; it is a move toward others, a joining, and a union. The healing being spoken of in this lesson is a healing of the mind, and not necessarily of the body. "Our function is to let our minds be healed, that we may carry healing to the world, exchanging...separation for the peace of God" (13:1).

Whatever the state of my body, it cannot interfere with this function. My body cannot restrain or limit my mind. "Minds that were walled off within a body [become] free to join with other minds, to be forever strong" (8:6). My task today, and every day, is to allow my mind to be healed, and to allow healing to flow through my mind to other minds, carrying healing to the world. That can occur whatever state my body is in. I do not normally realize how powerful my mind is, and how extensive the effects of its healing can be. "And as you let yourself be healed, you see all those around you, or who cross your mind, or whom you touch or those who seem to have no contact with you, healed along with you" (10:1).

As I open my mind to healing today, I realize that whatever the state of my body, "what is opposed to God does not exist" (11:3). When I refuse to accept sickness as my reality, my mind "becomes a haven where the weary can remain to rest" (11:3). Sickness is just a special case of "I am my body." So what we are called on to do is not just to refuse the limitations of sickness, but to refuse the limits of the body altogether. Today, I choose to let "thoughts of healing...go forth from what is healed to what must yet be healed" (12:6). I set aside some time, ten minutes in the morning and evening, and a minute every hour, to give my mind over to its function of sharing healing thoughts with the world. "Reach out to all your brothers, and touch them with the touch of Christ" (T-13.VI.8:2).

Today, I want to let healing be through me (15:1). I want to be a channel, a channel of blessing to the world. What other purpose could bring me such joy?

LESSON 138 ✦ MAY 18
"Heaven is the decision I must make."

Practice instructions

Purpose: To make the choice for Heaven, "the choice that time was made to help us make" (7:1).

Longer: Two—the first and last moments of your day, for five minutes.

Use these five minutes to make a firm, definitive choice for Heaven. Begin by saying, *"Heaven is the decision I must make. I make it now, and will not change my mind, because it is the only thing I want."* Then spend the rest of the time bringing your mind to a place where you truly mean these words. This will probably involve bringing to light unconscious beliefs that life is a terrifying exercise in which all hope is finally swallowed up in death, and in which death is, sadly, the only escape from conflict. Bring this belief system to light and call on Heaven's help, and you will see that this view is totally invalid, "nothing but an appearance of the truth" (11:2). Then set this hellish view of life, divested of all reality, next to the alternative: Heaven. If you do, you will see that choosing Heaven is so obvious and natural that it is no choice at all.

Shorter: Hourly, for a brief quiet time.

Consciously reaffirm the choice you made in the morning by saying, *"Heaven is the decision I must make. I make it now, and will not change my mind, because it is the only thing I want."* There is a real emphatic note in these lines, so you might want to emphasize "must" and "now" and "will not."

Remarks: Devote the evening practice to reaffirming the choice you made at the beginning of the day and reinforced every hour of the day. By ending in this way, you make the entire day about the choice for Heaven.

427

Commentary

The lesson makes some stark contrasts between this world and creation. One is a realm of duality, in which "opposition is part of being 'real'" (2:2). The other is a realm of unity, of perfect oneness: "Creation knows no opposite" (2:1). This is a classic discussion about what can be called duality and nonduality.

Nonduality, or oneness, is what is real. Where there is only oneness there can be no choice, because there is nothing between which to choose. If oneness is reality, then choice, any choice, is an illusion and nothing more. Choice is impossible, inconceivable. That is the reality.

Within our dream, however, choice is not only possible; it is inevitable, it is life. Within this world, truth cannot enter because it would be met only with fear; the choicelessness of oneness seems the ultimate threat to a mind that thinks duality is all there is. Therefore, in this world, we are learning to make one, final choice. It is a choice to end all choices, the choice between illusion and reality. Time exists for nothing but this choice, to "give us time" to make it. We are being asked to choose Heaven instead of hell.

Years ago, before I encountered the Course, I had been through a lot of things, read a lot of books, and attended a lot of seminars. I sat down one day to try to distill, in writing, what I had learned from life. I was writing for my sons, then in their teens. I recall quite clearly that at that point in my life, I felt I was only sure of two things:

One, you can trust the Universe.

Two, happiness is a decision I make.

I won't bother to comment on the first item here, but the second is something very fundamental to the Course, the realization that nothing outside my mind makes me happy or unhappy; my happiness is entirely the result of my own choice.

When I first read this lesson in the Workbook I was stunned by the similarity of the concept, even the very words. "Heaven is the decision I must make." Perhaps the fact that I had arrived at this conclusion on my own was one of the reasons I took so rapidly to the Course; it confirmed what, to me, was the essence of my own personal wisdom, words that as far as I knew were entirely my own. Here was this book, saying the same thing. In saying that we must choose Heaven, and that this is "the decision" we have to make, the Course is saying that learning this is what life is all about. It is "the choice that time was made to help us make" (7:1). It is a choice, a decision, that accepts the total responsibility of the mind for the way it perceives reality.

But the lesson is saying far more than this. The discussion of duality and nonduality in this lesson explains clearly why so many of us, indeed most of us, experience such tearing, inner conflict over accepting the simple truth. We have become convinced that opposites and conflict are not simply part of life, they *are* life. They *are* reality to us. "Life is seen as conflict" (7:4). This belief shows up, for instance, in the somewhat frivolous objection that Heaven, where nothing changes and there are no opposites, sounds boring. We are addicted to the drama, devoted to the delicious agony of indecision. To be without choices, to us, seems like death. To finally and completely resolve the conflict appears to us like the end of life itself.

Yet that is what the Course promises and asks of us: the end of all conflict. When this truly dawns on our minds, we often recoil in mortal terror.

> These mad beliefs can gain unconscious hold of great intensity and grip the mind with terror and anxiety so strong that it will not relinquish its ideas about its own protection. It must be saved from salvation.   (8:1–2)

It is unconscious; we do not realize what is going on. But we literally run away from the truth, and shrink from total love, not knowing what we are doing. Virtually everyone who works with the Course over any length of time experiences something like this in their life. It seems as though we are being asked to die. And in a sense, we are: die to life *as we have known it.*

The only way out is through. Through fear to love. "Heaven is chosen consciously" (9:1). For a decision to be conscious, *both* alternatives must be seen clearly. We have to see hell in the plain light of day, as well as Heaven. Our fear of hell, our terror of destruction, our agony of guilt must be "raised to understanding, to be judged again, this time with Heaven's help" (9:3). It was our own mind's desire for an alternative to Heaven that made hell, and we must understand that duality is a beast of our own making—and that our desire had no *real* effect.

"Who can decide between the clearly seen and the unrecognized? Yet who can fail to make a choice between alternatives when only one is seen as valuable; the other as a wholly worthless thing, a but imagined source of guilt and pain?" (10:2–3). Our making of duality has seemed like such a monstrous thing; buried in our unconscious, it was "made enormous, vengeful, pitiless with hate" (11:4), but when it is brought into conscious awareness, "now it is recognized as but a foolish, trivial mistake" (11:5). Our guilt over it is all that holds it in place. When we look at it again, "this time with Heaven's help," the choice to let it go becomes the only possible decision we can make. And in that decision, we are released.

LESSON 139 ✦ MAY 19
"I will accept Atonement for myself."

Practice instructions

Purpose: "To accept the truth about yourself, and go your way rejoicing in the endless Love of God" (10:2).

Longer: Two times—morning and evening—for five minutes.

- Begin by reviewing your mission: *"I will accept Atonement for myself. For I remain as God created me."*
- Then go into a meditation aimed at reconnecting with the knowledge of who you are. You haven't lost this knowledge. It is still there, deep within your memory. You may want to picture this knowledge as a light at the very center of your mind, and then focus on sinking down and inward to make contact with it. Increase your motivation to reach this knowledge by realizing that you can remember it for everyone (11:5). Whenever your mind wanders off, be sure to call it back by repeating the opening lines.

Shorter: Hourly, for several minutes.

Do a shorter version of the longer practice (begin by repeating, *"I will accept Atonement for myself. For I remain as God created me"*). Lay aside all distracting thoughts. Let all false beliefs about yourself be cleared away, and learn that the chains that would hide your Self from your awareness are nothing but fragile cobwebs.

Commentary

What does it mean to accept the Atonement for myself? This lesson puts an end to any idea that this is a selfish notion, or that it means my only concern is myself, or my personal happiness. Nothing could be clearer than this: "It is more than just our happiness alone we came to gain. What we accept as what we are proclaims what everyone must be, along with us" (9:4–5).

To accept the Atonement for myself means to accept the truth of what I am, to decide to "accept ourselves as God created us" (1:2). And what am I? I already know, in my heart of hearts, but I resist knowing. This lesson is magnificent in its trenchant dissection of the insanity of the way we question our Identity. It questions all our questioning. It raises all our doubts to doubt. It denies the possibility of denial. It belittles our thoughts of littleness. How can we be anything except what we are? How can we *not know* what we are? "The only thing that can be surely known by any living thing is what it is" (2:3).

God created us as extensions of His Love. That is our mission; it is what we are. To accept the Atonement is to accept this truth about ourselves. To accept the Atonement is to begin to function as God's Love in the world.

Every time we refuse to see the magnificence in another we are denying our own. We look on others with less than love because we refuse to see how much *we* merit it. We are God's representatives on earth; accepting the Atonement is to accept our mission. We are here to restore the grandeur of what we all are to every mind—not just to our own. This grandness, this magnificent inclusiveness, this divine generosity is our very being. We are the open heart that embraces the world, remembering "how much a part of us is every mind" (11:6).

In us our Father's Love can contain them all. Our heart is big enough for all the world.

This is Who we are. Today, let me remember. Today, let me accept my holy aim. Today, let me know myself as part of this great throbbing, all-embracing Heart of God.

LESSON 140 ✦ MAY 20
"Only salvation can be said to cure."

Practice instructions

Purpose: To seek healing for the mind, not the body, by hearing the Voice of healing, which God placed inside you, so close that you cannot lose it.

Longer: Two times—at beginning and end of day—for five minutes.

- Let all your interfering thoughts be laid aside as one, for there are all equally meaningless.
- With empty hands, lifted heart and listening mind, pray, *"Only salvation can be said to cure. Speak to us, Father, that we may be healed."* You are asking that the Voice of healing speak to you, to heal your mind, the source of all sickness.
- Then, in the silence of all thought, listen for God's Voice, Which will cure all ills, regardless of their size or shape. Feel His salvation blanket you with protection and deep peace, allowing no illusion to disturb your holy mind.

Remarks: You will succeed to the degree you realize there are no meaningful distinction among illusions. They are all unreal. That is why they can be cured.

Shorter: As the hour strikes, for a minute.

Do a short version of the longer practice period. Say, *"Only salvation can be said to cure. Speak to us, Father, that we may be healed."* Then listen in joyous silence, and hear God's answer.

Commentary

The "cure" that the Course is talking about is a healing of the mind, not of the body.

> The body needs no healing. But the mind that thinks it is a body is sick indeed!   (T-25.In.3:1–2)

> The lesson is the *mind* was sick that thought the body could
> be sick.   (T-28.II.11:7)

To seek a cure in the physical realm, by any means (even New Age means) is what the Course would call "magic." (Calling it "magic" doesn't mean we can't use it if our fear level requires it; the Course advocates a compromise approach in such circumstances. See T-2.IV.4–5 and T-2.V.2, which I discuss a bit later.) The Atonement heals the mind that thinks the body can be sick. "This is no magic" (6:4).

This lesson applies to bodily sickness, but it applies equally to any apparent "problem" in this material world: financial lack, loneliness, and so on. These problems all occur within the dream, and finding "a magic formula" within the dream is never the solution (2:2). We are "curing" the symptom and not the disease. The root of the problem is within the mind. "Let us not try today to seek to cure what cannot suffer sickness" (7:1). Our problems are not physical in nature. "We will not be misled today by what appears to us as sick" (9:1). "So do we lay aside our amulets [crystals? religious medallions?], our charms and medicines, our chants and bits of magic in whatever form they take" (10:1).

Early in the Text, Jesus makes it clear that magic is not evil. It just doesn't really work. It is only a stop-gap, an attempt to rid ourselves of symptoms without really curing the disease. Yet sometimes that is the best we can do. We have a headache, and with a splitting headache it is often difficult to quiet the mind and peacefully meditate ourselves well. So we use magic. We take the aspirin; there is no shame in this. Only let us not deceive ourselves that we have really done anything to cure the disease; we have simply masked the symptom. "If you are afraid to use the mind to heal, you should not attempt to do so" (T-2.V.2:2). If our fear level is high, a "compromise approach" may be necessary (T-2.IV.4:4–7).

"Only salvation can be said to cure." The magic of this world can mask symptoms but not cure. "The mind that brings illusions to the truth is really changed. There is no change but this" (7:4–5). Today we are asked to practice just this: bringing our illusions to the truth, allowing our guilt to be removed from our minds. *This* cures, and nothing else. "There is no place where He [God] is not" (5:5), and this includes our minds. Sin would keep Him out, but since He is everywhere, sin cannot be anywhere (see 5:1–7); sin cannot be in our minds. "This is the thought that cures" (6:1). Sin, and therefore sickness, cannot be real because God is in us; He has not left us, and what we think is sin cannot be so. In our awareness of His presence, guilt disappears, and with it, the cause of sickness.

IX

Review IV: Introduction and Lessons 141 - 150

INTRODUCTION

If you will recall, back in the Workbook introduction we were told, "The workbook is divided into two main sections, the first dealing with the undoing of the way you see now, and the second with the acquisition of true perception" (W-In.3:1). Although Part II does not begin for another eighty lessons, the introduction to Review IV announces that we are entering a transition stage of the Workbook, "preparing for the second part of learning how the truth can be applied" (1:1). Part II of the Workbook, if you will look at it, consists of lessons that are a half page long, or less. They give very few specific practice instructions, and offer us a great deal more latitude in exactly how we practice. They are geared to students who have begun to make the truths of the Course their own, and who are ready to apply them independently. This review gives us some preliminary exercises in that kind of independent practice. In Lesson 153, shortly after we complete this review, there will be a major shift in practice, as we shall see, which will set the pattern for the practice during the rest of Part I of the Workbook.

Therefore, following the practice instructions for this review is quite important, if we want to be prepared for what is to come. You'll notice that the reviews give us nothing but the theme thought for the review and the two theme ideas being reviewed; there is no additional commentary. In a sense, we are meant to supply that commentary for ourselves. We are meant to take the ideas and let the Holy Spirit open their meaning in our own minds, without the prop of printed words to help us. "Let each word shine with the meaning God has given it, as it was given to you through His Voice" (7:4).

Perhaps you do not feel ready for this. I confess that when I first did the Workbook I pretty much lost interest after Part I; I did the lessons but really all I did was read them, think about them for a minute or two, and then forget them. The reviews such as this one seemed particularly pointless to me. Two or three sentences wasn't enough to stimulate my mind, and I was not ready, apparently, to allow the Holy Spirit to "let each word shine" in my mind. You may find yourself in the same boat. Still, I would say, try to follow the instructions. Take the few lines given for each day, and ruminate on them. Chew them over. Think about what you know of their meaning, and ask to be shown more. If it works for you, try to initiate a dialogue with the Holy Spirit about the ideas. Turn them into prayers. Think how they can apply to your life. Be still before God and let the feeling of the ideas wash over you. Do whatever seems to work for you.

Maybe you won't feel that you're doing very well, but what is the purpose of practice, if not to learn to do something you don't know how to do well?

Notice the theme thought for the review: "My mind holds only what I think with God" (2:2; 5:3). The instructions tell us to spend five minutes letting this one thought, and this alone, engage our minds, and remove all other thoughts. What we are doing is clearing the stage, making way for the Holy Spirit to teach us. The five minutes spent with this idea each day is our warm-up period. We are making ourselves ready to receive the thoughts of God, through His Holy Spirit. We are preparing ourselves to hold communion with God.

Only after this five-minute warm up are we instructed to take the two thoughts for review, and let their meaning illuminate our minds. There is no time limit given here; we are to review them "slowly" (7:2) and with "no hurry" (7:3). Surely this will be more than a few seconds! More like several minutes, at the least. The best way is to be able to do this review without concern about time; if we take five minutes or twenty-five, it does not matter. The important thing is that we commune with God, and let His Thoughts fill our minds. As the review says of our hourly review sessions, we should take "time enough to see the gifts that they [the two ideas] contain for you, and let them be received where they were meant to be" (8:2). The exact amount of time you spend is left to you.

REVIEW IV PRACTICE INSTRUCTIONS

Purpose: To prepare for Part II of the Workbook (which does not begin for another eighty lessons). The next review (Review V) announces this same preparation. The Workbook seems to assume that we have gotten over some kind of hump (see, for instance, W-pI.122.10:2), and that now, with much of our resistance behind us, we can focus on getting ready for the pinnacle of the Workbook: Part II.

Longer: Two—beginning and ending of the day—for about seven minutes.

First, spend five minutes dwelling on the central idea of the review: "My mind holds only what I think with God." Quiet your mind, and repeat the idea over and over, very slowly, focusing on its meaning. Let it clear out and replace all of your normal thinking. Your usual thoughts (as paragraphs 3 and 4 explain) are really unforgiveness in disguise. Since these thoughts are not of God, they obscure the truth that your mind holds only what you think with God. By clearing them out and thinking only this one thought from the Course, you get in touch with your mind's true state, in which it thinks only Thoughts from God. This will prepare you for a day which reflects that true state, in which the thoughts that occur to you come from God (see 6:1-2).

If your normal thoughts try to intrude, dispel them with the central thought. One suggestion for this time is to use the imagery of 4:3. Picture your mind as the ocean. Placing one of your normal thoughts in your mind is like a child throwing a stick into the ocean. How can that change the grand rhythms of the ocean (the tides, the sun warming the water, the moon reflecting on the surface)? How can that change the grand thoughts you share with God?

After these five minutes, move on to the second phase. Read the two review ideas, close your eyes, and repeat them silently to yourself—very slowly. God placed a gift inside each word. Let your mind receive that gift. "Let each word shine with the meaning God has given it" (7:4). Receive the thought He placed in there for you, for such receiving is the true condition of your mind.

The purpose of the first phase is to prepare you for this second phase. By spending five minutes dwelling only on a thought from God, you prepare yourself to see in the two review ideas only the meaning placed in them by God.

Remarks: In the evening, repeat the same practice. Realize that the central thought has "made the day a special time of blessing" (9:3), both for you and for the world through your faithful practicing. Realize also that you drop off into sleep surrounded by God's gratitude for your practicing. For you are now learning to reclaim the inheritance He gave you.

Shorter: Hourly, for a quiet moment.

This is a miniature version of the morning and evening practice. Spend a quiet moment with the central thought, and then repeat the two review ideas, slowly, giving yourself time to see the precious gifts of meaning that God placed in them for you

THE OCEAN OF YOUR MIND

Aren't our minds a mess? They are the arena of a constant crazy dance of thoughts. Each thought seems to dance to its own music, and many of them seem to dance with no rhyme or reason at all. Furthermore, most of these thoughts are so petty, so self-centered, that we hardly want to report them with honesty to others. After a lifetime of seeing our minds filled with this ever-changing rush of erratic, selfish thoughts, what can we conclude but that this is the definitive statement on the nature of our minds? What can we conclude but that we are made of the fabric of chaos and pettiness?

Yet what if our whole experience of our minds is an illusion, a deception designed to camouflage their real nature? That is what is suggested in this passage from the Workbook of *A Course in Miracles*:

> And yet, your mind holds only what you think with God. Your self-deceptions cannot take the place of truth. No more than can a child who throws a stick into the ocean change the coming and the going of the tides, the warming of the water by the sun, the silver of the moon on it by night.
>
> (W-pI.rIV.In.4:1-3)

This passage contains a profound and evocative view of the mind, a view which I would like to spend this article drawing out. This passage is actually an elaboration on the first line of it. That line (put in first person) is the central theme of our practice for ten lessons in the Workbook, where we spend five minutes morning and evening dwelling on "My mind holds only what I think with God" (W-pI.rIV.In.).

So what does that line mean? Does it mean that all of the thoughts we entertain somehow mysteriously come from God, no matter how meaningless and random they seem? No, what it really means is that the mind of which I am aware is not my real mind. My conscious mind, filled with my erratic private thoughts, is an illusion of a mind. It is a mirage, floating above my real mind. My real mind is a limitless domain, at one with the Mind of God. In that mind, my thoughts are not tiny, fleeting events, like my conscious thoughts, but stable, eternal realities. These thoughts are not self-initiated, but rather stream from God through the center of my Identity, where they become my thoughts as much as they are His. That is the meaning of "My mind holds only what I think with God."

What, then, does the next line mean: "Your self-deceptions cannot take the place of truth"? Your self-deceptions are all the thoughts of which you are currently aware. They are self-deceptions precisely because they deceive you into thinking that your mind is not that infinite mind which thinks in unison with the Mind of God. As long as these thoughts engage you, your mind clearly seems to be a rather mean little creature, for only such a creature would crank out the small-minded thoughts you call your own. If you have ever been glad that no one can read your mind, because you were embarrassed over your thoughts, you know what I'm talking about. These thoughts, then, appear to be the proof that whatever exalted mind God gave you in the beginning has been replaced by this puny thing you call your mind now.

This passage is refuting what seems to be so obvious. Our current mind seems to be all there is to us, while the mind the Course is talking about is nowhere to be seen. Believing it exists at all seems to be a daring leap of faith. The Course is saying exactly the opposite. Our real mind, the mind that thinks with God, is all there is. What we call our mind, our conscious mind, does not actually exist at all. Believing in *it* is the daring leap of faith.

This brings us to the final sentence: "No more than can a child who throws a stick into the ocean change the coming and the going of the tides, the warming of the water by the sun, the silver of the moon on it by night." I see this line as sheer poetry. It uses an economy of words to capture a definite feeling. It begins with the busy activities of the child caught up in throwing his stick. Yet no matter how important his throwing seems to the child, it is reduced to utter insignificance in the face of the majesty of the ocean and its vast, perpetual rhythms. In this image one gets a sense of timeless cycles which are totally unheeding of our tiny human activities.

For me, this sense of timeless rhythm is enhanced by the rhythm of the poetic meter. These lines are written in iambic pentameter (where each line has five "feet" of two syllables each, with the accent on the second syllable of each foot: da-*dum* da-*dum* da-*dum* da-*dum* da-*dum*), and each of the ocean's three cycles that are mentioned has its own line of iambic pentameter:

> the coming and the going of the tides,
> the warming of the water by the sun,
> the silver of the moon on it by night.

When I read these lines and feel their rhythm, I get a sense of perpetually repeating cycles, in part because the lines themselves take the form of repeating cycles. Three times these lines repeat the same structure of five "heartbeats," five cycles of an unstressed followed by a stressed syllable. Through this repeating form, one can almost feel the repeating rhythms of the ocean. One can almost feel the days turning, as the tides go in and out, as the sun rises and then sinks in the sky, as the moonlight appears and shines peacefully upon the water, and as another day begins in which it all starts over again. Through both the form and content of these lines, one catches a sense of timelessness, of cycles that go on repeating forever, unaffected by what we humans do on the tiny shoreline. You might want to go back and read those three lines and see if you can catch this feeling from them.

The image of the stick thrown into the ocean, however, is not only designed to impart that feeling, it is carefully crafted to symbolize in detail the teaching the Course is giving us here. Let's explore how it does that.

The image, remember, symbolizes the relationship between our conscious mind and thoughts, on the one hand, and our true mind and the thoughts it thinks with God, on the other. The child on the beach is us, the thinker of our conscious thoughts. The child's act of throwing a stick into the ocean is our act of "throwing" a thought into our mind. The stick, therefore, represents one of our usual thoughts.

The ocean symbolizes our true mind, the mind that thinks with God. Our mind may seem like an insignificant little puddle, but that is the illusory mind. According to this image, our true mind is like an ocean. In this the Course is echoing an ancient tradition of seeing the ocean's depth and boundlessness as a symbol of the Divine, into which our individual identities eventually merge like rivers flowing into the sea. This image is usually associated with Hinduism, although it has been used in Christian mysticism as well. The Course's image is similar but slightly different, for here the ocean is not God, but our own true mind, which is one with the Mind of God but not absolutely identical.

What, then, do those three cycles symbolize—the tides, the sun warming the water, the moon reflecting on the surface? They must symbolize our true thoughts, the thoughts we think with God. After all, thoughts are events within the mind, and those cycles are events within the ocean. If the ocean is our true mind, then those cycles must represent the thoughts in our true mind. And what a beautiful symbol for our true thoughts. These thoughts are not the little mice we now find scurrying through our mind. They are more like the grand rhythms of the ocean.

One more point: Notice that all three cycles are a response to a celestial body. The tides are a response to the gravitational pull of the moon. The reflection of the moon is a response to its light. The warming of the water is a response to the sun's rays. This leads us to another bit of symbolism. The ocean's cycles are generated by the sun and moon; those cycles represent our true thoughts, and our true thoughts are generated by God. The sun and moon must therefore symbolize God.

Again the Course is echoing traditional symbolism. The sun is an ancient symbol for God and has often been worshipped itself as a god. The moon, too, has frequently been given religious significance. There is the famous image in Buddhism of the finger pointing at the moon, the moon representing enlightenment. Buddhism has also used the image of gazing on the moon's reflection in the water (or even in a still sea) as a symbol for enlightenment. That is very close to our image from the Course.

I find the ocean's response to the sun and moon to be a moving symbol for our mind's reception of God's Thoughts. The ocean cannot help but rise and fall in response to the pull of the moon. It cannot help but respond with warmth to the rays of the sun. It cannot help but receive and reflect the moonlight. The ocean is perfectly receptive to the action of these celestial bodies. Just so, our minds are perfectly receptive to the Thoughts of God. We cannot help but respond to His pull, be warmed by His sunshine, receive and reflect His moonlight. In our true mind, we yield to Him as naturally and completely as the ocean yields to the sun and the moon.

I want to stress that this image is merely a symbol. The Course places no actual significance in the ocean, sun, or moon, none whatsoever. The sun is not God, the ocean is not divine. When the Course is speaking literally, it makes it very clear that these things are illusions that will one day pass away (see, for instance, T-29.VI.2:7-10). Yet, even though things are mere illusions, I think you will admit that they can be excellent symbols for what is real.

Now that we have deciphered the symbolism, let's make use of this image. For it is not merely a fascinating and instructive symbolic picture; it can actually draw us toward that oceanic place in our minds. Let us, therefore, try to apply it to our own mind.

Imagine yourself as the child. When you think a thought, it is like the child throwing his stick. You may believe that your little thought actually molds and changes the nature of your mind. Perhaps you can accept that when God created your mind it was crystal clear, pure and immaculate. Yet each new stick you have thrown into it seems to have changed it into an increasingly stagnant pool, odorous and covered with algae.

Thinking this, however, is like the child on the shore thinking that his stick can actually change the ocean. Notice that he is not throwing a rock into the ocean. Whereas the rock has its way with the ocean—it sinks no matter what the ocean does—the ocean has *its* way with the stick. The stick simply floats harmlessly on the surface. As it floats, you see the water being slowly warmed as the sun shines down upon it. When the sun has set, you see the water calmly reflecting the moonlight. And while the wheel of the days and nights continues to turn, you see the tides come and go as they always have. These ageless cycles simply go on, as they have for millions of years gone by, as they will for millions of years to come, unheeding of your little stick.

In just this same way, the thoughts of which you are aware float on the surface of your true mind, not affecting that mind in the least. It simply continues, as it always has, as if your conscious mind were not even there.

Let us, then, try to reach down to this true mind in us. I find that this ocean image is an effective focus for meditation, so I want to suggest that we try using it for that. Imagine that, in a deep place within you, lies your true mind. If you will, take a moment and close your eyes and try to sink down and inward, into the center of your mind. From time to time, in order to keep your mind on track or pull it back from wandering, you may want to repeat "My mind holds only what I think with God." As you start to get past the mists that are your usual thoughts, realize that you approach an ancient shore. It is the shore of your real mind, which is as deep and as boundless as the ocean.

See the waves rolling onto this shore. And as you do, realize that these waves have been rolling thus for time beyond measure. They are unaware of your usual thoughts, of your problems and anxieties and responsibilities—of your sticks. Your human drama is irrelevant to them. Have you ever felt this at the ocean's edge? Have you ever felt released from your burdens by the vastness of the ocean and the fact that your problems mean nothing to it? That, of course, was the point of that image in the Course: The child's little drama meant nothing to the ocean. So try to get a sense of that now. Try to realize that here, on the shore of your true mind, your dramas are completely meaningless and irrelevant. Here, you are free of them.

Instead, focus your attention on the ocean. Realize that it is slowly, serenely, with majestic regularity, thinking with God. Realize that the tide is rising in response to the gravitational pull of God, and that this rising is a single grand thought which the ocean shares with God. Realize that the endless expanse of water is warming in response to God's sunshine, and that this is another vast thought it shares with God. See the day turn to night and God's moonlight reflecting on the water, and see this as yet another thought shared with God. The ocean of your mind, like a lover, is constantly moving in perfect response to the thoughts of its celestial Love.

Now realize that this ocean is not only there when you visit it. It has always been there and will always be. Further, it is not a special place hidden deep in your mind. It is the only place there really is. It is the only part of your mind that actually exists. The other part is just an illusion. Therefore, it only seems as if you left this ocean long ago and traveled far inland. Instead, you merely fell asleep there on the sand and dreamt of going somewhere else. And you are still there now. You have never left this ocean's shore. Yet even this is somehow an illusion. In truth, you never even climbed *onto* the shore. How can the ocean leave itself?

.

LESSON 141 ✦ MAY 21

Central theme:

"My mind holds only what I think with God."

Review of:

(121) "Forgiveness is the key to happiness."
(122) "Forgiveness offers everything I want."

 Practice instructions

See instructions on page 439.

Commentary

Forgiveness really does offer us everything we want, and without true forgiveness, happiness just isn't possible. We may not consciously and completely believe this as yet, but our right mind believes it, and always has. Forgiveness operates not just on what I think the world did to me (in reality it did nothing to me), but also on what it *did not* do that I wanted it to. The older one gets, the more disillusioned one becomes about the world. We speak of people becoming "world-weary" and cynical as they age, because despite the high hopes we had when younger, despite the brilliant promises the world seemed to make to us, it disappointed us. It did not make us happy. We discover that the world isn't fair, that good people don't always succeed, that we don't always get what we want. And even when we do, it isn't as good as we had hoped.

Forgiveness involves recognizing that we are the ones who laid these expectations on the world, and we are the ones who made it to disappoint us. We asked the impossible; nothing in this world will ever satisfy us or make us happy. Happiness is to be found in our native state and there alone, that is, in union with God and with the Sonship. To forgive the world means to stop begrudging its imperfections. We cannot blame the world for our pain, nor can we blame it for its failure to make us happy. We cannot blame it at all. When at last our teeth unclench, our fists relax, and our breath eases as we release these deep-seated grievances, what we discover is our own inherent happiness, there all along, but masked by our unforgiveness.

LESSON 142 ✦ MAY 22

Central theme:

"My mind holds only what I think with God."

Review of:

(123) "I thank my Father for His gifts to me."
(124) "Let me remember I am one with God."

 Practice instructions

    See instructions on page 439.

Commentary

That my mind holds only what I think with God is not something I have to work at to attain. It is not a thought to be repeated like a purgative, to drive out opposing thoughts, with the undertone of "I have to *make* my mind have only God's thoughts in it." That my mind holds only what I think with God is "a fact, and represents the truth of What you are and What your Father is" (W-pI.rIV.In.2:3).

As we were told early in the Workbook, when we think that we are thinking without God, we are not really thinking at all; our mind is actually blank. "While thoughtless ideas preoccupy your mind, the truth is blocked. Recognizing that your mind has been merely blank, rather than believing that it is filled with real ideas, is the first step to opening the way to vision" (W-pI.8.3:2–3). "Now we are emphasizing that the presence of these 'thoughts' means that you are not thinking" (W-pI.10.3:2).

The Thoughts of God that fill my mind in reality are my Father's gift to me. I am opening my mind, today, to His Thoughts. What I ordinarily think of as thoughts that interfere or conflict with God's Thoughts are like the static on a radio that interferes with the actual signal. They are not thoughts; they are static, they are noise. The signal is still there, but the static needs to be tuned out so that the signal can come through. The truth about me is that I am one with God; His Mind is my mind, His

Thoughts are my thoughts. I am not something other than what He is. This is "the truth of What you are and What your Father is."

To say that my mind holds only what I think with God can be a joyous affirmation of the truth. It can remind me of His gifts to me, and remind me that I am one with Him. That in me which seems contrary to God, distant from God, or opposed to God, is not who I am; it is not my reality. It is without meaning. There is nothing opposed to God in my mind. Another way of putting that is that what seems to be in me, opposing God, is actually nothing; it is an illusion or a hallucination, with no power and no strength of its own. It is empowered only when I believe in it. Today, I choose to deny that anything not of God has any power over me. I choose to remember what my reality is. I choose to remember that I am one with God.

LESSON 143 ✦ MAY 23

Central theme:

"My mind holds only what I think with God."

Review of:

(125) "In quiet I receive God's Word today."
(126) "All that I give is given to myself."

 Practice instructions

See instructions on page 439.

Commentary

God's Thought creates. We were created when God thought of us; His Mind extended outward, and what was in His Mind extended into and became our mind. Speaking of the main theme thought, "My mind holds only what I think with God," the review introduction says, "It is this thought by which the Father gave creation to the Son, establishing the Son as co-creator with Himself" (W-pI.rIV.In.2:4).

Our minds must therefore be like His, creating like His by extending our thoughts outward. We are God's Thoughts, and His Thoughts have His nature:

> As God's creative Thought proceeds from Him to you, so must your creative thought proceed from you to your creations. Only in this way can all creative power extend outward. God's accomplishments are not yours, but yours are like His. He created the Sonship and you increase it. You have the power to add to the Kingdom, though not to add to the Creator of the Kingdom. You claim this power when you become vigilant only for God and His Kingdom. By accepting this power as yours you have learned to remember what you are. (T-7.I.2:3–9)

As we receive God's Word today, so we must give it. If we receive it we *will* give it, because what we receive is a thought of sharing. We were created by this sharing of thought, this extending of God's Self; sharing, or giving ourselves, is our heritage, the essence of what we are. In the first thought we review for today are the words "I receive"; in the second thought are the words "I give."

Accepting or remembering what we are means realizing we are beings who extend, who give, who share. Created by Love, we are lovers. This is why the Course places such stress on accepting our *function* as saviors of the world; in accepting this, we are accepting our Self as God created It. We are merely taking our place in the creative process, choosing no longer to block the flow of love from God to us, and through us to the world.

> To create is to love. Love extends outward simply because
> it cannot be contained.   (T-7.I.3:3–4)

In quiet today I receive God's Word, which is the affirmation of His Love for all His creations. I open myself to acknowledge that Love, receiving it for myself. And then I step forth to give as I have received, knowing that in giving to my sisters and my brothers, I am indeed giving that Love to myself. My giving of it *is* my receiving of it. By my words, my thoughts, my expressions, and my attitudes I communicate to all around me the Word I have received: "You, too, are loved. You, too, are loving. You, too, are the expression and channel of the Love of God."

LESSON 144 ✦ MAY 24

Central theme:

"My mind holds only what I think with God."

Review of:

(127) "There is no love but God's."
(128) "The world I see holds nothing that I want."

 ### Practice instructions

See instructions on page 439.

Commentary

How is it that the theme thought for the review, that my mind holds only what I think with God, "fully guarantees salvation to the Son" (W-pI.rIV.In.3:5)? It means that there is nothing in my mind that opposes God. It means that what seems to be contrary to God's thoughts, the things I see within myself that are ungodlike or unloving, are misperceptions of myself. It means that there is nothing in reality that can keep me from completion as God's offspring. The enemies and obstacles that seem to stand in the way—most especially the ones that seem to be part of me—are not real, and have no substance.

If there is no love but God's, and my mind holds only what I think with Him, then the emptiness I sometimes feel within myself, the lack of love, the longing for a fully satisfying love that never fails and is always there, something I can depend upon in every situation, will be fulfilled. Thinking that I am seeking for love in this world is simply a mistake. The love I am looking for is within me, right in my own mind. I am not looking for anything in this world, although I so often think I am. I am looking for something I already have, but have denied. And the way to find it is to give it. To *be* it.

Love is not something I can possess. Love is something that can possess me, and in that possession is satisfaction. The attempt to collect love, to possess it and to hoard it brings me pain. My joy can be found in pouring love out, sharing it, blessing the world with it. To recognize that my mind holds only this love, and to open it to the world, is all that I truly want. This, and only this, will bring me happiness.

The words "The world I see holds nothing that I want" could be spoken in despair. The unspoken thought behind them might be, "Nothing here is good enough for me. Nothing here satisfies, and I will therefore never be satisfied." Or, these words can be spoken with joy. If I am driving a brand new car, exactly the kind I most want, equipped with every accessory I have ever desired, and I pass an auto junkyard, I can look at that junkyard and say, "That junkyard holds nothing that I want." I can speak the words with satisfaction. I can say the same thing as I pass a luxury car dealership, because I already have what I want. Likewise, if I already have what I want in God, there is no despair in the words "This world holds nothing that I want." My wants are all filled.

If there is no love but God's, and He has imparted Himself, His very Thought, to my mind, I can look calmly at the world and realize that there is nothing in it to compare with what I have. I have an artesian well of love springing up in my heart. I can never lack for love. I am that very love, and I see that same love in every being around me, springing from the same Source.

Love is all around me and within me, if I am only willing to see it. Let me look for God's Love today in everything I see, and let me rejoice every time I find it. Let me acknowledge it in every smile. Let me give it every chance I have to do so. Let me encourage every spark of it in others, and in myself. This is where salvation lies. This is my function and my happiness. And it is guaranteed, because my mind holds only God's loving Thoughts.

LESSON 145 ✦ MAY 25

Central theme:

"My mind holds only what I think with God."

Review of:

(129) "Beyond this world there is a world I want."
(130) "It is impossible to see two worlds."

 Practice instructions

See instructions on page 439.

Commentary

Though the mind of God's Son holds only what he thinks with God, "Lack of forgiveness blocks this thought from his awareness" (W-pI.rIV.In.2:7). Therefore, the world I see is a world shown to me by unforgiveness. It is "the delusional system of those made mad by guilt" (T-13.In.2:2). The only thing that keeps up the illusion of this world's reality, with its seeming punishment, pain, sorrow, separation, and death, is a lack of forgiveness. Why does my body seem to be what I am? Why does the pain I experience, mental, emotional, and physical, seem so real? Why does loss seem so real? All of its reality originates and is sustained by a lack of forgiveness in my mind. This is why, as Lesson 121 says, "Forgiveness is the key to happiness" (W-pI.121. Heading).

There is a world I truly want, a world that lies beyond this world. The Course calls it the real world. "The real world is the state of mind in which the only purpose of the world is seen to be forgiveness" (T-30.V.1:1). "The real world is attained simply by complete forgiveness of the old, the world you see without forgiveness" (T-17.II.5:1). My perception shifts from seeing the world of pain to seeing the real world by means of one thing: forgiveness.

This is why it is impossible to see two worlds. Either my mind is forgiving, or it is not. Either it condemns what it sees, or it accepts in merciful forgiveness. Let me begin within myself: how unkind I am to myself in the way I think of myself! How merciless I am in judging my mistakes! This harshness with myself is the origin of the harsh world I see.

There is within me, and within us all, a vast space of kindness, an enormity of heart that embraces everything in love. This is the Mind I share with God. Within me, too, is a fearful child, awash in pain, believing it has eternally damaged the universe. Let me turn with love to that hurt part of myself and open my arms in comfort and gentle loving-kindness. My heart is big enough to hold this pain instead of rejecting it. The love I share with God is vast enough to grant mercy to myself. Let me not shut myself out of my own heart any longer. Let me take myself in, in warmth and gentle welcome.

Let me look on the ones close to me, as well, with this same gentle, kind acceptance. Here is the cure for my loneliness and pain, for there is nothing so painful as a closed heart. Indeed there is no pain but this. Pain is constricting the heart. Pain is denying the love that I am. In this subtle, internal gesture of rejection lies the origin of the world I see. In the undoing of this contraction of pain is my salvation, and the salvation of the world. Here is the entry to the real world, a world bright with love, radiant with hope, certain in its joyfulness.

Beyond this world, there is a world I want, and the key to open the door is forgiveness.

LESSON 146 ✦ MAY 26

Central theme:

"My mind holds only what I think with God."

Review of:

(131) "No one can fail who seeks to reach the truth."
(132) "I loose the world from all I thought it was."

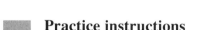

Practice instructions

See instructions on page 439.

Commentary

Continuing to develop some ideas from the review about the theme thought, I was struck by these words, from paragraphs 2 and 4 of the introduction:

> Yet it is forever true [that my mind holds only what I think with God]. (W-pI.rIV.In.2:8)

> And yet, your mind holds only what you think with God. Your self-deceptions cannot take the place of truth. No more than can a child who throws a stick into the ocean change the coming and the going of the tides, the warming of the water by the sun, the silver of the moon on it by night. (W-pI.rIV.In.4:1–3)

It is "forever true" that my mind holds only what it thinks with God. It was true when God created me. It will be true when the journey is over and I am home with God. And it is true *right now*. "Forever true." The third paragraph talks about the many forms of unforgiveness, the way unforgiveness is "carefully concealed" in my mind, the defenses of the ego, its illusions, its use of self-deception to keep the mindless game going. Yet, despite this, "My mind holds only what I think with God." Nothing I do affects this fact. All the self-deception in the world can only hide the truth, not change it. "Your self-deceptions cannot take the

457

place of truth" (W-pI.rIV.In.4:2).

The image of the child throwing a stick into the ocean is just perfect. I remember as a very young boy I used to go to Cape Cod. I would stand in the surf, with waves perhaps two or three feet high breaking before me, and I would punch the waves, battling with them, driving my fist through them. To me at the time, I was like a warrior, fighting against the ocean. I'm sure the ocean was deeply concerned! I'm sure my mighty efforts slowed down the tide a bit, at least. Sure they did. Right, of course.

Our "rebellion" against God has had about that much effect. In other words, none. The very idea that we could alter God's creation is as ludicrous as the child with the stick seriously believing he had damaged the ocean when he threw the stick in.

This is why "no one can fail who seeks to reach the truth." Because the truth is right there, in my mind, where it always has been and forever will be. I can't fail to find it because I haven't lost it! I've still got it.

I have looked upon this world and believed it to be a place where God is not. I've seen what appears to be an outrageous lack of love. I've been deeply disappointed with the world. Well, "I loose the world from all I thought it was." I let all those impressions of the world drop away, because it can't be what I thought it was, not if all of our minds still hold only what we think with God. Something is wrong with this picture! Just when I thought I had begun to figure out the world, along comes the Course and says, "Not even warm." So I let my judgments about the world fall away, and open my mind to be taught anew. Maybe, just maybe, the way I've seen it had something to do with what I was thinking about myself, with my belief that my mind was at war with God. Maybe I've seen a world at war with God because that is how I imagine my mind to be, and I've projected that onto the world. And maybe, if I let go of my foolish ideas about myself, my image of the world will change, too. I'm willing to give it a try.

LESSON 147 ✦ MAY 27

Central theme:

"My mind holds only what I think with God."

Review of:

(133) "I will not value what is valueless."
(134) "Let me perceive forgiveness as it is."

 ### Practice instructions

See instructions on page 439.

Commentary

Let me, today, look at the things I value and reconsider them all. Why am I doing this particular thing? What is it I am valuing here? The things we value are often quite foolish when we look at them. For instance, when I have begun to experience the nourishing warmth of true intimacy in relationship, nothing seems worth the closing off of that warmth. I recall reading about a fundamentalist church that split up over the issue of whether or not it was sinful to plug in a guitar. How, I wondered, could anyone value *anything* like that enough to shut out from their hearts people who had once been close friends? So many relationships break up over issues that seem just as trivial.

Forgiveness sees that nothing is worth shutting another child of God out of my heart. We have so many absolutes in our consciousness, things we consider more important than love, more important than unity, more important than our own peace of mind. Have I come, yet, to value peace of mind above everything else? Have I come to the point where anything that interferes with the flow of love through me is quickly discarded?

We need to become aware of the source of our own pain. We ache when we close down our hearts. We ache when we refuse to forgive, when we latch on to the wrongs that have been done to us and fondle them over and over, refusing to let them go. "Love holds no grievances"

459

(W-pI.68.Heading). Forgiveness is a gift to myself; it is a release from my own pain. What am I valuing above the free flow of love, the warmth of union with my brother or sister? Let me choose to no longer value this valueless thing, and choose to forgive.

Let me take five minutes this morning, and five minutes tonight, to open my mind and clear it of all thoughts that would deceive (W-pI.rIV.In.5:2). Let me brush aside lesser values, and remember that my mind holds God's own thoughts. Let me value these thoughts above all else. Let me rejoice in the congruence of my mind and God's Mind, and recognize that this blending of my mind with God's, this sharing of His thoughts, is all that is truly valuable to me.

LESSON 148 ✦ MAY 28

Central theme:

"My mind holds only what I think with God."

Review of:

(135) "If I defend myself I am attacked."
(136) "Sickness is a defense against the truth."

 ## Practice instructions

See instructions on page 439.

Commentary

What seem to me to be obstacles within my mind, out-of-control thoughts that hinder me on my spiritual path, are my defenses against the truth. Nothing enters my mind without my permission. No one is thinking thoughts in my mind except me (and God). As Lesson 26 taught us, my attack thoughts are attacking my own invulnerability. I may think I am attacking someone else, but I am really attacking my own Identity with God.

My ego has built up a clever, multi-layered defense system against the truth, and has hidden it in obscurity and disguise. The process the Course sets before me is one of uncovering these defenses, becoming aware of them, judging them as insane, and letting them go. All of them are false, and what is false cannot affect what is true. Beneath all the camouflage of the ego, my mind still holds only what I think with God. The rest is elaborate illusion with no real power to cause any effects whatsoever.

Sickness is one very prominent and very effective defense system of the ego. In sickness, something my mind has caused appears to be an attack from the outside, a visible or invisible enemy with very visible effects on my body. It is something I must continually defend against, and fight with every resource when it strikes. As soon as one disease is conquered, another seems to arise with even more devastating effects.

Most of mankind is not ready to accept that sickness is only of the mind. I have not fully accepted it myself; my level of fear is still too high. So there is every reason to continue to alleviate diseases in the ways we have been doing, yet we must realize that we are only muting the symptoms and not eradicating the cause. Only as more and more of us begin to realize that our minds hold only what we think with God, and that everything which seems to be other than from God is an illusion of our creation, will the need for the compromise approach of physical medicine begin to disappear.

Today in my practice I am contributing to the ultimate cure of every disease. As I search out my own inner defenses, which are actually forms of self-attack, and let them go, I am collaborating with the power of God to free mankind from disease, and not only disease, but every such ego-based system of defense against the truth. As I clear my mind of all thoughts that would deceive (W-pI.rIV.In.5:2), and place God's Mind in charge of the thoughts I receive (W-pI.rIV.In.5:4), I am not working alone. "They [the thoughts] will not come from you alone, for they will all be shared with Him" (W-pI.rIV.In.6:1).

Let me, then, take the assigned times today to remember the true Source of all my thoughts, and to allow the Holy Spirit to clear the cobwebs of deception from my mind. Let me take five minutes in the morning to "set the day along the lines which God appointed" (W-pI.rIV.In.5:4). Each time I do so, each day I remember my practice, I bring myself and all the world nearer the day when all deception will vanish in the light.

LESSON 149 ✦ MAY 29
Central theme:

"My mind holds only what I think with God."

Review of:

(137) "When I am healed I am not healed alone."
(138) "Heaven is the decision I must make."

 Practice instructions

See instructions on page 439.

Commentary

More and more, as we progress through the Workbook, what we are being asked to do is really to commune with God. Or, to put it in more mundane terms, to get back into communication with Him:

> You taught yourself the most unnatural habit of not communicating with your Creator. Yet you remain in close communication with Him, and with everything that is within Him, as it is within yourself. Unlearn isolation through His loving guidance, and learn of all the happy communication that you have thrown away but could not lose. (T-14.III.18:1–3)

As we clear our minds of lesser thoughts and tune in to the thoughts we share with God, thoughts will come to our minds, and they won't be from ourselves alone:

> And so each one will bring the message of His Love to you, returning messages of yours to Him. So will communion with the Lord of Hosts be yours, as He Himself has willed it be. (W-pI.rIV.In.6:2–3)

Connecting in my mind with God connects me, as well, with my

463

brothers and sisters, because all of us are connected to the Source. I am not healed alone.

I could use a "message of His Love" today; how about you? And I wouldn't mind returning my message of love to Him, as well. There are moments in a loving relationship where the love just seems to be ping-ponging back and forth so fast you can't follow it, you can't even be sure whose love is whose. It outstrips ping-ponging, in fact; it transcends the back-and-forth motion implied by that analogy and becomes a constant, cyclical current of love, going both ways simultaneously. You don't even feel as though you are *doing* anything; you are just caught in the current, possessed by love. Sort of the way you might feel when you look into your beloved's eyes and feel you are falling in, when the love coming back at you is almost too much to bear, and the love you are feeling threatens to blow your circuits. I'd like a moment like that today with my Beloved. Well, I'd like a moment like that *this year*. I've had such moments, but they are rare.

Why are they rare? Having those moments of communion, which are a foretaste of Heaven, is up to me. It's a decision I must make; no, *the* decision I must make:

> The instant in which magnitude dawns upon you is but as far away as your desire for it. As long as you desire it not and cherish littleness instead, by so much is it far from you. By so much as you want it will you bring it nearer.
>
> (T-15.IV.2:2–4)

It is nearer than my own heart, so close. This ecstasy of love, this communion with God, is actually going on right now. My right mind has never ceased to be in perfect communication with Him (see T-13.XI.8). "The part of your mind in which truth abides is in constant communication with God, whether you are aware of it or not" (W-pI.49.1:2).

So all that is necessary is to decide that I want it, and it is there. I just plug in to it. What is it that prevents me from choosing it? What keeps me from letting myself fall in love with God? What holds me back? Am I willing to be in love with everyone, or am I afraid of appearing too "mooshy"? Am I afraid of being out of control? Am I afraid of being too vulnerable? What holds me back? Let me look at myself today and ask myself, "Why am I not experiencing being in Heaven right now?"

When you realize that you could just "switch over" at any instant—and that you don't!—it is a sobering moment. All of a sudden you can't blame anyone or anything for experiencing anything less than Heaven. You recognize that you are choosing it; "I am doing this to myself" (see T-27.VIII.10:1). There is literally nothing to prevent me from experiencing the holy instant right now. Nothing but my refusal to accept it; nothing but my fear. "So we begin today considering the choice that time was made to help us make" (W-pI.138.7:1). There is no rush; we have all of time to make this choice. But why wait? Why not now?

LESSON 150 ✦ MAY 30

Central theme:

"My mind holds only what I think with God."

Review of:

(139) "I will accept Atonement for myself."
(140) "Only salvation can be said to cure."

 Practice instructions

See instructions on page 439.

Commentary

Accepting Atonement for myself means, to me, allowing God to release me from all kinds of guilt. Letting go of all my judgments against myself, all my diminishing self-evaluations. It means accepting that I am not my thoughts and, above all, I am not my ego. I am not what I have thought I am. I am not what I am afraid I am. Accepting the Atonement for myself means that I can look upon my own ego without condemnation, recognizing it as no more than a foolish mistake about myself that can be corrected.

When I accept Atonement for myself, I stop measuring myself against arbitrary standards and accept myself just as I am. I am able to look upon myself with love, to view myself with merciful acceptance. In the holy instant, I accept the Atonement, and to enter such a moment it is not necessary that I have no thoughts that are not pure, only that I have no thoughts that I want to keep (see T-15.IV.9:1–2). I recognize that I have made mistakes, but I am willing for every mistake to be corrected, and I accept no guilt concerning those mistakes. I do not allow my mistakes to keep me from the holy instant, because the holy instant is the place those mistakes can be corrected, and their consequences undone.

This is salvation. This is the undoing of errors, the correction of mistakes.

> Salvation is undoing in the sense that it does nothing, failing to support the world of dreams and malice. Thus it lets illusions go. By not supporting them, it merely lets them quietly go down to dust. (W-pII.2.3:1–3)

This is the only thing that can be said to truly cure. Anything less than this is mere alleviation of symptoms, mere shifting of form without any change in content. The root cause of guilt must be undone. "The Holy Spirit knows that all salvation is escape from guilt" (T-14.III.13:4).

To know that my mind holds only what I think with God is to escape from guilt. To know that my mind holds only what I think with God is salvation, and truly cures my ills. Atonement is God's answer to everything within my mind that appears to be other than God. It erases every thought opposed to truth and leaves me with the clean, crisp truth of my own innocence. I can bring every impure thought, every unworthy thought, every guilty thought, every thought of isolation and separateness, every thought of pain and vengeance and despair to this miraculous place of Atonement, lay it there on the altar, and watch it disappear:

> This is the shift that true perception brings: What was projected out is seen within, and there forgiveness lets it disappear. For there the altar to the Son is set, and there his Father is remembered. Here are all illusions brought to truth and laid upon the altar. What is seen outside must lie beyond forgiveness, for it seems to be forever sinful. Where is hope while sin is seen as outside? What remedy can guilt expect? But seen within your mind, guilt and forgiveness for an instant lie together, side by side, upon one altar. There at last are sickness and its single remedy joined in one healing brightness. God has come to claim His Own. Forgiveness is complete. (C-4.6:1–10)

X

Lessons 151 - 170

LESSON 151 ✦ MAY 31

"All things are echoes of the Voice for God."

Practice instructions

Morning/evening practice: Fifteen minutes.

Repeat the idea slowly, just once. Then watch your mind; observe your thoughts. As each thought crosses your mind, give it to the Holy Spirit. Then listen as He gives it back in purified form. What He will do is take your thought and strip away all the egoic elements in it, leaving only whatever light that was contained in it: the love, the kindness, the pure intentions, your desire for peace and for God (for teaching on this idea, see T-5.IV.8:1-6). For example, let's say the thought you give Him is "I'm running out of time to get this task done." The purified version that you receive back from Him might be "I really want to do this right. I want to do right by the people this affects." In other words, you will be giving Him thoughts that are very mixed bags—patterns of darkness interlaced with threads of light. When He gives them back, however, only the threads of light will be left. They will be pure light, and so will reveal the light in you.

And you will see them come together into a single, perfect thought, which will shed its blessing on everyone.

Remarks: This process of purification of your thoughts will resurrect your mind, making today your personal Eastertime. It will also inaugurate your ministry. For your ministry is simply to extend your purified thoughts, which will release everyone from guilt and teach them their sanctity.

Shorter: Hourly.

Repeat the idea (which basically means that you can see in all things—in the world and in your mind—the interpretation that the Holy Spirit has given that thing. You can experience all things as echoes of the Voice for God). Thank the Holy Spirit for the purified thoughts He gives you, and trust that the world will happily accept those thoughts as its own. This seems to imply that on the hour you will do a miniature version of the longer practice—perhaps giving a thought to the Holy Spirit and listening for Him to give you back a purified version of that thought.

Commentary

The world as we see it seems to bear unrelenting witness to separation, sin, death, hatred, and the transient nature of everything. The world seen with the vision of Christ, as the Holy Spirit sees it, bears witness to the truth, to unity, holiness, life, love, and the eternal nature of everything. *Everything* is echoing the Voice for God, all the time, but we do not hear it. We hear the ego's voice with relentless consistency. The two views could not be more stark in their contrast. Why do we display such a prejudice for the ego's view?

The early part of this lesson points out that the reason the world so often seems so solidly real to us is because of our underlying doubt of its reality. It asks us to look at the fact that the ego goes too far in its stubborn insistence that what our eyes and ears show us is solidly reliable. It says that, although we know very well from our experience that our senses often deceive us, and our judgments are often wide of the mark, we irrationally continue to believe them down to the last detail. We show surprise whenever we discover that what we thought was true is not, in fact, true, even though we have had this experience hundreds or thousands of times. And it asks:

> Why would you trust them [your senses] so implicitly?
> Why but because of underlying doubt, which you would
> hide with show of certainty? (2:5–6)

It is like the line in Shakespeare's *Hamlet*: "The lady doth protest too much, methinks." It is the behavior of someone who is trying to shout down their doubts with protestations of absolute certainty. So, to the Holy Spirit, our very "certainty" of the world's reality is a proof of underlying doubt! We are certain even when it is unreasonable to be certain, and that is a certain evidence of hidden uncertainty.

We who study the Course are used to the idea that we project our guilt and anger onto others. Here, however, the Course introduces the idea that there is a way in which our egos project themselves onto us. The ego doubts. The ego condemns itself. The ego alone feels guilt. Only the ego is in despair (see 5:1–6). But it projects all of these things onto us, and tries to convince us "its evil is your own" (6:2). It plays this trick on us by showing us the world through its eyes, and introducing the things of the world as witnesses to our evil, our guilt, our doubt and despair. The ego is desperate for us to see the world as it wants us to because the ego's world is what proves to us that we are identical with the ego. For instance, it leads us to evaluate our own spiritual progress and to find ourselves wanting; it induces us to despair. Why? Because *it* [the ego] is feeling despair. It knows (without admitting it) that it is going to lose. This is why spiritual despair so often strikes after a major spiritual advance. The ego feels despair, and projects that despair onto our minds, trying to convince us the despair is *ours* rather than *its*.

This is why the ego is so insistent on convincing us of the world's reality. It needs the world to build its case.

The lesson asks us to raise all our evaluations, which we have learned from the ego, to question, and to doubt the evidence of our senses. It asks us to let the Holy Spirit be the Judge of what we are, and of everything that seems to happen to us (8:1; 9:6). If we try to judge things by ourselves, we will be deceived by our own egos, and the way in which we see ourselves and the world will become a witness to the ego's reality. If, however, we let go of our judgments and accept the judgment of the Holy Spirit, He will bear witness to our beautiful creation as God's Son. Everything we see, if we look with Him, will show us God.

Read the eleventh paragraph; it describes perfectly just how the Holy Spirit accomplishes this retranslation of everything. When we give Him our thoughts, He gives them back as miracles (14:1).

Let me, then, give my thoughts to Him today. Let me not hide my thoughts from Him, nor try to alter them myself before I expose them to His sight. Let me ask Him to work His alchemy on them, to transmute the lead into gold before my eyes. That is His job. Every thought has elements of truth in it, to which we have added falsehood and illusion. The Holy Spirit strips away the false, and leaves the golden kernel of truth. He does not attack our thoughts; He purifies them. He shows "the love beyond the hate, the constancy in change, the pure in sin" (11:3). He does this with our very thoughts, and so reveals to us the gentle face of Christ as our very Self.

LESSON 152 ✦ JUNE 1
"The power of decision is my own."

Practice instructions

Purpose: To be truly humble and lay aside my self-concepts, which arrogantly claim that I am weak and sinful, and accept the power of my true Self.

Morning/evening practice: Five minutes.

- Repeat these lines: *"The power of decision is my own. This day I will accept myself as what my Father's Will created me to be."* You could rephrase this as: *"With the unlimited power of my decision, I will accept the unlimited power of my Self."*

- Then spend some time giving up your self-concepts, which are just lies you've told yourself about who you are. They say that you are weak, at the mercy of a world you did not make. They say that you are sinful, and should be ashamed of what you are. Lay aside all of these self-concepts, recognizing that their littleness is actually arrogant, since they imply that God is wrong about you.

- Then wait in silence, as you humbly ask your Self to reveal Himself to you in all His mightiness, changelessness, and wholeness. Lift your heart in true humility to your Creator, and allow Him to show you the infinite Son that He created as you. Expect His Voice to respond, and to replace your false self-concepts with the realization of your true Self. Whenever your mind wanders, repeat the opening lines again, and return to waiting.

Shorter: Hourly.

Do a miniature version of the longer practice, inviting the realization of your Self with these words: *"The power of decision is my own. This day I will accept myself as what my Father's Will created me to be."*

473

Commentary

The central appeal of this lesson is to get me to "accept [my] rightful place as co-creator of the universe" (8:3). It attempts, through its logical arguments, to persuade me to accept the fact that I made the world I see (6:1). "Nothing occurs but represents your wish, and nothing is omitted that you choose" (1:5).

If that is true, and I accept it, then the main thought of the lesson makes sense: "The power of decision is my own." My choice makes the world. What grants our illusion of pain, sin, and death such apparent solidity is that we believe it exists outside of our power; that we are *not* responsible for it. If, however, I can accept that I made it what it is, then I can recognize the possibility of exercising the same power of choice to make it disappear. If I deny that I made it I cannot unmake it.

If, however, I recognize that I have made the world I see, I am accepting at the same time that God did *not* make it. The absurdity of the idea that God created this world is clearly stated here:

> To think that God made chaos, contradicts His will, invented opposites to truth, and suffers death to triumph over life; all this is arrogance. Humility would see at once these things are not of him. (7:1–2)

If they are not of Him, they must be of me—my fabrications, the results of my power of decision, and therefore things that I can undo.

Applied to myself, these ideas mean that I must be still whole, unchanged by mistakes:

> As God created you, you must remain unchangeable, with transitory states by definition false. And that includes all shifts in feeling, alterations in conditions of the body and the mind; in all awareness and in all response. (5:1–2)

I love those words "transitory states by definition false." If it changes, it is not real. Wow! What does that do to any concerns I might have about mood swings? About aging? About sickness? About the level of my income? ("Transitory" seems so apropos in regard to income!) How about alterations in awareness? Transitory, therefore false. Alterations in my response to the Course? Transitory, therefore false. Truth is true, and only truth is true; any and all alterations are "contradictions introduced by [me]" (4:4).

I have begun to learn that when I feel bummed out, for any reason, I can remind myself that this feeling is transitory and therefore false; nothing to be concerned about. This doesn't always immediately dispel my feeling bummed out, but it *does* prevent me from feeling guilty about feeling bummed out, or feeling anxious that something is seriously wrong with me. As a result, the negative feeling does not last as long as it used to, because I am no longer adding additional layers of self-condemnation on top of the original feeling.

Such an attitude somehow distances me from the transitory feelings or shifts in my awareness. Instead of relating *from* the feeling I begin to relate *to* it, with gentleness and merciful forgiveness. Some have expressed the difference in words by saying things like "My body is sick" instead of "I am sick," or "I am experiencing a depression" instead of "I am depressed." Instead of the passing thought or feeling being mistaken for "me," I am aware of "me" over here, consistent and unchanging, but experiencing this transitory state of mind. "I" am distinct from, and not identified with, the passing show of my mind. And in that situation, I can recognize: "The power of decision is my own."

LESSON 153 ✦ JUNE 2

"In my defenselessness my safety lies."

Practice instructions

Purpose: To learn that "defenselessness is strength" (6:1), for it rests on awareness of Christ's strength in us, a strength so great that it can never be attacked.

Morning/evening quiet time: At least five minutes; ideally, thirty or more.

This practice sounds the same as yesterday's, where you laid aside the self-concepts that portray you as weak, and let the awareness of your true Self arise in you. Here, you do the same thing, with special emphasis on getting in touch with His strength in you. If you succeed, you will realize that you have no need for defense, for you were created unassailable. Let the morning time be your preparation for a day of defenselessness. Clothe yourself in the strength of Christ.

Hourly remembrance: One or two minutes as the hour strikes (reduce if circumstances do not permit).

- Repeat the idea, remembering while you do that Christ remains beside you, giving you His strength, making defending yourself unnecessary.
- Then sit quietly and wait on God. Thank Him for His gifts in the previous hour. And let His Voice tell you what He wants you to do in the coming hour.

Response to temptation: Whenever you feel tempted to defend yourself.

Repeat the idea as a way of calling upon the strength of Christ in you. Then pause a moment and listen for Him saying, "I am here" (19:6).

Overall remarks: The Workbook clearly considers this lesson a turning point. We are given here our practice instructions for the next *forty-eight lessons*! And we are told (in paragraph 20), that our "practicing will now begin to take the earnestness of love"

(20:1). Rather than being a fulfillment of duty, it will be a sincere and natural expression of our heart. Let us take this step forward in confidence. Jesus asks us to "be not afraid or timid" (20:2), because we simply cannot fail. God will make sure that we make it to our goal.

Commentary

In regard to our practice, notice that this lesson presents instructions that are to be followed "for quite a while" (15:1). Specifically, the form of practice given today continues for every lesson through Lesson 170. They are given this once and not referred to again except in brief mentions; we are supposed to remember the instructions from this lesson. Notice, too, that the instructions about what we are to do in this five- to thirty-minute period each day are rather vague. Mostly they are summed up as "giving our attention to the daily thought as long as possible" (15:2). We are told that our "practicing will now begin to take the earnestness of love" (20:1). The longer practice periods have become "a time to spend with God" (15:5); we enjoy His loving Presence so much that half an hour seems too short! To some degree, by this time, our practicing has switched from sessions with a drill sergeant to a rendezvous with our Lover. If that hasn't happened for us yet, it will: "There can be no doubt that you will reach your final goal" (20:3).

The lesson opens by pointing out that this world is *not* a safe place: "It is rooted in attack" (1:3). Peace of mind in *this* world is impossible (1:5). On every side are things that provoke us to defensiveness (2:1–2). But defenses affect not only what is outside of us; they affect ourselves. They reinforce our sense of weakness (2:4), and since they ultimately do not work (2:4), they betray us. We are betrayed by the world outside and by our own defenses within (2:5–6).

> It is as if a circle held it [the mind] fast, wherein another circle bound it and another one in that, until escape no longer can be hoped for nor obtained. (3:1)

We are trapped in concentric vicious circles of attack and defense; we find ourselves unable to break out of the attack-defense cycle (3:2–3).

We do not realize how profoundly our minds are threatened by the world around us. If we try as hard as we can to conceive of someone caught deep in a frenzy of intense fear, "The sense of threat the world encourages is so much deeper, and so far beyond the frenzy and intensity of which you can conceive, that you have no idea of all the devastation it has wrought" (4:3). All of us, the Course is saying, are living in blind panic masked by a superficial act of being calm. Panic is always there, just below the surface. Think of the things that threaten us constantly, and the attention that is paid to them in our personal lives and in the media. Nuclear holocaust. Street gangs. Drunk drivers. *All* drivers. Corrupt politicians. The greedy power structure. Threatening economic collapse. Food additives, depletion of the ozone layer, vitamin-depleted foods, growth hormones in our milk, nitrates in the bacon, cholesterol, saturated fat, sugar, polluted water supplies, drought, heat waves, blizzards, floods, hurricanes, tornados, earthquakes, alien invasion, lying news media, insects in our homes, aging bodies, untrustworthy love partners or business partners, AIDS, cancer, heart disease—the list could go on and on. And we have not begun to speak of the threat of foreign invasion or economic takeover, racial animosities, or religious intolerance.

We are slaves of the world's threat (5:1). "You do not know what you do, in fear of it. You do not understand how much you have been made to sacrifice, who feel its iron grip upon your heart" (5:2–3). Try to imagine, for a moment, what it would be like to be completely *without* any and all fear concerning the things we have mentioned. If you are like me, you can't even *imagine* it. We have become so accustomed to the subliminal hum of fear! Nor do we realize how much we have sabotaged our own peace by our stance of constant defensiveness (5:4).

The choice this lesson presents to us (6:3) is between two things: the "silly game" (6:4) of defensiveness, played by tired children too sleepy to remember what they want (a bit like how I feel right now!), and the "game that happy children play" (12:1), a joyous game that teaches us that the game of fear is gone. The happy game is "salvation" (12:1), or functioning as a minister of God in the world, offering the light to all our brothers. In brief, we can spend our time trying to defend ourselves, or we can drop our defenses and reach out in love to the world. Those are the only options.

The game of defensiveness is a deadly one. In defensiveness "lies madness in a form so grim that hope of sanity seems but to be an idle dream, beyond the possible" (4:2). Defenses bind us into an attack-defense cycle that never ends.

Defenselessness is based on the reality of what we are. "We need no defense because we are created unassailable" (9:1). It witnesses to our strength. As God's ministers we are protected. We need no defense *because* we are "the ones who are among the chosen ones of God, by His election and [our] own as well" (10:6).

To choose defenselessness is to choose the strength of Christ, instead of our own weakness. To reach out to heal, instead of contracting inward in self-defense, puts us in an unassailable position. Our true safety lies, not in protecting what we have, but in giving it away, because this firmly identifies us with the Christ.

LESSON 154 ✦ JUNE 3

"I am among the ministers of God."

Practice instructions

Purpose: To be God's minister in this world, to give Him our voice, hands, and feet. Through this we unite with His Will and thus unite with all the gifts contained in His Will.

Morning/evening quiet time: At least five minutes; ideally, thirty or more.

Repeat, *"I am among the ministers of God, and I am grateful that I have the means by which to recognize that I am free."* "The means" refers to giving God's messages to your brothers. Spend the practice period letting the truth of these words sink into your mind. Let the world recede as you focus totally on these words. Let them light up your mind; let them change your mind. Do this in whatever way works for you.

The purpose of this practice period is to prepare you to use those "means"—to go out and minister to your brothers. Unlike other lessons, the main focus in this lesson is on what you will do *after* the practice period. During the day, show you understood the words you practiced by giving God your voice, so that He can speak words of love through you to your brothers. Give Him your hands, so that He can use them to deliver messages of love to your brothers. Give Him your feet, so that He can direct them to wherever someone is in need.

By doing this, you will be uniting your will with God's Will. And when His Will is yours, all the gifts contained in His Will will be yours as well. By being His instrument you will gain His treasures.

Hourly remembrance: One or two minutes as the hour strikes (reduce if circumstances do not permit).

Repeat the idea and then sit silently and wait on God. Ask Him how He would have you minister to your brothers in the hour to come, and then listen intently for the answer of His Voice.

Commentary

As I see it, this lesson has two main things to say to me:

1. My function on earth is to be a minister (or messenger) of God, and the specific form that function takes is determined, not by me, but by the Holy Spirit.

2. As a messenger, my function is to receive God's messages for myself, and then to give them away, as directed by the Holy Spirit. By giving away the messages I will recognize and understand the messages I have received.

The Holy Spirit knows me to the core. He knows my individual strengths and weaknesses; He knows the "larger plan" (1:5) I cannot possibly know; He knows how best to use my particular strengths, "where they can best be applied, for what, to whom, and when" (2:2). Therefore, it is unwise to try to evaluate myself or to direct my own functioning in this world, and far wiser to place myself in His hands. Because of this, I will "choose no roles that are not given [me] by His authority" (7:3). He chooses my function for me, tells me what it is, gives me strength to do it and to succeed in everything related to it (3:2).

A major part of the training program in the Workbook is learning to hear His Voice and to submit to Its authority. Learning to hear His Voice isn't something that comes without any effort. Indeed, it takes effort and great willingness (T-5.II.3:9–10). I may feel at first that I don't know how to hear His Voice, but that is *exactly* why I need this practice. I don't know, as I begin, how to tell the Voice of the Holy Spirit apart from my own ego's voice; I need training in that discernment, and some of it will be trial and error. But if I will follow the instructions in this book, I will learn.

The second point is really an encouragement to take up the function given me by God, which in a generic sense is to be His messenger:

> He needs our voice that He may speak through us. He needs our hands to hold His messages, and carry them to those whom He appoints. He needs our feet to bring us where He wills, that those who wait in misery may be at last delivered. And He needs our will united with His Own, that we may be the true receivers of the gifts He gives.
>
> (11:2–5)

Clearly, He directs me very specifically, choosing where I go physically, whom I speak to, and what I say. Yet the main thing is that I accept this overall function of "messenger" for my life; if I accept that, the specifics will follow.

There is a three-step process clearly delineated in this lesson: 1) *receive*, 2) *give*, and 3) *recognize*.

First, I receive the message for myself, accept it, and apply it to my own life. I accept the Atonement for myself, seeing that the appearance of guilt within me is an illusion, and recognizing the innocence it hides. I accept my acceptance with God. I let go of my false and guilty self-concept.

Second, I give this message to those to whom the Holy Spirit sends me. This can be with words, with actions, or simply with the attitude of mercy and acceptance I show to those I meet. I give the message I have received. I show them the mercy God has shown to me. I see in them what I have begun to see in myself.

Third, as a result of giving, I recognize the reality of what I have received. "No one can receive and understand he has received until he gives" (8:6). Giving away the message cements it and validates it in my own mind. "We will not recognize what we receive until we give it" (12:1).

The second step is an essential part of the whole process. Without giving away the message, the cycle cannot be completed; my own recognition of salvation cannot become complete. It is not enough simply to receive the messages of God. "Yet another part of your appointed task is yet to be accomplished" (9:4). The messages must be given away, shared, in order to be fully received. I must take up my function as the messenger of God if I am to understand what I have been given.

Notice that the practice instructions are adapted from Lesson 153, where we were told "we practice in a form we will maintain for quite a while" (W-pI.153.15:1). These instructions will be followed until new ones are given in Lesson 171 (Review V), and apply to Lessons 181–200 as well.

LESSON 155 ✦ JUNE 4
"I will step back and let Him lead the way."

Practice instructions

Morning/evening quiet time: At least five minutes; ideally, thirty or more.

We are obviously getting fewer instructions for what to do during the longer practice periods. We are meant to increasingly rely on what has worked for us before and what the Holy Spirit inspires us to do in the moment. During today's longer practice, we are meant to mentally link up with God, Who will speak to us, telling us how much He loves us and how He has entrusted our brothers to us, trusting perfectly that we will lead them home to Him. So repeat the words given (*"I will step back and let Him lead the way, for I would walk along the road to Him"*), and then enter deeply into your mind, listening quietly for His Voice. Remember your training in how to do this: listen in stillness, in confidence, and in patience, repeating the lines when your mind wanders.

The purpose of the morning practice is to firmly take hold of His Hand, so that He can lead you, while you in turn lead your brothers. By preparing you to serve your brothers, the purpose of today's practice is essentially the same as that of yesterday's.

Hourly remembrance: One or two minutes as the hour strikes (reduce if circumstances do not permit).

Repeat the idea and then listen quietly for God's Voice. Ask Him how He would lead you in the coming hour, how He wants you to guide your brothers along the way to Him. And thank Him for His leading in the hour gone by.

Commentary

"There is a way of living in the world that is not here, although it seems to be" (1:1). And to this way of living we all aspire. The remarkable thing about the Course is that it offers what might be called a middle way between renouncing the world and diving into it. Many, perhaps the majority, of spiritual seekers make the mistake of thinking that a spiritual life must somehow look different. Some dress differently; some abjure the modern conveniences; some find spirituality in vegetables; some fill their homes with incense; some live in poverty, or apart from normal worldly concourse.

This lesson is one of the clearest statements in the Course that a good Course student does not change appearance—except that perhaps he smiles more frequently. There are spiritual paths that demand a changed appearance—a shaved head, difference in dress—and this is not to put down these other paths. But they are not the way of the Course. One of the more difficult lessons for students of the Course, in my observation, seems to be learning to be normal. A true student of the Course is like anyone else, so much so that "those who have not yet perceived the way will…believe that you are like them, as you were before" (1:5).

Yet we are different. The difference is inward; we have stepped back, taken our hands off the controls of our lives, and we are letting our Inner Guide lead the way to God. Everyone, including ourselves, came to this world by choice, "seeking for a place where they can be illusions, and avoid their own reality" (2:2). But we have discovered that we cannot escape our reality, and we have chosen to place diminishing importance on the illusions, and to follow the truth. We have taken up our function, and we recognize that we are here now, not for ourselves alone, but to serve those around us as we serve ourselves (5:4). We walk to God, and we lead the world to God with us (12:1; 13:1). We step back, and let Him lead the way.

LESSON 156 ✦ JUNE 5
"I walk with God in perfect holiness."

Practice instructions

Morning/evening quiet time: At least five minutes; ideally, thirty or more.

Although we are not given specific instructions for particular practice periods, we are told how to practice generally today. Before we set our feet on the path, we walked around unconsciously believing that we walked alone, accompanied only by our sinfulness. We carried the weight of what we thought we had done like a heavy rock on our shoulders. Once we stepped onto the path, we opened our mind to the idea that God was walking with us, that His Being was inseparable from our being, and that therefore we carried holiness with us, not sinfulness. Now we are of *two* minds, at times believing we walk alone in sinfulness, at times believing we walk with God in holiness.

Our practice, then, consists in asking ourselves, *"Who walks with me?"* Meaning, is it God or sin? As we ask, we need to realize this is a genuine question; we are really not sure yet what the answer is. And then we need to answer with these words: *"I walk with God in perfect holiness. I light the world, I light my mind and all the minds which God created one with me."* As we say these words, we need to realize that they are not just our own words trying to answer our question. They are the words that God has given us; they are Him answering for us (8:4).

If we can truly embrace this answer, then our holiness will shine forth for all to see. As paragraph 4 says, even the waves, flowers, trees, and wind will respond to us as if we are visiting royalty (bowing down in front of us, laying a carpet before us, shielding our head from the heat, filling the air with sweet-smelling incense), for they will innately sense the heavenly King walking with us.

Hourly remembrance: One or two minutes as the hour strikes (reduce if circumstances do not permit).

- Ask the question: *"Who walks with me [God or sin]?"* And then answer with the lines, *"I walk with God in perfect holiness. I light the world, I light my mind and all the minds which God created one with me."*
- Then thank God for walking with you in the hour gone by. You might even think of events from that hour that were evidence of Him walking with you.
- And finally, ask Him for guidance for the coming hour: where He wants you to walk and what He wants you to do.

Suggestion: You may want to do this practice of asking the question (*"Who walks with me?"*) and repeating the response (*"I walk with God..."*) many times during each hour. The lesson mentions doing it a thousand times a day, or approximately once every waking minute. This remarkable frequency is perhaps a bit beyond our current level of discipline. We will experience powerful benefits even if we do it a few times each hour.

Commentary

"Ideas leave not their source" (1:3). When a mind thinks an idea, that idea stays in the mind; it does not become a separate thing, apart from the mind that thought it. And I am a Thought of God; therefore, I cannot possibly be apart from Him. I have thought I was separate. Indeed, much of the time I still think and behave as though I were separate from God. But I am not; I cannot be.

To be apart from God is impossible. God *is* Being; He is Existence. Whatever exists is in Him. He is Life; whatever lives, lives in Him. "He is what your life is. Where you are He is. There is one life. That life you share with Him. Nothing can be apart from Him and live" (2:5–9).

God is also holy. If God is holy, and I am in him, I am holy, too. "What lives is holy as Himself" (3:3). Therefore, "I walk with God in perfect holiness." I could "no more be sinful than the sun could choose to be of ice" (3:3). This is not a feeble hope; it is a fact. It is the truth about me, and about you, and about everyone who lives.

Yet we have taught ourselves that this truth is not true. It fascinates me to see what contradictory ideas arise in my mind when I repeat this statement. It would be a useful exercise to write today's idea as an affirmation, ten times or more, and in a second column, write down the response of the mind to this idea. You might get things like this:

"I walk with God in perfect holiness." "I'm not so holy." "I walk with God in perfect holiness." "I have a long way to go to be holy." "I walk with God in perfect holiness." "I don't like being called holy." "I walk with God in perfect holiness." "Most of the time I walk alone."

And so on. What's interesting about such an exercise is that it reveals the train of thought that dominates my mind, that opposes today's idea and constantly counteracts it. It is this chain of negative thought that blocks the light in me. All the responses are some form of the idea "I am a sinner," which I would probably vehemently deny that I believe, if anyone asked me. And yet, faced with the affirmation that I walk with God in perfect holiness, these forms of that idea arise "spontaneously." Where are they coming from? Obviously from a backlog of very careful mind training by the ego, very effective brainwashing, so well done that I don't even realize my mind has been programmed.

Do I believe I am a sinner? "You have wasted many, many years on just this foolish thought" says the lesson (7:1). Yes, indeed I do. But when I am made aware of these negative thoughts about myself, I can let them go. I can "step back," and stop accusing myself. When I do, "the light in you steps forward and encompasses the world" (6:2).

How can we counter the programming of the ego? One way, clearly recommended by this lesson, is explicit counter-programming. It recommends that a thousand times a day we ask ourselves the question "Who walks with me?" And then, that we answer it by hearing the Voice for God, saying for us:

I walk with God in perfect holiness. I light the world, I light my mind and all the minds which God created one with me.

(8:5–6)

Certainty of our holiness does not come with a single repetition of today's idea. We need thousands of repetitions. We need to keep repeating it until we *are* certain of it. If we took this literally, repeating the idea a thousand times would mean repeating it a little more often than once per minute, all day long, assuming we are awake sixteen hours. That's a lot of repetition!

Let me today see the "quaint absurdity" (6:4) of the idea of sin, and laugh at the thought. Let me begin to absorb the wonderful teaching of the Course that sin "is a foolish thought, a silly dream, not frightening, ridiculous perhaps" (6:5). And let the wonder of it steal over me: "I walk with God in perfect holiness."

LESSON 157 ✦ JUNE 6
"Into His Presence would I enter now."

Practice instructions

Purpose: To usher in our first direct experience of Heaven. This is a holy day, a crucial turning point in the curriculum, the beginning of a new journey. Today will launch your ministry. Your only purpose now will be to bring to the world the vision that reflects what you experience today. And you will be given power to touch everyone with that vision.

Morning/evening quiet time: At least five minutes; ideally, thirty or more.

Approach this practice with a sense of sanctity, for you are attempting to pass beyond the veil of the world and walk into Heaven. Repeat the idea (you may want to repeat it over and over again), and let it bring you into that deep place in your mind, the place of stillness and rest. Then wait there "in still anticipation and in quiet joy" (4:3), for the experience promised you. Trust that your Self will carry you to where you need to go. He will lift your mind to the highest reaches of perception, to the holiest vision possible. Here at "the door where learning ceases" (2:3), you will pause for a moment, and then walk through that doorway into eternity. You will pass beyond all form and briefly enter Heaven.

Today is meant to be your first experience of what the Text calls revelation, direct union with God and your Self. Yet if it happens (and tomorrow's lesson will seem to acknowledge the obvious fact that it may not; see W-pI.158.11:1), it will not be your last. You will come into this experience increasingly. Each time will bring both you and the world closer to the day when this experience will be yours for all eternity.

Hourly remembrance: One or two minutes as the hour strikes (reduce if circumstances do not permit).

Repeat the idea and spend a quiet moment with it, seeking to enter into the Presence of your Self. Then thank God for His gifts to you in the previous hour, and let His Voice tell you what He wants you to do in the next hour.

Commentary

Today I'd like to share some thoughts about *experience* and *vision*, thoughts based mainly on Lesson 157, but with some references to Lesson 158 also. This lesson introduces a series of lessons designed to lead us into the holy instant, which is a major goal of the Workbook. From this point on, "Every lesson, faithfully rehearsed, brings you more swiftly to this holy place" (3:3).

The Course talks here of both an experience and of vision which results from the experience. The holy instant contains a moment of knowledge—something beyond all perception—from which we return with the vision of Christ in our minds, which we can offer to everyone.

The experience spoken of here is simply entering the Presence of God. It is "a different kind of feeling and awareness" (1:4) in which we "learn to feel the joy of life" (1:6). It is called elsewhere the holy instant. Lesson 157 calls it "a touch of Heaven" (3:1) and a moment in which we are left to our Self. It is an instant in which "the world is quietly forgot, and Heaven is remembered for a while" (6:3). We leave time for a moment and walk into eternity (3:2). It is not something we do ourselves; the Holy Spirit, the "Giver of the happy dreams of life" and "Translator of perception into truth," will lead us (8:2).

The vision spoken of is the result of the experience. This is not "a vision," something that is seen, but "vision," a way of seeing. We are not talking of some trance state, some appearance within our minds of mystical sights. We are talking about a different way of seeing the world, a different mechanism of sight, something other than the physical senses. Eastern religion might talk about opening the Third Eye to indicate the same sort of thing.

In experiencing the holy instant, we have awakened a different way of seeing. That new sort of vision does not disappear when we "come back to the world," so to speak (7:1). It is only a figure of speech to say we come back. We never left. Or perhaps better, since Heaven is what is real and this world is the illusion, we never came here at all. What "comes back" with us, into the dream, is the remembrance of God and Heaven, the remembrance of what we saw in that holy instant. We continue to see glimpses of it beyond the sight of the world, seeing the "real world" beyond the world, and beyond that, Heaven.

Each (apparently separate) holy instant we experience strengthens this new vision, this new mechanism of seeing. This is the purpose of the Workbook's recommendations for daily morning and evening periods of meditation; they are practice sessions, exercises to develop our new vision. We are meant, of course, to exercise this vision constantly during the day, to have repeated holy instants all day long. If we compare this to learning a language, the meditation sessions are like language labs and grammar studies. The concentrated language exercises are not an end in themselves but are meant to prepare us and improve our speech and understanding as we go out and actually use the language. Likewise, meditation is not an end in itself. It is an exercise to strengthen spiritual vision, but the purpose is to go out into daily life and begin using that new vision as often as possible.

Lesson 157 says, "We cannot give experience like this directly. Yet it leaves a vision in our eyes which we can offer everyone" (6:2–3). I can't give you a holy instant directly. I can tell you about it, but you have to do the work yourself and have the experience yourself.

What I can give you or offer to you is the new vision, the new way of seeing the world. The vision we can all teach, as fledgling teachers of God, is that of forgiveness and love within the world. I can teach you that it is possible to see the invisible beyond the visible, to see the undimmed truth behind the clouds of doubt, fear and defense. I can teach you to "see no one as a body. Greet him as the Son of God he is, acknowledging that he is one with you in holiness" (W-pI.158.8:3–4). By seeing you without guilt I teach you that seeing without guilt is possible.

And in willingness to practice the vision, willingness to ask to be shown a different way of seeing, the experience of the holy instant comes.

LESSON 158 ✦ JUNE 7

"Today I learn to give as I receive."

Practice instructions

Purpose: To practice seeing your brothers with Christ's vision, seeing past their bodies, their mistakes, and their fearful thoughts, to the pure, untainted holiness of their true Identity.

Morning/evening quiet time: At least five minutes; ideally, thirty or more.

Begin, as always, by repeating the idea for the day. Its meaning can seem vague, but the lesson makes it clear. It means: *"Today I learn to give my brothers a vision of Who they really are, as I receive from God the knowledge of Who I really am."* The *knowledge* God gives you cannot be given directly; you can only give it in reflected form, by giving to others your *vision* of their holiness.

Then use the rest of the time as the Spirit moves you and as the Workbook has taught you to do. The main thing you have been taught to do during these longer practice periods is to quiet your mind and sink down and inward to the deep sanctuary within you, keeping your focus and drawing your mind back from wandering by repeating the idea for the day.

Today, do this with the intent of getting in touch with the knowledge of Who you are, so that you will have something to give your brothers. By dipping into this deep well within you, you will gain the awareness that we are not our bodies, and this is the awareness you are to give your brothers today.

Hourly remembrance: One or two minutes as the hour strikes (reduce if circumstances do not permit).

- Repeat the idea and then (this is my recommendation) spend some time trying to see a particular brother through the eyes of Christ. Consciously try to see past his body and personality to the holy light of his true reality.
- Then thank your Father for the gifts He gave in the

previous hour—perhaps gifts of seeing past a certain brother's appearance to his reality.

• Finally, ask for guidance for the coming hour. You may want to think of people whom you might meet up with, and prepare yourself for those meetings by intentionally seeing past each person's body to the holiness that shines beyond.

Frequent reminder: Whenever you encounter someone.

Remember to see each brother you meet with the Christ's vision. See him as God's Son, at one with you, not as a separate mind housed in a separate body. To motivate yourself, remember that whatever you see in him you see in yourself. If you see him with Christ's vision, then that vision will shine on you.

Commentary

This lesson has a lot of profound metaphysics in it, particularly the stuff about time. If you'd like to dig into the Course's concept of time, a terrific starting place is Ken Wapnick's book *A Vast Illusion: Time in 'A Course in Miracles.'* I can't write a book tonight and you probably don't want to read one right now! So I'm going to skip over most of that stuff.

The practical point this lesson is trying to make is that "knowledge," which lies in the sphere of Heaven, is outside the scope of this Course. We *all* received knowledge when we were created; every living thing knows, inherently, that it is still connected to its Source: "a mind, in Mind and purely mind, sinless forever, wholly unafraid because you were created out of love" (1:2). It may seem to us that this is something we do *not* have, and that it is this we are trying to give to others and to receive for ourselves. But we can't give it because everyone already has it. It exists outside of time entirely. The point in time at which the experience of this knowledge reveals itself to us is already determined, by our own minds (2:9). When it happens, it will happen.

Within time—which is an illusion—what we can give, and receive, is forgiveness. Forgiveness is the gift that reflects true knowledge "in a way so accurate its image shares its unseen holiness" (11:2). What we can give is a vision of sinlessness, "Christ's vision." We can look past the body and see a light; look past what can be touched and see an idea; look past the mistakes and fears in our brothers and sisters, and see their inherent purity. We can greet one another and in each one, see him "as the Son of God he is, acknowledging that he is one with you in holiness" (8:4).

We are not giving knowledge. When we meet someone, we can give them our vision of themselves as sinless. In the way that we perceive them, they can find a new perception of themselves, one they have not found on their own. As they respond to our merciful vision, they will reflect that vision back to us, enabling us to perceive the Love of God within ourselves. When we forgive another, we have simultaneously forgiven our own sins, because "in your brother you but see yourself" (10:3).

We cannot know when revelation of truth, the experience of our reality, will come to us. The time is set; the drama is being played out; there is not one step we take only by chance (3:1–3). And yet, each act of forgiveness brings the day nearer. Our concern, then, is not with the final experience, but with the practice of vision, seeing with the eyes of Christ. This is something we can attain; this is something we can do something about. And we can do so *today*. Right now.

"This can be taught; and must be taught by all who would achieve it" (8:1). The way to learn the vision of Christ is to give it. The way to achieve the vision of ourselves as Christ sees us is to practice seeing others with His eyes. We give it to have it. This is the whole plan of the Course.

LESSON 159 ✦ JUNE 8

"I give the miracles I have received."

Practice instructions

Purpose: To open Christ's treasure house deep in your mind, gather lilies of forgiveness from it, and then give them away to your brothers. Only by giving them away will you realize that you have received them.

Morning/evening quiet time: At least five minutes; ideally, thirty or more.

As is usual at this stage, we are not given explicit instructions for what to do during our practice periods. So what follows is a suggestion based on the content of the lesson.

Close your eyes, repeat the idea, and sink down deep into your mind. As you approach the quiet center of your mind, you see a treasure house, a beautiful, gleaming structure that radiates a sense of holiness. You approach the massive doorway, wondering if you will be able to get in. Yet the lesson reminds us, "No one will be turned away from this new home, where his salvation waits" (7:4). The door swings silently open before you, and as you enter in you behold the treasure that is stored in this place. Rather than gold and silver, you see a sacred garden of the most amazing lilies you have ever laid eyes on. They literally shine with holiness. You can swear you hear the faint singing of heavenly choirs in the air around them. You realize that these are the lilies of forgiveness. These are miracles. You also realize that the soil they are growing in is Christ's vision, "the miracle in which all miracles are born" (4:1).

You are here to gather these miracles and take them back to the world. So walk into the garden and begin to pick the lilies. Don't be shy; that is what they are for. As you pick each one, notice that two more spring up in its place. Now, with an armful of lilies, you are ready to go out into your day, ready to give these miracles to everyone you encounter.

After the practice period, as you go through your day, imagine yourself giving one of these lilies to each person you meet. Your lily is your acknowledgment that this person is the Christ, washed clean of his past, ready to arise from the tomb of his sins and be reborn. So as you give the lily, you might say silently, *"You are forgiven. This is your Eastertime."*

Hourly remembrance: One or two minutes as the hour strikes (reduce if circumstances do not permit).

I suggest repeating the idea and then choosing one person. Then imagine giving this person a lily, while you say, *"You are forgiven. This is your Eastertime."* Then ask God what lilies He would have you give in the coming hour, and thank Him for the lilies He gave through you in the hour gone by.

Commentary

You might notice that today's lesson title is almost the same as yesterday's: "Today I learn to give as I receive." There is definitely a commonality of thought that runs through these two lessons, even extending two lessons back. They all talk of Christ's vision. They are all presenting a picture of the holy instant as a key part of our spiritual practice, although that term is not specifically mentioned in every lesson.

The general picture being presented is of our ongoing spiritual practice. It is this: We enter frequently into a holy instant. There, we experience a touch of eternity or Heaven, a taste of the knowledge of the truth. While we cannot carry this experience back with us to the world, we can carry back what that experience is like, translated into perception; this is called "the vision of Christ," which is manifested in forgiveness.

In this lesson, the holy instant is only hinted at by such phrases as "Let us an instant dream with Him" (10:6), or "Receive them now by opening the storehouse of your mind, where they are laid" (2:5). The Holy Instant is the "treasure house" we come to, the place in which we receive the gifts of Christ's vision. We must receive before we can give.

But we cannot recognize, or become fully aware of, what we have received until we give it away: "To give is how to recognize you have received. It is the proof that what you have is yours" (1:7–8). The extension of Christ's vision is an integral part of the plan of salvation presented by the Course. It is what brings us to certainty. This is quite similar to the principle taught by AA, that you stay sober by helping someone else to stay sober. Here,

> You understand that you are healed when you give healing. You accept forgiveness as accomplished in yourself when you forgive. (2:1–2)

It is only as we bring the "lilies" of forgiveness from the holy instant, where we received them, and distribute them into the world that we truly know we are forgiven. It is in giving away miracles that we receive them.

Father, help me today to realize that I am rich. The storehouse of my mind is filled with miracles. I can come to this storehouse and, in this holy instant, receive them. You entrust them to me for the giving. Let me pause often today, to meet here with You, and then carry these treasures forth to offer them to the world. This is my whole purpose in life; this is why I am here.

LESSON 160 ✦ JUNE 9

"I am at home. Fear is the stranger here."

Practice instructions

Morning/evening quiet time: At least five minutes; ideally, thirty or more.

My suggestion: Begin by realizing that the experience of *fear* and the experience of *home* are mutually exclusive. When you feel truly at home, you feel a sense of shelter and safety, a sense of joining and belonging, a sense of comfort and peace. When you feel afraid, you feel the absence of all these things. In essence, you feel homeless.

Now spend some time trying to get in touch with each state. First, imagine feeling completely at home inside yourself, regardless of what goes on outside you. Imagine knowing who you are, feeling at home with yourself. Imagine feeling at home with God, enfolded in His Love. Imagine fear being a thought loitering on the periphery of your mind, trying to invade the peace of this inner home, knocking on the door, tapping at the window, but unable to get in.

Then switch to getting in touch with the state of fear, the state that we all live in. Notice how in this state, fear, anxiety, and worry are your most natural reactions to the happenings of the world, so natural as to be automatic reflexes. This leaves you feeling that you have no safe harbor, no true shelter. You feel separate from God and alienated from yourself. It is as if *you* are loitering on the outside, while fear sits unchallenged on the throne of your mind.

Now ask yourself with real sincerity, *"Who is the stranger?"* Is it fear or is it you? Who sits at home in your mind, and who is on the outside, wandering homeless? Is it fear or is it you? Which of the states you just reviewed is the truth and which is the lie?

Now answer with the words that God has given you: *"I am at home. Fear is the stranger here."* Realize that this answer is true because it comes from God. Repeat it over and over. Try to feel

497

the truth in it.

Finally, let this idea draw you down into your mind, to the place where you are at home and where fear has no place. Feel the attraction of home drawing you deep within. Sink down to where you are at one with your Self, at home in your Creator. To renew your focus, from time to time repeat, *"I am at home."* And whenever a thought wanders into this holy home, say, *"I am at home. This thought is the stranger here."*

Hourly remembrance: One or two minutes as the hour strikes (reduce if circumstances do not permit).

Repeat the idea, letting it draw you to a place in your mind where you feel truly at home. Thank your Father for the letters from home He sent you in the previous hour, in the form of loving interactions and shifts in perception. And ask Him what to do in the coming hour.

Response to temptation: When you are tempted to be afraid or to see a brother as a stranger.

1. When you tempted to be afraid, say, *"I am at home. This thought of fear is the stranger here."* While you do, imagine yourself at home within your mind while the thought of fear loiters outside, powerless to get in.

2. When you are tempted to see a brother as a stranger, remember that he is part of your Self. You might say silently to this brother, *"You are at home with me. There are no strangers here."*

Commentary

Fear in this lesson is virtually synonymous with "ego." The picture being given is that we have invited fear, personified as a stranger, into our house, and the stranger has taken over and declared that he is us. He has taken over our identity almost completely. And the insane part of it all is that we have gone along with the stranger. We have accepted that this stranger is really us, and we have given our home over to him completely. We have been dispossessed.

Who is the stranger? You, or the ego? It is so easy, when thoughts of fear occupy our minds, to believe that the fear is us. The anger is us. The loneliness is us. The sense of helplessness is us. We have habituated ourselves to identifying with our thoughts and feelings of fear; we believe they are us. The thrust of this lesson is that all of these manifestations of fear are an interloper, not a genuine part of us at all. You are not the ego; the ego is not you.

Stephen Levine, in several of his books, talks about relating *to* our fear rather than relating *from* it. The distinction he is making is between identifying with the fear (relating from it) or distinguishing our self from it (relating to it). When I relate from my fear, I am in its grips. The fear runs me; the fear is me. When I relate to my fear, however, I can look on it with dispassionate mercy. I can react to it with mercy, and heal instead of go into panic. It is the difference between saying, "I am afraid," and saying, "I am having thoughts of fear" or "I am experiencing fear." My thoughts are not me. I am the thinker who is thinking the thoughts, but I am not the thoughts.

When we can separate ourselves from the fear we feel, we already have identified with our true Self. Our Self is certain of Itself, and It operates to heal our minds, to call us home. As we give this Self welcome in our minds, we remember who we are.

Yet this new vision of ourselves, of necessity, includes everyone. It is as though God were offering us a pair of glasses and saying, "If you put these on, you will see your true Self." But when we discover that, in putting them on, we see not only ourselves in a new light, but everyone, we rebel. We want to see ourselves as innocent, but we are unwilling to see everyone that way. If we refuse to see those around us as innocent, we will put down the glasses, refuse the vision of Christ, and we will not be able to recognize ourselves (10:5). "You will not remember Him [God] until you look on all as He does" (10:4).

When thoughts of fear enter my mind today, let me recognize that they are the stranger, the interloper, and that I am the one who is at home—not fear. Fear does not belong. I do not need to accept it in my mind. But let me not fight against it; let me look on my own thoughts of fear with compassion and understanding, recognizing them as merely a mistake, and not a sin. There is no guilt in feeling fear, or there need not be. I can step back from these thoughts, step back into my Self, and see them as the illusions that they are. I can look upon myself with love. And from this same place of merciful awareness, I see all my brothers in the same light: caught in fear, mistaking the fear for themselves, and needing not judgment and attack, but forgiveness, kindness, and mercy.

LESSON 161 ✦ JUNE 10

"Give me your blessing, holy Son of God."

Practice instructions

Purpose: To "take a stand against our anger" (1:1). To remove the fears we have projected onto our brothers and see the divine savior that they really are.

Morning/evening quiet time: At least five minutes; ideally, thirty or more.

- Select one brother as a symbol of all brothers. Through forgiving him, you forgive everyone.
- Visualize him as clearly as you can: his face, hands, feet, and clothing, his smile, his familiar gestures. Doing this gets you in touch with all the negative meanings you have projected onto him. As the lesson said earlier, the body of another is a great projection screen.
- Then realize that what you are seeing blocks the vision of your savior. Deep inside this person is a holy being who, like a great spiritual master, can enlighten you with his blessing, can free you from your self-imposed chains. If you saw him for Who he really is, you would be tempted to kneel at his feet.
- Ask this holy being to set you free. Say, *"Give me your blessing, holy son of God. I would behold you with the eyes of Christ, and see my perfect sinlessness in you."* Repeat these lines over and over, in the same spirit in which you would ask the blessing of an enlightened master.
- You have called on the Christ in him, and the Christ in him will answer you. The scales will fall off your eyes and you will realize that you have been completely wrong about who this person is. "Behold him now, whom you have seen as merely flesh and bone, and recognize that Christ has come to you" (12:3)—come to you to reveal the Christ in *you.*

Hourly remembrance: One or two minutes as the hour strikes (reduce if circumstances do not permit).

Repeat the idea, perhaps applying it to a particular person. Then thank God for the blessings He has given you in the hour gone by. And ask Him for His direction for the hour to come.

Response to temptation: Whenever you are tempted to attack a brother.

Use the idea instantly. Let it help you see past the appearance of a devil (12:6), or a wild animal itching to rip you apart (8:2-4), to the reality that here before you is the Christ.

Commentary

[Today's comments are something I wrote several years back while I was working as a computer consultant in New York City. On this particular day, I had expected to be able to work from home, via modem, but my client had insisted I come into the office. This threw off my plans for a long "quiet time." The comments that follow were what came to me as I read over the lesson.]

"Today we...take a stand against our anger, that our fears may disappear and offer room to love" (1:1). How "coincidental" that I begin this lesson with flares of anger at having to rush off to work! When a brother or a circumstance seems to cause anger in me, instead of listening to the ego and agreeing that the brother or circumstance is the cause of my anger, let me see that the brother is giving me a blessing by revealing to me that I am angry, that I have dropped the hand of Jesus.

Think about it logically for a moment. If I am totally connected to the Love of God in my heart, nothing will be able to disturb my peace. If something comes along that does (seemingly) disturb my peace, something must have happened beforehand. I must have disconnected from God's Love first, in order to react as I do. That something, then, instead of causing my upset, is merely revealing it to me. I can therefore see my brother's action, or the circumstance, as a blessing, a message from God, a lesson God would have me learn.

"Complete abstraction is the natural condition of the mind" (2:1). Abstraction is the concern with content rather than form. It separates the inherent qualities or properties of something from the actual physical object to which they belong. The natural state of mind considers content "apart from concrete existence" (American Heritage Dictionary).

Part of the mind, says Jesus here, has become concrete and specific rather than abstract. It sees fragments of the whole, rather than the whole. This is the only way we could see "the world." "The purpose of all seeing is to show you what you wish to see" (2:5). If I am seeing something that "makes me" angry or upset, it is because I wish to see it. The mind, dealing in the abstract, has already separated from the Love of God (or thinks it has, or wishes to, since that separation is inherently impossible). Therefore, it splinters reality, sees specific forms that seem to justify its separation, upset and anger. It creates illusions that seemingly give valid reasons for being upset.

It accomplishes this only by seeing fragments instead of the Whole. If I could see the whole picture, as God does, including things I cannot even imagine from my limited perspective, I would never be upset. I have made up those specifics. Since I have made them up, and am immersed in specifics that were made for the purpose of justifying my separation from God, "now it is specifics we must use in practicing" (3:2). The Holy Spirit will take the specific circumstances I have made as an attack on God and use them to bring me back. How?

> We give them to the Holy Spirit, that He may employ them
> for a purpose which is different from the one we gave to
> them. Yet He can use but what we made...   (3:3–4)

(In other words, all we have to work with are the specifics we've made up, so He will use them.)

> ...to teach us from a different point of view, so we can see
> a different use in everything.   (3:4)

"The mind that taught itself to think specifically can no longer grasp abstraction in the sense that it is all-encompassing" (4:7). Ideas like "All minds are joined" and "One brother is every brother" mean absolutely nothing to us! We cannot grasp them. These abstract statements simply don't help us, immersed in the illusion as we are.

We cling to the specifics, to symbols like the body, because our egos want fear, and that is the only way fear can seem real. There is no reality to fear itself, but the symbol of fear can seem very real. So we focus on the symbols, the specifics, the body. We feel limited by our own body, and by other bodies; we see bodies as attacking us.

What I see, when I see a brother as a body attacking me, is my own fear external to myself, poised to attack (paragraph 8). We tend to think that when we project fear, we see people who are afraid; not so, what we see are people who seem to be *making us* afraid. We see a monster that "shrieks in wrath, and claws the air in frantic hope it can reach to its maker and devour him" (8:4). When I am upset and angry at my client for "forcing me" to come to in to the office, that external specific is actually revealing to me my own fear of God's Love! It is giving me the opportunity to see beyond the apparent attack and to ask him for a blessing, to show me my own perfect sinlessness.

If I allow the Holy Spirit to show me my brother as he is, instead of how my fear has made him, what I see will be so awesome that I will hardly be able to keep from kneeling at his feet in adoration (9:3). And yet what he is, I am, and so I will, instead of kneeling, take his hand (9:4).

I call upon the Christ in him [my client] to bless me. I am seeing only a symbol of my own fear of God. I bring that fear to the Holy Spirit now. And as I do, I begin to feel a spark of true gratitude to my brother for offering me this salvation from fear. I feel the resentment about having to commute into the city melting away. This, too, is a lesson, and a very good one. Thank you, Jesus, for this lesson. And thank you, my brother.

LESSON 162 ✦ JUNE 11
"I am as God created me."

Practice instructions

Purpose: To accept the perfect holiness that is your right, to recognize the Son of God in you. And to thereby bring this acceptance and recognition to everyone.

Morning/evening quiet time: At least five minutes; ideally, thirty or more.

My suggestion: Spend this time in deep meditation. Let the power of these sacred words ("I am as God created me") carry you to the place in your mind where you experience the Self that God created as you. You might want to begin this meditation by reviewing the various images you hold of yourself, stating each one in the form *"I see myself as..."* and letting each one go by affirming, *"But I am as God created me."*

Hourly remembrance: One or two minutes as the hour strikes (reduce if circumstances do not permit).

Dwell on the idea and let it carry your mind to stillness. Then thank your Father for His gifts in the hour gone by. And ask His guidance for the hour to come.

Overall remarks: I recommend making a conscious decision to steep your mind in these words today. Begin the day with them, end the day with them, and try to keep them with you all the time in between. If you do so, you will experience their power to uplift your condition. They can transform your mind into the treasure house in which all of God's gifts are stored, ready for you to distribute them to the world. Today's lesson assumes that your understanding of this idea has deepened, for whereas in earlier occurrences of it (94 and 110), you were given additional lines to repeat, this lesson says you need no extra thoughts to draw out its meaning (4:2).

Commentary

For the third time we encounter as the main thought of a lesson what may be the single most repeated thought in the Course. (The first two lessons were 94 and 110; the idea was featured in Lesson 93 as well.) The phrase "as God created" occurs 105 times in the Course. We will see it as a focus of our Workbook review period in another twenty lessons, 201–220.

Why is this idea so important and repeated so often? "This single thought, held firmly in the mind, would save the world" (1:1). In the Text, our entire spiritual journey is characterized in terms of this idea: "You but emerge from an illusion of what you are to the acceptance of yourself as God created you" (T-24.II.14:5). If these statements are true, it is reason enough to memorize this idea and repeat it over and over until it becomes part of our pattern of thought. We might say that the entire Course is aimed at nothing more, and nothing less, than bringing us to the point where we hold this thought firmly in our minds.

In paragraph 4 our practice for the day is described as a very simple practice. All we need are the words of the main idea: "They need no thoughts beyond themselves to change the mind of him who uses them" (4:2). The change of mind the Course aims at is simply the acceptance of ourselves as God created us. By focusing on this thought, meditating on it, repeating it, and chewing it over in our minds, we accelerate this change of mind. "And thus you learn to think with God. Christ's vision has restored your sight by salvaging your mind" (4:4–5).

In Lesson 93, there was a useful addition to the words that helped clarify their meaning for me:

> Salvation requires the acceptance of but one thought;— you are as God created you, not what you made of yourself. Whatever evil you may think you did, you are as God created you. Whatever mistakes you made, the truth about you is unchanged. Creation is eternal and unalterable.
>
> (W-pI.93.7:1–4)

We are not what we made of ourselves. Our mistakes have not changed the truth about us. That is what accepting this idea means: the recognition that nothing we have done has been able to alter our relationship to God in the slightest, nor to change our nature, given us by God in creation. Our most shameful acts, the thoughts we would never want exposed to the world, have, none of them, changed God's creation in the slightest. There is no reason for guilt, no cause to shrink from God in fear; our imagined "sins" have had no effect. We are still safe, and complete, and healed, and whole.

How are we to use this thought? "Holy indeed is he who makes these words his own; arising with them in his mind, recalling them throughout the day, at night bringing them with him as he goes to sleep" (3:1). It reminds me of the words written about the words of God in the Old Testament: "And thou shalt teach them diligently unto thy children, and shalt talk of them when thou sittest in thine house, and when thou walkest by the way, and when thou liest down, and when thou risest up" (Dt 6:7). In other words, make them a part of your entire life, especially on rising in the morning and when going to bed.

To acknowledge that "I am as God created me" is to recognize the Son of God. It is to be free of guilt. It is to know the innocence of every living thing. It is to acknowledge God as perfect Creator. It is to release the past. It is to forgive the world. In these words is everything we need: "I am as God created me."

LESSON 163 ✦ JUNE 12

"There is no death. The Son of God is free."

Practice instructions

Purpose: To take a stand against every form of death; to realize that, unless God is dead, death itself must be unreal. To look past the outward appearance of death (which is all around us), and see the true life which shines in all things. Thus we release all those who worship the idea of death.

Morning/evening quiet time: At least five minutes; ideally, thirty or more.

Begin with the prayer at the end of the lesson (this is the Workbook's first prayer). Make it your prayer for the day. It asks that God bless your eyes, to give them power to see beyond the illusion of death that confronts you everywhere, and to see the eternal life that shines in all things. Through this sight, you abandon the religion of worshipping death, and you rescue others from this same dangerous cult.

After the prayer, do whatever you feel guided to do with the practice period. Since the prayer focuses on seeing with Christ's vision, you may want to try to sink down in your mind and join with the Christ in you, so that His eyes become your eyes.

Hourly remembrance: One or two minutes as the hour strikes (reduce if circumstances do not permit).

Repeat the idea. You may also want to pray the prayer again; I highly recommend that. Then thank God for His gifts in the previous hour, and let His Voice tell you what He wants you to do in the next hour.

Response to temptation: Whenever you are tempted to believe in a form of death.

Forms of death include anything where life—in the broadest sense of the word—appears to be losing the battle. This would include sadness, fear, anxiety, doubt, anger, envy; in short, any negative emotion (see 1:2), as well as sickness and physical death. In the face of these, immediately repeat the idea for the day. Realize it means that life and death cannot both be real, since they contradict each other. And since life is of God and God can't be killed, unlimited life is the only reality there can be. We are not imprisoned by the power of death. We are free in God's unlimited life.

Commentary

When the Course says, "There is no death," it is not talking about the death of the body. In fact, elsewhere it states that the body does not die, for the simple reason that it never has lived (T-28.VI.2:4; T-6.V(A).1:4). To talk of physical immortality and to base it on ACIM is foolishness. How could what never lives live forever?

"Death," says the lesson, "is a thought" (1:1). Not an event in the physical world, but a thought. In its simplest form it is the thought "Life ends." It is from this root thought that many different forms spring forth. Sadness is the thought of death. Fear is the thought of death. Anxiety is the thought of death. Lack of trust is the thought of death. Concern for the body is the thought of death. Even "all forms in which the wish to be as you are not" are really variants on the thought of death (1:2). My concern with my body and wishing to lose weight is a veiled form of a death thought. Part of the motivation to avoid being overweight is to "live longer." But if the body is not alive at all, what are we talking about?

Even the apparently spiritual thought of desiring to leave the body behind and to be free of it is a way of seeing physical death as some sort of salvation. "My body is a wholly neutral thing" (W-pII.294.Heading). It is neither a holy thing, destined to exist forever if we become sufficiently spiritual, nor is it a trap, prison, or real limitation on spirit. Being in a body does not keep me from being completely spiritual. Being in a body does not make me an ego. Rather, it is being an ego that makes the body!

In the world's way of thinking, death is the only certainty. Everything else is "too quickly lost however hard to gain" (3:1). As the Preacher of Ecclesiastes cries, "Vanity of vanities! All is vanity, futility and striving after wind" (Eccl 1:2, 14, paraphrased). Wealth, luxury, family, friends, nothing satisfies, and nothing lasts forever. Death takes them all in the end. Death never fails to triumph over life.

The Course says that to accept this thought system—which we all do to a greater or lesser degree, and far more extensively than any of us recognize—is to proclaim the opposite of God (death) "as lord of all creation, stronger than God's Will for life" (4:3). Each apparent triumph of death is a witness that God is dead (5:1–3). He Whose Will is life could not stop this death, so He must be dead. And as we watch the deadly drama, we "whisper fearfully that it is so" (5:4).

We may respond by saying we don't want to believe it. We don't want to worship death; we don't want to die; we want to believe in God and believe in life. In fact, however, we do want to believe in death, at least in certain forms of it. We've already pointed out that anger is a death thought. In anger, we want something or someone to "go away" or "not be," which in its essence means we want them to die. We actually hold on to guilt because we think guilt is useful; we are afraid that without guilt everything would be chaos. Guilt or condemnation is a judgment that some certain aspect of things does not deserve to exist. It is a wish for death, death of part of ourselves or of another. And certainly we hold on tenaciously to "the wish to be as you are not" (1:2).

We try to compromise. We want to hold on to certain death thoughts while letting others go. The lesson says this is impossible. You can't "select a few [forms of the death thought] you would not cherish and would yet avoid, while still believing in the rest" (6:1). Why? Because "death is total. Either all things die, or else they live and cannot die. No compromise is possible" (6:2–4).

If death exists at all, it totally contradicts life. It is life's opposite; surely that is clear. The lesson says, "What contradicts one thought entirely can not be true, unless its opposite is proven false" (6:5). In concrete terms we could paraphrase these words in this way: Death contradicts life entirely, and cannot be true unless life is proven false. The reverse is also true: Life contradicts death entirely, and cannot be true, unless death is proven false.

If God is the Will to life, how can death exist? Something must be there contradicting His Will, something more powerful than God. Anything more powerful than what we call God must actually be God, the real God. So if we are saying death is real in any form—physical death, or anger, or envy, or fear—we are saying death is God, and the God of life is dead.

Here again we find an echo of the profound words from the Text's introduction: "Nothing real can be threatened. Nothing unreal exists" (T-In.2:2–3). Life cannot be threatened. Death does not exist.

"The idea of the death of God is so preposterous that even the insane have difficulty in believing it" (7:1). It is absurd to believe that God died! Yet, the point the Course is making here is that this is what we *must* believe if we believe in death in any form.

"Death's worshippers may be afraid" (8:1). He's speaking about us, about you and me. We are afraid of death, let's be honest about that.

> And yet, can thoughts like these be fearful? If they saw that it is only this which they believe, they would be instantly released. (8:2–3)

In other words, can the thought that God died be fearful? It is so patently absurd, so utterly ridiculous, so absolutely, obviously untrue. If we saw that this is what we are believing, when we believe in death in any of its myriad forms, we would be instantly released. We would laugh at ourselves!

Belief in death is just another form of the "tiny, mad idea" at which "the Son of God remembered not [i.e., forgot] to laugh" (T-27.VIII.6:2). If we truly saw that worry about physical death, sadness, anger, envy, anxiety, fear, doubt, mistrust, concern for bodies, and the desire for change are all just forms of the idea "God is dead," we would laugh at them! We would see that all of this is no big deal, all of it is just a silly idea that is downright impossible and therefore nothing to worry about at all.

And so,

> There is no death, and we renounce it now in every form, for their salvation [those around us who believe in death] and our own as well. God made not death. Whatever form it takes must therefore be illusion. This is the stand we take today. And it is given us to look past death, and see the life beyond. (8:5–9)

No one is saying this is easy. In the illusion of time it does not happen overnight. In practice, it takes countless repetitions, constant vigilance of the mind, until we learn to uproot and deny all the forms that denial of truth has taken in our minds. To believe in death in any form is to deny life and thus deny truth. Our function here is "to deny the denial of truth" (T-12.II.1:5). It is to recognize the thoughts based on death and see they are simply silly and meaningless.

When I find myself being worried, anxious, or sad, I can ask myself, "Is God dead?" Somehow I find that helps me see the absurdity of it all. I lift a bag of groceries and the bottom falls out, spilling food all over the floor, and I am flushed with anger and deep sadness, in the form of feeling sorry for myself. Suppose in that moment I ask myself, "Is God dead?" For that is what my anger and sadness is proclaiming: God is dead. It suddenly seems so absurd for me to leap from spilled groceries to the death of God, so absurd I can laugh. And pick up the groceries.

More seriously, perhaps I experience "a great loss." My loved one dies, or perhaps I go through a wrenching divorce. The sorrow seems unending, and I feel as if life is over. "Is God dead?" In contrast to the magnitude of God, my personal [and illusory] loss is as nothing. Do I really believe that what happens in my little life can destroy the reality of God? Of course not. Especially if what I believe happened isn't even real.

Naturally in such profoundly disturbing circumstances I don't recover as quickly as I might over a bag of spilled groceries. Yet the same thoughts suggested by this lesson can be of immense comfort. Nothing dies. Nothing real can be threatened. Whatever form death takes must be illusion. When a body "dies" nothing really dies. When a divorce rips a beloved body out of my experience, nothing has truly been lost. I've been attached to an illusion, but God is still alive.

The pain and agony of loss through death or divorce can continue for months. Denying what I feel is simply not healthy, and I do not mean to suggest that we should attempt to stuff our grief with idealistic affirmations that "Death isn't real" and "Nothing has been lost." Rather, as the Course so often suggests, I can simply look at what I am thinking and feeling and recognize that, however real it feels, it is based on a denial of the truth. I can remind myself, "I'm believing that death is real, and loss is real. I'm believing that God is dead, and that's just a foolish notion. This pain, which I am indeed feeling, is therefore not real and is nothing to be concerned about. I'm okay, and God is still alive."

You might call it lucid living, similar to lucid dreaming. Although the experience you are going through seems terribly real, and the grief and sadness are real in proportion to your belief in the reality of the loss, there is still a part of you that is aware that you are dreaming, that you are being fooled by an illusion. You are fooled by the illusion, you do suffer the grief and sadness, but part of you knows it isn't really real.

That's all the Course is asking us to do. We're not being asked to abruptly jettison our feelings and our misthoughts. All the Course asks is that we recognize that they are based on a lie, that really they are proclaiming God is dead, and that simply isn't true. If we do that, the Holy Spirit will do the rest. Bit by bit, gradually (so it seems to us), the shadows of illusion will begin to lift from our minds. The form of "life beyond" the death we see will begin to take on definition and shape in our minds, and the illusion will become more and more shadowy. Our belief in death's many forms will weaken, and our belief in life will strengthen. The events of the illusion will have less and less effect on us, and we will experience the second phrase of this lesson's title: "The Son of God is free." We will know that we are eternally alive, and always have been, and there is nothing to fear.

LESSON 164 ✦ JUNE 13
"Now are we one with Him Who is our Source."

Practice instructions

Morning/evening quiet time: At least five minutes; ideally, thirty or more.

Enormous promises are attached to today's practice, if we do it faithfully (4:5), if we "practice in earnest" (9:5). So let's bring every ounce of willingness we have to this practice today.

Begin by going through a process of "letting go all things you think you want" (8:1). Go through a list of things your ego is attached to, and with each one, be willing to consider, just for the duration of this practice period, that it has no real value. You might imagine that you are inside the room of your mind, a room cluttered up with all the "trifling treasures" (8:2) you are attached to. One by one, clear out those worthless "treasures" from this room.

Now you have a clean and open room, ready to receive real treasure from Christ, "the treasure of salvation" (8:2). Let this room fill with "an ancient peace you carry in your heart and have not lost" (4:2). Let it be pervaded by "a sense of holiness in you the thought of sin has never touched" (4:3). Hear your Father calling to you, and then hear the Christ in you answer for you. Most of all, try to let in Christ's vision. Open the curtains in this room; let in the light. Through these open windows, you now can "see the world anew, shining in innocence, alive with hope" (W-pI.189.1:7).

Now the room of your mind has become His treasure house, filled with the gold and silver of His miracles. Now, wherever you look, your eyes deliver these miracles, as you bless what you see with your loving gaze. Step out into your day knowing that this is your job, to heal everyone you see by looking on them with "His forgiving vision" (7:6).

Hourly remembrance: One or two minutes as the hour strikes (reduce if circumstances do not permit).

513

Repeat the idea as a way of entering the treasure house of your mind and feeling your oneness with God. Then thank Him for the treasures He bestowed on you in the last hour. And ask Him what He would have you do in the next hour.

Commentary

To anyone who has done the Workbook lessons to this point, it is clear that the recent lessons are reaching for some new kind of level. There is a consistent emphasis on what the Course calls the holy instant, although many of the lessons do not use the term. But when a lesson, as this one, speaks of "this instant, now" as the time in which we come "to look upon what is forever there" (1:3), or of the time we give to spend in quiet "with Him, beyond the world" (3:2), it is clearly indicating times in which we enter the holy instant, a moment of eternity within time.

The practice being asked of us (since Lesson 153), day after day, is to set aside times of no less than five minutes, and as much as a half hour or more, morning and evening, to exercise our spiritual sight and hearing. We are being asked to listen to "the song of Heaven" (1:6) that is continually sounding beyond all the sounds of this world. This "melody from far beyond the world" (2:3) is the song of love, the call of our hearts to Him, and of His to ours.

These times are periods in which we forget all our sins and sorrows (3:3), and remember the gifts of God to us (3:4). We practice setting aside the sights and sounds of the world that constantly witness to us of the ego's message of fear, and we listen to the song of Heaven. We quiet ourselves, still our minds, and try to get in touch with the "silence into which the world can not intrude" (4:1), the "ancient peace you carry in your heart and have not lost" (4:2), and the "sense of holiness in you the thought of sin has never touched" (4:3). All of this, as the first paragraph says, "is forever there; not in our sight, but in the eyes of Christ" (1:3). We are not creating it; we are not making it happen; we are brushing away everything within our minds that veils it from our sight. "Now is what is really there made visible, while all the shadows which appeared to hide it merely sink away" (5:2).

Such practicing puts our minds in a state in which we feel pure joy. Joy is the word that comes to my mind to describe what a holy instant "feels like." There is a sense of contentment, an assurance that, despite all evidence to the contrary, all is well. There is a peaceful relaxation into the mind of God. Our minds naturally reach out in love to all the world from within this holy place, blessing rather than judging.

It may be difficult for us at this juncture to fully understand how such quiet practice, something that takes place completely within our own minds, can "save the world" (6:3). The lesson states in no uncertain terms that, by means of this practice, "We can change the world" (9:2). How can that be? It is so because all minds are joined, and while we may understand the concept, our sense of its reality may be very weak. That is normal; the effect on the world proceeds whether we are aware of it or not. We can, for the time being, focus on the personal benefit: "But this you can surely want; you can exchange all suffering for joy this very day" (9:4).

If you are like me, the reality and importance of this practice grows slowly. There are many days we let "slip by" without taking the time to do the work on our minds the Workbook calls for. The details of life, the press of business, the daily crises shriek for our attention, drawing us away, as they are meant to do. It takes some determination to put this "quiet time" with God first, above all else. But when we do so, an amazing thing happens. As Lesson 286 puts it: "Father, how still today! How quietly do all things fall in place!" (W-pI.286.1:1–2). I recall, long ago, reading how Martin Luther once wrote, "I have so many things to do today, I must spend three hours in prayer to prepare myself." There was a man who understood, within his own context, that preparing his mind with God was the most important thing, and that the more pressing the world seemed, the more he needed that quiet time in God's presence.

LESSON 165 ✦ JUNE 14
"Let not my mind deny the Thought of God."

Practice instructions

Purpose: To stop denying the Thought of God; to experience it and then abandon all else as worthless in comparison.

Morning/evening quiet time: At least five minutes; ideally, thirty or more.

Practice in whatever way the Holy Spirit inspires you to, but the essence of it should be undoing your denial of the Thought that created you and sustains you, and asking to know that Thought. Thus, there should be both a *negative* focus on letting go of your denial, your resistance, and a *positive* focus on asking for the experience of the Thought of God, the experience of Heaven. "Ask with desire" (5:1) and with hope (7:1). It is all right if you doubt how much you want this. Certainty will only come through experiencing what you ask for. This will carry you past all your doubts, to where you know that this experience is indeed the only thing you want.

Hourly remembrance: One or two minutes as the hour strikes (reduce if circumstances do not permit).

Repeat the idea, trying to let go of your denial and inviting the awareness of Heaven. Then thank God for His gifts in the hour gone by, and ask for His guidance for the hour to come.

Commentary

Today's lesson, tomorrow's, and those just before and after, are a strong encouragement to move forward. The Course, in these days, is trying to draw us past the point of hesitation and into a firm commitment.

> What makes this world seem real except your own denial of the truth that lies beyond?...What could keep from you what you already have except your choice to see it not, denying it is there? (1:1, 4)

Ken Wilber, the author of many books on transpersonal psychology and spiritual growth, points out that, viewed as evolution, spiritual growth proceeds to the degree we are willing to die to the lower level of life in order to transcend it and remember (or re-member) the higher level. The fact that our experience is on an ego level is not because the higher is not already here, it is because we have chosen the lower as a substitute for the higher, and we do so in every instant. It is not until the lower level is lived out, tried to the fullest, in a sense, and found lacking, that motivation exists to move us higher.

We need to become disillusioned with the ego to the point that we begin to see through its illusions. The degree to which the ego seems real to us is the measure of our denial of "the truth that lies beyond" (1:1). We can't see the real world because *we don't want to*. We are actively denying it. The reality of the real world, if perceived and accepted, will mean the end of reality as we now know it. Heaven appears to us as a threat to our imagined comfort on the ego level.

Jesus appeals to us,

> Deny not Heaven. It is yours today, but for the asking. Nor need you perceive how great the gift, how changed your mind will be before it comes to you. Ask to receive, and it is given you. Conviction lies within it. Till you welcome it as yours, uncertainty remains. Yet God is fair. Sureness is not required to receive what only your acceptance can bestow. (4:1–8)

You don't have to be sure before asking for Heaven. You don't have to be certain. "Sureness is not required" (4:8). In fact, you cannot be sure or certain before asking because "conviction lies within it" (4:5); that is, you don't find the conviction, the sureness, the certainty until you have Heaven, and you can't know you have it until you ask.

As we live thinking we are egos, considering moving forward, considering leaving the ego behind, the ego fights for its own existence. "You don't know what you are getting into here," it tells us. "How can you be sure you'd like it? You'd better make sure before you make a move."

Certainty, sureness, and conviction come from experience. When you have experienced the real world, even a glimpse, you will know you want it, you will know it is what you want and what you have mistakenly been seeking in the shadow world of the ego's illusions. So ask for Heaven.

Another comfort is that we don't have to understand all that Heaven, or the real world, is, before we experience it. You don't have to have a clear idea of what you're asking for, of "how changed your mind will be" (4:3). That change of mind does not precede the decision to ask, it follows it. It is the desire that allows it to come.

You don't even need to be sure that Heaven is the only thing you want!

> You need not be sure that you request the only thing you want. But when you have received, you will be sure you have the treasure you have always sought. (5:2–3)

It's all right to go into this with reservations, such as "Maybe I can have the real world and still hold onto my special relationships. Or maybe I can have inner peace and still enjoy my little pleasures." Those reservations will vanish once you taste the real thing. A very poor analogy, but one that makes the point: "How can you keep them down on the farm after they've seen Paris?" Once you taste "the treasure you have always sought" why would you go back to lesser things?

We already have the certainty within ourselves, in reality. That's part of what we've covered over with ego illusions. When we find the Self, we find it complete with certainty. The process of the Course, of "removing blocks to the awareness of love's presence" (T-In.1:7), is restated here in terms of that inner certainty: "This course removes all doubts which you have interposed between Him and your certainty of Him" (7:6).

The process consists of becoming aware of our doubts, owning them, acknowledging them, and then not taking them seriously. This is exactly the same process we go through with other such blocks, like anger and sadness and pain. See them clearly so you can see that the doubts, too, are part of the illusion. They are "meaningless, for God is certain" (7:3). "His sureness lies beyond our every doubt" (8:3).

Certainty is not something we can generate for ourselves. "We count on God, and not upon ourselves, to give us certainty" (8:1). But for that to happen, we must be willing to move forward, to be willing to "die" to the level of life we know now and to ask for something more, a different way of seeing, a different kind of vision. We need to be willing to ask that "the Thought of God" enter our minds and displace the distorted thinking we have been doing. We need to "follow the instructions," so to speak, given in the Course; if we do, certainty is sure to come to us.

LESSON 166 ✦ JUNE 15
"I am entrusted with the gifts of God."

Practice instructions

Purpose: To give the gifts of God to those who still walk the lonely road you are escaping. To demonstrate through your happiness what it means to receive the gifts of God.

Morning/evening quiet time: At least five minutes; ideally, thirty or more.

My suggestion: Spend time feeling the touch of Christ. You have made a false self that is akin to a mentally ill homeless person (see 4:4). As a result, you wander about feeling alone and impoverished. In your meditation, let Christ tap you on the shoulder and give you the awareness that you are not alone and you are not impoverished. Experience the joy that comes from feeling His touch.

This will prepare you for a day in which "your hand becomes the giver of Christ's touch" (14:5), in which you become the reminder to the "homeless" people around you that *they* are not alone and are not impoverished. You do this primarily by demonstrating the joy you have received from Christ. "Be witness in your happiness to how transformed the mind becomes which chooses to accept His gifts and feel the touch of Christ" (15:4).

Hourly remembrance: One or two minutes as the hour strikes (reduce if circumstances do not permit).

Repeat the idea and try to feel the touch of Christ. Then thank God for the gifts He placed in your hands in the past hour. And ask Him how He would have you give these gifts in the coming hour.

Response to temptation: Whenever you are tempted to be sorrowful, fearful, tearful, or sick.

My suggestion: Repeat the idea in order to dispel these feelings, for they betray your trust, your mission. Whenever you

520

are afraid, hear Christ reply with, "It is not so" (11:3). When you feel poor, let Him point out His gifts to you. When you feel lonely, let Him speak of His companionship.

Commentary

This lesson carries on the general tone of the previous one, attempting to persuade us to keep moving forward, past the illusion of ourselves we have been content to live with. It opens with the idea that God trusts us so much He has given everything to us. Everything. He knows His Son, and just because He knows us, He gives us everything without exception. His trust in us is limitless. We doubt our own certainty, but God's we can depend on.

I trust God's trust in me.

What we fear is that trust in God is "treachery" to ourselves (3:2). We are attached to this world we made.

To admit it is not real is to betray myself. If I have progressed beyond the point of believing that I can create like God, that I can make a world that is perfect somehow, at least I want to cling to the notion that I can unmake what God made, that I can destroy the world and shatter its perfection. To be told my actions, my sins, my denials, my doubts, and all their like are without effect is demeaning to my ego self. So I contradict the truth of Heaven to preserve what I have made.

There is a part of each of us that wants to be "a tragic figure," like some hero or heroine in an opera (6:1 and following). We want to be able to say, "Behold how nobly I withstand the slings and arrows of outrageous fortune." We think, all unconsciously, that without the "outrageous fortune" our nobility would be lost.

When I listen to my ego, this is how I want to see myself. Such a tragic figure! Poor thing, so weary and worn. Look at his threadbare clothing! How he must have been deprived! And his feet—Oh! Poor thing! They are bleeding.

We can all identify with this figure. "Everyone who comes here [to this world] has pursued the path he follows, and has felt defeat and hopelessness as he is feeling them" (6:2). You know what this is talking about. You've been there, maybe you are there now. You know what "defeat and hopelessness" means, you've felt it too.

Yet is he really tragic, when you see that he is following the

way he chose, and need but realize Who walks with him
and open up his treasures to be free? (6:3)

Is "he," the tragic hero [who is you and me], really tragic? Or is he
just foolish? Is he just making a silly mistake? When you see that he is
choosing his path and could choose otherwise, can you consider his
suffering tragic?

"This is your chosen self, the one you made as a replacement for
reality" (7:1). This, folks, is the ego self we have chosen to be. It's how
we've seen ourselves. This is the self we are defending. This is the
person we have become, and we resist all the evidence and witnesses
that prove that this is not us.

Jesus calls on us to drop the victim act and recognize that "I am not
the victim of the world I see" (W-pI.31.Heading), that

> I *am* responsible for what I see. I choose the feelings I
> experience, and I decide upon the goal I would achieve.
> And everything that seems to happen to me, I ask for and
> receive as I have asked. (T-21.II.2:3–5)

You see yourself as this tragic figure, but Jesus' response is: "[Christ]
would make you laugh at this perception of yourself" (8:3).

I'd like to meditate on that a while. Jesus wants to make me laugh!
Jesus is a frustrated comedian. Well, maybe not frustrated; look at what
he accomplishes through Marianne Williamson. He wants us to laugh at
our egos! He wants me to see the humor of my position, pleading
tragedy when I've deliberately chosen to be what I am.

> Where is self-pity then? And what becomes of all the
> tragedy you sought to make for him whom God intended
> only joy? (8:4–5)

The self-pity and the tragedy just disappear, that's what happens.
When you laugh at the "sorry figure" of the ego, the tragedy vanishes.

The next paragraph describes very well where some of us are right
now, just starting to realize that we are not the ego. This lesson is written
on many levels, addressing first, as we've seen, the person hiding in the
ego illusion of tragedy; then, in these next sentences, the person who has
begun to realize that the miserable ego is not his true Identity; and

finally, in paragraph 11 on, the person who has clearly seen and accepted that "you are not what you pretend to be" (11:2).

In paragraph 9 we see the person in the middle—feeling torn, afraid, almost under attack by God, Whom he has habitually avoided all his life. Let's listen in to our responses as Jesus tries to make us laugh, and see alongside it the humorous truth.

First, we sense the presence of God, Whom we have been hiding from: "Your ancient fear has come upon you now, and justice has caught up with you at last" (9:1).

Our reaction: *Oh, rats! It's God! Now I'm going to get it.*

Jesus: It's silly to be afraid of God, silly to think He is your Enemy and wants to hurt you. What a laughable idea, to be afraid of God!

The lesson: "Christ's hand has touched your shoulder..." (9:2).

Our reaction: *What was that really weird feeling? Oh, Christ—was it Christ? Is that His Voice in my mind? I must be losing it.*

Jesus: It is your brother, and he wants to bring you home. How foolish to fear him!

The lesson: "...and you feel that you are not alone" (9:2).

Our reaction: *And I'm not sure I like the idea of someone always with me, looking over my shoulder.*

Jesus: What a funny reaction! I am your Comforter and Teacher, not your judge. It's silly to think you prefer being alone.

The lesson: "You even think the miserable self you thought was you may not be your Identity. Perhaps God's Word is truer than your own" (9:3–4).

Our reaction: *I can't believe I've started to doubt these things I've believed all my life! I must be insane!*

Jesus: On the other hand, who has more chance of being right: you, or God? Be real!

The lesson: "Perhaps His gifts to you are real" (9:5).

Our reaction: *Yeah, and maybe it's just my imagination.*

Jesus: But what if they really are real, these gifts? Isn't it foolish not to find out?

The lesson: "Perhaps He has not wholly been outwitted by your plan to keep His Son in deep oblivion, and go the way you chose without your Self" (9:6).

Our reaction: *Yeah, and maybe He has. Maybe I've screwed it up so bad that even God can't fix it.*

Jesus: Now that's truly funny! You, outwitting God? Right, sure, that's really brilliant thinking. God decides He wants something and you are going to keep it from happening?

Our reaction: *But if I didn't outwit Him, then I must still be what He made me to be. I'm not sure I want to give up believing in what I've always thought I am. I feel threatened.*

Jesus: So, okay. Hold on to the picture of yourself you've always had; I'm sure you've really enjoyed being you, that way. Right? God isn't fighting it.

The lesson: "God's Will does not oppose. It merely is" (10:1–2).

You're not fighting with God, and He is not fighting with you. He doesn't fight, He doesn't oppose. He merely is. What you are fighting (and this is fall-down, bust-a-gut funny) is reality itself. Thinking you are separate from God is about as smart as a drop of water deciding it's not in the ocean any more. It's like a lion deciding it wants to be a mouse. You're trying to be what you are not; that's what causes all the strain, when it should cause nothing but laughter. The fight is all on your side against an imagined enemy. You are the Answer to all your own questions. There is nothing to be afraid of here. The truth about yourself is wonderful, not frightening.

In the remainder of the lesson, Jesus talks of three things we need to know. First, all the gifts that God has given us, that is, the real Self that we are, whole, healed, and abundant. Second, His Presence with us, our Companion on the journey. And third, that the gifts we have are made for giving away; we have a purpose here, to give these gifts to "all who chose the lonely road you have escaped" (13:1).

In a sense those are the three main thrusts of *A Course in Miracles*. First, learning the true nature of Self, the holiness and joy of our own being. Second, and equally important until we leave this world, is the sure knowledge of His Companionship on the way, the help we need to make it through. And finally, that the nature we have realized is that of Giver and Lover; to know we have the gift, we must give it. We must teach the world by showing it "the happiness that comes to those who feel the touch of Christ" (13:5).

Our mission is just that: to be happy. "Your change of mind becomes the proof that who accepts God's gifts can never suffer anything" (14:5).

We are here to become the living proof of what Christ's touch can offer everyone…Be witness in your happiness to how transformed the mind becomes which chooses to accept His gifts, and feel the touch of Christ. Such is your mission now.   (15:2, 4–5)

Recognize His gifts. Feel His touch. And share His gifts with the world through our happiness (not through beating people over the head with them). Those are the three stages of moving forward.

Another way to put it: Drop the victim act and take responsibility as the source of your life. Choose Heaven instead of hell, ask your Companion for His help. And be the proof of Heaven's reality by your radiant joy and refusal to suffer anything.

LESSON 167 ✦ JUNE 16

"There is one life, and that I share with God."

Practice instructions

Purpose: To accept that the life God gave us has no opposite, cannot change, cannot die, and cannot even sleep. To strive to keep our mind as He created it, to let Him be Lord of our thoughts today. This is a companion lesson to 163, "There is no death. The Son of God is free."

Morning/evening quiet time: At least five minutes; ideally, thirty or more.

Remember that during the longer practice periods, at this point in the Workbook, you are supposed to do what you feel guided to do and what has worked for you up until this point.

My suggestion for today is to try to get in touch with "mind awake" (8:1). This lesson teaches that our experience of death is not thrust upon us from the outside, but is solely the result of our "idea of death" (2:3). Under the sway of this idea, it says, our mind seems to fall asleep in Heaven and dream of a life separate from God, a life in this world. And yet, says this lesson, the mind "merely *seems* to go to sleep" (9:2; italics mine). In fact, the mind "cannot change what is its waking state" (6:2). Thus, the appearance of your mind as a volatile, changing field, with thoughts of fear and hope constantly sweeping across it, is an illusion. Your mind is really eternally awake, and as such is completely changeless and unlimited. That is the reality of your mind. Try, then, in your meditation, to get in touch with this reality. Try to leave behind the illusion of your mind as a restless sea, and experience its reality as a boundless and steady light.

Hourly remembrance: One or two minutes as the hour strikes (reduce if circumstances do not permit).

Repeat the idea and then spend a moment resting in the wakefulness that is the reality of your mind. Then thank God for His gifts in the last hour. And ask Him how you can express the truth that there is no death in the hour to come.

> *Response to temptation:* (Suggestion) whenever you feel tempted to acknowledge death in any form—as sorrow, anxiety, weariness, discomfort.
>
> Repeat the idea immediately. Realize that your negative emotion is a denial of life, and use the idea to remind yourself that life is the only reality.

Commentary

There is a repetition here, or perhaps a statement that I anticipated when, in writing about Lesson 163, I said, "Belief in death is just another form of the 'tiny, mad idea' at which 'the Son of God remembered not [i.e., forgot] to laugh.'" This lesson says that death "is but an idea, irrelevant to what is seen as physical" (3:2). Later it says, "Death is the thought that you are separate from your Creator" (4:1). That is the essence of the idea of death: separation from Life.

This is why we can say, "There is no death." It is simply impossible. God is Life, and what He creates must be living. To cease living would be to separate from God, to become His opposite. Since God has no opposite, there is no death.

> There is no death because what God created shares His Life. There is no death because an opposite to God does not exist. There is no death because the Father and the Son are one. (1:5–7)

"Ideas leave not their source" (3:6). That idea is central to the Course. Ideas exist only in the mind that thinks them. Ideas do not exude out from mind, take on an independent existence, become self-sustaining, and become capable of opposition to the mind that created them. They simply don't do that.

I am an idea in God's Mind. I am the thought of "me." I cannot depart from God's Mind, live independently of Him, dependent only on myself, capable of a will that opposes God's. I simply cannot do it. I can only imagine I am doing it.

> [Death] is the fixed belief ideas can leave their source, and take on qualities the source does not contain, becoming different from their own origin, apart from it in kind as well

as distance, time and form.   (4:3)

I cannot do that; I cannot leave my Source and take on qualities not contained in that Source. Therefore, I cannot die.

We need to see that, as Lesson 163 (paragraph 1) said, death takes many forms. The "attraction of death" spoken of in the "Obstacles to Peace" section (T-19.IV) reflects all those forms. This lesson lists a few more:

> Yet we have learned that the idea of death takes many forms. It is the one idea which underlies all feelings that are not supremely happy. It is the alarm to which you give response of any kind that is not perfect joy. All sorrow, loss, anxiety and suffering and pain, even a little sigh of weariness, a slight discomfort or the merest frown, acknowledge death. And thus deny you live.   (2:3–7)

What is death? Any feeling that is not supremely happy. Any response to anything in our life that is not perfect joy. Can we see how anything less than supreme happiness and perfect joy is a denial of life and an affirmation of death? To be less than perfectly joyful is to assert there is something other than God, other than Life, other than Love; something "other" that dilutes the radiant Being of God.

I am not advocating becoming a bliss idiot, walking around in total denial of the pain and suffering of our lives and of those around us, frantically asserting, "Everything is perfect. None of this is real. It's all illusion, ignore it. Only God exists."

Rather, I am encouraging the exact opposite. I am suggesting that we need to start noticing just how much the idea of death influences us. We need to notice those little sighs of weariness, those twinges of anxiety, and recognize that the idea of death underlies them all, the idea that separation from God is real, that something other than God exists, opposing and nullifying His radiance. We need to notice how we believe we are that "something other," or at least part of it. Notice, and say to God, "I'm believing in death again. I'm feeling separated from You. And I know, therefore, this feeling doesn't mean anything, because there is one life, and I share it with You."

It is only when you recognize that you are responsible for those death thoughts that you can truly understand they have no reality except in your own mind. To affirm they have no reality without first taking responsibility for them is unhealthy denial. It leaves them without a source, and they must have a source. So your mind supplies an imagined source in God or somewhere outside yourself, and you are back to the separation thought again, because there is nothing outside God nor outside you. By screaming, "It's all illusion!" without truly knowing that you are the illusionist, you make the idea of death into something real, something to be fought against and repressed.

To recognize death thoughts as illusion does not require that you do violence to your mind. Seeing beyond illusion is the most natural thing in the world when it happens naturally, as the result of taking responsibility for the illusion. To see the world as illusion does not require concerted and sustained effort. It is not something you can try to do. If you are trying, you're doing it backwards.

The same principle operates when people say, "I'm trying to see the Christ in him." You can't try to see Christ in a person; you either do or you don't. When your eyes are open and nothing is in the way you don't have to try to see! You just see.

Spiritual vision is the same. Christ is there, in every person, and you are quite capable of seeing Him there. The problem is, you've erected many barriers, many screens, that block your sight. You're seeing the reflection of your own ideas instead of seeing who the person really is, which is Christ.

The way to spiritual sight, the way to see Christ in a brother, therefore, is to become aware of all the screens you are throwing up, all the illusions you are projecting from your own mind, blocking true vision. Paradoxically, you don't see Christ in a brother by looking at him, squinting and trying to pretend he is a loving being; you see Christ in him by looking at your own mind, your own thoughts, which are the barrier to vision.

Perhaps you are afraid of the person in some way. He appears to you as a threat of some sort, perhaps prone to attack you physically, or to take your money. Instead of trying to see through that picture of him as a bad person, a threat to yourself, look at that picture itself and ask where it came from. With the Holy Spirit's help, you will see that it originated entirely in your own mind. It is the sum of your own judgments solidified into an opinion. It is how you have taught yourself to see your brother. And that is all.

You know, or you should, that you are not capable of judgment. You cannot possibly have all the evidence. So you can turn to the Holy Spirit and say, "I recognize that my opinion of my brother is my own creation. It is based on the idea of death, of something separate from and other than God. As such, I know it is only a bad dream. It has no meaning. My brother is not what I think he is, and I am not a bad person for having this thought; I'm just making a mistake. I am willing to let go of it, and since I am its only source, I can let go of it."

You may go on feeling afraid. The key difference is not whether or not the fear disappears, as it sometimes will. The key difference is that, if the fear (or whatever feeling or judgment it may be) is present, you are aware that you are making it up and it isn't real. This opens the way for a different vision to dawn on you. If what you have been seeing is illusion, there must be something else, some other way of seeing, that is real.

The vision of Christ, which is what the Course calls this different way of seeing, may not burst on your sight after one application of this mental process. It probably won't. We've got lots and lots of barriers to that vision, and you may have recognized only one of many things preventing you from seeing Christ in your brother. That's okay. You've understood that this particular barrier is an illusion, and affirmed there is another way of seeing your brother. That's all you have to do. You don't have to try to find the other way! When you are ready, when the barriers are recognized as something you make up, the vision will just be there.

It will "just be there" because it is already there. The Christ in you already recognizes Himself in your brother. The process is similar to tuning out static in a radio with electronic filters. There is a signal you want to hear, but too much noise and static prevents its being heard. You identify the static, isolate it, electronically "instruct" your equipment to ignore it, and eventually, the clear signal comes through.

What you are doing in the process the Course recommends—looking at the ego and its thoughts of death, identifying them, and deciding to ignore them because they come from an undependable source—is tuning out the static. Keep doing that, and the clear signal of Christ's vision will come through. It is there, in you, right now. You just can't "hear" it for all the noise the ego is making.

LESSON 168 ✦ JUNE 17
"Your grace is given me. I claim it now."

Practice instructions

Purpose: To ask for and experience the gift of God's grace, which will give us first the gift of vision, and then eternal knowledge. This will momentarily lift us into Heaven, restore all forgotten memories and give us certainty of Love. This is a new and holy day.

Morning/evening quiet time: At least five minutes; ideally, thirty or more.

Begin with the prayer at the end of the lesson: *"Your grace is given me. I claim it now. Father, I come to You. And You will come to me who ask. I am the son You love."* Make this prayer as heartfelt as you can. In it, you are lifting your heart to God and asking Him for the gift of grace, in which He leans down to you and raises you up to Him, restoring you to full awareness of Him and His Love. The next lesson will explain that such moments will only "replace the thought of time but for a little while" (W-pI.169.12:3), but this little while can change your life forever. So ask for it with all the desire you can, and then hold your mind in silent expectancy, poised, motionless, waiting for the descent of His grace. And when your mind wanders, repeat the prayer again to bring it back to that motionless waiting.

Hourly remembrance: One or two minutes as the hour strikes (reduce if circumstances do not permit).

Repeat the prayer and spend a moment waiting in stillness for God's grace. Then thank Him for the reflections of grace you experienced in the hour gone by. And ask Him what He would have you do in the hour to come.

Commentary

What is grace?

This lesson answers not in the impassive terms of a formal definition, but in the picture of a warm, personal conversation with God. "God speaks to us. Shall we not speak to Him?" (1:1–2). Grace is the concomitant of God's Love, something that comes along with it as part of the package. He has always loved us (1:7–11). Grace is the effect or application of that love which guarantees His Love will be fully recognized and received. Grace is whatever it takes to bring us out of our sleep. It is the movement of love that woos us back to Him, the quiet whisper of His Voice in our minds that will not let us go, the careful planning of our curriculum to help us unlearn everything we have taught ourselves of fear, the activity of Spirit that works constantly to win back our trust, restore our joy, assuage our guilt. It is His answer to our despair. It is the means by which we recognize His Will (2:3–4).

His grace is given me. His grace is "a given," a certainty, part of what it means that God is Love. It is a gift, always available, always being given, awaiting only my acknowledgment (2:5). It is "the gift by which God leans to us and lifts us up" (3:2). And ultimately, grace is that aspect of His Love in which "finally He comes Himself, and takes us in His Arms and sweeps away the cobwebs of our sleep" (3:4).

Shall I not, then, today, sit down for a few minutes of quiet conversation with this God of Love? Can I not take the time even to ask Him to grant me this grace, which He has already granted? Can I not express my willingness to receive it, to allow this sorry world to disappear from my sight, replaced by true vision? Can I not tell Him that I long, at least in part of myself, to be swept into His Arms? I may feel as though I am making some kind of surrender or concession; I may believe I am giving something up, or losing something dear to me. Yet if this opening to grace is surrender at all, it is surrender only to Love. It is a sigh of lost resistance to what I have always, always wanted. It is a loss of pretense, a falling back into what I have always been. It is surrender to my Self. It is capitulation to my Beloved; nothing more than that, and nothing less. It is the ultimate manifestation of "falling in Love."

Do I doubt my own capacity to love, and to respond adequately to God's immaculate, eternal Love? "Our faith lies in the Giver, not our own acceptance" (5:2). It is not the power of my choice or my faith that works the miracle, it is the power of Him Who gives it. His grace gives me the means to lay down all my errors (5:3), even when I doubt my own ability to do so. That is what grace is for. Grace supplies everything I think I lack. As God once said to the Apostle Paul, "My grace is sufficient for thee" (2 Cor 12:9). What is grace? Everything we need to bring us home to God, whatever form that might take.

LESSON 169 ✦ JUNE 18
"By grace I live. By grace I am released."

Practice instructions

Purpose: To ask for grace, and the temporary experience of Heaven that comes from grace. And then to return and bring to others the gifts that you received from grace.

Morning/evening quiet time: At least five minutes; ideally, thirty or more.

Today you are again asking for the gift of grace, which will momentarily lift you into the knowledge of Heaven. Begin with this prayer: *"By grace I live. By grace I am released. By grace I give. By grace I will release."* The first half of this prayer asks that your mind be raised up into the daylight of reality, where you will experience pure oneness. This is the "experience we try to hasten" (7:1). This is not the final revelation that will one day come to you, in which you finally disappear from time and space altogether, but it does signify that that day is coming. This is essentially a meditation in which you are going for it all, so bring to it all that you have learned about meditation, as well as all of your desire for God.

The second half of the prayer speaks of the aftereffects of the moment of grace. Once you emerge from your instant of timelessness, people will "see the light that lingers in your face" (13:2), and you will give them the miracles that were laid in your mind in that holy instant.

Hourly remembrance: One or two minutes as the hour strikes (reduce if circumstances do not permit).

Repeat the prayer used in the longer practice, asking again for God's grace. And then thank God for whatever reflections of grace came your way in the previous hour. And ask Him how, in the coming hour, He would have you give the gifts you received in your meditation.

Commentary

Grace, Jesus tells us, "is an aspect of the Love of God which is most like the state prevailing in the unity of truth" (1:1).

I suppose one might say that to live by grace means to live with full, conscious awareness of Love's Presence while in the world. In that sense, it is equivalent to living in the real world.

This fits in with the rest of the first paragraph. The state of grace, or living by grace and constantly receiving grace, is something beyond learning. Learning only prepares us for it, for learning is purely in this world. Really, what we are doing is unlearning all our denial of the truth about our Self.

"It is…the goal of learning, for grace cannot come until the mind prepares itself for true acceptance" (1:3). Learning prepares us to accept grace. It does not give us grace, but it prepares us to receive it, to accept it, which implies that grace is already available but we are not able to accept it.

"Grace becomes inevitable instantly in those who have prepared [a place in themselves where it can be] willingly received" (1:4). Grace is simply there, instantly, whenever we are ready to receive it. Learning is necessary to produce the state of willingness; then the grace just pours in. We don't have to do anything to bring it, but we do have to progress through (un)learning to remove our unwillingness to receive.

There then follows what is perhaps the best definition of grace in the lesson: "Grace is acceptance of the Love of God within a world of seeming hate and fear" (2:1).

Grace means seeing through the illusion. I am still in this world of "seeming hate and fear" and yet, somehow, I accept the Love of God. I accept that He is wholly Love, not angry and vengeful, not something to be feared because of my sin, not someone to be blamed for the seeming ills of the world: God is Love. Instead of seeing the world as solid and real, and wondering how God can be loving when all this is going on, "those whose minds are lighted by the gift of grace can not believe the world of fear is real" (2:2). Those who know grace know that God is real, love is real, and it is the world of fear that is the illusion.

> Grace is not learned. The final step must go beyond all
> learning.   (3:1–2)

This is not something you learn. It cannot be learned. It must come from outside the context in which learning occurs, which is purely the ego context. The Course often says there is no learning in Heaven, or in God. How could there be learning where everything is known?

> Grace is not the goal this course aspires to attain. Yet we prepare for grace in that an open mind can hear the Call to waken. It is not shut tight against God's Voice. It has become aware that there are things it does not know, and thus is ready to accept a state completely different from experience with which it is familiarly at home.   (3:3–6)

So, since learning is the goal of the Course, grace is not; it is beyond what the Course teaches because it cannot be taught. But the learning of the Course, which is really unlearning, prepares us for grace by loosening the tight grip of the ego on our minds. The goal of the Course, as seen in this paragraph, is an open mind and an awareness that there are things we don't know.

We do not realize the extent to which our minds have been closed, "shut tight against God's Voice." That is what we must learn. What we learn is all the ways we shut God out. When we learn that completely, there is nothing left to shut Him out and He is simply there, as He has always been.

The lesson then goes on to talk of the state of Heaven or oneness. I don't have time to comment on it here; the lesson speaks for itself when it says, "We cannot speak nor write nor even think of this at all" (6:1).

> Yet forgiveness, taught and learned, brings with it the experiences which bear witness that the time the mind itself determined to abandon all but this is now at hand.   (7:2)

In other words, forgiveness is what we now teach and learn, not grace. Forgiveness is the learning process, the preparation for grace, and it gives us witness experiences, foretastes of what it is like to live in grace.

> Now we have work to do, for those in time can speak of things beyond, and listen to words which explain what is to come is past already. Yet what meaning can the words

convey to those who count the hours still, and rise and
work and go to sleep by them?   (10:3–4)

We are still in time. Let's be real and practical here. Talking about
"things beyond" and trying to understand how "what is to come"
(enlightenment or awakening, which is in our future, as we perceive it)
"is past already" (that is, the journey is already over, we're already
enlightened, and oneness is a constant state which is here now, forever
as it always was)—talking about these things can be fascinating, a little
encouraging perhaps, but how on earth can we understand it? We can't!
The words convey very little meaning to us while we live and order our
lives by time, by counting the hours.

It is good to think of these things a little, but to do so is not our main
task. In fact, it can be a waste of time if it distracts us from the fact that
"we have work to do" here, now. Forgiveness work. Sitting around
discussing what it means to live constantly by grace, in the real world,
or what follows in the experience of Heaven, is meaningless without
that very real and practical work of forgiveness going on in our lives.

We won't understand Heaven until we get there. Grace foreshadows
Heaven, and we can't even understand that yet, not fully. We can have
tastes of it, though, in the holy instants in which we connect with God
and with Love in our minds. So,

now we ask for grace...Experience that grace provides will
end in time...[it does] not replace the thought of time but
for a little while.   (12:2–3)

The experiences of grace come, and they go. We experience being
outside of time "but for a little while." These experiences, which come
in moments of true forgiveness, are all we need for now. "The interval
suffices" (13:1). The holy instants, the "little while" of each forgiveness
experience, is enough. It is all we need.

"It is here that miracles are laid" (13:2). In other words, the holy
instant opens us to miracles. It is the way that miracles flow into our
lives, "to be returned by you from holy instants you receive, through
grace in your experience, to all who see the light that lingers in your
face" (13:2). When you "come back" from the holy instant, there is a
light that lingers in your face. Other people see it, and to them, you bring
the miracles you received in that moment.

> What is the face of Christ but his who went a moment into
> timelessness... (13:3)

This is talking about you and me. The face of Christ is your face, my face, when we have received a holy instant and "return" to the world of time; our faces glow with the light of Heaven.

> ...and brought a clear reflection of the unity he felt an
> instant back to bless the world? (13:3)

That is our function here in the world: to bring a clear reflection of Heaven's unity back to bless the world. To ask for grace, to open our mind to receiving grace from God, to choose, as often as we can, to "go" into that holy instant in which we feel the unity of Heaven, and then to return with a reflection of that to bless the world. Notice that the unity is "felt" and not just intellectually accepted and understood. It is felt. That is what happens in a holy instant.

We hear about living the in the real world, or what it must be like to live in a constant state of oneness (Heaven), and we want it. We want it now. We get frustrated because the holy instants come and go, they last "but for a little while" and we find that disappointing. Jesus is explaining here that the learning stage is absolutely necessary, and we should not feel frustrated, we should not think we are failing in our work if the holy instants don't last.

> How could you finally attain to it forever, while a part of
> you remains outside, unknowing, unawakened, and in need
> of you as witness to the truth? (13:4)

Your brothers around you in the world, "unknowing, unawakened," are your own thoughts in form. They are "a part of you" which "remains outside." You have a mission here, a purpose to fulfill. Awakening must be communicated. You want a steady state of "holy instant-ness," but Jesus asks, "How could you attain that if part of you is outside that state of oneness, unknowing, unawakened, unaware?" Your oneness must include them.

Jesus says we should actually be grateful to "come back" from these holy instants, back to the world of time. Listen:

> Be grateful to return, as you were glad to go an instant,
> and accept the gifts that grace provided you. You carry
> them back to yourself.   (14:1–2)

If the holy instant is a moment in which you are aware of oneness, in a sense you have to come back. You have to come back because you are aware of your oneness with those who haven't seen yet. They are part of you, and so you have to "go back" to bring the gifts of grace to that part of yourself that is still not awake, as you see that reflected in your brothers.

Jesus tells us clearly to be content with this, to "not ask for the unaskable" (14:7). To want Heaven for myself while leaving my brothers behind is to fly in the face of what Heaven is: the awareness of oneness. A private salvation is unaskable. We go together or we go not at all.

Some might react to this as though the mass of humanity is holding us back and preventing our full enlightenment. Such a thought is still based on a consciousness of separation and so is totally alien to grace and Heaven. The world you see is not a force separate from you, restraining you. It is a reflection of your own self-restraint, your own resistance which has yet to be overcome or unlearned. The world is not outside your mind, but in it. You are the world, that is what you are learning.

You become what you always have been by accepting your role as savior to the world. Your salvation is the world's salvation. They are not two things, they are the same.

We "come back" to save the world. That doesn't mean that we have our little moment of bliss and then come back to preach to the world about it and tell them how enlightened we are, and why don't they get with it? If your salvation is the world's salvation, the reverse is true: the world's salvation is your own. You save the world by working on yourself. "The sole responsibility of the miracle worker is to accept the Atonement for himself" (T-2.V.5:1). You save the world by changing your own mind, because that is where the world is, in your mind. There is only one mind, only one of us here.

When you are at a movie, if there is a problem on the screen you don't run to the screen to fix it; you find the projector and fix that. Those "unenlightened people" you see out there are parts of your own mind that you haven't recognized as part of you; you don't bring them with you by trying to work to fix the screen (those separate people out there), you do it by working with the projector, the cause (your own mind).

Be glad to go an instant, and be grateful also to return, to bring the light of God to the world. You bring it to yourself. It is in seeing that fact that you will be saved. The returning is not a step back into time. No, it is a step forward in your own awakening, the means by which you bring all the world with you into timelessness, there to be the oneness you have touched and known.

LESSON 170 ✦ JUNE 19
"There is no cruelty in God and none in me."

Practice instructions

Purpose: To stand before your devotion to cruelty as a means of safety, see it as a meaningless idol, and choose to serve this idol no longer.

Morning/evening quiet time: At least five minutes; ideally, thirty or more.

We need to look honestly at our belief that attacking others in self-defense keeps us safe. This amounts to a belief that *cruelty* keeps us safe, since all attack intends to hurt and the intent to hurt is cruel. This has enthroned cruelty as a god in our mind, a god we dare not question.

Yet today, we must question this god. We must look dispassionately at our belief that cruelty means safety. So first, get in touch with this belief in you. Note how you do believe that, when attacked, your attack in return will keep you safe. Then be willing to question this belief. Consider the possibility that your own defense against an attack is what gives it power in your eyes. Consider the possibility that your own cruelty is ultimately what makes you afraid. And consider that this belief that cruelty equals safety is just that—a belief, an idea to be calmly re-examined, not a god to be worshipped.

Now turn to another aspect of this belief. You realize that God wants you to lay down your arms, to give up attack and defense. This makes Him appear to be cruel, for He seems to want to strip you of your protection. He apparently wants you to be all meek and saintly while you get run over. As soon as you see cruelty as the god that protects you, then the real God of Love will seem cruel, as if your protection does not matter to Him. Look at this belief. Be willing to question it. Is it possible that He wants your safety more than you do? Is it possible that "love is your safety" (W-pII.5.5:4)?

In looking at both beliefs—that cruelty is your god and that

God is cruel—you are standing before the same idol, and making a choice. "Will you restore to love what you have sought to wrest from it and lay before this mindless piece of stone?" (8:4). While trying to make this choice, keep repeating the idea *"There is no cruelty in God and none in me."* Consider that God is only Love and that your nature is like His, that cruelty is quite simply unnatural for you. Genuinely try to "look for the last time upon this bit of carven stone you made, and call it god no longer" (11:2).

If you succeed, you will walk out upon a new world, which you will see through new eyes. You will look on the same people, but whereas before you saw danger in them, now you will see God's glory in them. Where before your heart was filled with fear and cruelty, now it will be filled with nothing but love.

Hourly remembrance: One or two minutes as the hour strikes (reduce if circumstances do not permit).

Repeat the idea, trying to renounce your allegiance to cruelty and to accept the love that is your true nature. Then thank God for the gifts of His Love that came your way in the hour gone by. And let Him tell you how to express the newfound love in your heart in the hour to come.

Commentary

The basic thought today's lesson contains is that our attempts at defending ourselves are what make external attack seem real to us.

We fear because we believe, somewhere deep in our hearts, that we have attacked, and deserve punishment for our attack. We sense within ourselves a belief that "to hurt another brings [us] freedom" (1:4). This belief lies behind every attack we attribute to self-defense. No matter how hard we try to justify our attacks, something in us knows that our intent is to hurt the other person because we believe that hurting them will somehow free us from something. In a nutshell, we believe that we are inherently cruel.

We project our belief in attack onto something external; we see the attack as coming from outside of our own mind. In reality, there is nothing outside of our mind; we are the ones who attack ourselves by our guilt, but we believe we see the attack external to ourselves, justifying further attack on our part. Thus fear and defense become the means of preserving ourselves. And "love is endowed with the attributes of fear" (5:3); that is, because love would counsel us to lay down our defenses, it becomes something to fear. Love becomes dangerous.

From this perspective, fear and cruelty become a "god," an idol, something to be preserved at all costs. To let go of fear becomes the ultimate danger. We fear being without fear more than anything else; we cling to our fear, believing that it protects us.

Taken to the extreme, this "worship" of fear and cruelty ends up being projected onto God Himself; we see Him as a vengeful God, breathing fire, threatening us with hell, ready to dupe us with His talk of love, laughing with savage glee as we go down to defeat. In fact, it is our fear of God, buried as well as we can bury it, disguised in many forms when it leaks out of our unconscious, but ever present, that is "the basic premise which enthrones the thought of fear as god" (9:4). Ultimately, all our defenses are defenses against God. Buried deep in our psyche is our conviction that the universe is out to get us. Most of our lives, if we look at them with honesty, are spent in buttressing our fortifications against "things" that seem to threaten us.

The Course calls on us to lay down our defenses as the only way of discovering that the threat is unreal (2:6–7). God is not angry. The universe is not out to get us. If God appears to us to be separate from us, only the walls we have erected make it seem so. We are the victims only of our own defenses.

We have no reason to fear. We are not cruel; we cannot be, for God Who created us has no cruelty in Him. There is no punishment hanging over our heads. We are the innocent Son of God, the Son He loves. Without that primal fear, there is nothing to project upon others; when we cease to project our fear, there is no perception of attack from without; when no attack is perceived without, there is no need for defense.

If we assess our "god" of fear and defense honestly we have to see that it is made of stone. It has no life; it cannot save us. Fear begets fear; attack begets attack. The wars of the world testify to this endlessly. Hurting others *never* makes us safe; it only adds to the cycle of fear and attack.

To realize that our trusted method of securing safety is worthless, that our champion warrior is a traitor, can be a terrifying moment. The missile silos in which we have placed all our trust are pointed at our own hearts! "This moment can be terrible. But it can also be the time of your release from abject slavery" (8:1–2). To think of giving up defense entirely can momentarily paralyze us with fear. But it can be the moment in which we are free to recognize that what we fear does not exist, and the "enemy" we have striven to keep out is allowed to enter, bringing His peace with Him.

XI

Review V: Introduction and Lessons 171 - 180

REVIEW V PRACTICE INSTRUCTIONS

Purpose: To prepare for Part II of the Workbook. To give more time and effort to practicing, that you may pick up your pace on the journey to God. To recognize the truth in the central idea ("God is but Love, and therefore so am I"). Make this review a gift to Jesus and a time in which you share with him a new yet ancient experience.

The prayer: Use the prayer in paragraphs 2 and 3 to dedicate the review to God. It asks God to lead your practicing and to call you back to it when your practice lags, so that you can make quicker progress on the road to Him.

The central thought: The review really revolves around this idea ("God is but Love, and therefore so am I"). The purpose of the review is to bring us to a place where truly understand and experience the truth of the idea. And the purpose of the ideas being reviewed is to support the central idea, draw out different aspects of it, and make it "more meaningful, more personal and true" (W-pI.rV.In.4:2). Therefore, have this idea pervade every day of this ten-day review. Start and end the day with it, start and

545

end each practice period with it, and surround every repetition of the review ideas with it.

Morning/evening quiet time: At least five minutes; ideally, thirty or more.

Spend a moment repeating the central thought (*"God is but Love, and therefore so am I"*) and the two review ideas. Surround each review idea with the central idea. Use the review ideas to illumine some aspect of the central thought and make it more meaningful to you.

Then enter what I call "Open Mind Meditation." Hold your mind still and quiet, empty of all words. Words are like signposts—they point to meaning, but now you are seeking the direct experience of meaning, and for this, words only get in the way. In this verbal void, simply wait in "silent expectancy" (W-pI.94.4:1) for the experience of what the words speak of, the experience of your true Self. Your whole focus is on waiting "in still anticipation" (W-pI.157.4:3). Your mind is at rest, yet also poised. Your whole awareness is waiting for the dawn of realization to spread over it. Hold this focus wordlessly. However, when your mind wanders, which will happen regularly, repeat the central thought to remind you of what you are waiting for—the realization of your true Self—and then return to your wordless waiting.

Close by repeating the central thought once again.

Hourly remembrance: One or two minutes as the hour strikes (reduce if circumstances do not permit).

Suggestion: Repeat the two review thoughts, surrounding each one with the central thought. Then thank God for his gifts in the previous hour and ask His guidance for the coming hour. Close with the central thought.

LESSON 171 ✦ JUNE 20

Central theme:

"God is but Love, and therefore so am I."

Review of:

(151) "All things are echoes of the Voice for God."
(152) "The power of decision is my own."

Practice instructions

See instructions on page 545.

Commentary

Another review! As you read through the introduction to the review, you will notice that there are no detailed practice instructions. The summary, given in paragraph 11, is the only reference to the actual practice we are meant to follow. A morning time, an evening time, and keeping the idea in our remembrance throughout the day—that's all the instruction we are given. Actually, the full instructions were given in Lesson 153, paragraphs 15–18. There, the instructions were said to be "a form we will maintain for quite a while" (W-pI.153.15:1). That "while" is still continuing.

In the ten days of review, I will be commenting mainly on the review introduction, rather than the daily ideas being reviewed. Today I'll cover the first three paragraphs, and then one paragraph a day for the remaining nine review lessons. The theme idea for the review is: "God is but Love, and therefore so am I." We are told (4:2) that each of the twenty thoughts we are reviewing clarifies some aspect of the theme thought; I will also attempt to point out some ways the theme is connected to each day's two thoughts.

The introduction to our review opens with a powerful appeal to us to take our practicing seriously, to "give more effort and more time to what we undertake" (1:2). Once again, as in Review IV, we are reminded that this series of lessons is meant to help us in "preparing for another phase

547

of understanding" (1:3). Review IV made it clear that this is a reference to the second part of the Workbook: "This time...we are preparing for the second part of learning how the truth can be applied" (W-pI.rIV.In.1:1). The realization that we are preparing for something more, a shift into another phase, is meant to motivate our efforts so that we "take this step completely, that we may go on again more certain, more sincere, with faith upheld more surely" (1:4). One gets the sense that the effectiveness of the second half of the Workbook depends, in large measure, on how much time and effort we are willing to put into our practicing right now.

I remember the first few times I did the Workbook, I always felt the second half was a bust. Anticlimactic. I also remember that I made no serious effort to follow the practice instructions; I just read the lesson every morning. I am absolutely certain that there is a direct connection between those two facts: my feeble practice, and my sense of anticlimax.

The Workbook recognizes that we have been wavering, and that we have had doubts that caused us to be less than diligent in practicing. It does not berate us over this, but it does make clear that if we want the results, we have to follow the program. The reward will be "a greater certainty, a firmer purpose and a surer goal" (1:6).

The prayer in paragraphs two and three would be, in my opinion, a good one to use every day during this review. It needs no comment; the meaning of every line is quite clear. It is a prayer for diligence in practicing. It is an affirmation of faith that, even if we forget, stumble, or wander off, God will remember for us, raise us up, and call us back.

Today's two thoughts connect easily to the theme idea. If God is only Love, and I am also only love, then everything echoes His Voice. Everything is nothing but an aspect of Him. The decision I face, today and every day, is whether or not to accept this fact. Will I live today as an expression of the Love of God, or will I choose to attempt what must be impossible: to be something else?

LESSON 172 ✦ JUNE 21

Central theme:

"God is but Love, and therefore so am I."

Review of:

(153) "In my defenselessness my safety lies."
(154) "I am among the ministers of God."

 ## Practice instructions

See instructions on page 545.

Commentary

Paragraph 4 of the review introduction:

"This is the thought..." (4:1). The words refer to sentence 3 of the paragraph, the theme thought for the review. As we review, we are to dwell on this thought first, every day, every morning and evening, and often through the day. Each additional thought from the previous lessons "clarifies some aspect of this thought, or helps it be more meaningful, more personal and true, and more descriptive of the holy Self we share and now prepare to know again" (4:2). It would be good, in our reviewing, to meditate on how this central thought relates to the other two ideas. The focus is on the theme thought; the additional thoughts are meant to clarify it or expand on it.

Notice the word "prepare" used again in sentence 2. The new "phase of understanding" (1:3) that we are preparing for will have something to do with once again coming to know our true Self. The first half of the Workbook has concentrated on undoing our old thought system; the second half will move us on into reclaiming the knowledge of the Self we thought we had lost.

The holy Self we are is simply an extension of God. He is Love; so are we. We are what He is, extended. That is what we are preparing to remember; more than simply to remember, to *know*. That one word implies worlds. I can write the words, I can agree with them, but do I *know* what I am saying? Knowing that I am an extension of God's Love will change everything about my life, banish all fear, and give me a sense of holy purpose unparalleled by anything I have ever before experienced.

What is this Self, which I am, like? It is "perfectly consistent in Its thoughts; knows Its Creator, understands Itself, is perfect in Its knowledge and Its love, and never changes from Its constant state of union with Its Father and Itself" (4:5). This is a description of me and you as God created us. This is what our practicing is preparing us to "know again."

Isn't this a goal worth "more effort and more time"? (1:2). Try to imagine what it will be like (not "would be" but "will be") to be perfectly consistent in all your thoughts. Try to get a sense of what it will be like to know God and yourself perfectly. Try to imagine living in a constant state of union with the Father, and with your Self, without variation or change in that state of union.

Today's two review ideas help us to see the way to our goal, negatively and positively. If I am Love, how can I be defensive? To be what I am in truth, I must lay down my defensiveness. And if I am Love, what can I be but a minister of God? What can my purpose here be but to extend His Love, to reach out and touch my brothers with the touch of Christ?

LESSON 173 ✦ JUNE 22

Central theme:

"God is but Love, and therefore so am I."

Review of:

(155) "I will step back and let Him lead the way."
(156) "I walk with God in perfect holiness."

Practice instructions

See instructions on page 545.

Commentary

Paragraph 5 of the review introduction:

The Self that is only Love, perfectly consistent in Its thoughts, is what "waits to meet us at the journey's ending" (5:1). I often need to remind myself of what it is I am "going for" in this spiritual walk. Sometimes it seems like such a long journey—"countless situations...through time that seems to have no end" (T-24.VI.7:2). Keeping the goal in view, in the forefront of my mind, is a necessity for me. "This," with a capital "T" (at least in some editions of the Course), "is promised us" (5:4). I am on a journey to find my Self, and at the end of the journey, it is promised, I will find It. A Self in constant union with God. A Self at perfect peace within Itself. This is worth "going for."

The journey seems long, but every step brings me a little nearer (5:2). Each time I pause for a minute to remember brings me nearer. Each time I open my heart in love to a brother brings me nearer. Each morning or evening I take the time to practice, sitting in silence, listening, brings me nearer. The path offered by the Course is not a flashy one. It is not, sometimes, a very exciting one. But it works. It is so clear to me that this work *must* be done somehow; the twisted thoughts of my ego must be undone and replaced with something else. The multitude of fear's disguises must be unmasked and replaced with love. Sometimes I wish it could happen overnight. Sometimes I wonder why it seems to take so long and proceed so slowly. And then I catch my own thoughts, turning me away, delaying me, and I know why. Occasionally I even feel gratitude that God does not force anything on me against my will, because, when at last I end the journey, there will be not one shred of uncertainty that it is my will, as well as His. And I return to the steady work the Course sets forth, knowing that—for me, at least—this is the only way I have found that works.

"This review"—done as we are asked to do it, of course—"will shorten time immeasurably" (5:3). So if I feel impatient, here is the means to shorten the time it takes. The means are being given to me, handed to me on a silver platter, put before my eyes day after day. Will I take them? Will I use the means given me to shorten time? I say so often that I want the journey to proceed more quickly. Yet if, given the means to shorten the time, I do not use them, what does that say about my wanting? My regularity in practice is the measure of my true desire.

If I practice with the goal in mind, if I remember why I am doing it, the benefit will be maximal. If, however, I trudge through the practice as if it were some kind of duty being imposed on me, a tedious chore, I will benefit less.

Today let me raise my heart from dust to life as I remember (5:4). Let me lift up my eyes and recall the glorious goal, the completeness of my Self that awaits my remembering. Let the inner hunger that never leaves me have its way and draw me onward.

Today's two review ideas dovetail nicely with the ideas in the paragraph from the review introduction. I "step back and let Him lead the way," willingly following His direction. And I am encouraged on my journey in knowing that as I go, "I walk with God in perfect holiness."

> This course was sent to open up the path of light to us, and teach us, step by step, how to return to the eternal Self we thought we lost. (5:5)

Thank You, Father, for this course. Thank You for its step-by-step instructions. Thank You for this time of review, for the times I can spend with You, quietly, listening, waiting, knowing that every minute draws me nearer to my goal, every minute saves immeasurable time. Thank You for opening up the path of light.

LESSON 174 ✦ JUNE 23

Central theme:

"God is but Love, and therefore so am I."

Review of:

(157) "Into His Presence would I enter now."
(158) "Today I learn to give as I receive."

Practice instructions

See instructions on page 545.

Commentary

Paragraph 6 of the review introduction:

In this paragraph, Jesus speaks in the first person: "I take the journey with you" (6:1). One aspect of the Course that seems to get less attention than many others is the personal presence of the author in our lives. No doubt many of us, feeling we have "escaped" from what we perceived as restrictive Christian backgrounds, many of which emphasized a "personal Savior" and the actual worship of Jesus as God's only Son, find ourselves uncomfortable with the notion of having Jesus by our side as we make this journey. It is too much like what we left behind.

In the Clarification of Terms section in the Manual for Teachers, we are reminded that "some bitter idols have been made of him who would be only brother to the world" (C-5.5:7). One relationship that may need healing is our relationship with him; we may carry with us many "shadow figures" from the past that distort our perceptions of him. We are asked, here in the Manual, to "forgive him your illusions, and behold how dear a brother he would be to you" (C-5.5:8). Yet the Course takes this issue, as it does all such issues, gently. "It is possible to read his words and benefit from them without accepting him into your life. Yet he would help you yet a little more if you will share your pains and joys with him" (C-5.6:6–7). So if you find this idea of relating with him a little unsettling or even distasteful, be at peace; it's okay.

Jesus offers to share our doubts and fears in order to make himself accessible to us. We can know he understands what we go through because he has been this way before. Even though he has reached a place where uncertainty and pain have no meaning, he understands them when we experience them. We don't have to feel that we are approaching some remote figure, high and mighty, who will dismiss our uncertainty as irrelevant with a wave of his hand. He sees what we see. He is aware of all the illusions that terrify us, and the reality they seem to have to us. But he holds in his mind "the way that led him out, and now will lead you out with him" (6:5). He is like an elder brother who has finished the journey, but has come back now to lead us home with him. He knows that the Sonship is not complete until we have walked the same way he walked. He is with us now, leading the way for us.

In my quiet time today, then, let me be aware of his presence. As I enter into God's Presence, let me be conscious of one who is at my side, perhaps holding my hand if I feel fearful. Let me be willing to bring my uncertainty and pain to him, so that he can help me overcome them. As I receive the grace from him enabling me to set aside my fears and doubts, let me learn to give as I receive. Let me come forth from this time with him to share what I have received with those around me. Let me act as God's representative in the world, to forgive the "sins" of those around me, ease their minds, and offer them the peace that has been given me.

LESSON 175 ✦ JUNE 24

Central theme:

"God is but Love, and therefore so am I."

Review of:

(159) "I give the miracles I have received."
(160) "I am at home. Fear is the stranger here."

Practice instructions

See instructions on page 545.

Commentary

Paragraph 7 of the review introduction:

You know, from the way Jesus talks in the first sentence, it sounds like this is something he has experienced more than once! "My resurrection comes again each time I lead a brother safely to the place at which the journey ends and is forgot" (7:1). I'd certainly like to think that there have been more than just him; it would be disheartening if he were the only one so far. I think, today, that there have probably been far more than we realize who have reached the journey's end with him. Sometimes we wonder why there seem to be so few in this world who seem to have "made it," but if I think about it, it seems to me that "this world" is the last place we are likely to find such people! I'm just glad that Jesus, at least, has decided to hang around and be a "savior…with those he teaches" (6:5). (Actually, the Course implies that there are others as well; see Section 26 of the Manual, "Can God Be Reached Directly?" first two paragraphs.)

There is something uplifting about the idea that when I learn, in some circumstance, the way out of "misery and pain" (7:2), that Jesus is "renewed." Actually, of course, that is true of all of us; every one of us is renewed when a brother learns the way out of pain. Everyone we touch with a miracle enriches us when they receive it. When anyone shares an account of a miracle in their life, everyone who hears is

555

renewed; that is what makes the sharing so refreshing. My own walk with God is strengthened every time I realize that something I have said helped someone. The Course often says that those we help help us, that our brothers see in us more than we can see in ourselves; that is how we learn to remember what we are.

Let me remember, today, that every time I turn my mind to the light within myself, and look for Him, Christ is reborn. This is how the Second Coming happens (see W-pII.9.3:2, "What Is the Second Coming?"). When we all have given our minds wholly to Christ, the Second Coming will be complete. Each time I turn to the light within, I bring it nearer. Each time today that I remember "God is but Love, and therefore so am I," I hasten that day. Each time I choose to give the miracles I have received, each time I remember that my Self, and not fear, is at home in me, Christ is reborn in the world.

No one has been forgotten. I love Marianne Williamson's line, "God hasn't lost your file." I like to imagine the hustle and bustle in the "heavenly office," with all sorts of entities working on my behalf, all unknown to me. Planting little clues where I'll find them. Arranging for me to meet the right people, stumble over the right books, and go through the experiences I need to go through.

But all of this needs my cooperation. The last sentence is almost paradoxical, stating that Jesus needs *my help* to lead me back to where the journey was begun. But it makes sense, for as the Course says all along, the one essential is my willingness. He *leads* me, he doesn't force me. My help consists in being willing to follow, stopping now and then to listen for directions. And in doing the practice he gives me to do.

I notice that he is leading me backwards (!) to where the journey began, in order that I can make "another choice" (7:5). All of his work with me is to take me back to that moment when I made the wrong choice, so that I can make it differently. Nothing, then, is irrevocable. Even the pivotal choice that began the nightmare can be undone, and will be undone, and *has been* undone. He is leading us up the ladder that separation led us down (T-28.III.1:2). Each mistaken choice that I allow him to undo today is another step back up the ladder to the memory of my original state, to the memory of the fact that "God is but Love, and therefore so am I."

We give the miracles we have received, and as we do, we remember we are at home, and it is fear that is the stranger.

LESSON 176 ✦ JUNE 25

Central theme:

"God is but Love, and therefore so am I."

Review of:

(161) "Give me your blessing, holy Son of God."
(162) "I am as God created me."

Practice instructions

See instructions on page 545.

Commentary

Paragraph 8 of the review introduction:

Our practicing somehow releases Christ to the world. Opening our minds to the Holy Spirit makes us available as channels to those around us. The Holy Spirit, of course, is "Him Who sees your bitter need, and knows the answer God has given Him" (8:1). One of the things that makes the Course so unique, I think, is the way in which it both acknowledges our "bitter need" and yet affirms that in reality we have no needs. It is as if He is saying to us, "I know that the world of pain and loss is only an illusion and nothing to be disturbed about, but I also know that, to you, it is very, very real, and I am ready to work with you on that basis."

Quite clearly, we are being encouraged to develop a relationship with Jesus and the Holy Spirit. We review "together" (8:2). We devote our time and effort to these review thoughts "together" (8:3). We are not simply individuals practicing some kind of mind manipulation; we are engaging in a relationship, a collaborative venture:

> Healing does not come from anyone else. You must accept guidance from within. The guidance must be what you want, or it will be meaningless to you. That is why healing is a collaborative venture. I can tell you what to do, but you must

collaborate by believing that I know what you should do.

(T-8.IV.4:5–9)

So we are reviewing these thoughts *with him*. We are not just mulling them over by ourselves, but listening to that guidance from within as we do so.

"And together we will teach them to our brothers" (8:4). Have you noticed how nearly every time the Course talks about the process we are going through, it ends up with some aspect of sharing or extension, some kind of giving what we have received to our brothers? The Course is not a personal path of salvation. Indeed it teaches there *is* no such thing as individual salvation, because "individual" is an illusion. We are not alone. We are not separate individuals who can be individually saved. We are part of a whole, and when we begin to receive what the Holy Spirit has to teach, we *must* share it, because sharing is what He is teaching. We teach "by actions or thoughts; in words or soundlessly; in any language or in no language; in any place or time or manner" (M-1.3:6).

We share precisely because the whole is not whole until everyone is included. As Jesus is incomplete without us, we are incomplete without our brothers. We, like Jesus, may recognize the wholeness in ourselves and in so doing, recognize it in our brothers. The wholeness is already there, but unacknowledged and unrecognized: "I am as God created me," as one of our thoughts for review reminds us. Our "ancient home" is being "kept unchanged by time, immaculate and safe" (8:8). We cannot lose it, but we *have* lost awareness of it, and that awareness is what we share with each other.

As we begin to accept our own wholeness we become reminders to the world of the wholeness that is also theirs, and that we share with them. There is no "preaching" quality, no spiritual elite telling the rest of the world "how it is." It is the happy communication that "You are whole, as I am. I am as God created me, and you are as God created you." We come to our brothers not as superiors, but asking their blessing on us, acknowledging them as the holy Son of God, along with us: "Give me your blessing, holy Son of God."

Your holiness is the salvation of the world. It lets you
teach the world that it is one with you, not by preaching to

it, not by telling it anything, but merely by your quiet recognition that in your holiness are all things blessed along with you.   (W-pI.37.3:1–2)

LESSON 177 ✦ JUNE 26

Central theme:

"God is but Love, and therefore so am I."

Review of:

(163) "There is no death. The Son of God is free."
(164) "Now are we one with Him Who is our Source."

 Practice instructions

See instructions on page 545.

Commentary

Paragraph 9 of the review introduction:

Four more days of this review; four more days of our "gift" to him. Of course, every moment we connect with our right mind, every moment we taste the one holy instant, is a gift as well. This paragraph has a wonderful flavor to it: our hearing his words; us giving them to the world; Christ working through us to save the world; walking together to God with him; taking the hand of our brother as we go. A wonderful connective energy, all part of a magnificent whole which is our Self, sourced from God. The energy flows to us and through us, from us to our brothers and from them to us, weaving us all together in the divine fabric. We are one with Him Who is our Source.

"For this alone I need; that you will hear the words I speak, and give them to the world. You are my voice, my eyes, my feet, my hands through which I save the world" (9:2–3). This is the real purpose of my existence and my experience here in the world. I may feel confusion, day to day, about my purpose and the form it is taking. I may have my doubts about those with whom my life is now interacting, wondering how in Heaven's name they could ever be part of any divine plan. I may wonder the same about myself. But Jesus speaks in these words from the Course saying, in effect, "My only need is you. I need your physical presence to reach through you to the others who are lost in the illusion of bodies."

How can this be? How, in the mess I find myself in, can this happen? I don't know. But I believe that the Holy Spirit knows. All I can do is to make myself available, to be willing for it to happen. Let me remember that these thoughts of anxiety, doubt, lack of trust, and sadness are all just forms of the belief in death, and let them go, placing them in His hands. Let me place myself in His hands as well, remembering that I am one with Him Who is my Source; I am Love as God is, I am the extension of His Being, as are we all. If I can believe this I am free.

Donna Cary has written a wonderful song, one of many based on her experience with the Course. The chorus of it repeats over and over, "He's asking me to give myself to Him, Calling me to give myself to Him." The song speaks of the fear that arises when we hear this call. Can I say, today, "He needs me. He wants my hands, my feet, my eyes and my voice. Father, I am frightened, but here I am. Use me"? Let me be the instrument of His peace. Or, in the words of a Christian poet of the last century, Amy Carmichael:

> Love through me, Love of God.
> Make me like Thy clear air,
> Through which, unhindered, colors pass
> As though it were not there.[1]

God is nothing but Love, and "therefore, so am I." Let that Love flow through me, unhindered by anything. Let me be clear and clean. Remind me, God, that I am free today; there is no death, there is no opposite to Love, or to life. Let my life be an expression of that truth.

---

1. Amy Carmichael, in *Toward Jerusalem* (Fort Washington, Penn.: Christian Literature Crusade, 1989).

LESSON 178 ✦ JUNE 27

Central theme:

"God is but Love, and therefore so am I."

Review of:

(165) "Let not my mind deny the Thought of God."
(166) "I am entrusted with the gifts of God."

 ## Practice instructions

See instructions on page 545.

Commentary

Paragraph 10 of the review introduction:

The practice of the Workbook is meant to induce not just new thoughts and new permutations of thoughts, but an experience: "a new experience for you, yet one as old as time and older still" (10:1). How can an experience be older than time? How but in being part of eternity? "The holy instant reaches to eternity, and to the Mind of God" (T-15.V.11:5). "The holy instant is a miniature of eternity" (T-17.IV.11:4). These times spent in quiet with God are occasions when we step out of time and into timelessness; what we experience here is older than time, incredibly ancient and yet immediately present, always present.

We are experiencing our Self. "Hallowed your name. Your glory undefiled forever" (10:2–3). These are words that sound to us (if our background is Christian, at any rate) as if they should be spoken of God. Yet here they are spoken of *you* and of me. What is it like to experience such a thing? What is it like to know yourself as one of whom these words can be spoken, one who is entrusted with the gifts of God? I do not think words can convey it, although many have attempted to do so. What is required is an experience; then, words become unnecessary and even unwanted.

"There is a kind of experience so different from anything the ego can offer that you will never want to cover or hide it again" (T-4.III.5:1). That is what we are seeking in these quiet times. Not desperately or anxiously, not with concern or fear that it will not come to us, but peacefully, quietly, trustingly. We cannot force it to happen, we can only "let" it happen. We do not seek to add anything to ourselves, we simply seek to stop *denying* the Thought of God, which is the whole truth about us.

In this moment we can experience our "wholeness now complete, as God established it" (10:4). Once you have known your own wholeness, why would you ever again want to cover or hide it? Only the lie that what you are is something you do not want to know could have ever persuaded you to hide it. Outside the holy instant our Self is surrounded by a ring of fear; we shy away from approaching the Self because we have been tricked into believing that what we will find is fearful.

The time it seems to take to find the holy instant is not because it is mysterious and inaccessible; the time is only the measure of our fear of our Self. It takes this time to gently still our fears, until we are ready to find the Self that lies outside of time, older than time itself, whole and complete as God created It. This Self is the Thought of God. Our unawareness of it is only our denial of this Thought. Our experience of it is only the ending of our denial. The Self does not change, nor come and go. It *is*.

In this Self we are "completing His extension in [our] own" (10:5). The creative extension of God is made complete as we, in turn, extend ourselves. The Love that made us flows through us to enliven others. We are practicing what we have always known; we knew it before the ancient truth seemed to disappear into illusion, and we will know it again. In the holy instant we know it now. And what we know is this: We are entrusted with the gifts of God. Our giving of them completes His giving. "We remind the world that it is free of all illusions every time we say: *God is but Love, and therefore so am I*" (10:7–8).

LESSON 179 ✦ JUNE 28

Central theme:

"God is but Love, and therefore so am I."

Review of:

(167) "There is one life, and that I share with God."
(168) "Your grace is given me. I claim it now."

 Practice instructions

See instructions on page 545.

Commentary

Paragraph 11 of the review introduction:

The paragraph is once again about specifics of Workbook practice. I don't mean to belabor this point, but since I am simply following the content of this introduction, the emphasis is really not mine but that of the Course itself.

The Workbook places a great emphasis on repetition of the ideas it presents. Repetition is one of the primary techniques for mind training that it encourages. If we are doing it as directed—and I am the first to admit that I am still far short of doing so—we will be meditating on this theme thought for a minimum of five minutes in the morning and evening, with up to half an hour each time being even better. We will be recalling it every hour, and using the theme idea, "God is but Love, and therefore so am I," to frame the two additional thoughts we are reviewing for the day.

This is not a radical or strange idea. Repetition of spiritual thoughts is common in many religions. I even ran into it in fundamentalist Christianity. A teacher at an evening class I once attended at Moody Bible Institute in Chicago, in 1959, taught his students what he called Bible meditation. The general idea was to memorize verses from the Bible so as to have them handy in one's mind, and to meditate on them all during the day—upon arising, as you walked from place to place, whenever you sat waiting for anything, riding the bus or the train, and again at night just before sleeping. He defined meditation as "Sharing with the Lord His own Word, prayerfully, and with personal application." This teacher claimed that such meditation had revolutionized his life.

It revolutionized my life as well. In time I memorized more than a thousand Bible verses. I knew entire chapters by heart, word for word. I'm sure that the practice is a good part of what took me, eventually, beyond the confines of fundamentalism.

I still remember one of the first times that I set aside time right before sleeping to meditate. I sat up for five or ten minutes, ruminating on the verses for that day, turning them into prayer, communing with God over them, applying them to my life. Then I fell asleep with the words still going through my mind.

The next morning, I woke up and lay in that half-awake state just before you open your eyes. And there in my mind, like a mantra, the words were still being repeated. I believed then, and do now, that they had been playing over and over like a tape loop in my mind all during the night. I woke that morning with a joyful burst of faith, realizing that I was truly feeding my mind with nourishing thoughts.

It is a wonderful thing to find the words of the Course springing into your mind spontaneously during the day, or as you wake up. But that doesn't happen without a lot of repetition. Without practice of these thoughts, the tape loops running in our minds are something very different, because we have already trained our minds very well, but with the wrong thoughts. It takes a conscious effort, repeated choices to remember the thoughts for the day and to repeat them, to meditate on them, and to apply them to our lives. This is a course in mind training, and "training" means "training."

When we enter wholeheartedly into the training, there will be results. "We will have recognized the words we speak are true" (11:5). So let us remember today, and often, that "there is one life, and that I share with God." Let us affirm to ourselves, constantly, every time we can, "Your grace is given me. I claim it now."

Don't be discouraged if you forget. I still forget often. But I remember more often than I used to. If you have done nothing more before today than read over the lesson in the morning, then if today you remember just one time during the day, or take a few minutes before sleeping, thank God. Try to remember today just one more time than yesterday. If, yesterday, you forgot entirely, then resolve today to remember at least once. Every time you remember is a great step forward.

The paragraph we will cover tomorrow reminds us that the words are only aids, and the practice is just a means to produce an experience. Don't make a ritual out of the practice; the experience is what counts.

LESSON 180 ✦ JUNE 29

Central theme:

"God is but Love, and therefore so am I."

Review of:

(169) "By grace I live. By grace I am released."
(170) "There is no cruelty in God and none in me."

 Practice instructions

See instructions on page 545.

Commentary

Paragraph 12 of the review introduction:

Yesterday we thought again about the means of practice that we are being taught, the frequent repetition of the thoughts for the day. Today's paragraph reminds us that the words are only aids. Their purpose is simply to "recall the mind, as needed, to its purpose" (12:1). The purpose is in the experience, the communion with God experienced during the holy instants we spend. "We place faith in the experience that comes from practice, not the means we use" (12:2).

What is the mind's purpose to which we are being recalled? It is remembering Who we are, and sharing that with the world, reminding others of their true Self, shared with us. The repetition of words only brings us back to this memory of a Self that is in constant union with Its Father and Itself, His natural extension. The goal of our practice is to experience that state of right-mindedness, even if only for a brief moment. We are remembering that what we are is only Love, because that is all that God is. If that is so, there can be no cruelty in God, nor any cruelty in us.

The experience of the Self is what brings conviction (12:3). The words "God is but Love, and therefore so am I" or "By grace I live" cannot bring conviction or certainty. The experience of it not only *can* bring conviction, it *does* bring conviction. The goal of practice is to go beyond the words to the experience, to their meaning, "which is far beyond their sound" (12:4).

How does that happen? I can't tell you; no one can. But I can tell you that it does happen. It won't happen without practice. Practice does not make it happen, but it prepares the mind. It opens the door. It washes the mind clean with crystal pure thoughts, and readies it for the experience that is always there, always waiting. And in that experience, we find our rest.

About the Authors

Allen Watson is a staff writer and teacher with the Circle of Atonement, and is the author, or co-author with Robert Perry, of several popular books on the Course, as well as numerous articles in Course magazines and newsletters. He is well known around the world for his helpful daily commentaries, which are on the Internet as well as in book form (*A Workbook Companion, Volumes I & II*). Allen is also internationally known as a speaker on the Course. His gifted and spirited writing and teaching help students to unlock the meaning of the Course for themselves.

Robert Perry has been a student of *A Course in Miracles* (ACIM) since 1981. He taught at Miracle Distribution Center in California from 1986 to 1989, and in 1993 founded the Circle of Atonement in Sedona, Arizona. The Circle is an organization composed of several teachers dedicated to helping establish the Course as an authentic spiritual tradition.

One of the most respected voices on ACIM, Robert has traveled extensively, speaking throughout the U.S. and internationally. In addition to contributing scores of articles to various Course publications, he is the author or co-author of twenty books and booklets, including *Path of Light: Stepping into Peace with* A Course in Miracles. Robert's goal has always been to provide a complete picture of what the Course is—as a thought system and as a path meant to be lived in the world on a daily basis—and to support students in walking along that path.

www.circlepublishing.org

Circle Publishing is a division of the
Circle of Atonement Teaching and Healing Center.

The Circle of Atonement offers a wide range of teaching materials
designed to help the student walk the transformative path of
A Course in Miracles. It offers a vision of the Course that is both
faithful to it and practical for the student. Visit the Circle's website
at www.circleofa.org for a wealth of free materials, including
articles by Robert Perry, Daily Lesson Commentaries by Allen
Watson, and Course Q&A's by Greg Mackie. You may also sign
up to receive the Circle's free e-newsletter, *A Better Way*, or to
receive Allen's Lesson Commentaries or Robert's weekly class
notes by e-mail.

Contact:
The Circle of Atonement
P.O. Box 4238
West Sedona, AZ 86340
Phone: (928) 282 0790
E-mail: info@circleofa.org
www.circleofa.org